AMERICAN ORIENTAL SERIES

VOLUME 86

INCENSE AT THE ALTAR:
PIONEERING SINOLOGISTS AND THE
DEVELOPMENT OF CLASSICAL CHINESE PHILOLOGY

AMERICAN ORIENTAL SERIES

VOLUME 86

AMERICAN ORIENTAL SOCIETY

NEW HAVEN, CONNECTICUT

2001

INCENSE AT THE ALTAR:
PIONEERING SINOLOGISTS AND THE
DEVELOPMENT OF CLASSICAL CHINESE PHILOLOGY

By

DAVID B. HONEY

AMERICAN ORIENTAL SOCIETY

NEW HAVEN, CONNECTICUT

2001

CONTENTS

PREFACE AND ACKNOWLEDGMENTS

"Review the old and know the new and one may become a teacher."
—Confucius

"Grasp on to the way of the ancients to manage the matters of the present."
—Lao Tzu

The full history of Western Sinology has yet to be written. The several general bibliographic and biographical surveys that come to mind, Herbert Franke, Leslie and Davidson, and José Frèches in the West, C. Y. Tao and Ishida Mikinosuke in the East, are rather catalogues of authors and titles à la J.E. Sandys;[1] what we need is an analytical history in the mode of Rudolf Pfeiffer's magisterial *History of Classical Scholarship*.[2] Regretfully, the present work is not that history. It is merely a preliminary attempt, through a survey of selected representatives of the most important schools, to provide a narrative history based on the development of the one discipline of modern sinology that helps to form the foundation for every other endeavor, whether in the realms of art, archaeology, history, economics, anthropology, linguistics, literary criticism, or whatever. I am speaking, of course, of the honorable—if sometimes merely preparatory—calling of philology. This work attempts to outline and illustrate some of the main principles of classical Chinese philology as

---

[1]Hebert Franke, *Sinologie* (Bern: A. Francke, 1953); Donald Leslie and Jeremy Davidson, *Author Catalogues of Western Sinologists* (Canberra: Dept. of Far Eastern History, Australian National University, 1966); José Frèches, *La Sinologie* (Paris: Presses Universitaires de France, 1975); C. Y. Tao (T'ao Chen-yü), *Shih-chieh ke-kuo Han-hsüeh yen-chiu lun-wen-chi* (Taipei: Kuo-fang yen-chiu-yüan, 1962); Ishida Mikinosuke, *Ō-Bei ni okeru Shina kenkyū* (Tokyo, 1942); J.E. Sandys, *A History of Classical Scholarship*, 3 vols. (1903-1908; rpt. Boston, 1958).

[2]Rudolph Pfeiffer, *History of Classical Scholarship*, 2 vols. (Oxford: Oxford University Press, 1968-1976).

developed and personified by their most brilliant exponents in the West. Therefore, this work of academic biography, scholarly summary, and textual evaluation, like incense at an altar, is meant to invoke blessings—not from above but from the past; not for spiritual comfort nor material prosperity, but for methodological rectitude—and an increased awareness of the heritage of sinology.

Sinology has traditionally been regarded as the humanistic study of pre-modern Chinese civilization through written records. The title "sinologist," coined circa 1838, hence has historically been equivalent to "philologist": "If it means anything," mused Frederick Mote, "sinology means Chinese philology."[3] Wolfgang Franke adds the endorsement that, "until recently sinology was largely equated with Chinese philology."[4] This once firmly-entrenched connection between a discipline and a field is, of course, no longer valid. Yet the multivalent application of the term "sinology," appearing sometime after 1860 (and initially most often spelled as "sinologue" when used to refer to practitioners, still in occasional use by modern European sinologists),[5] is seen in the approaches adopted by two very different books. George Kennedy's famous handbook, *An Introduction to Sinology: Being a Guide to the Tz'u Hai (Ci hai)*, takes us through those philological principles necessary to utilize the famous dictionary in accessing traditional Chinese sources; yet Kiang Kang-Hu's own rudimentary syllabus, *Chinese Civilization: An Introduction to Sinology*, functions rather as a general historical and cultural guide for China Hands, incorporating everything from customs to law, cuisine to kinship terms.[6] This confusion has led to some understandable reaction

---

[3]Mote,"The Case for the Integrity of Sinology," *JAS* 23 (1964): 531.

[4]Franke, *China and the West*, trans. R.A. Wilson (Oxford: Basil Blackwell, 1967), 145.

[5]An early example is John Chalmers, "Is Sinology as Science?" *China Review* 2 (1873): 169-73; two modern examples are Michael Gasster, "Hellmut Wilhelm, Sinologue," *Newsletter for Modern Chinese History* 8 (1989): 27-51, and Donald Holzman and Denis Twitchett, "The Life and Work of Robert des Rotours," *T'ang Studies* 13 (1995): 13-31.

[6]Kennedy, *An Introduction to Sinology: Being a Guide to the Tz'u Hai (Ci hai)*. (1953; rpt. New Haven: Far Eastern Publications, 1981); Kiang, *Chinese Civilization: An Introduction to Sinology* (Shanghai: Chun Hwa Book Co., 1935).

against the use of this ambiguous term, and a welcome methodological reorientation among some modern scholars of China who, being more concerned with economic, sociological, or anthropological questions, are less dependent on the discipline of philology. And some historians, wishing to distance what to them are bold new interpretive stances from older, entrenched trends, dismiss the outdated history as the "old sinology." Hence, in this work I do not suggest that modern sinology should revert, in a flush of reactionary reverence for the past, to its historical roots in philology. But the choice of the main title for this work, *Pioneering Sinologists and the Development of Classical Chinese Philology*, was made with the historical connection between sinology and philology in mind.

The use of the term "classical Chinese philology" is itself purposeful, and is based on an even more intransigent tradition: studies in the Greek and Latin classics have always been called "classical philology." Witness the original German title of Wilamowitz's *History of Classical Scholarship*: "Geschichte der Philology."[7] Wilamowitz's successor at Berlin, Werner Jaeger, further confirms this with his own essay on the Classics department at Berlin from 1870 to 1945, as does the early history of classical scholarship of Guillaume Budé (1468-1540), the first classical scholar of France, entitled *De Philologia*.[8] Recent studies of specific individuals also prove this point, as in the work of Anthony Grafton on Joseph Scaliger, or C.O. Brink's treatment of three prominent textual critics, Bentley, Porson, and Housman, packaged boldly as *English Classical Scholarship*.[9] Our excursions in the history of sinology through the lives of prominent philologists, then, is entirely warranted both historically and

---

[7]U. von Wilamowitz-Moellendorff, *History of Classical Scholarship*, trans. Alan Harris, edited with introduction and notes by Hugh Lloyd-Jones (Baltimore: Johns Hopkins University Press, 1982).

[8]Jaeger, "Classical Philology at the University of Berlin: 1870 to 1945," in *Five Essays*, trans. Adele M. Fiske, R.S.C.J. (Montreal: Mario Casalini, 1966), 45-74; Budé, *De Philologia* (Paris, 1532).

[9]Grafton, *Joseph Scaliger: A Study in the History of Classical Scholarship*, vol. 1: *Textual Criticism and Exegesis* (Oxford: Oxford University Press, 1983); Brink, *English Classical Scholarship* (Cambridge: James Clarke and Co., 1986).

methodologically.

The father of this group, Edouard Chavannes (1865-1918), initiated the professionalism of classical Chinese philology among Western scholars. Previous to him, the field had been dominated by part-time practitioners; in the terminology of Andrew Walls,[10] they were hyphenated missionary-sinologists, official-sinologists, or businessmen-sinologists—who stole time from their regular duties to introduce the China they knew to the West. The few professional sinologists, such as Hirth, Schlegel, De Groot, produced works admirable for the results obtained under the research conditions of the times; yet much of what they produced is today flawed in many instances, based as it was upon an erroneous assumption about the nature of the Chinese language, an insufficient base in traditional bibliography, and the handicap of lacking the tool of historical phonology—something not yet developed at the time they labored.

The reason we may consider Chavannes to be the founder of professional sinology is that nothing he wrote is outdated today in terms of either intellectual assumption, conceptual clarity, or methodological approach. That his works may need updating is something true of every scholarly production in the face of the advancement of knowledge. Yet his oeuvre retains its worth today as an entirety much better than that of his contemporaries because of his painstaking care for completeness, caution where proof was lacking, and mastery of a variety of sources. He was furthermore careful not to base too many conclusions on either comparative philology or historical phonology, since the science of Chinese linguistics was just getting started. Whatever use he made of historical phonology was carefully phrased in provisional terms, and as an adjunct to conclusions already reached by other means. Actually, his disciples Pelliot and Maspero were the first to utilize historical phonology in a systematic, sound way as a scholarly tool (not as the major object of research as was done by the sinological linguist Bernhard Karlgren or his predecessors).

Paul Pelliot (1878-1945) became the greatest philologist of Chinese

---

[10]Walls, "The Nineteenth-Century Missionary as Scholar," in *Misjonskall og forskerglede*, ed. Nils E. Block-Hoell (Oslo: Universitetsforlaget, 1975), 209-21.

of this century. His tenacity of memory enabled him to marshal the facts of Chinese history, textual criticism, bibliography, and biography on almost any subject or period of time and analyze them in an orderly way. His store of knowledge was immense, enabling him to act as the final arbiter of sinological questions. However, his erudition was sometimes burdening, as his sense of order was such that he could hardly ever bring himself to synthesize all that he knew to form provisional historical statements; he would rather gather his facts and bring them to bear on one problem at a time. His forte, then, was providing exhaustive annotations for translations of important Chinese sources, and discussing *seriatim* a series of topical problems found in the course of translation. A mechanical dryness sometimes resulted from his precise approach to sinology, abetted by the technical nature of some of his more obscure concerns. But his example of textual explication, in the exactness of procedure and thoroughness of result, remains unparalleled today.

His classmate Henri Maspero (1883-1945) was scarcely less skilled as an annotator and textual commentator, but he also possessed a highly developed feel for history that allowed him to summarize his research and to state provisional conclusions. His research specialties, especially Taoism, ancient mythology, and history, were also more humanistic than Pelliot's in that they were more accessible to the concern and ken of the ordinary educated person of intelligence. Even his more technical works on phonology and the oral language somehow were infused more by a humanistic than a scientific spirit. His contemporaries, Marcel Granet (1884-1940) in the sociology of ancient China and Bernhard Karlgren (1889-1978) in historical phonology, specialized in what to Maspero were general interests, and developed independent disciplines; but neither they nor Maspero can be appreciated without accounting for their mutual influence and tit-for-tat exchanges in the journals.

Georg von der Gabelentz (1840-1893), Wilhelm Grube (1855-1908), August Conrady (1864-1925), Walter Simon (1893-1981), and many other German sinologues, though less well-known today, played their parts in developing the dialogue between a sinologue and the community of colleagues—establishing journals à la Bruno Schindler (1882-1964)—and between a sinologist and the educated public in the style of Richard

Wilhelm (1873-1930). The imposing figures among this group are Otto Franke (1863-1946) in historiography, and Gustav Haloun (1898-1951) in textual criticism.[11]

British sinology developed out of the service of Protestant missionaries in China, chiefly the Scots Robert Morrison (1782-1834) in lexicography and biblical translation, Alexander Wylie (1815-1887) in bibliography, astronomy, and mathematics, and James Legge (1815-1897) in classics. Legge gained an international reputation for his meticulous approach to the translation of the classics; his grasp of the commentarial tradition rivaled that of native scholars in China, where he was considered a specialist on the *Shih-ching* in the sense of old-school Chinese exegesis on the classics. Herbert Giles (1845-1935) was one of the last of the consular officials to turn to academics, and functions as a transitional figure in the painful process that transformed British sinology from a part-time endeavor to a full-time occupation. His Victorian rhymes from the Chinese, along with the even more impressionistic literary effusions of Ernest Fenollosa, led on the one hand to the Vorticism of Ezra Pound, and on the other to Waley's own variations on sprung rhythm.

Arthur Waley (1889-1966) was the pre-eminent poet among sinologists. As a polished stylist, his English versions not only popularized the reading of Chinese and Japanese literature in translation but set an almost inimitable standard that in the main remained as accurate—for his purposes—as it was readable. Another side of the scholarly Waley was his command of world anthropology. His translations of Chinese classical texts and philosophers were informed with cultural insights gained from a broad comparative perspective. He was the last and best of the line of self-taught sinologists fathered by nineteenth-century ecclesiastical, commercial, and political interests. But, standing outside the institutional orb of professional sinology, he drew it rather into the realm of Western literature as he unofficially represented the Orient as a kind of literary

---

[11]An epitome of the treatment of German sinology in this book has appeared as "Cultural Missionaries of China to the West: An Overview of German Sinology," in *Sino-German Relations Since 1800: Multidisciplinary Explorations*, ed. Ricardo K.S. Mak and Danny S.L. Paau (Frankfurt am Main: Peter Lang, 2000), 149-65.

ambassador.

American sinology had missionary and consular roots similar to the British. Two nineteenth-century American missionaries, Elijah Coleman Bridgman (1801-1861) and Samuel Wells Williams (1812-1888), represent the first flowering of this tradition before the maturation of the social sciences finally subdivided the field. William F. Rockhill (1854-1914) and Arthur W. Hummel (1884-1975) personify the diplomatic and institutional aspects of American sinology of the early twentieth century. Highly specialized studies in the worlds of natural history, technology, and anthropology were pioneered by Berthold Laufer (1874-1934), the only eminent American sinologist of his generation, even if German-born and trained. Homer H. Dubs (1892-1969) at Oxford, L. Carrington Goodrich (1894-1986) at Columbia, and George A. Kennedy (1901-1960) at Yale, all either born or raised in China, were the last of the breed to spring from the missionary heritage of the nineteenth century.

Three Harvard men conclude this general survey of American sinology. Two of them represent the development of the field of history from narrative historiography to area studies. Charles Gardner (1900-1966) considered the historical document as source, and left a concise theoretical treatise on philology for historians. John King Fairbank (1907-1992) regarded a whole series of documents as data base to draw from in fleshing out his theoretical paradigms; whether he or a native collaborator accessed such a data base was ultimately irrelevant to the course of his scholarship. A third Harvard professor, Francis W. Cleaves (1911-1995), illustrated in masterful and powerful style the philological principles explained by Gardner in many annotated translations of Chinese and Mongolian texts.

Finally, the two most brilliant lights of the Berkeley school receive separate treatment. Peter A. Boodberg (1903-1972) equaled Pelliot's intellectual incisiveness and strength of memory if not his international profile, and exceeded Maspero's humanity as he unabashedly harnessed the work of the philologist to a universal humanism. He attempted to add the philologist, in his role as curator of the records of the ages, to the ranks of the philosophers and prophets in seeking the best in the creative spirit and cultural heritage of all nations. Each of Boodberg's works in his small oeuvre breathes brilliance, at times accessible only to minds attuned to the voices of the classicists, the medievalists, and the poets of the past. Many of his contemporary sinologists, blinded to the lofty purposes of his scholarly approach by his penchant for coining arcane neologisms, and distracted by some of his odd personal traits, dismissed his scholarship in the end as quackery, and attached to his memory only a reputation for engaging in quixotic philological crusading. His conceptual foil in the debate on the nature of the Chinese script, the historian Herlee G. Creel (1905-1994), founded the Chicago school that still remains prominent in fields that he pioneered: early Chinese history, intellectual history, and archaeology.

Boodberg's pupil Edward H. Schafer (1913-1991) was equally brilliant in the scope and depth of his scholarship, but had that rare ability to communicate even to those outside academia those hardly definable qualities of art and literature that make for masterpieces. If Boodberg failed to found a new philosophy based on scholarship, as Werner Jaeger had failed with his Third Humanism in the field of classics, Schafer succeeded in establishing a new genre of learned writing. His extensive works directed poetical insight and illustration to concrete manifestations of culture. His explorations of the natural, material, and imaginary worlds of T'ang China were accompanied by virtuoso exploitations of both medieval Chinese and world literature. His humanism was thus directly conveyed to inhabitants of the globe, learned or lay, who were not necessarily sinologists but who nevertheless were entranced by the exoticism of many of his subjects, the erudition of his argumentation, and the elegance of his prose.

All of these scholars, whether occupied with problems of textual filiation or exploitation, grammatical analysis or phonological reconstruction, historical translation or poetical appreciation, were masters of handling the technical arsenal of philology. These and other means of analyzing texts and accessing textual data constitute what I term philology in this work. The range of tools available to the philologist was once enumerated by Edward Schafer when he supplied his own definition of the term philology: it is "the analysis and interpretation of textual remains, employing such aids as epigraphy, palaeography, exegesis, the lower and higher criticisms, leading to the study of literature as an immediate expression of the intricacies of culture and the subtleties of the human mind."[12]   Historically, it is true, until the end of the fifteenth century philology in the West encompassed both the sum of learning—the so-called Seven Liberal Arts[13]—and the means of acquiring it.[14] Giambattista Vico (1668-1744), in countering Descartes' philosophy of rationalism, restored to science the philological focus of the particulars of history as found in texts and other "artifacts of the spirit,"[15] building on linguistic momentum generated by earlier treatises on the methods of study such as Erasmus' *De ratione studii*.[16]   In China, the foundational role of the discipline of philology for classicists, even for Sung-period scholiasts interested more in questions of ethical hermeneutics than exegetical glossing, never lost its importance.[17]   Understanding how scholars of both East and West produced the works they did—the methodologies of lasting value—is just as important as accessing the scholarly conclusions reached—the transient phase of understanding that may be changed with the latest archaeological discovery or publication of a *magnum opus*. "Our chief need now," announced Hugh Lloyd-Jones in 1976 after reviewing the second volume

---

[12]"Communication to the Editors," *JAOS* 78 (1958): 119; *JAS* 17 (1958): 509.

[13]The Seven Liberal Arts were grouped into an initial trio or *trivium* of grammar, rhetoric, and logic, and second quartet or *quadrivium* of arithmetic, geometry, astronomy, and music; see Charles Homer Haskins, *The Rise of Universities* (1923; rpt. Ithaca: Cornell University Press, 1965), 27-29.

[14]Witness Matianus Capella's satire *De Nuptius Mercurii et Philologiae* or *The Marriage of Mercury and Philology* (fifth century); for the historical development of philology, see Karl D. Uitti, "Philology," in *The Johns Hopkins Guide to Literary Theory and Criticism*, ed. Michael Groden and Martin Kreiswirth (Baltimore: Johns Hopkins University Press, 1994), 567-74.

[15]Uitti, "Philology," 570; for a particularly detailed defense of philology, especially the approach of textual criticism, see Vico, *On the Study Methods of Our Times*, trans. Elio Gianturco (Ithaca: Cornell University Press, 1990), 76.

[16]Translated by Brian McGregor as "On the Method of Study," in *Collected Works of Erasmus*, vols. 23-24: *Literary and Educational Writings* (Toronto: University of Toronto Press, 1978), 24:661-91.

[17]For a comprehensive introduction to traditional Chinese philology in relationship to classical studies, see Ch'ien Chi-po, "Monograph on Philology" ("Hsiao-hsüeh chih"), in *Ching-hsüeh t'ung-chih: Ching-hsüeh ts'ung-shu ch'u-pien* (Taipei: Hsüeh-hai ch'u-pan-she, 1985), 215-52.

of Pfeiffer's great work, "is for detailed studies giving an exact description of the actual procedures of scholars in successive periods of the history of the subject."[18]   Although falling far short of this lofty aim, this work at least attempts, through a discussion of selected published offerings, to illustrate how our chosen scholars functioned as philologists.

My procedure itself is unavoidably documentary as I follow the old-fashioned translation-annotation approach and select works normative in the philological side of sinology and comment at length on their inner processes. This venerable commentarial tradition, of course, is ultimately derived from generations of Chinese scholiasts and Confucian moralists who bequeathed their methodological mind-sets and textually biased frameworks to the first Occidental sinologists. In this I cannot escape a type of reverse Orientalism that would make such a critic of culture as Edward Said happy even as it would disappoint an Arthur Wright, the philologist-turned-historian. Although my reactions to their critiques of traditional sinology are reserved for the Envoi that concludes this work, nevertheless it may be helpful to stress for now that I adopt such a philological approach not in willful ignorance of the advances made in the historical or social-science side of sinology, nor out of perverse gadflyism in the Taoist mode. Intellectual history is just not my purpose. Hence, despite many fine methodological models to follow in other fields, I do not attempt either to construct the field of sinology as a hegemonic discourse or to deconstruct it, in Foucauldian terms, as an archeological paradigm. My sinologists—their scholarship more than their lives—are treated like documentary evidence and subjected to both interpretive translation and copious annotation. In other words, in adopting a genealogical framework I concentrate on the individual, not the field; in fine, I ignore the forest of sinology for the trees of the sinologists and their various methodological branches.

No doubt many other sinologists could have been included in this study, perhaps even selected as a major focus of attention. I have in mind

---

[18]Lloyd-Jones, review of Pfeiffer, *History of Classical Scholarship,* vol. 2, in *Times Literary Supplement,* 20 August 1976; rpt. in *Classical Survivals: The Classics in the Modern World* (London: Duckworth, 1982), 19.

such notables as Etienne Balasz, Derk Bodde, Arthur Wright, Wolfram Eberhard, Paul Demiéville, Timoteus Pokora, or Piet van der Loon, not to mention Asian *Han-hsüeh-chia* such as Wang Kuo-wei, Ku Chieh-kang, Ch'en Yin-k'o, Ch'ien Mu, Yang Lien-sheng, William Hung, Yoshikawa Kōjirō, Morohashi Tetsuji, or Shima Kunio. But, to take the group of Asian sinologists first, this work is intended for students of China, in the roundest sense of the term, at Western universities. Quite apart from this is the problem inherent in discussing the classical language in modern Chinese or Japanese: most often lines of poetry or prose, just what the Western reader wants analyzed, are cited without comment because it is taken for granted that they are apprehended and appreciated by the reader. And the Western sinologists cited above, although many were master philologists, most often harnessed philology as an adjunct to questions more properly the concern of other disciplines, from economics to sociology. To my mind, the principles of philology are best illustrated by works that are themselves mainly philological in intent: literary criticism, textual criticism, translation, and the like.

The sinologists treated in this work, all deceased, are distributed along national or, in the case of the Anglo-Americans, linguistic, lines. Despite only eight sinologists meriting chapter-length treatment, I have attempted to provide the historical background and intellectual context for the careers of many of the major sinologists, and to identify if not always trace in detail lines of discipleship. This wider setting is provided through an introductory chapter on Jesuit translators and the first professional sinologists in France, pioneers of the German, British, and American sinological traditions, and the appearance of many others either in the text or notes. The works treated are not always the most important or well-known contributions of our sinologists. But, in my view, they exemplify the philological method at its best. Other criteria led Chou Fa-kao, in his *Han-hsüeh lun-wen*, to group Granet along with Pelliot, Maspero, and Franke as the leading lights of Western sinology.[19] But my concern

---

[19]Only these four twentieth-century Western sinologists merit appended biographies in Chou Fa-kao, *Han-hsüeh lun-chi* ([Hong Kong]: Ke-ta shu-chü, 1964), 149-62.

remains more narrow: the development and utilization of philology; hence Granet, although treated in conjunction with the career of Maspero, does not merit an independent chapter. This same narrow concern further explains the absence of all but two or three Russian sinologists in this study. The history of sinology cannot afford to overlook the Russian school; but for a study of the development of classical Chinese philology in the West, the Russians played a lesser role. Regardless, I have had to choose exemplars more linguistically accessible to me. This narrow concentration on philology also explains the absence of any women in this study. For even such a giant as Anna Seidel offered little in the way of methodological innovation even while influencing the field and advancing many careers both by the power of her personality as well as the brilliance of her published work. But her approach, if not her specific themes, had been pioneered earlier by Maspero and Schafer.

With the above caveats and well-meant *mea culpa*, I turn to what I intend to accomplish with this study. Rather than introduce the specific techniques of the philological approach and trace their utilization and refinement from sinologist to sinologist, my approach instead will center on one major scholar at a time. And, while all important methodological aspects of an individual's scholarship will be covered, most of the major sinological biographies will frame an extensive discussion of one or more particular tools, whether historical phonology, epigraphy, bibliography, textual criticism, etc. I usually offset this discussion by introducing the development of similar techniques in both the West and in China.

If this book leads to more attention being paid to the works of the pioneering figures in the field, a victory will have been won for the ecologists of sinology who are dismayed to see the giants of the past cut down and tossed aside for the sake of streamlined degree programs or specialization in newer methodologies that assume sophistication in the niceties of philology but do not always teach it. Of course, not everyone should specialize in philological work—the wide field of sinology would soon turn barren and risk losing significance for humanities in general. And, in commenting on the methods of the social scientists, most often historians, I do not mean to set up an oppositional polemic or to devalue these disciplines against other approaches. Nevertheless, it can only be methodologically healthy for sinologists of any disciplinary orientation or stage of development to reflect on the pioneers of the past and to appreciate their accomplishments, if not necessarily to imitate them.

Graduate students and young professionals who jump into research by applying new and exacting methodologies have not normally, in the course of their studies, been able to attain sufficient depth of understanding of the textual tradition. Premature publication is, unfortunately, an unavoidable evil in the drive for tenure, but not necessarily conducive to enduring scholarship. The problems of studying traditional Chinese sources of any type are so formidable that more than graduate training is necessary—life-long dedication is required. For this reason, sure grounding in the techniques and targets of philological analysis, including close translation and textual explication, criticism and appreciation, historical phonology and linguistics, paleography and epigraphy, and finally that unavoidable auxiliary, bibliography, should be among the mainstays of graduate study so that a scholar is prepared with the tools to be self-taught and self-directed throughout a lifetime to explore or utilize the literature in a personal direction. In this regard, this work treats philology as a set of techniques open to utilization whenever needed. I am not trying to advance the "cause" of philology as a discipline in order to convert more students to departments of Chinese language and literature!

Compared to such departments, the social sciences and their equally honorable endeavors lend themselves to a fast graduation track and quick publication at first; they furthermore generally focus on questions that are, or seem to be, of a more immediate political, social, or humanitarian relevancy. They therefore tend to be popular in the U.S. system of education. But it is for this very reason that at least the outlines of the history of sinology, as revealed by the story of its founding figures, is essential reading for fledgling scholars, so that approaches and models from the social sciences may more fruitfully be applied to the Chinese textual tradition. Of course, it is up to the philologists to obtain an equally firm grasp of any discipline they may seek to utilize from the social sciences, but that is a different story. Europe, with its educational system of senior professors occupying endowed chairs of eminent pedigrees, seems to be more respectful of its traditions, even if such traditions limit the scope of action of junior faculty and perhaps restrain the field. At least methodologically speaking, a sinologist who aspires to become a "full" professor (in the American sense) must expect to be among the leading experts in his or her field, discipline, period, or specific set of texts. Such an expectation is not realized without a thorough grasp of questions that have traditionally been the concern of philology.

This work began in a graduate seminar at the University of California, Berkeley in 1984, shared with Stephen Bokenkamp (currently Professor of Chinese at Indiana University). The seminar was the creation of the late Edward H. Schafer, master philologist and proud conservator of a noble tradition. Like any arduous training for a religious order, the seminar was a bracing baptism into the history of sinology and its most venerable saints. For his earnest tutelage and enduring example, this work is inevitably and gratefully dedicated to the memory of Edward H. Schafer.

Funding for various research trips and research assistants is gratefully acknowledged from the following campus institutions: Department of Asian and Near Eastern Languages, College of Humanities, and the David M. Kennedy Center for International Studies. Former department chairs Kazzy Watabe and Van Gessel, as well as the current chair Dil Parkinson, have been unfailingly supportive of this project; their patience, encouragement, and liberality with funds dispersed on my behalf have meant a great deal to me.

Many colleagues at home and abroad generously offered thoughtful criticism. Professors Chauncey S. Goodrich and Paul W. Kroll read the entire manuscript with the ruthless eyes of professional editors and supplied abundant corrections and stylistic suggestions. Later, as the editor of the American Oriental Society monograph series, Professor Kroll gave the manuscript yet another careful inspection. His and Professor Goodrich's mastery of the history of sinology and its major figures provided many corrective insights to my sometimes parochial vision. In a visit in late 1995 to the University of Chicago, Professor Edward Shaughnessy and the students in his graduate seminar on the history of sinology provided a stimulating setting for airing abstract intellectual questions that arise out of concrete methodological choices. His late-night discussions on sinology and sinologists are particularly appreciated. Professor Victor Mair helped me attempt to transcend my residual and inherent Berkeley bias, and see beyond the broadly published philologist to the master pedagogues of philology in the classrooms, museums, and the field. David Helliwell of the Bodleian, Professor Robert Chard, St Anne's College, Oxford, and Professor Denis Twitchett, Cambridge, provided a warm welcome on two research trips to Great Britain and greatly smoothed the way in accessing sources and making crucial contacts in the confusing arena of Oxbridge. Professor Twitchett's insightful recollections of Arthur Waley, Gustav Haloun, and Walter Simon are especially treasured. Professor Anne Birrell of Clare Hall, Cambridge, helped make one visit both comfortable as well as socially and academically meaningful.

Helpful comments, timely words of support, and valuable materials were gratefully received from Profs. William Boltz, Bruce Brooks, Elizabeth Endicott-West, Scott Galer, Norman Girardot, Grant Hardy, David Knechtges, William H. Nienhauser, Jr., Lauren Pfister, Denis Sinor, Hartmut Walravens, and Wong Man-kong.. My co-workers at Brigham Young University, Dr. Gail King, and Profs. Paul Hyer, Sechin Jagchid, Scott Miller, Van Gessel, and David C. Wright (now of the University of Calgary), were equally supportive. My former and immediate colleagues in the Chinese section of my department deserve my fullest expression of thanks for support, encouragement, and comradeship over the years; they are Professors Gary Williams, Dana Bourgerie, Matthew Christensen, Tang Yanfang, and Edward Peng. Jennifer Myers prepared the camera-ready copy with skill and dedication. For her efforts and sacrifice, I thank her. Eliza Moody shouldered the onerous task of compiling the index; I hope she does not feel that it was a thankless one.

Lastly, Professor Herbert Franke has been unstinting of his time in reading various stages of the manuscript, and providing first-hand observations, crucial corrections, and warm encouragement. His example of a rigorous philological technique harnessed to authoritative historical research in many fields, including the history of sinology, all infused with a pervasive humanistic spirit, marks the culmination of many trends treated in this work. His career honors sinology.

ABBREVIATIONS

AM	*Asia Major*
BEFEO	*Bulletin de l'Ecole française d'Extrême-Orient*
BSOAS	*Bulletin of the School of Oriental and African Studies*
BSOS	*Bulletin of the School of Oriental Studies*
CLEAR	*Chinese Literature: Essays, Articles, Reviews*
FEQ	*Far Eastern Quarterly*
HJAS	*Harvard Journal of Asiatic Studies*
JA	*Journal Asiatique*
JAOS	*Journal of the American Oriental Society*
JAS	*Journal of Asian Studies*
JESHO	*Journal of the Social and Economic History of the Orient*
MS	*Monumenta Serica*
OE	*Oriens Extremus*
OLZ	*Oriental Literaturzeitung*
PEW	*Philosophy East and West*
TP	*T'oung Pao*
ZDMG	*Zeitschrift der deutschen morgenländischen Gesellschaft*

INTRODUCTION

i. THE SCHOLARLY MISSIONARIES

"The Chinese language is for us like a language from another world. And if one were to give a definition of language according to which all the other idioms are called languages, then one would have to admit that Chinese is not a language at all, just as the Chinese people are not a people."

—Friedrich Schelling (1775-1854)[1]

"It took a long time before European scholars began to study Chinese language and literature, and still today such study is not cultivated as it ought to be, considering the value and practical usefulness of Chinese."

—Theophilus Bayer (1694-1738)[2]

The Iberian Phase

A hazy historical awareness of the existence of China by the West, either as the legendary land of the Seres, as Ptolemy's Sinae, or the Cathay of the Moslem historians, was the backdrop generated by medieval travelogues such as those by Marco Polo and Ibn Battutah (1303-1378), or the reports of the papal emissaries to the court of the Mongols and elsewhere, to an uninformed appreciation for many of her exotic cultural quirks and delightful material goods.[3] Factual knowledge of China,

---

[1]Cited in Christopher Harbsmeier, "John Webb and the Early History of the Study of the Classical Language in the West," in *Europe Studies China: Papers from an International Conference on the History of European Sinology* (London: Han-Shan Tang Books, 1995), 332.

[2]Knud Lundbaek, *T.S. Bayer (1694-1738): Pioneer Sinologist* (London: Curzon Press, 1986), 39.

[3]The first place one must always turn to for Western contacts with Asia remains Donald F. Lach's magnificent, multi-volumed study *Asia in the Making of Europe*, 2 vols. (5 books) (Chicago: University of Chicago Press, 1965-1970); Lach and Edwin J. Van Kley, vol. 3 (4 books) (Chicago: University of Chicago Press, 1993). Raymond Dawson, *The Chinese Chameleon: An Analysis of European Conceptions of Chinese Civilization* (London: Oxford University Press, 1967) introduces European impressions of China up

although less encrusted by error and fancy as the tales kept filtering in, was still hard to acquire. Donald Lach provides a lucid and elegant encapsulation of the situation at the inception of Asian-Western contacts in the epilogue to volume two of *Asia in the Making of Europe*, a volume aptly entitled "A Century of Wonder":

> All sixteenth-century Europeans inherited from the pre-discovery era a picture of the East as a shadowy place obscured by the mists of time and space. The broad public, informed by the medieval tradition as preserved in the romance of Alexander, the encyclopedias, cosmographies, sermon books, and bestiaries, continued to visualize Asia as a rich region inhabited by strange peoples who practiced mysterious and magical arts, excelled in a number of unknown and exotic crafts, and lived exemplary lives. Isolated examples of Asian art, technology, and ideas had migrated to Europe before 500, but their provenance was not usually recognized; in the sixteenth century also, artistic motifs, tools, devices, and mathematical ideas were borrowed, sometimes only semiconsciously, from Asian originals. Most Europeans were unable to distinguish between the Islamic

---

to modern times. Brief historical overviews are W.E. Soothill, *China and the West: A Sketch of their Intercourse* (London: Oxford University Press, 1925); Arnold H. Rowbotham, "A Brief Account of the Early Development of Sinology," *The Chinese Social and Political Science Review* 7 (1923): 113-38; Robert H. Gassmann, "Sinologie, Chinakunde, Chinawissenschaft: Eine Standortbestimmung," *Asiatische Studien* 39 (1985): 147-68, and David E. Mungello, *The Great Encounter of China and the West, 1500-1800* (New York: Rowman and Littlefield Publishers, 1999). The specific case of England in the eighteenth century is covered in Fan Tsen-chung, *Dr. Johnson and Chinese Culture* (London: The China Society, 1945). Both Marco Polo and Ibn Battutah are too well known to need documentation, as are the accounts of the missionaries. A densely detailed but swift overview of early travelers to China and their reports, plus an account of the Jesuits in China, is found in the preface to Bayer's *Museum Sinicum*, a virtual history of sinology up to his time. Its most relevant sections are translated and annotated in Lundbaek, *T.S. Bayer*, 39-97; see further Donald W. Treadgold, *The West in Russia and China: Religious and Secular Thought in Modern Times*, vol. 2: *China 1582-1949* (Cambridge: Cambridge University Press, 1973), 1-34. Much of the same ground is covered more critically and in greater depth in Paul Demiéville, "Aperçu historique des études sinologiques en France," rpt. in his *Choix d'études sinologiques (1921-1970)* (Leiden: E.J. Brill, 1973), 443-87.

Orient and the rest of Asia. Consequently, the growing fear of an Ottoman attack upon central Europe was accompanied by anxiety and uneasiness about invasions of strange and unfathomable ideas from the distant East; many writers connected the Portuguese wars against the Muslims in India with the unrelenting struggle against the hostile Turks. Thus for the public in all parts of Europe the East was the homeland of the Islamic enemy as well as of fabulous peoples, magical arts, superior craftsmanship, moral kings, and mass armies.[4]

It was not until Portuguese and Spanish navigators published the narratives of their maritime expeditions, which first landed on the China coast in 1513, that comparatively reliable sources became widely accessible.[5]

The distinguished humanist and bureaucrat Joao de Barros (1496-1570) was the leading Portuguese historian to utilize these travelogues. His *Third Decade of the Asia of Joao de Barros: of the Deeds which the Portuguese Did in the Discovery and Conquest of the Seas and Lands of the East* was published in Lisbon in 1563.[6] The Dutch narrative of Jan Huygen van Linschoten (1563-1611), called *Travel Account of the Portuguese to the Orient* (1595) compiled both from personal experience and from Portuguese archival materials, soon impelled the Dutch on their commercial ventures in the Orient.[7] However, the most widely read general history of China was written by one, who like Liu Yü-hsi composing his poetry on Chinling, had not even visited the scene of his record. Juan González de Mendoza, *Historia de las cosas más notables, ritos y costumbres de gran Reyno*

---

[4]Lach and van Kley, *Asia in the Making of Europe*, vol. III, Book 3, p. 557. It is curious that, although Marco Polo and his *Il milione* receive extended treatment by Lach, Ibn Battutah is not even mentioned.

[5]An introduction to the Spanish and Portuguese roles much more narrowly focused than Lach's great work is C.R. Crone, *The Discovery of the East* (New York: St. Martin's Press, 1972); more abbreviated still is Michael Cooper, "The Portuguese in the Far East: Missionaries and Traders," *Arts of Asia* 7 (1977): 25-33.

[6]See C.R. Boxer, *Joao de Barros: Portuguese Humanist and Historian of Asia* (New Delhi: Concept Publishing Company, 1981); Lach, *Asia in the Making of Europe*, vol. I, Book 1, p. 190.

[7]J.J.L. Duyvendak, *Holland's Contribution to Chinese Studies* (London: The China Society, 1950), 4-5; Lach, *Asia in the Making of Europe*, vol. 1, Book 1, p. 201.

de la China (Rome, 1585), went through thirty editions in various European languages before the century was out.[8] It was, however, based on the reports of two first-hand informants, the Dominican friar Gaspar da Cruz, and the Augustinian friar Martin de Rada.[9] It informed the work of many European thinkers and scholars, Francis Bacon for one, and inspired a like number of explorers, among them Sir Walter Raleigh.

The great classicist Joseph Scaliger read it two years after it was printed, and mined it for his work on world calendrical systems:

> The Sinese [Latin *Sinae*] (whom the Spanish call Chinese [*Chinas*], for reasons unfathomable to me) reckon 4,282 years from their ancient king Vitey to Honog, who ruled after the year of the Lord 1570. For they count 2,257 years from Vitey to Tzintzom, the last of the race of Vitey. He separated the Tartars from the Sinese by a continuous wall. From him to Honog, around the years of the Lord 1570, 1571, 1572, etc., they reckon 2,025 years. This sum amounts to 4,282 years, as we said before. Hence Vitey is far older than Abraham.[10]

If precise data such as dates were derived from Mendoza, the impossible spelling of Chinese names, whether in translation or transcription, nevertheless betrays the abysmally low level of general understanding about China, let alone linguistic sophistication—Mendoza's original "Bonog" for Scaliger's "Honog" notwithstanding. Scaliger's knowledge of the twelve branches of the Chinese zodiac is another instance of a loose grasp of facts being misplaced in a culturally misunderstood context. He

---

[8]The English translation was published 1588. A physical description of this book, its contents and sources, plus citations for further bibliographical information, is in John Lust, *Western Books on China Published up to 1850 in the Library of the School of Oriental and African Studies, University of London* (London: Bamboo Publishing Ltd, 1987), 7; see further Lach, *Asia in the Making of Europe*, vol. 1, Book 1, p. 184; Book 2, p. 562.

[9]Both reports are reprinted in English translation in C.R. Boxer, ed. *South China in the Sixteenth Century* (London: Hakluyt Society, 1953); for evaluations, see Lach, *Asia in the Making of Europe*, vol. 1, Book 2, pp. 536, 749-50.

[10]Quoted in Anthony Grafton, *Joseph Scaliger: A Study in the History of Classical Scholarship*, II: *Historical Chronology* (Oxford: Clarendon Press, 1993), 406.

derived the basic set of animal names from Ignatius, the Patriarch of Antioch, through correspondence, yet mistook their fundamental nature: "He did not realize that the names formed a fixed sequence of a cycle and could not be used by way of poetic description of the nature of a certain year."[11]

But Mendoza's *Historia* can hardly be blamed for all the shortcomings and mistaken impressions of China, let alone the constricted compass of the medieval world-view itself. It was not superseded until the publication of Matteo Ricci's (1552-1610) journal-narrative, called *De propagatione Christiana apud Sinas* (On the Propogation of Christianity among the Chinese) (Augsburg, 1615),[12] and later Martino Martini's (1614-1661) *De Bello Tartarico historia* (Antwerp, 1654), called by Giuliano Bertuccioli the first "serious, detailed, systematic scientific attempt to present Chinese history to Europeans."[13]   The latter's *Atlas Sinensis* (Amsterdam, 1655), containing seven maps, was the first atlas to show the topography of China, and his *Sinica historia decas prima* was the first European work on ancient Chinese history.[14]

The earliest intellectual steps of nascent sixteenth-century sinology, briefly sketched above,[15] are aptly termed the "Iberian Phase" by Timothy

---

[11]J.J.L. Duyvendak, "Early Chinese Studies in Holland," *TP* 32 (1936): 294.

[12]Translated from the original Italian and edited by Nichola Trigault, S.J. (1577-1628). English version: *China in the Sixteenth Century: The Journals of Matteo Ricci, 1583-1610*, trans. Louis J. Gallagher, S.J. (New York, 1953). See the discussion of this work and of the respective contributions of Ricci and Trigault in David E. Mungello, *Curious Land: Jesuit Accommodation and the Origins of Sinology* (Wiesbaden: Franz Steiner, 1985), 46-49.

[13]Bertuccioli, "Sinology in Italy 1600-1950," in *Europe Studies China*, 69.

[14]His work is briefly summarized by Bertuccioli, "Sinology in Italy 1600-1950," 68-69. See further Giorgio Melis, ed. *Martino Martini: Geografo, cartografo, storico, teologo* (Trento, 1983), and Giorgio Melis, "Ferdinand Verbiest and Martino Martini," in *Ferdinand Verbiest, S.J* (1623-1688): *Jesuit Missionary, Scientist, Engineer and Diplomat* (Nettetal: Steyler Velag, 1994), 471-84.

[15]The above historical epitome is based on Boxer, ed. *South China in the Sixteenth Century*, introduction; C.R. Boxer, "Some Aspects of Western Historical Writing on the Far East, 1500-1800," in *Historians of China and Japan*, ed. E.G. Pulleyblank and W.G. Beasley (London: Oxford University Press, 1961), 306-21; and Frèches, *La Sinologie*, 9-16.

Barrett.[16] It consisted of outside impressions obtained by foreign visitors through personal observation or via native informants. It edged into true sinology—the study of China through Chinese texts—with the limited efforts of the Dominicans in the Philippines, and the more substantial contributions of the Jesuits on the mainland of China.

The Dominicans in Manila

A printing press operating in Manila between 1593 and 1607 produced nine works on the Catholic faith, doctrine, and ordinances: three in classical Chinese, one in a mixture of classical Chinese and vernacular Hokkien, one in Spanish and Tagalog, three in Tagalog, and one in Latin.[17] These works were designed to benefit the Chinese immigrant community, and, while produced by the Chinese themselves, were original compositions of the Dominicans. The spiritual impulse behind the work of translation and printing is clarified by Domingo de Nieva, author of the *Memorial de la vida christiana en lengua china* (1606) and the first Dominican to apply himself for an extended period to learning Chinese:

> When religion does not use language it is obstructed; when faith is explained in an unknown script it will not be recognized. In compliance with our religion and faith I wandered to this place, where I was fortunate in conversing with scholars of the Great Ming dynasty. After I had acquired a rough knowledge of their script and language I was very grateful, so I passed on to them the contents of an old work, which I rendered in the script and language of the Great Ming. I publish this book in order to guide those who become members of our faith.[18]

But learning to write Chinese characters to promulgate the faith is much different than learning to read Chinese books. Still, the methods involved

---

[16]See Barrett, *Singular Listlessness: A Short History of Chinese Books and British Scholars* (London: Wellsweep, 1989), 26-29, for further documentation.

[17]Piet van der Loon, "The Manila Incunabula and Early Hokkien Studies, Part I," *AM* n.s.12 (1966): 1-45.

[18]van der Loon, "The Manila Incunabula," 30.

to master either form were much the same, and we cannot discount the importance of the early vocabularies and dictionaries compiled by the Spanish Dominicans for private use merely because of the purpose to which they were applied.[19] Similar activities by the Dominicans in China were overshadowed by the superior accomplishments of the Jesuits.[20]

The Jesuits in China

Greater strides were attempted by Jesuits on the Chinese mainland.[21] For instance, the earliest syllabary composed by the Jesuits was written at the tail-end of the sixteenth century.[22] Matteo Ricci's dictionary was utilized by the Jesuits in China but never published.[23] These attempts, however, were soon overtaken by the linguistic achievements of the new generation of Jesuits in the seventeenth century. This next stage of incipient sinology saw the compiling of the first full-fledged dictionaries and the production of the first large-scale translations.

The Polish Jesuit Michael Boym (1612-1659) published the first two dictionaries of Chinese, a Chinese-Latin one in 1667 and a Chinese-French edition in 1670.[24] Since he also produced works on Chinese language,

---

[19]On these early manuscript vocabularies, grammars, and dictionaries, see van der Loon, "The Manila Incunabula and Early Hokkien Studies, Part II," *AM* 13 n.s. (1968): 95-186.

[20]See P. Jose Maria Gonzales, O.P., *Misiones Dominicanos en china (1700-1750)*, 2 vols. (Madrid: Consejo Superior de investigaciones cientificos Instituto Santo Toribio de Mogrovejo, 1952).

[21]The summary below is indebted to Mungello, *Curious Land*; and Bertuccioli, "Sinology in Italy 1600-1950." Some guidance on isolating representative figures from the crowd is derived from Edward H. Schafer, "Rudiments of a Syllabus on Sinological History," unpublished manuscript, Berkeley, n.d. Schafer's views were formulated by his personal perusal of rare books in the University of California-Berkeley library, supplemented by the evaluations of Henri Cordier.

[22]van der Loon, "The Manila Incunabula, part II," 102.

[23]Boleslaw Szczésniak, "The Beginnings of Chinese Lexicography in Europe with Particular Reference to the Work of Michael Boym (1612-1659)," *JAOS* 67 (1947): 160-65.

[24]Szczésniak, "The Beginnings of Chinese Lexicography in Europe," and "The First Chinese Dictionary Published in Europe," in *American Oriental Society Middle West Branch Semi-Centennial Volume*, ed. Denis Sinor (Bloomington: University of Indiana, 1969), 217-27. See further Paul Pelliot, "Michael Boym," *TP* 31 (1935): 95-151. The

medicine, cartography, geography, and botany, he may be considered—as he is by his modern compatriot Boleslaw Szczésniak—as "perhaps the first Sinologist of the true learning, who contributed most considerably to the foundation of Chinese studies in the Western World."[25] Basilio Brollo's Chinese-Latin dictionary of 1694, revised in 1699, was more comprehensive than that of Boym; it contained 7,000 characters in the first version and 9,000 in the second. Unfortunately, it circulated only in manuscript, and was plagiarized as the unacknowledged basis of Chrétian Louis Joseph de Guignes' 1813 dictionary.[26] Another important Italian Jesuit, from Sicily, was Prosper Intorcetta (1625-1696), who translated some of the Chinese classics into Latin (*Chung-yung*, for instance), and produced the *Sapienta sinica* (1662) and *Sinarum scientia politica-moralis* (1669).[27] The first grammar to be published, concerned exclusively with the spoken language, was the *Arte de la Lengua Mandarina* (Canton, 1703) of Francisco Varo, a Spanish Dominican who arrived in China in 1654.[28] Unfortunately, "this pioneering grammar," laments Christopher Harbsmeier, "avoided the use of characters and introduced the Chinese language entirely on the basis of transliteration." Although it circulated in manuscript in China, including among the Jesuits, it was very rare in Europe, yet it became one of the unacknowledged sources utilized by Fourmont in his *Grammatica duplex*,

---

authorship of these dictionaries is disputed by Walter Simon, "The Attribution to Michael Boym of Two Early Achievements of Western Sinology," *AM* n.s. 7 (1959): 165-69.

[25]Szczésniak, "The First Chinese Dictionary Published in Europe," 217.

[26]Bertuccioli, "Sinology in Italy 1600-1950," 69-70.

[27]An abridged translation appeared later: *The Morals of Confucius A Chinese Philosopher* (London, 1691).

[28]Edward Schafer puts this achievement into the context of general European scholarship by reminding us that this Chinese grammar was produced long after grammars on virtually all major languages had been completed: Spanish (1492); Arabic (1505); English (1586); Hebrew, Aramaic, Italian, French, and many South American Indian languages (16th century); Japanese (1604), Tagalog, Malay, Turkish, Ilocano, Persian, and Vietnamese (17th century). See Schafer, *What and How is Sinology?* Inaugural Lecture for the Department of Oriental Languages and Literatures, University of Colorado, Boulder, 14 October 1982 (University of Colorado, 1982), 5.

to be discussed below.[29] Ferdinand Verbiest (1623-1688), a Belgian Jesuit, cannon maker for the K'ang-hsi emperor, and supervisor of the Board of Astronomy, wrote a contemporary account of early Ch'ing history, the *Voyages de l'Empereur de la Chine dans la Tartarie* (Paris, 1695). Such was the esteem the emperor placed in Verbiest for his numerous contributions as astronomer, mathematician, geographer, engineer, translator, and diplomat, that he became the first Westerner to be granted a Chinese posthumous title.[30] The culmination of such individual efforts in translating texts and composing historical narratives came with the collaborative project first initiated by Ricci and finally orchestrated by Philippe Couplet (1622-1693), the Belgian Jesuit who edited the group translation of three of the "Four Books" (excluding *Mencius*), *Confucius Sinarum philosophus*. It was published at Paris in 1687 in a folio edition of 412 pages plus illustrations. Sixteen Jesuits are listed as contributors, but as many as one hundred sixteen may have participated.[31]

Matteo Ricci and Conversion Through Acculturation

The dominant Jesuit figure in China was, of course, the pioneer, Matteo Ricci.[32] Born in 1552, he studied at the Roman College under Christopher Clavius, the leader of Jesuit astronomy and author of the

---

[29]Harbsmeier, "John Webb and the Early History of the Study of the Classical Language in the West," 329.

[30]See the recent conference volume, John W. Witek, S.J., ed., *Ferdinand Verbiest, S.J.*, (Nettetal: Steyler Verlag, 1994). His *Astronomia Europaea* recently has been translated by Noel Golvers, *The "Astronomia Europaea" of Ferdinand Verbiest, S.J. (Dillingen, 1687): Text, Translation, Notes and Commentaries* (Nettetal: Steyler Verlag, 1993).

[31]Bertuccioli, "Sinology in Italy 1600-1950," 76, n. 13 lists four Jesuit editors: Intorcetta, Couplet, Christiani Herdtrich, and Francisci Rougemont. Mungello, *Curious Land*, devotes over fifty pages to this work (247-99). On Couplet, see Jerome Heyndrickx, C.I.C.M., ed., *Philippe Couplet, S.J. (1623-1693): The Man Who Brought China to Europe* (Nettetal: Steyler Verlag, 1990).

[32]Most authorities isolate three Jesuits as *primi inter pares*, at least in terms of making an impact on the Chinese intellect, whether through Christian thought or Western science: the Italian Ricci, the German Johann Adam von Schall (1592-1666), and Ferdinand Verbiest of Belgium; see *Ferdinand Verbiest, S.J.*, 17, 184, 329. Their tombs in Peking were repaired at government expense in 1978.

Gregorian calendar.[33] Ricci commenced his missionary labors in Macao in 1582, and arrived in Canton one year later. He spent the next twenty-eight years of his life preaching his gospel of salvation to the Chinese until his death in 1610, utilizing a novel approach that differed radically from earlier Spanish and Portuguese missionaries. Initially, he learned Chinese to impress the Chinese of his sincerity.[34] It soon came to be a proselytizing approach. For, instead of regarding the Chinese as idolatrous pagans, Ricci sought an accommodation with the powers that be through cultivated studies, considering them like-minded literati approachable on the level of learning.[35] That is, he utilized his European education in science, classical rhetoric, memory techniques, and the like, presented to the Chinese in elegant essays in classical Chinese, to find common ground with the Juist literati class. He was, at base, "a humanist and a scholar." As Howard Goodman and Anthony Grafton see him, "he worked with texts: Confucian classics that he mastered as the price of entrance to conversations with the Chinese elite and Western classics that gave him the authority to offer an alternative to Confucianism."[36] As Ricci stated,

> We have been living here in China for well-nigh thirty years and have traveled through its most important provinces. Moreover, we have lived in friendly intercourse with the nobles, the supreme magistrates, and the most distinguished men of letters in the kingdom. We speak the native language of the country, have set ourselves to the study of their customs and laws and finally, which is of the highest importance, we have devoted ourselves day and night to the perusal of their literature.[37]

---

[33]For Clavius, see Lach, *Asia in the Making of Europe*, vol. 2, bk. 3, 413; 480.

[34]John D. Young, *East-West Synthesis: Matteo Ricci and Confucianism* (Hong Kong: Centre of Asian Studies, University of Hong Kong, 1980), 14.

[35]It was after Ricci replaced Fr. Ruggierie in 1588 as the superior of the mission that the Jesuits abandoned the *kāsyāpa* of Buddhist priest and donned the robe of Juist scholar; Lionel M. Jensen, "The Invention of 'Confucius' and His Chinese Other, 'Kong Fuzi,'" *Positions* 1 (Fall 1993): 426.

[36]Howard L. Goodman and Anthony Grafton, "Ricci, the Chinese, and the Toolkits of Textualists," *AM* 3rd ser. 3 (1990): 102.

[37]Quoted in Mungello, *Curious Land*, 48.

Once a rapport was established and mutual respect shared, Ricci felt that the Christian sources of both his learning and his amity would be given a fair hearing.[38] He also extended a limited spiritual accommodation to certain Chinese beliefs and rituals that was later judged to have compromised "true" Catholic doctrine.[39] Yet his novel approach was merely the practical result of a spiritual movement current in Jesuit circles in Europe known as "Ancient Theology," which taught "a more open stance towards pagan religious expression," from Plato to Confucius.[40] The European debate between supporters of Ancient Theology and more mainstream Catholics culminated in the Rites Controversy and its wrangling over the nomenclature of translation.[41]

Like the Dominican Domingo de Nieva, Ricci utilized both spoken and written Chinese to facilitate his missionary work. But unlike the Dominicans and most of his fellow Jesuits, Ricci was more oriented to the written than to the spoken word. As Jonathan Spence explains,

> Ricci shared with all these men [i.e., his learned Chinese converts] a love of books and printing. He had an exaggerated view of the extent of Chinese literacy—"few are there here among them who don't know something of books"—but he noted correctly that all religious groupings tended to spread their message through books rather than

---

[38]For Ricci's accommodation policy and his scientific erudition, see Young, *East-West Synthesis*; Henri Bernhard, S.J., *Mattco Ricci's Scientific Contribution to China*, trans. Edward Chalmers Werner (Westport, Conn.: Hyperion Press, 1973); Mungello, *Curious Land*, 44-73; and Jonathan D. Spence, *The Memory Palace of Matteo Ricci* (New York: Viking, 1984).

[39]See Willard Peterson, "Learning from Heaven: the introduction of Christianity and other Western ideas into late Ming China," in *The Cambridge History of China*, vol. 8: *The Ming Dynasty, 1368-1644, Part 2*, ed. Denis Twitchett and Frederick W. Mote (Cambridge: Cambridge University Press, 1998), 789-839.

[40]Ibid., 792.

[41]For the effects of this accommodation on the so-called Rites Controversy, and especially Confucian accommodation to the Christian message, see Erik Zürcher, "Jesuit Accommodation and the Chinese Cultural Imperative," in *The Chinese Rites Controversy: Its History and Meaning*, ed. D.E. Mungello (Nettetal: Steyler Verlag, 1994), 31-64.

through preaching or public discourses.[42]

Hence the theoretical justification for translating religious tracts into Chinese, and the motivation for adopting the policy of accommodation through mutual acculturation. Part of this process, of course, was to learn more of China and to spread this understanding among people of good will in Europe. This accounts both for the translation work that Ricci and his colleagues supported, the composition of surveys of Chinese culture and history, and the private journals and letters published in Europe, among them Ricci's own posthumously published journals.

The Oriental Renaissance: Baroque Sinophilia and the *Clavis sinica*

Ricci and a legion of colleagues began a stream of translations from the Chinese that flooded into a Europe made increasingly receptive to foreign ideas with the eighteenth-century Enlightenment.[43] An important component of this intellectual awakening was what Raymond Schwab calls the Oriental Renaissance, first manifested in the intense preoccupation with things Persian, especially the material trappings of culture; later Indian and Chinese objects came to the fore.[44] On the intellectual plane, this trend came to be called "baroque sinophily."[45] Yet the foundation of this Renaissance in its maturity, like that of the earlier one in Europe, was philology.[46] As such, explains Lois Dussieux, "Oriental erudition is the

---

[42]Spence, *The Memory Palace of Matteo Ricci*, 154.

[43]See, for instance, Ting Tchao-ts'ing, *Les Descriptions de la Chine par les Française, 1650-1750* (Paris, 1928). The influence on the literary consciousness of the French made by these reports is treated by P. Martino, *L'Orient dans la littérature francaise au XIIIe et au XVIIIe siècle* (Paris, 1906).

[44]Raymond Schwab, *La Renaissance orientale* (Paris: Editions Payot, 1950); English edition, *The Oriental Renaissance: Europe's Rediscovery of India and the East, 1680-1880*, trans. Gene Patterson-Black and Victor Reinking (New York: Columbia University Press, 1984).

[45]Herbert Franke, "In Search of China: Some General Remarks on the History of European Sinology," *in Europe Studies China*, 12.

[46]As recently reiterated by Alain Peyraube, "Orientalism et linguistique," in *Livre blanc de l'orientalisme française* (Paris: Société Asiatique, 1993), 101-3. For the European Renaissance, cf. Craig R. Thompson, ed., *Collected Works of Erasmus*, vol. 23 (Toronto:

complement of the Renaissance."[47]

Dorothy Figueira explains the intellectual hold the Oriental Renaissance exerted on the minds of Europe in terms of its dual role in replacing the Western classics and furthering psychological self-identification:

> With the "decoding" of languages such as Sanskrit, Oriental wisdom became a complement to the vision of the Renaissance. No less a commentator than Victor Hugo notes in his *Journal* that Oriental literature had become, for superior souls, what Greek literature had been for the savant of the sixteenth century. Moreover, the Orient authorized the European observer to pose, from a position of prestige, the question of *difference*. Not only was it different from the unique model of Western culture, it was also the locus of a multitude of European aspirations.[48]

One scholarly preoccupation of the age lent intellectual energy to the ostensibly religious pursuits of the translators. This was the search for a universal language that would trace all tongues back to the biblical confusion at Babel.[49] Comparing all language versions of the Old Testament as an aid in exegesis was one scholarly by-product. This search resulted, among other curiosities, in the pious but misguided etymologies of the Dutch minister Phillippe Masson, who equated *manna*, the bread of the Hebrews distilled from Heaven, with Chinese *man-t'ou*, the popular bread bun from Shantung, or the Messianic title *Shiloh* with Chinese *shih-lo*, "Joy of the Ages."[50] Historians of both centuries who sought the origin of Chinese culture in Babylonia or among Egyptian colonists committed

---

University of Toronto Press, 1978), xxi: "The rebirth or 'renaissance' of arts and letters...is said by Erasmus in 1518 to date from 'about eighty years ago,' and although it extended to various arts the basis was philological: the sound recovery of Latin."

[47] As cited in Schwab, *The Oriental Renaissance*, 15.

[48] Dorothy Matilda Figueira, *Translating the Orient* (New York: State University of New York Press, 1991), 1.

[49] For this fascination with a universal language, see Mungello, *Curious Land*, 174-207.

[50] Duyvendak, *Holland's Contribution to Chinese Studies*, 13.

the same sin to a more egregious degree.[51]

Ancillary to this search was finding a methodological "key" to learning Chinese such as Andreas Müller's (1630-94) work on a *clavis sinica*, so that this language could be mastered and quickly placed within a pedigree chart of languages.[52] Yet, despite the use of linguistic tools unavailable to the previous generation, the academic debates and spiritual controversies that supercharged the intellectual atmosphere of the century tended to draw what should have been straightforward translations towards one camp or another to support personal agendas, either scholarly or religious. For instance, the over-spiritualized translations of earlier Jesuits become over-rationalized in the *Confucius Sinarum philosophus*.[53] In the words of David Mungello, "source materials were chosen with an eye to triumph rather than truth,"[54] cresting with the polemics of the Rites Controversy of 1700.[55]

Jesuit Translators versus Proto-Sinologists

Eighteenth-century translation work from the Chinese came to be dominated by the French Jesuits, not ending until the dissolution of the order in 1773. By this time, some 456 Jesuits, including converted natives, had labored in China.[56] This flood of translation activity began in earnest

---

[51]See, *inter alia*, Joseph de Guignes, *Memoire dans lequel on preuve, que les Chinois sont une colonie Egyptienne* (Paris, 1759), and Terrien de Lacouperie, *The Western Origin of the Early Chinese Civilization from 2300 BC to 200 AD* (London, 1884).

[52]Müller as the reputed founder of German sinology is treated in chapter four below.

[53]See Mungello, *Curious Land*, 258 for a passage from the *Ta-hsüeh*.

[54]Mungello, *Curious Land*, 331.

[55]The entire complicated question of historical bias and intellectual prejudice of both Jesuit and secular sinologists is put into context by Paul A. Rule, *K'ung-tzu or Confucius: The Jesuit Interpretations of Confucianism* (Sydney: Allen and Unwin, 1986), 183-98. For the Rites Controversy, see D.E. Mungello, ed., *The Chinese Rites Controversy: Its History and Meaning*.

[56]Kenneth S. Latourette, *A History of Christian Missions in China* (New York, 1929), 167. For the Jesuits in China, consult first Arnold H. Rowbothan, *Missionary and Mandarin: The Jesuits at the Court of China* (Berkeley: University of California Press, 1942); George Dunne, *Generation of Giants: The Story of the Jesuits in China in the Last Decades*

with the first French mission to China, led by Jean de Fontaney (1643-1710) and consisting of Jesuit mathematicians.[57] The greatest French Jesuit sinologue resident in Peking was Antonine Gaubil (1689-1759), who arrived in 1733 and remained there until his death twenty-six years later.[58] His main works include *Histoire abrégée de l'astronomie chinoise* (1729), *Histoire de Yen-tchis-can et de la dynastie de Mongou* (1739), *Le Chou-king, un des libre sacrés des Chinois* (1770), and *Traité de la chronologie Chinoise divisé en 3 parties* (1814). Unfortunately, most of his writings were published only after his death. Gaubil's scholarly approach is summarized by C. R. Boxer: "He made no pretence at being an original author, but explained that he was trying to give Europeans some exact and critical notions of Chinese history as related by the most reliable Chinese historians."[59] Moreover, he was one of the few Jesuits, along with Joseph de Mailla, to acknowledge his dependence upon native informants, once complaining of the dearth of capable assistants.[60]

Despite such an objective chronicler as Gaubil, there was initially little likelihood of the development of a science of sinology that evaluated China on her own terms. For, as the living embodiment of both *pro* and *con* arguments of the virtues of enlightened, non-Christian despotism, China was ineluctably drawn into the debate between the *esprits forts*—rational attackers of Christianity such as Voltaire and Bayle—and the defenders of pious orthodoxy such as Montesquieu and Turgot. On top of all of this, many of the major productions of the period were burdened with double biases—occidental interpretations of China as gleaned from

---

of the Ming Dynasty (South Bend: Notre Dame University Press, 1962); and Charles Ronan and Bonnie Oh, eds., *East Meets West: The Jesuits in China, 1582-1773* (Chicago: Loyola University Press, 1988).

[57]Recounted in Mungello, *Curious Land*, 329-31.

[58]For his biography, see Abel Rémusat, *Nouveaux mélanges asiatiques*, 2 vols. (Paris, 1829), 2:277-90.

[59]Boxer, "Some Aspects of Western Historical Writing on the Far East, 1500-1800," 314.

[60]Ibid., 315.

Manchu historiography,[61] set against the idealizations of the fetish for chinoiserie.[62]   Lively correspondence across the seas, conveying facile impressions and uninformed attitudes, took the place of dispassionate if less intriguing analysis.[63] Yet the scholarship that was produced by non-Jesuits tended to be equally polemical.   David Mungello has pronounced the earlier Jesuit missionaries, at least on the linguistic level, as more scholarly in both their aims and their methods than the so-called secular "proto-sinologists" of Europe; at least the published works of most Jesuits were grounded in Chinese or Manchu language sources.[64] Nevertheless, even if studies such as Joseph de Mailla's *Histoire générale de la Chine* (1777-1783) drew upon original sources and strove for a balanced presentation—and even this objectivity is questionable—[65]other sources were closer to the

---

[61]E.g., Jean-Francois Gerbillon (1654-1707), *Observations historiques sur la Grande Tartaire*. Since he helped mediate a border dispute with Russia on behalf of the Chinese crown, his pro-Manchu leanings are understandable.

[62]Highly readable is the study of Hugh Honour, *Chinoiserie: The Vision of Cathay* (London: John Murray, 1961), which treats everything from the image of Kublai Khan to the cult of Chinese gardens, from the preoccupation with porcelain products to the institutionalization of tea drinking.

[63]For a popular account, see Isabelle and Jean-Louise Vissière, *Letters édifiantes et curieuses de Chine par des missionnaires jésuits 1702-1776* (Paris: Garnier-Flammarion, 1979), which is based on the massive compilation *Lettres édifiantes et curieuses écrites des missions étrangèrs*, 34 vols. (Paris, 1703-76).

[64]For a less ponderous entrée to the nature and reliability of Jesuit scholarship than Mungello, consult Paul A. Rule, "Jesuit Sources," in *Essays on the Sources For Chinese History*, ed. Donald Leslie et al. (Columbia: University of South Carolina Press, 1973), 176-87, and E. Zürcher, "From 'Jesuit Studies' to 'Western Learning," in *Europe Studies China*, 264-79. The historical background, with a brief bibliographical survey, is offered by Frèches, *La Sinologie*, 16-24. Asian perspectives are provided by Mikinosuke, *Ō-Bei ni okeru Shina kenkyū*, 5-29; and Fang Hao, *Fang Hao liu-shih tzu-ting kao* (Taipei: Student Book Co., 1969).

[65]Joseph de Moyriac de Mailla, *Historia général de la Chine ou annales de cet empire*, 13 vols. (Paris, 1777-1783), was based largely on original translations from Chu Hsi, *T'ung-chien kang-mu*. Marianne Bastid-Bruguiere regards de Mailla's work, together with the edifying and curious letters of the Jesuits, as "the last major attempt of the Jesuits to rescue China's image as well as their own credibility." See her "Some Themes of 19th and 20th Century Historiography on China," in *Europe Studies China*, 229.

spirit of du Halde's *Description de l'empire de la Chine*, the "bible of European sinophilia,"[66] which avoided anything unsympathetic to the Chinese.[67]

Learned clerics like Andreas Müller or Athanasius Kircher (1602-80) integrated their sinological studies into a broad research agenda that extended well beyond China. Hence, such scholars were regarded more as intellectually independent proto-sinologists than Jesuit apologists for China, and occupied a position analogous to the Cold War "China Hand." Their specialized sinological work, having no obvious propagandist purpose, was therefore well received. For instance, Kircher's most influential production was read throughout Europe, the *China monumentis qua sacris profanis, nec non variis naturae & artis spectaculis, aliarumque rerum memorabilium argumentis illustrata* [China elucidated through its sacred and profane (literary) monuments, as well as by items of natural art, and through evidence of other remarkable things] (Amsterdam, 1667).[68] Its purpose, almost concealed amidst the overabundance of information, was to establish the authenticity of the Nestorian monument. As such, it included such relevant topics as the various routes to China; history of Christianity in China; old overland routes; a description of Tibet; depictions of the religions of China, Japan, and India; sketches of the government, customs, geography, fauna, flora, and mechanical arts of China; a treatise on the language of China, and a long Chinese-Latin dictionary.[69] But despite the merits of the work of these and other proto-

---

[66]According to the view of Zürcher, "From 'Jesuit Studies' to 'Western Learning,'" 268.

[67]Jean-Baptiste du Halde (1674-1743), editor of eighteen of the thirty-four volumes (vols. 9-26) of *Lettres édifiantes et curieuses*, authored *Description géographique, historique, chronologique, politique et physique de l'Empire de la Chine*, 4 vols. (Paris, 1735); this was largely derived from Martini, *Sinicae historiae* (Munich, 1658), Le Comte, *Nouveaux mémoires sur l'etat présent de la Chine* (Paris, 1696), and Jesuit reports sent to du Halde from Peking. See the evaluations of C.R. Boxer, "Some Aspects of Western Historical Writing on the Far East, 1500-1800;" and Mungello, *Curious Land*, 125.

[68]See Conor Really, *Athanasius Kircher: Master of a Hundred Arts* (Rome, 1974); and Jocelyn Godwin, *Athanasius Kircher: A Renaissance Man in Quest of Lost Knowledge* (London, 1979).

[69]Lach, *Asia in the Making of Europe*, vol. 3; Book 1, pp. 485-86.

sinologists, their secular scholarship was in fact too heavily informed with the Christian ideal of an all-embracing Hermeticism—the attempt to find vestiges of the true religion amid pagan literary remains. For instance, Kircher is remembered today less for his work on China than for his great synthesis of Hermeticism, *Oedipus Aegyptiacus*, 4 vols. (Rome, 1652-54).[70] The discovery of a paean to the nativity scene of the infant Christ in the *Shih-ching* (Mao #245) is an especially popular example.[71] Also amusing is his thesis that Ham and his sons brought Chinese characters to their new colony when they migrated from Egypt.[72] The proto-sinologists, therefore, turn out to be just as religious in their assumptions and apologetics as the more mainstream Jesuits, with of course a different academic program to pursue. And adding intellectual insult to objective injury, the proto-sinologists were heavily dependent on both oral and written reports of the Jesuits resident in China. For example, Müller's unfinished *Clavis sinica* was derived from secondary sources, for he knew little Chinese. In short, the proto-sinologists functioned more as compilers and editors than as researchers and writers.[73] Their ideas, then, would be best characterized as mental *chinoiserie*, and enjoyed as such.

---

[70] Mungello, *Curious Land*, pp. 134-73 treats the Hermeticism of Kircher in depth; cf. 307-11 for the same tendencies in the Figurism of Joachim Bouvet (1656-1730), and Claudia von Collani, *P. Joachim Bouvet S. J. Sein Leben und sein Werk* (Nettetal: Steyler Verlag, 1985).

[71] See Knud Lundbaek, *Joseph Prémare (1666-1736), S.J.: Chinese Philology and Figurism* (Aarhus: Aarhus University Press, 1991), 134-35.

[72] Lach, *Asia in the Making of Europe*, vol. 3, Book 3, pp. 1717-18.

[73] Mungello, *Curious Land*, 135.

ii. LEARNED LAITY AND THE FIRST PROFESSIONALS

"Nous allons aborder une terre déserte et encore en friche. La langue don't nous nous occuperons dans ce cours, n'est connue que de nom en Europe....Nous n'avons aucun modèle à suivre, aucun conseil à espérer; nous devons, en un mot, nous suffire à nous-mêmes, et tout puiser dans notre propre fonds."

—Jean-Pierre Abel Rémusat (1788-1832)[1]

It is true that the pioneer Abel Rémusat must have felt overwhelmed by the enormity of the task he faced. Yet, as Maspero has pointed out, China had long before developed its own system of scientific investigation of its native literature, and had assembled a large panoply of scholarly aids: dictionaries, bibliographies, general and specialized histories, encyclopedias, collections of geographical and epigraphical data, etc.[2] As opposed to the student of the classics in the West, then, the neophyte sinologist already had many of the tools of his trade, if he knew how to find them and make use of them. But, since both text and dictionary, history and commentary, were composed in the same lofty language, it must have seemed of dubious utility to handle such unwieldy tools. At any rate, it devolved upon the first professional sinologists to develop their own investigative agendas, methodologies, and most fundamentally, research aids and translations.

Eighteenth-century intellectual life in Europe was dominated by Catholic France, whose fanaticism at that time helped impel the reactionary tide of humanism; it is there that we must seek the origins of modern sinology.[3] For the first occupant of a professional chair of

---

[1]Rémusat, *Mélanges asiatiques*, 2: 2-3.

[2]Henri Maspero, "La Sinologie," *Societé asiatique, Le Livre de Centenaire, 1822-1922* (Paris, 1922), 261.

[3]Five bibliographical or biographical studies by Cordier on eighteenth-century French sinology are listed on the first page of his "Les Etudes chinoises sous la révolution et l'empire," *TP* 19 (1920): 59-103; six more on nineteenth-century developments are listed as well. *Deux siècles de sinologie française* (Peking: Centre franco-chinois d'études sinologiques, 1943), is a catalogue of the exhibit of pioneering works by eighteenth- and

sinology in Europe was a Frenchman, Rémusat, whose work in sinology was preceded by that of two countrymen, De Guignes and his teacher, the erudite if unscrupulous Jesuit Etienne Fourmont.

Etienne Fourmont

Fourmont (1683-1745) was educated in Mazarin College, where he indulged his fascination with languages. A Latin textbook he wrote while still in school was one product of this indulgence. The Hebrew, Arabic, and Chinese grammars that he eventually completed were all unfortunately analyzed on the basis of Latin grammatical categories. This "universalizing" tendency was part of the spirit of the times.

As a professor of Arabic at the Collège Royal, he enlarged the scope of his academic stewardship to include the Chinese language. He made his reputation as a sinologue off the hard work of his learned assistant, one Arcadius Huang (1679-1716), a Christian Chinese from Fukien. Huang had arrived in Europe in 1703 with a Catholic delegation, and was assigned to oversee the royal library and charged with compiling a dictionary.[4] The dictionary remained incomplete at Huang's untimely death in 1716, and was immediately appropriated by Fourmont. A catalogue initiated by Huang was completed by Fourmont, the *Catalogus Codicum Manuscriptorum Bibliothecae Regiae* (Paris, 1737). Fourmont's most notable work, *Grammatica Duplex*,[5] was based entirely on Varo's

---

nineteenth-century French sinologists, Jesuit or otherwise, as noted in the sub-title: *Exposition des principaux ouvrages d'autuers française publiés au xviiie et au xixe siècle et rassemblés a Pékin.* It includes short biographical notices along with bibliographical descriptions of the books that were placed on display. Frèches, *La Sinologie*, 24-33, treats the development of sinology among lay scholars in Europe from 1650 to 1800.

[4]Huang is included among those introduced by Abel Rémusat, "Sur les Chinois qui sont venus en France," *Nouveaux mélanges asiatiques*, 1:258-65. New light on Huang's personal life in Paris is shed by Jonathan D. Spence from archival material, "The Paris Years of Arcadio Huang," in *China Roundabout: Essays in History and Culture* (New York: W.W. Norton, 1992), 11-24.

[5]*Linguae Sinarum mandarinicae hieroglyphicae grammatica duplex latine et cum characteribus Sinensium. Item sinicorum regiae bibliothecae librorum catalogue denuo cum*

earlier grammar with the exception of the addition of Chinese characters. A font of 80,000 Chinese graphs engraved on wooden blocks, which took five craftsmen twenty years to carve, seems to be Fourmont's single independent contribution to incipient French sinology, and was an administrative, not scholarly, achievement.[6]

As a person, Fourmont was an unlovely, despicable character, who freely plagiarized the work of others, namely Huang, Varo, and Prémare. Cordier's characterization of this man is devastating and need not be reproduced here. Cordier felt so strongly about this unlikely father of French sinology that he repeated his unflattering dismissal of him in several works.[7] Rémusat avoided *ad hominem* attack, and limited himself to appraising Fourmont's scholarship, sometimes negatively, it is true.[8] Henri Maspero, with characteristic charity, merely states that the eighteenth-century missionaries believed one could only learn the languages and civilizations of the Far East in residence, and that the unhappy attempts of Fourmont had done nothing to change this opinion.[9]

Still, Fourmont was an enthusiastic student of the Chinese language; he worked his entire life on unfinished Chinese-French dictionaries, and was especially exercised by the contemporary vogue of searching for the "key" to Chinese by way of the 214 radicals—a *clavis sinica* being the Holy Grail of the proto-sinologists and French sinological orientalists. He never did learn to read integral texts, though, a failing that troubled him greatly. He contributed a reconciliation of Chinese and biblical calendrical

---

Notis amplioribus & Caractere Sinico editus (Paris, 1737).

[6]For an evaluation of Fourmont's influence on French sinology and his scholarship, especially his grammars and the "Port Royal" pedagogical approach he espoused, see Cécile Leung, "Etienne Fourmont (1683-1745): The Birth of Sinology in the Context of the Institutions of Learning in Eighteenth-Century France," *Sino-Western Cultural Relations Journal* 17 (1995): 38-56. My colleague Dr. Gail King kindly introduced this article to me and provided a copy.

[7]See Cordier, "Les Etudes chinoises sous la révolution et l'empire," 60.

[8]See Rémusat, *Nouvel Mélanges Asiatiques*, 2:291-304.

[9]Maspero, "La Sinologie," 261-62.

systems,[10] and seems to have been the earliest French sinologue to argue that Chinese was the original universal language.[11] He left an incomplete draft of a *Dictionar Historium Geographicum*, bound in three hefty volumes, which, along with his library catalogue, serves as the earliest French exemplar of the later spirit of bibliographic classification that gripped both Cordier and Pelliot so firmly. As Cécile Leung summarizes,

> If Fourmont's other works were to enable the student to learn the language, this dictionary was to help the reader explore the geography of China and become acquainted with its history, a compelling necessity for any serious scholar of the first half of the eighteenth century, when the gathering and organization of knowledge was foremost in the minds of the intellectual elite.[12]

Given his plagiarizing ways and lack of philological ability in Chinese, if Fourmont cannot in all honor serve as the founder of the premodern French school of sinology, at least he may be considered as the programmatic precursor.

Theophilus Bayer

A true scholar of independent judgement and accomplishment was Theophilus Siegfried Bayer (1694-1738).[13] This Prussian classicist was self-taught in Chinese; like Fourmont, he was a professional scholar, but of Greek and Roman antiquities. After working as a librarian in the Royal Library in Berlin, he was recruited to come to the newly established Academy of Sciences of Peter the Great at the latter's eponymous capital.

---

[10]"Dissertation sur les Annales Chinoises." Paper presented at the Académie des Inscriptions et Belles-Lettres, 18 May 1734.

[11]As evinced by the first subtitle of his earliest grammar, *Meditationes sinicae, in quibus I considerature linguae philosophicae atque universalis natura qualis esse, aut debeat, aut possit; II lingua Sinarum mandarinica...* (Paris, 1737).

[12]Leung, "Etienne Fourmont," 56.

[13]Lundbaek, *T.S. Bayer*; Dr. Franz Babinger, *Gottlieb Siegfried Bayer (1694-1738), ein Beitrag zur Geschichte der morgenländischen Studien im 18. Jahrhundert* (Leipzig: Harrassowitz, 1916).

But Bayer's increasing commitment to Chinese studies led to the creation of a new position for him, professor of Oriental Antiquities. Not until the arrival of Vassili Mikhailovitch Alekseev (1881-1951), student of Chavannes and last pupil of V.P. Vasil'ev (1818-1900), did St Petersburg boast an equally brilliant Orientalist, this time a fully-trained sinologist.[14]

Bayer's modern biographer Knud Lundbaek contrasts Bayer and Fourmont, the two earliest semi-professional sinologists, as follows:

---

[14]Universally regarded as the founder of the modern Russian school of sinology, Alekseev graduated from St Petersburg University in 1902. He continued his sinological studies in England, France, and Germany. While in Paris his classmates included Maspero, Granet, and Pelliot; he considered Pelliot his closest friend throughout the rest of his life. He was appointed the equivalent of "assistant professor" at St Petersburg upon his return from Europe, serving concurrently as Curator of Chinese books and manuscripts at the Asiatic Museum of the Academy of Sciences. He translated many volumes of Chinese literature, studied Chinese aesthetics, literary criticism, lexicography, bibliography, and the history of sinology. Five volumes of posthumous materials have been published, and a like amount remains in manuscript. For his life and works, see Hartmut Walravens, "V.M. Alekseev—Leben und Werk: Eine Bibliographie," *OE* 21 (1974): 67-95; L.N. Men'shikov, "Academician Vasilii Mikhailovich Alekseev (1881-1951) and his School of Russian Sinology," in *Europe Studies China*, 136-48; L.Z. Ejdlin, "The Academician V.M. Alexeev as a Historian of Chinese Literatrue," trans. Francis Woodman Cleaves, *HJAS* 10 (1947): 48-59; and Frèches, *La Sinologie*, 82-83. For the history and development of Russian sinology, see Vladislav F. Sorokin, "Two and a Half Centuries of Russian Sinology," in *Europe Studies China*, 111-28; Nikolai Speshnev, "Teaching and Research on Chinese Language at St Petersburg University in the 19th and 20th Centuries," in *Europe Studies China*, 129-35; Wilhelm Barthold, *La Découverte de l'Asie: Histoire de 'Orientalismé en Europe et en Russia* (Paris, 1947); C. Kiriloff, "Russian Sources," in *Essays on the Sources for Chinese History*, 188-202; Tung-Li Yuan, *Russian Works on China, 1918-1960* (New Haven: Far Eastern Publications, 1961); E. Stuart Kirby, *Russian Studies of China: Progress and Problems of Soviet Sinology* (New Jersey: Rowman and Littlefield, 1976); and B.G. Gafurov and Y.V. Gankovsky, eds. *Fifty Years of Soviet Oriental Studies: Brief Reviews (1917-1962)* (Moscow: Nauka, 1967). The missionary background to the earliest Chinese language studies is set by Eric Widmer, *The Russian Ecclesiastical Mission in Peking During the 18th Century* (Cambridge, Mass.: Harvard University Press, 1976).

The personality of the two men was as different as can be imagined: here was pious and timid Bayer, there was arrogant and virulent Fourmont. Their situations were also very different: Bayer in a newly-founded Academy in the small, new modern-style capital of Peter the Great's Russia, Fourmont in one of the famous old academies in Paris....As to their facilities for indulging in Chinese studies, as a young man Bayer had sat for less than a year in the Royal Library in Berlin, copying from a missionary vocabulary and from old Jesuit manuscripts and letters. When he came to St Petersburg in 1726 he found no Chinese books there and no works by China missionaries. In his last years he had the benefit of being advised by the learned Jesuits in Peking, but it usually took a year or more before a letter from St Petersburg was received in Peking and the same time before a reply arrived. Fourmont had the large Chinese collections of the Bibliothèque royale at his disposal and for some years he had a young French-speaking Chinese to help him.[15]

Bayer's most influential work was the *Museum sinicum*, a collection of theoretical essays, long and short, on the Chinese language, literature, grammar, origins of the script, lexicography, dialects, and materials leading towards a full-fledged dictionary, based largely on the works of earlier Jesuits, and freely acknowledged as such.[16]

Joseph and Chrétian Louis De Guignes

Fourmont's chief disciple was Joseph De Guignes (1721-1800). Professor of Syrian at the Royal College, De Guignes is known today as the imagination behind the theory that the Chinese were originally Egyptian colonists, mentioned above.[17] His sole production retaining value for sinology today is *Histoire générale des Huns, des Turcs, des Mongols et des autres Tartares occidentaux*, 5 vols. (Paris, 1758), which indicates the true

---

[15]Lundbaek, *T.S. Bayer*, 1
[16]Analyzed in depth by Lundbaek, *T.S. Bayer*, 39-140.
[17]*Mémoire dans lequel on preuve, que les Chinois sont une colonie Egyptienne.* A synopsis is presented at Schafer, *What and How is Sinology*, 6.

thrust of his studies, Asian rather than sinological, however broadly conceived.[18] His son Chrétian Louis Joseph De Guignes served in the French consulate in Canton as a royal envoy and interpreter, and he published three narrative volumes of his experiences in China.[19] More importantly, he was commissioned by Napoleon to edit the manuscript dictionary of Chinese by Basilio Brollo (1648-1703) which had been included among the 100 paintings, busts and vases, along with 500 manuscripts, from the Vatican that had formed the spoils of war (according to the treaty of Telontino of 1798 after Napolean's victorious first Italian campaign). De Guignes began in 1808 using characters already engraved by Fourmont. This *Dictionnaire chinois, francais et latin* was printed in Paris in 1813 under de Guignes' own name.[20]

Despite the work of Fourmont, the two De Guignes', and another pupil of Fourmont, Deshauterayes, the condition of sinological studies in France during this period, as characterized by Cordier, was one of haphazard and aimless individual effort, vitiated by fantastic theories and lacking method. Michel le Roux Deshauterayes (1724-95), professor of Arabic at the Collège de France and nephew of Fourmont, illustrates at least the haphazard and aimless side of sinology at the time. His main works, evincing no common thread, include a translation of the *Ch'un-ch'iu*, a history of the Buddha, and a treatise on Chinese cereal grains! The true creator of Chinese studies in France was one who was able to bring

---

[18]Cordier, "Les Etudes chinoises sous la révolution et l'empire," 64. Eight unpublished manuscripts of De Guignes on Chinese history, script, astronomy, calendars, and religion, plus a partial translation of the *Ch'un-ch'iu*, are listed by Cordier on p. 86.

[19]*Voyages à Peking, Manille et l'Ile de France faits dans l'intervalle des années 1784 à 1801*, 3 vols. (Paris, 1808).

[20]A more complete title was *Dictionnaire chinois-française et latin, publié d'apres l'ordre de Sa Majesté l'Empereur et Rois Napoleon le Grand; par M. de Guignes, résident de France à la Chine*....It has been assessed by Cordier, "Les Etudes chinoises sous la révolution et l'empire," 93-98; and Knud Lundbæk, "The Establishment of European Sinology 1801-1815," in *Cultural Encounters: China, Japan, and the West. Essays Commemorating 25 Years of East Asian Studies at the University of Aarhus*, ed. Søren Clausen, et al. (Aarhus: Aarhus University Press, 1995), 17-18, 34-35.

order and direction to the field, the great Abel Rémusat.

Jean-Pierre Abel Rémusat

Jean-Pierre Abel Rémusat (1788-1832) obtained a doctorate in medicine in 1813, but already a Chinese herbal had attracted his attention to sinological studies. He was self-taught with the help of the traditional Chinese dictionary *Cheng tzu t'ung;* after assuming the newly established chair in Chinese, he gained access to manuscript grammars and dictionaries deposited in the imperial library, notably Prémare's *Notitia linguae sinicae* (1728), which source he gratefully acknowledged.[21] According to Maspero, Rémusat was the first auto-didactic savant in Europe to acquire a profound knowledge of Chinese.[22] At the tender age of twenty-three he published a work later termed brilliant by Cordier, an *Essai sur la langue et la littérature chinoises* (Paris, 1811).[23] Another essay published in Latin in 1813 concentrates on the nature of the Chinese script, and such aspects of the classical language as monosyllabism, binomial expressions, grammatical particles, and the like: "Utrum Lingua Sinica sit vere monosyllabica? Disputatio philologica, in qua de Grammat ica Sinica obiter agitur; autore Abelo de Remusat."[24] His next few publications further augmented his reputation, and brought about the creation of a chair in Chinese for him

---

[21]This work by the Jesuit Joseph Menri-Marie de Prémare (1666-1736), was, in the view of Christopher Harbsmeier, the most important Chinese grammar of the eighteenth century. For technical reasons it remained unprinted in Paris, and only appeared in Malacca in 1831. Nevertheless, in manuscript form it much influenced Rémusat's grammar. "For its time," concludes Harbsmeier, "it is a simply astonishing scholarly achievement vastly superior to what preceded it and quite arguably much superior to more celebrated works," including that of Rémusat; see Harbsmeier, "John Webb," in *Europe Studies China*, 330. For Prémare; see Lundbaek, *Joseph Prémare*; a lengthy analysis of *Notitia linguae sinicae* is found on 64-103.

[22]Maspero, "La Sinologie," 262.

[23]Summarized by Lundbæk, "The Establishment of European Sinology," 41-43.

[24]*Mines de l'Orient* 3 (1813): 279-88; rpt. in French as "Sur la nature monosyllabique attribuée communément à la langue chinoise," *Mélanges asiatiques*, II:47-61.

at the Collège de France on November 29, 1814.[25] This, according to Herbert Franke, was the birth-year of sinology.[26] Knud Lundbaek argues rather that it was not until Abel Rémusat presented his inaugural lecture in this chair on January 16, 1815, that academic sinology was formally established.[27] Edward Schafer highlights Rémusat's career as follows:

> Rémusat, in addition to Chinese, had studied Mongol, Tibetan, and other East Asian languages. His work, accordingly, displays one of the hallmarks of the French school of sinology, destined to be refined and perfected by Paul Pelliot at the beginning of the twentieth century. I shall only suggest Rémusat's distinguished career by naming one title from among his many publications: *Eléments de la Grammaire Chinoise ou Principes généraux du Kou-wen ou style antique, et du Kouan-hou, c'est-à-dire, de la langue commune généralement usitée dans l'empire chinois.* This was published in 1822. In addition to such basic studies as this, he published many significant reports and translations in the fields of literature, philosophy, religion, and history. He was editor of the *Journal des Savants*, to which he contributed articles on China. He was the first secretary of the Asiatic Society of Paris, whose organ is the still important *Journal Asiatique.*[28]

His course at the college already points toward the strict philological methods of the mature French school: three sessions per week

---

[25]A chair in Sanskrit was endowed at the same time.

[26]Franke, "In Search of China," 13.

[27]Lundbæk, "The Establishment of European Sinology," 15. The history of the Chinese chair in Paris, from its endowment and first occupancy by Abel Rémusat, through Julien, Hervey de Saint-Denys, and Chavannes, is treated by the latter's successor, Henri Maspero, in "La Chaire de Langues et Littératures chinoises et tartares-mandchoues," in *Le Collège de France, Livre jubilaire composé à l'occasion de son quatrième centenaire* (Paris, 1932), 355-66.

[28]Schafer, *What and How is Sinology?*, 7. An absorbing account of the intellectual excitement animating the newly founded Société Asiatique is Schwab, *The Oriental Renaissance*, 80-84.

were divided between lectures on grammar and the explication of texts, among them the *Shang-shu, Lao-tzu, Kan-ying p'ien*, the life of Confucius both in Chinese and Manchu, the Nestorian stele, and novels. His lecture notes culminated in the *Eléments de la grammaire chinoise* mentioned above and became the first scientific exposition of Chinese in Europe, even if not wholly original.[29] This work inspired Wilhelm von Humboldt to compose his now famous philosophical epistle *Lettre à M. Abel Rémusat sur la nature des formes grammaticales en général, et sur le génie de la langue chinoise en particulier* (1827), and it served as the standard primer for French sinologists throughout the century. Maspero described its virtues in these generous terms:

> Marshman and Morrison had each published a new grammar, the first in 1814 and the second in 1815, but this was the first to treat both the written language and the spoken, each occupying one part. Above all, this was the first in which the grammar was isolated to take account of the proper spirit of the Chinese language, and not just as a translation exercise where all the grammatical forms of the European languages with their conjugations, declensions, etc., imposed their individual patterns.[30]

This work laid the foundation for Rémusat to exploit systematically and methodically the riches of Chinese literature. A similar work by Rémusat on the "Tartar" languages of Asia, i.e., the non-Chinese tongues of Mongolian, Manchu, Tibetan, and Eastern Turkic, had appeared earlier in 1820, viz. *Recherches sur les langues tartares*. This was the first attempt to classify these languages systematically.[31]

As a translator, at least with the most difficult works such as the *Fo-*

---

[29]His debt to Prémare' grammar is analyzed by Lundbaek, *Joseph De Prémare*, 176-82.

[30]Maspero, "La Chaire de Langues et Littératures chinoises et tartares-mandchoues," 357-58.

[31]Maspero, "La Sinologie," 262.

kuo chi, Rémusat fell prey to a debilitating habit of eighteenth-century sinologists, that of presenting paraphrase instead of rendering the literal sense. "If he attained the general sense, it was due to the intuition of a prodigy rather than correct analysis." Nevertheless, continues Maspero, this particular translation was "remarquable pour le epoque," especially given the paucity of historical and geographic knowledge of Central Asia and India of the times.[32]

Commissioned to inventory the Chinese sources in the royal library, Rémusat conceived the plan of translating the bibliographical sections of the *Wen-hsien t'ung-k'ao* of Ma Tuan-lin to help lay the foundation of bibliography on a firm footing. Only the first volume, on the "classics" was completed, and Rémusat died of cholera before it could be printed. Among his several students, Julien, Fresnel, and Pauthier, the first was chosen to succeed him.

Stanislas Julien

Stanislas Julien (1797-1873) came late to scholarship due to the poverty of his family; when he had the chance he applied himself diligently to catch up. His scholarship eventually ripened, and he became the dominant European sinologist of the age; except for the missionary-sinologue Legge, no sinologist enjoyed a like reputation until Chavannes. His estate funded a prize in his honor to be awarded annually for the outstanding contribution to sinology. Unfortunately, according to Paul Demiéville, his character was execrable.[33] (It is unknown whether his personality was responsible for the unflattering epithet of Victor Pavie,

---

[32]Ibid., 263.

[33]Demiéville, "Aperçu historique des études sinologiques en France," 154. Cf. 458: "Il avait un caractère aussi abominable que sa science était irréprochable. Jaloux, colérique, acariâtre, il accapara les charges et écarta tout concurrent." And speaking of several scurrilous pamphlets issued by Julien, little more than *ad hominem* attacks on fellow sinologists, Demiéville concludes: "Ces titres divertissants montrent que les moeurs de la sinologie française ne s'etaient pas adoucies en France depuis la Querelle des Rites et les disputes épiques de Fréret et de Fourmont au XVIIIe siècle."

"philological animal"—in the plural form, *bestiae linguaces*, including fellow savant Francisque Michel in this learned menagerie).[34]

After studies at the college in Orléans, he transferred to the Collège de France and devoted himself to Greek, branching out into Arabic, Hebrew, Persian, and Sanskrit.   In 1824, six months after meeting Rémusat, he began his own translation of the *Mencius* in Latin, partly through two Manchu versions, having recently added that language to his arsenal. It took four months, and was burdened with the lengthy title of *Meng Tseu vel Mencium inter Sinenses philosophos, ingenio, doctrina, nominisque claritate Confucio proximum, edidit, Latina interpretatione, ad interpretationem Tartaricam utramque recensita, instruixit, et perpetuo commentario, e Sinicis deprompto, illustravit Stanislaus Julien*, 2 vols. (Paris, 1824-29). It was praised fulsomely by his teacher, who set forth the virtues of Julien's methodology in detail.[35] For instance:

> En premier lieu, M. Julien s'est livré à une lecture assidue du texte de Mencius; il a étudié le style de cet auteur, et s'est pénétré de tout ce que son langage offre de particulier. Une comparaison répétée de tous les passages qui contiennent quelques difficultés dans un même écrivain, suffirait souvent pour donner la clef du plus grand number: c'est ce qui arrive en chinois comme dans les autres langues.[36]

Julien consulted ten different editions of the Chinese text, a feat even more notable for his day and place than was the editing of Horace out of ten Latin editions by Lambinus (Denys Lambin, 1520-72) in 1561. Julien's translation of the *Tao-te ching* (Paris, 1842) evinced the same concern for clarifying the textual tradition before hazarding an interpretation, for he again consulted all available editions (seven). His overall superiority as a sinologist, according to Maspero, rested upon the soundness of his

---

[34]Schwab, *The Oriental Renaissance*, 335.
[35]*Mélanges asiatiques*, 2:298-310.
[36]Ibid., 2:302.

translations, commencing with Mencius.[37]

In his teaching Julien dispensed with lectures on grammar in the abstract, and devoted himself instead to conducting his pupils through extended readings in the texts: *San-tzu ching, Ch'ien-tzu wen, Shang-shu, Lun-yü, Tso-chuan,* and *Li-chi.* However, he insisted on attention to syntax as the key to reading, and produced his *Syntax nouvelle de la langue chinoise* (Paris, 1869) both to defend his approach from his detractors, notably G. Pauthier,[38] and to teach this crucial science.[39] It incorporated the results of much recent Chinese philological work; for instance, pp. 151-231 includes much of Wang Yin-chih's study of particles, the *Ching-chuan shih-tz'u* of 1798.

Julien translated most of the classics and many works of history and literature for his students, but never saw fit to publish them. What he produced in the first part of his career during the decade of 1830 was more in the popular vein: Yüan dramas and Ming and Ch'ing novels that were rendered in a masterful style. This was done in part out of the desire to study the social life of the people, something that could not be done without first-hand observation (as justified by Maspero, who chirped with snobbish elitism that otherwise "their banality and mediocre construction scarcely compensated the effort of the translator").[40] Julien's skill in the intricacies of the language made it possible for him to do justice to the prose narrative of the novels as well as to the numerous passages in verse

---

[37]Maspero, "La Sinologie," 267.

[38]Jean-Pierre-Guillaume Pauthier (1801-73) started as a poet and ended up as a popularizer of the Orient, with an intermediate career as an Indianist. The protracted confrontation between Julien and Pauthier, scarcely to be dignified by characterizing it as a debate, is documented by Henri Cordier, *Bibliotheca sinica: Dictionnaire bibliographique des ouvrages relatifs à l'empire chinois,* 5 vols. (rpt. Taipei: Ch'eng-wen, 1966), 3:1731-34; see also the discussion by Schwab, *The Oriental Renaissance,* 326-28.

[39]Julien had first been struck by reading a vague mention of syntax in Marshman's *Clavis sinica,* who had himself been anticipated by Varo in his *Arte de la Lengua Mandarina* (19), but it took Julien's work to clarify and illustrate this principle.

[40]Maspero, "La Sinologie," 264.

scattered about the texts. Indeed, it was both the novelty as well as the difficulty inherent in such texts, with their combination of classical and vernacular registers, that challenged Julien's interests and virtuosity. His success in this dual challenge illustrated the need for competency in both classical and colloquial languages in order truly to master Chinese literature.[41]

Later in his career his interests expanded to include China in an Asian setting. His translation of the life of Hsüan-tsang was produced in 1851; in 1856 appeared the ancillary *Mémoires sur les contrées occidentales*. With the *Histoire de la vie de Hiouen-Thsang* Julien became the first sinologist to go beyond the native commentators and produce a work of independent judgement; as such, this work constitutes an important milestone in the development of sinology. And both of these works, with their transcriptions of Sanskrit words, helped lay a firm scholarly foundation for Indianists.

One methodologically instructive pamphlet derived from Julien's work on Hsüan-tsang, *Méthode pour déchiffre et transcrire les noms sanscrits qui se rencontrent dans les livres chinois* (1861). Admittedly its results are flawed because Julien depended on modern forms for both Sanskrit and Chinese and ignored the chronological difficulties of his comparisons. Nevertheless, it served as an empirical model for comparing transcriptions in a controlled and methodical way, and helped eliminate the most fanciful restitutions of later scholars and served as a guide for all sinological study of Buddhism.[42]

Documents sur les Tou-kiue came out between 1864 and 1867. Julien's articles in the *Journal Asiatique* devoted to the bibliography,

---

[41]This necessity has been reiterated and illustrated in David Hawkes, "Classical, Modern, and Humane," in *Classical, Modern and Humane: Essays in Chinese Literature* (Hong Kong: Chinese University Press, 1989), 3-23.

[42]Maspero, "La Sinologie," 267. See the short evaluation by Edwin G. Pulleyblank, "European Studies on Chinese Phonology: The First Phase," in *Europe Studies China*, 340.

history, and geography of India were reprinted as *Mélanges de géographie asiatique et philologies Sino-indienne* (1864).

At the urging of the ministry of public works, Julien also explored the history of Chinese technology, and produced works on the silk industry, porcelain,[43] and *Les Industries anciennes et modernes de l'empire chinois* (1869), a collection of miscellaneous bagetelles treating vegetable and mineral colors, metals, engraving, tea, and the like. This paralleled the study of Chinese technology being pioneered by contemporary missionaries in China, especially Alexander Wylie.

In sum, the modern French school of sinology was to be indebted to both Julien's insistence on complete command of Chinese sources and his expanded vision of China within the Asian setting. The ascendancy of the French school that began with Rémusat reached its zenith with Julien, not to be regained until the career of Chavannes.

At Julien's passing in 1873 most of his accomplished students had already predeceased him: Biot, the translator of the *Chou-li*,[44] Bazin, author of two works of grammar, *Mémoire sur les principles généraux du chinois vulgaire* (1854) and *Grammaire mandarine* (1856), and the first occupant of the chair in modern Chinese at l'Ecole des langues orientales established in 1841,[45] and the clergyman Méthivier. One of Julien's least accomplished disciples remained to succeed to his chair in Chinese, Mongolian, and Manchu languages and literature.

---

[43]*Histoire et fabrication de la porcelaine chinoise* (1856), which was a translation of an original source, the *Ching-te-chen t'ao-lu*.

[44]Berthold Laufer characterized this translation by Biot as "a monument of stupendous and sagacious erudition and remains the only work of Chinese literature heretofore translated into any foreign language with a complete rendering of all commentaries;" Laufer, *Jade: A Study in Chinese Archaeology and Religion* (1912; rpt. New York: Kraus, 1967), 15. Biot also translated the Bamboo Annals, *Tchou chou ki nien* (1841), and compiled several catalogues on Chinese astronomy, *Catalogue des étoiles filantes* (1841), and *Comètes obervées en Chine* (1846).

[45]The history of this chair is traced by Paul Demiéville, *Choix d'études sinologiques (1921-1970)*, 152-61.

Marquis d'Hervey de Saint-Denys

The Marquis d'Hervey de Saint-Denys (1823-92) had studied Chinese under Bazin at the Ecole des langues orientales and later with Julien. Under the latter's direction Saint-Denys translated the last few chapters of the *Chou-li* left incomplete at the death of Biot. But despite his work in the canonical literature and ability in modern Chinese, Saint-Denys is known as the pioneer translator of Chinese poetry, who popularized it before it became the fashionable thing to do. His principal works were *Poésies de l'époque des T'ang* (1862), and the *Li sao* (1870). As to the former, "I can testify," asserted Edward Schafer, "that these translations of more than a century ago are equal to most and superior to many versions of T'ang poetry made by American literary scholars today."[46] His translation of the "Li-sao" was judged less successful by Demiéville, who concluded that it was distinguished neither by philological acrobatics nor by the elegance of its French. Nevertheless, it did have a notable second life in the literary salons of the Second Empire.[47] One valuable aberration from the literary field was *Ethnographie des peuples étrangers à la Chine* (1876-83), a translation of two sections of the *Wen-hsien t'ung-k'ao* that dealt with foreign countries. In this work, Saint-Denys returned to his roots—the author Ma Tuan-lin who was first utilized by Rémusat and the field that was first exploited by Julien. Perhaps Saint-Denys avoided more studies in the classics because he was incapable of the philological feats of his predecessors.

Maspero, even more critically, lamented that when Legge's *Chinese Classics* first appeared (1861-1872), French sinology was not advanced enough to profit, and that included Saint-Denys:

The twenty years during which he occupied the chair (1874-1892) added little to the luster of French science, which, little by little, had

---

[46]Schafer, *What and How is Sinology?*, 8.
[47]Demiéville, "Aperçu historique des études sinologiques en France," 459.

been eclipsed by the remarkable pleiade of English savants of this period, Wylie, Legge, Watters, Mayers, Edkins, and the American Wells Williams. D'Hervey de St-Denys lacked the surety in translation of Julien, and had little critical sense.[48]

This surprising admission from Maspero makes Chavannes' accomplishments in the next generation all the more remarkable.

Much more than just a chair in classical Chinese was passed down from Rémusat through Julien to Saint-Denys, many items in their personal libraries were handed down as well. One example was an anonymous manuscript dictionary of Chinese in Spanish: "It had belonged to...Saint Denys..., whose library was sold two years after his death, and before him Stanislaus Julien...who bought it at the sale of the books of his predecessor at the Collège de France, Rémusat."[49] But of much greater import were the research methodologies and fields they inherited, developed, and bequeathed to the next generation.

From Orientalism to Cultural Parallelomania

Cordier was correct in claiming that the work of the earliest French *sinologues de chambre* was haphazard and aimless, vitiated by fantastic theories, and lacking in method. If Rémusat and his followers were able to impose order and method in the field, fantastic theories and unconscious biases continued to haunt the work of occidental sinologists in both China and the West. After all scholars, no less sinologists, work in the intellectual climate of their time, and react and respond according to contemporary concerns. The overall intellectual mind-set of the eighteenth and nineteenth centuries for western sinologists was Orientalism.

"Sinological Orientalism" is the term adopted by Norman Girardot and Lauren Pfister, in their respective forthcoming volumes on James

---

[48]Maspero, "La Sinologie," 269.
[49]van der Loon, "The Manila Incunabula and Early Hokkien Studies," 97.

Legge to characterize the scholarship on China of the nineteenth century.[50] As part of the mentality of contemporary Orientalism, sinologists adopted the same program of study and fell prey to the same psychological assumptions and cultural blinders as their Indianist and Arabicist confreres.

Orientalism commenced with the discovery that there was a world beyond the mental horizons of European culture, a horizon firmly fixed ever since the Greeks had studiously ignored Asia.[51] Beyond this horizon were languages that transcended the classical trio of Hebrew, Greek, and Latin, and religions and philosophies not delimited by the Judaeo-Christian paradigms of divinity and morality. The philological movement called the Oriental Renaissance, as mentioned above, consisted of the aggressive study of languages and cultures of the Orient, an enterprise chronicled with sure insight and sympathy by Raymond Schwab.[52] Sanskrit was the centerpiece of this movement. As a language cognate with ancient Greek and Latin, Sanskrit and the critical attention it attracted from William Jones and other comparative philologists of the nineteenth century such as Ernest Renan (1823-92) and Max Müller (1823-1900) turned the debate from the search for a universal language that was ultimately derived from the divine Adamic tongue to the lost civilization of Indo-European ancestors.[53] The Great Debate was no longer carried on in religious terms, for it had moved

---

[50]Girardot, *The Victorian Translation of China: James Legge's Oriental and Oxonian Pilgrimage* (Berkeley and London: University of California Press, forthcoming), and Pfister, *In Pursuit of the Whole Duty of Man: James Legge and the Sino-Scottish Encounter in 19th Century China,* unpublished manuscript. The discussion that follows has been greatly strengthened both through the theoretical issues raised by Girardot and Pfister and the riches of their capacious bibliographies.

[51]See Arnaldo Momigliano, "The Fault of the Greeks," in *Essays in Ancient and Modern Historiography* (Middletown, Conn.: Wesleyan University Press, 1982), 9-23.

[52]Schwab, *The Oriental Renaissance.*

[53]Maurice Olender, "Europe, or How to Escape Babel," *History and Theory* 33 (1994): 5-25, treats the interplay between these two traditions and the linguistic developments that led to the shift in attention. See further Olender, *The Languages of Paradise: Race, Religion, and Philology in the Nineteenth Century* (Cambridge, Mass.: Harvard University Press, 1992).

beyond biblical exegesis and conversion through acculturation. Instead, the concern was secular, the academic recovery of the roots of a culture. Aryanism was the result, which, tragically, yielded theoretical justification for the racial politics and genocide of our own century.

The institutional program of Orientalism and its major figures have been described by Schwab. But the term encompasses much more, as forcefully postulated by Edward Said in *Orientalism*.[54] In fact, so broad is it that Said never hazards a definition; rather he qualifies it differently at different places for the discussion at hand. First, Orientalism is what Orientalists do. Second, it is a "style of thought" that epistemologically opposes the Orient and the Occident. Finally, it is a "corporate institution for dealing with the Orient" that exerts hegemonic control over its sources, and in turn, conceptualizes it and presents it in Western (read "mythical" and "stereotypical") terms.[55] Said's arguments rest overwhelmingly on his analysis of the engagement of the West with the Middle East. China, Japan, and Southeast Asia, by way of contrast, seem to have suffered less from that aspect of Orientalism that encouraged an aggressive intellectual imperialism.[56] At least in the case of China, this was due largely to the fact that sinologists worked from within the literati tradition and shared the same textual outlook, philological methodologies, and canonized research agenda. They functioned, therefore, more as cultural apologists for China than as imperialist exploiters of its documentary riches.[57]

If nineteenth-century sinologists did not participate in active

---

[54]Edward W. Said, *Orientalism* (New York: Vintage, 1979).

[55]See James Clifford, review of Said, *Orientalism*, in *History and Theory* 19 (1980): 204-23 for the philosophical and political underpinnings of *Orientalism*; 209-10 are good for Said's difficulties with definition.

[56]See the essays by Robert Kapp, Michael Dalby, David Kopf, and Richard H. Minear in the review symposium on Said's *Orientalism* in *JAS* 39 (1980): 481-517.

[57]Arthur Wright, "The Study of Chinese Civilization," *Journal of the History of Ideas* 21 (1960): 233-55, treats the problems of sinologists working from within the Chinese tradition instead of squarely and objectively outside of it. My reactions to the issues raised by Wright are reserved for the Envoi that concludes this book.

intellectual colonialism as did their fellow Orientalists, they nevertheless subscribed to the same set of subconscious assumptions that animated the scholarly discourse of the times. If, as stated above, the debate had shifted from the religious to the secular arena, then sinologists shifted as well. Hence, when the preoccupation with a universal language eventually gave way to the effort to uncover ancient Indo-European roots, sinologists naturally partook enthusiastically of the new linguistic game. Methodologically speaking, the theoretically mushy concern with a conceptual *clavis sinica* yielded to the technically explicit tool of syntax, just as on the conceptual level Hermeticism yielded to Aryanism.

The worst excesses of Orientalism are aptly described, in the happy phrase of Girardot, as a "cultural parallelomania." Works from G. Pauthier, *Sinico-Ægyptiaca* (Paris: Typographie de Firmin Didot frères, 1842) and Joseph de Guignes, *Memoire dans lequel on preuve, que les Chinois sont une colonie Egyptienne* (Paris, 1759) to Terrien de Lacouperie, *The Western Origin of the early Chinese Civilization from 2300 BC to 200 AD* (London, 1884), determined to uncover the Aryan roots of Chinese civilization. Among the most active Aryanists of the nineteenth century were the sinologists Joseph Edkins (1823-1905) and Gustav Schlegel (1840-1903). In 1871 Edkins published in London *China's Place in Philology: An Attempt to Show that the Languages of Europe and Asia have a Common Origin*.[58] Edkins' most noteworthy comparison was probably "On the Three Words 'I Hi Wei' [夷希微] in the Tau Te King."[59] In this short article Edkins combined the Hermetic attempt to find traces of the original revealed religion with the effort to elucidate the Chinese cultural and linguistic connection with the Aryans; these three Chinese words, it turns

---

[58]Further examples from Edkins, "Sino-Babylonian" comparisons include "Early Connections of Babylon with China," *China Review* 16 (1887-1888): 371; "The Foreign Origin of Taoism," *China Review* 19 (1891):397-99; *Ancient Symbolism* (London, 1889); "Primeaval Revelation," *China Review* 21 (1891):22-23; and *The Early Spread of Religious Ideas* (London, 1893). Most of these examples are culled from Girardot's manuscript, *The Victorian Translation of China*.

[59]*China Review* 17 (1986):306-9.

out, are the names of the Trinity!

The inaugural address of the new president of the newly founded Shanghai Literary and Scientific Society, Rev. E.C. Bridgman, admirably sums up the essence of this outlook:

> If the ancient Chinese were surpassed by any of their contemporary pagan nations in the west—Egyptian, Phoenician, Greek, or Roman—as most modern historians and philosophers maintain, it was, no doubt, only because those occidentals enjoyed some faint rays of light derived from the early patriarchs of the human family. Moreover, as touching the earliest generations of the Chinese, it is quite probable that some knowledge—radiating from the same point of high antiquity, where men, after the flood, built their first altars to the one true God—did take an eastern direction, travel over the vast regions of eastern Asia, and eventually, on this far off domain, (subsequently referred to in prophetic vision as "the land of Sinim,") did kindle up here the bright fires of civilization. Admitting it to have been thus, then the founders of this empire were only a few generations removed from the founders of the earliest kingdoms of the west, and both alike must have shared, in some degree, in whatever of literary and scientific knowledge survived the Deluge.[60]

More broadly conceived was the work of missionary John Chalmers, *The Origin of the Chinese: An Attempt to Trace the Connection of the Chinese with Western Nations...*(Hong Kong, 1894). *Sino-Aryaca* of Gustav Schlegel (Batavia, 1872) was another prominent example of at least the linguistic side of the comparative search. Even the Protestant pioneers Robert Morrison (1782-1834) and James Legge (1815-97) accepted without argument the Western origin of certain Chinese cultural reflections.[61]

---

[60]Bridgman, "Inaugural Address," *Journal of the Shanghai Literary and Scientific Society* 1 (1858): 2.

[61]See Robert Morrison, *A Dictionary of the Chinese Language in Three Parts* (Macao: East India Company's Press, 1815-23), xii-xvi for the deluge of Yao; and James Legge, *The Religions of China* (London: Hodder and Stoughton, 1880), 221 for his initial

China Coast Sinologists and Sociology

Despite this scholarly preoccupation with Aryanism, most of which seldom rose above a no-holds-barred cultural parallelomania, it was during the decade of the 1870's that sociological sinology was born in China. The China Coast sinologists, according to Maurice Freedman, were the first students of Chinese popular life and thought. As opposed to the China of the sinologues—"early China and the normative culture of the classics"—"there had grown up a Western literature on China that, not always the work of men literate in Chinese, attempted to convey the notion of what Chinese life was at that time and of the popular elements in it."[62] Prominent examples of this kind of work include Justus Doolittle, *Social Life of the Chinese* (1865), and N.B. Dennys, *The Folklore of China, and its Affinities with that of the Aryan and Semitic Races* (1876). Nascent social anthropology, ethnography, folklore, dialectology, and the first attempts at gathering data through fieldwork rather than from literary sources, were made by the China Coast sinologists.[63] Unfortunately, their lead was not followed up until the work of D. H. Kulp, who began to teach sociology in Shanghai in 1913. In fact, among the most promising forerunners, J.J.M. de Groot (d. 1921) turned from the popular and the contemporary back to the classical and ancient with his later work.[64] It took the towering figure of Chavannes to begin the integration of library-bound philological research with first-hand fieldwork in non-traditional sources, and the example of his ecumenical scholarship to broaden the field so as to incorporate the concerns of non-elite cultures and social strata.

---

acceptance of the theories of Edkins, which Legge traced back to Amiot and Montucci, and Rémusat. It was not until Julien published his translation of the *Tao-te ching* that Legge renounced this view.

[62]Maurice Freedman, "Sinology and the Social Sciences," *Ethnos* 40 (1975): 198-99.

[63]For Gregory Guldin, sociology did not arrive on the scene until the early twentieth century; see his *The Saga of Anthropology in China: From Malinowski to Moscow to Mao* (Armonk, N.Y: M.E. Sharpe, 1994), 23-49.

[64]The two representative works of his sociological tendencies are *Les fetes annuellement célébrées a Emoui* (1886) and *The Religious System of China.* (1892-1910).

PART TWO: FRENCH PHILOLOGY AND A TRIO OF GIANTS

"Rheingold! Rheingold! Reines Gold!
leuchtete noch in der Tiefe dein lautrer Tand!
Traulich und treu ist's nur in der Tiefe:
falsch und feigt ist, was dort oben sich freut!"
— Richard Wagner, *Das Rheingold*, Act One, Scene Four

If the value of philology is compared with the treasure of the Rhinegold, then the trio of scholarly Rhinemaidens who guarded it best, until its luster faded after World War II, was inevitably the French masters Edouard Chavannes and his pupils Paul Pelliot and Henri Maspero. Unlike our treatment of German, English, and American schools of sinology, where it is necessary to survey the work of a large number of scholars, Part Two is focused largely on the work of three men alone, these three giants of sinology.

1. EDOUARD CHAVANNES (1865-1918): THE FATHER OF PHILOLOGY

"I open a dictionary as if I summoned the souls
He enchanted into mute signs on a page,
And I try to visualize him, a lover,
To have some comfort in my mortality."
— Czeslaw Milosz, "Philology," from *Provinces*

Emmanuel-Edouard Chavannes was the first representative of the modern period of French sinology. Although French Jesuit missionaries were still active in China, and wrote much that is admirable,[1] the stage had

---

[1] Nineteenth-century Jesuit scholarship was epitomized by two figures. First was Séraphin Couvreur (1835-1919), notable for his *Dictionnaire classique de la langue chinoise*

41

unalterably shifted to the professional sinologists. Chavannes soon came to enjoy the widest European reputation of any sinologist since Julien.[2] He exemplified this masterful tradition by not only combining sound analysis of specific textual matters with a thorough knowledge of a wide range of primary sources, but added to the store of primary sources through first-hand archaeological work in the field. But his scholarship was based upon a long and distinguished tradition of sinology in France, as we have seen, and was immediately influenced by his first teacher, Cordier.

Henri Cordier

Henri Cordier (1849-1925) was born in New Orleans of a French father and an Alabama girl of French extraction, but grew up in France.[3] Although he originally desired to study cartography, his father foresaw a

---

(1890) and translations of the classics, namely *Cheu king* (1896), *Chou king* (1897), *Les Quatres Livres* (1910), *Mémoires sur les bienséances et les cérémonies* (1913), and *Tc'ouen Ts'iou et Tso Tchouan* (1914). He won the Prix Julien four times. Second was Léon Wieger (1856-1933), who was a prolific translator of religious and historical sources, among them *Texts historiques* (1903-5), drawn principally from the *T'ung-chien kang-mu*; *Textes philosophiques* (1906); and *Bouddhisme chinois* (1910-13). A minor figure of this period was Angelo Zottoli (1826-1902). His *Cursus Litteraturae Sinicae*, 5 vols. (Shanghai, 1878-82), was the largest anthology of classical Chinese translated into a Western language. For nineteenth-century occidental sinology in general, both in Europe and in China, see Frèches, *La Sinologie*, 34-61. Specifically devoted to the French school, including the Jesuits, is *Deux siècles de sinologies française.*

[2]Cf. the view of Henri Maspero: "La sinologie française au XIXe siècle est dominée par les noms de deux savants, Stanislas Julien et Edouard Chavannes....C'est à eux que la science française doit la maîtrise incontestée don't elle jouit dans le domaine de la sinologie;" Maspero, "La Sinologie," 283. The same sentiments are voiced by Jacques Gernet, "Henri Maspero and Paul Demiéville: Two Great Masters of French Sinology," in *Europe Studies China*, 45.

[3]For his life and work, see Paul Pelliot, "Henri Cordier (1849-1925)," *TP* 24 (1926):1-15; L. Aurousseau, "Henri Cordier," *BEFEO* 25 (1925):279-86; W. Perceval Yetts, *BSOAS* 3 (1925):854-55; and Zoe Zwecker, "Henri Cordier and the Meeting of East and West," in *Asia and the West: Encounters and Exchanges from the Age of Exploration*, ed. Cyriac K. Pullapilly and Edwin J. Van Kley (Notre Dame: Cross Cultural Publications, 1986), 309-29. Cordier himself published his personal bibliography, *Bibliographie des oeuvres de Henri Cordier* (Paris, 1924).

career in business for him. He was then sent off to Shanghai to enter an American firm there. After two years he became Honorary Librarian of the North China Branch of the Royal Asiatic Society. He returned to France in 1876 on leave. While there he was asked by the Chinese government to take charge of a group of Chinese students then in Europe. He was destined never to return to China. But while discharging his duty at the Chinese mission, he became acquainted with Charles Schefer, a celebrated Near Eastern scholar who was the administrator of the Ecole des Langues Orientales Vivantes. Impressed by Cordier's knowledge of China, Shefer invited him to teach courses on the history, geography, and law of the Far East. Becoming a professor in 1888, Cordier held this post until his death.

As Zoe Zwecker points out, Cordier scarcely qualifies as a sinologist, since his knowledge of the Chinese language was superficial and hardly utilized in his studies.[4] Nevertheless, transcending the narrow parameters of sinology as philology, Cordier profoundly influenced the field as mentor, as historian, and especially as bibliographer.

Cordier was most renowned for his *Bibliotheca Sinica*, four volumes of bibliography of everything published in European languages on China, Korea, Manchuria, Tibet, and Mongolia since the West first became aware of the Far East up to the year 1924. Cordier also included articles on Central Asia, but according to Pelliot, this section was the least comprehensive. *Bibliotheca Sinica* was initially published between the years 1878 and 1885 in a two-volume set. The second edition expanded to four volumes, appearing between 1904 and 1908; a fifth volume of supplements was published in 1924.[5] The idea for the *Bibliotheca Sinica* was first conceived while Cordier was compiling the catalogue of the library of the North China Branch of the Royal Asiatic Society; many of the entries were based on the holdings of that library and of Alexander Wylie's private

---

[4]Zwecker, "Henri Cordier and the Meeting of East and West," 309.

[5]*Bibliotheca Sinica: Dictionnaire bibliographique des ouvrages relatifs à l'empire chinois*, 5 vols. (rpt. Taipei: Ch'eng-wen, 1966).

collection.[6]   The first edition was awarded the Prix Stanislas Julien. Cordier repeated this astounding feat of tabulation and endurance twice afterwards, producing four volumes of *Bibliotheca Indosinica*, dealing with Indochina, and a one-volume *Bibliotheca Japonica*.[7]   Cordier hence established the basis of bibliographic access to secondary sources on the Far East,[8] and contributed much in the way of his personal scholarship—his own output numbered over one thousand items, mainly on East-West commercial and diplomatic intercourse.

Cordier's other major contributions to sinology were in the fields of historical geography, Sino-Western relations, and the history of sinology.[9] His completion and revision of Yule's annotated translation of Marco Polo remains indispensable today for its many notes on cultural, geographical, and historical matters.[10]   A late publication, *Histoire générale de la Chine*, 4 vols. (1921), showed his skill in synthesis; for, according to Maspero, it was the first historical exposition of China that was not simply a translation or analysis of a Chinese source.[11]   And it happened that such an authority on Western bibliography on the Orient, with a particular aptitude to place the study of China within a continental context, became the teacher of the founder of modern sinology.

Education

Born in Lyons on October 5, 1865, Edouard Chavannes first studied philosophy at the Ecole Normale Supérieure.[12]   Upon the advice

---

[6]See Cordier, "The Life and Labors of Alexander Wylie," in Alexander Wylie, *Chinese Researches* (1897; rpt. Taipei: Ch'eng-wen, 1966), 7-18, especially 7-8; and *Bibliotheca Sinica*, 1: xiii-iv.

[7]Other offerings by the indefatigable Cordier in this vein include bibliographies on the works of Alain-Rene Lesage, Deaumarchais, Gaston Maspero, and Stendhal.

[8]For an analysis of his bibliographic studies, see Zoe Zwecker, "Henri Cordier and the Meeting of East and West," 314-16.

[9]Ibid., 316-22.

[10]Henry Yule, *The Book of Ser Marco Polo*, 2 vols. third edition (London, 1903). Cordier also revised Yule, *Cathay and the Way Hither*, 4 vols. (London, 1913-16).

[11]Maspero, "La Sinologie," 272.

[12]For biographical information on Chavannes, see the necrologies published by Henri Cordier, *TP* 18 (1917): 114-47 and *Journal Asiatique*, 11th ser. 40.2 (March-April

of the school's director, he turned towards the study of China. Intending to emphasize Chinese philosophy, he was redirected instead to history by Cordier, who suggested he translate one of the dynastic histories, which he would eventually do.

After gaining a good command of modern Chinese at the Ecole des Langues Orientales Vivantes with Cordier and classical Chinese at the Collège de France under Le Marquis d'Hervey de Saint-Denis, Chavannes was sent to Peking in 1889 and attached to the French legation.

The quality and value of his work had been recognized very early. In 1893, after studying Chinese for only five years, he was appointed Professor of the Chair of Chinese at the Collège de France, succeeding his teacher de Saint-Denis. Besides teaching, he fully participated in the social side of sinological circles—attending conferences, reading papers, sitting on editorial boards and the award committee for the Julien Prize—and was also active in the wider social circles of French academic life. He was a member of the Institut de France, a corresponding or honorary member of several foreign societies, and from 1904 to 1916 co-editor of T'oung Pao. In 1915 he became the President of the Academy of Inscriptions and Belles-Lettres.

The *Shih-chi* and Translation Style

It was during his first stay in China, from 1889 to 1891, that Chavannes decided to translate Ssu-ma Ch'ien's *Shih-chi*. Five volumes of introduction, translation, notes and appendices appeared during the period from 1895 to 1905.[13] The value of this great work, which "placed historical studies on a new and solid basis," according to Berthold Laufer,[14] was formally recognized by academic circles when his second volume was awarded the Julien Prize. Maspero later termed it the most considerable

---

1918):197-248; Louis de la Vallée Poussin,   BSOAS 1 (1918): 147-51; Paul Pelliot, *Bulletin Arch. Musée Guimet* 1 (1921): 11-15; and Berthold Laufer, *JAOS* 21 (1922): 202-5. A Chinese perspective on Chavannes and some of his most notable works is Li Huang, *Fa-kuo Han-hsüeh lun-chi* (Kowloon: Chu Hai College, 1975), 19-45.

[13]*Les Mémoires historiques de Se-ma Ts'ien*, 5 vols. (Paris: E. Leroux, 1895-1905); vol. 6 (Paris: Adrien Maisonneuve, 1969).

[14]*JAOS* 21 (1922): 203.

work of sinology since Legge's *Chinese Classics*.[15] After a short visit back to France in 1891 during which he was married, Chavannes returned to China and continued his monumental work on Ssu-ma Ch'ien. But after ten years and five volumes, during which he translated and annotated the first 47 of the 130 chapters, other research interests finally crowded out any remaining time or enthusiasm for the *Shih-chi*. This is mildly surprising, since Chavannes had all along pursued several different research projects concurrently, all densely detailed and of high quality.[16] But after ten years of continual effort, he gave up "cette interminable affaire" for good.[17] His translation, still indispensable today, was praised by Laufer as "one of the most splendid and lasting monuments produced by French scholarship."[18] A modern team of translators of the *Shih-chi*, headed up by William H. Nienhauser, regards it as "in many ways still the best" available.[19]

One of the side excursuses finished while Chavannes was still working on the *Shih-chi* was a translation of the travelogue of the T'ang monk I-ching, which received the Julien prize in 1894.[20] Soon after

---

[15]Maspero, "La Sinologie," 273.

[16]For instance, "Pei Yuan Lou: Récit d'un voyage dans le nord," *TP* 5 (1904): 163-93.

[17]Chavannes had apparently finished translating all 130 chapters while still in Peking; William H. Nienhauser, ed., *The Grand Scribe's Records*, vol. 1: *The Basic Annals of Pre-Han China* (Bloomington: Indiana University Press, 1994); xv, n. 64; xix, n. 77. Nienhauser, "A Note on Édouard Chavannes' Unpublished Translations of the *Shih-chi* ¥v°O," unpublished manuscript, Madison, Wisconsin, 1997, analyzes extant unpublished translations of chapters 23-30 and 40-130 in various stages of completion still preserved in the Musée Guimet.

[18]Laufer, *Chinese Pottery of the Han Dynasty* (1909; 2nd ed. Rutland, VT: Charles E. Tuttle, 1962), 214.

[19]*The Grand Scribe's Records*, 1: xv.

[20]*Voyages des pelerins bouddhistes: Les Religieux éminents qui allerent chercher la loi dans les pays d'occident, mémoire composé à l'époque de la grande dynastie T'ang par I-tsing, traduit en française* (Paris: Ernest Leroux, 1894). Chavannes' colleague, the Indianist Sylvain Lévi (1863-1935), had steered Chavannes towards translating those Chinese texts that contributed to the historical knowledge of India little known from Sanskrit sources. This helps explain Chavannes' early interest in Buddhist literature in general and travelogues in particular.

Lévi did for Buddhist scholarship what the Hebrew exegetes of the eighteenth

abandoning Ssu-ma Ch'ien, Chavannes published another travelogue, worth considering in depth as an example of his methodology.

In his "Voyage de Song Yün dans l'Udyana et Gandhara (518-522 p.C.),"[21] Chavannes translated and annotated that part of Yang Hsüan-chih's *Lo-yang ch'ieh-lan chi* which contains the account of the journey of Sung Yün and Hui Seng through Central Asia. Apart from valuable data on the regions visited, these travelers brought back important religious manuscripts which contributed to the expansion of Buddhist knowledge and interest, as well as exact measurements and models of stupas which enabled Chinese craftsmen to reproduce them faithfully. Chavannes' purpose in contributing to the scholarship on this travel account was to "clear up some points that remain obscure."[22]

Much more than this, his annotated translation is exemplary in its concern for detail, thoroughness, and accuracy. He consulted all available editions of the text, and pointed out any differences. This helped especially in dealing with proper names. His thoroughness enabled him to note where geographical names had shifted from Han to T'ang times; and he verified or modified such geographical data by comparing other sources. He also supplied biographical and bibliographical background on the people or works mentioned in the text. His translation was followed by an appendix of eleven pages containing "Notes on Diverse Works Relative to India which were Published in China before the T'ang Epoch."

If one compares his style of translation to a modern English version, we see that Chavannes more faithfully reflects the diction and syntax of the Chinese.[23] And his broad utilization of primary and secondary sources in

---

century had done for biblical studies, for he sought all versions of the Buddhist canon, whether in Sanskrit, Chinese, Pali, or Tibetan, in the attempt to establish the texts by collating definitive editions. Maspero credits this approach as a new methodology; "La Sinologie," p. 278. For the life and works of this great Indianist, see Louis Renou in *Mémorial Sylvain Lévi* (Paris: P. Hartmann, 1937), xll-li. A short scholarly evaluation is J.W. de Jong, *A Brief History of Buddhist Studies in Europe and America* (New Delhi: Bharat-Bharati, 1976), 40-43.

[21]*BEFEO* 3 (1903): 379-441.

[22]Ibid., 379.

[23]W.J.F. Jenner, *Memories of Lo-yang* (Oxford: Oxford University Press, 1981).

his annotations not only explains the question or makes the identification at hand, but also refers the reader to other sources. As in all his works, respect for the integrity of the text and establishing its meaning and degree of independence leave the reader in no doubt as to the primacy of the text, its importance, and its message; hence it becomes a solid foundation for other scholars to build on.

The breadth of his research was remarkable. His publications, regardless of theme, all evince the same careful, detailed, thorough, and imaginative treatment. And what a range of themes: historical documents, especially on nomadic peoples,[24] religious texts, including Buddhist, Taoist, Confucian, and Nestorian Christian documents and popular cults,[25] geographical treatises,[26] biographies,[27] book reviews, and comments on modern Chinese politics.[28]

Founding a New Discipline: Epigraphy

A major characteristic of much of Chavannes' work was the exploitation of new or neglected sources. For instance, in translating inscriptions which he had usually collected himself in the field, he founded a new discipline,[29] and his scholarship "inaugurated sound archaeological

---

[24]*Documents sur les Tou-kiu (Turks) occidentaux* (St. Petersberg, 1903).

[25]Among many other religious studies, see "Le Nestorianisme et l'inscription de Kara-balgassoun," *JA* 9th ser. (Jan.-Feb. 1897): 43-85; *Cinq cents contes et apologues extraits du Tripitaka chinois et traduits en français*, 3 vols. (Paris: Ernest Leroux, 1910-11); "Une version chinois de conte bouddhique de Kalyanamkara et Papamkara," *TP* (1914): 469-500; and the collaborative work with Pelliot on Manichaeanism treated in chapter two below.

[26]"Les Pays d'occident d'après le Wei Lio," *TP* 6 (1905): 519-71; "Les Pays d'occident d'après le *Heou Han Chou*," *TP* 7 (1907): 149-234.

[27]"Trois généraux chinois de la dynastie des Han Orientaux," *TP* 7 (1906): 210-69; "Seng-Houei +280 p.C," *TP* 10 (1909): 199-212.

[28]Many of his book reviews are listed at Cordier, *TP* 18 (1917): 134-43; for comments on modern Chinese politics, see 131-47 *passim*.

[29]According to La Vallée Poussin, *BSOS* 1 (1918):150. Among his most important epigraphical, archaeological, and art studies are *La Sculpture sur pierre en Chine au temps des deux dynasties Han* (Paris: Ernest Leroux, 1893); *Mission archéologique dans la Chine Septentrional, tome I. Premier partie: La Sculpture à l'époque des Han; Deuxieme partie: La Sculpture bouddhique* (Paris Ernest Leroux, 1913-1915); *Ars asiatica: Etudes et documents*

research."[30] He must have kept close to his heart something like the dictum of Erasmus: "We must hold fast to the knowledge of antiquity which is culled not only from ancient authors but also from old coins, inscriptions, and stones."[31]

Inscriptions preserve texts that are trustworthy—taking account of the usual encomium of most monuments and grave epitaphs—both because of their contemporary provenance and their imperviousness to corruption in the process of textual transmission. Studying the case of the historian Seutonius and his account of the reign of Nero, Narka Nelson stated that "For the period of the Empire epigraphic evidence is overwhelming, and in its pure and uncorrupted light the accounts of Tacitus and Suetonius can be examined." Nelson then sums up the value of epigraphic evidence for his purpose: "...It cannot be denied that an inscription which can be deciphered presents evidence which is reliable and contemporary. Here are cold facts, and hard, cold facts are what we need to test the veracity of Suetonius, for veracity has not been regarded as one of Suetonius' virtues."[32] Nelson concludes that "Suetonius' account of Nero does not suffer when put to the test of epigraphic investigation and interpretation."[33]

Although collections of inscriptions in manuscript form still survive from the fifteenth century, it was the generation of Poggio Bracciolini (1380-1459), that great collector of scattered manuscripts, which devoted itself as well to epigraphical and archaeological material. Flavio Biono (1392-1463) devised a four-part classification system of public, private, religious, and military antiquities in his *Roma triumphans* (1456-60). Among his other works are *Roma instaurate* (1440-63) and *Italia instaurata* (1456-60), which surveyed both ancient monuments and topography. The Dutch scholar Janus Gruter's (1560-1627) *Corpus inscriptionum antiquarum*

---

publiés sous la direction de Victor Goloubew, I: La Peinture chinoise au Musée Cernuschi Avril-Juin 1912; II: Six monuments de la sculpture chinoise (Bruselles and Paris: G. van Oest, 1914).

[30]Laufer, *JAOS* 22 (1922): 203.

[31]Erasmus, "De ratione studii," 674.

[32]Narka Nelson, "The Value of Epigraphic Evidence in the Interpretation of Latin Historical Literature," *The Classical Journal* 37 (1942): 282.

[33]Ibid., 290.

(1602) was the greatest of the medieval collections of inscriptions; its fame earned the author the post of librarian in Heidelberg. Joseph Scaliger supplied much of the material, and provided the twenty-four methodical indexes. In the field of numismatics and meteorology, Guillaume Budé (1468-1540), the inspiration behind the founding of the Collège Royal in 1530 (later becoming the Collège de France), authored *De Asse eiusque partibus* (1514), which immediately became the definitive handbook on Roman coins and metal objects. Its popularity led to ten editions over the next twenty years.   August Boeckh (1785-1867) edited the *Corpus Inscriptionum Graecarum*, 4 vols. and *Index* (Berlin, 1828-77), which ultimately gave way to a newly organized and newly edited corpus, instigated by U. von Wilamowitz-Moellendorff (1848-1931), the *Inscriptiones Graecae*, 10 vols. (Berlin, 1906-72; 3rd ed., 1981-93). Finally, it was Theodor Mommsen (1817–1903) who turned from historical research almost wholly to philological publishing, as he spent a large part of his life editing the *Corpus Inscriptionum Latinarum*, 16 vols. (Berlin, 1863-). Today, many theoretical introductions, bibliographies, collections of transcriptions or photographs of inscriptions are available to classicists, both for historical and linguistic research.[34]

Four hundred years earlier than in Europe, Sung period China saw the first active investigation into and collection of archaeological remains, especially stone monuments and bronze inscriptions. Edward Shaughnessy notes:

> According to modern tabulations, during the 170 years of the Northern Song well over five hundred Shang and Zhou bronzes were

---

[34]The literature for classical epigraphy is, of course, massive. Yet, listing a few titles will at least provide an inkling of the type of sources available. For Greek inscriptions, see A.G. Woodhead, *The Study of Greek Inscriptions* (Cambridge, 1959); W. Larfeld, *Grieschische Epigraphik* (3rd ed. Munich, 1914). For Latin inscriptions, see J.E. Sandys, *Latin Epigraphy: An Introduction to the Study of Latin Inscriptions*, 2nd ed., ed. S.G. Campell (Cambridge, 1927); and A. E. Gordon, *Illustrated Introduction to Latin Epigraphy* (Berkeley and Los Angeles: University of California Press, 1983). See the respective entries in *The Oxford Classical Dictionary*, 3rd ed., ed. Simon Hornblower and Antony Spawforth (Oxford: Oxford University Press, 1996), 539-46.

unearthed. Consistent with the trend at this period to categorize knowledge about antiquity...the inscriptions on these vessels were collected in some thirty different publications. One of the first of these was the *Xian-Qin guqi lu* (by Liu Chang [1019-68])....Although no longer extant, Liu's work, which is the first work known to have included drawings of the vessels, is important for the influence it had on the *Jigulu bawei*, edited by Ouyang Xiu in 1069, the earliest specialized study of bronze inscriptions still extant.[35]

In the *Chi-ku lu pa-wei* 集古錄跋尾 , 10 *chüan*, Ou-yang Hsiu preserved over four hundred colophons to the rubbings of metal and stone he had collected over the years in an unpublished work of 1,000 *chüan*.[36] The *Ssu-k'u* editors cited one of its virtues as helping to confirm the texts of documents, revealing interpolations and deletions by comparison with unchanging stone inscriptions.[37]

More useful to the modern student than colophons are the texts of the inscriptions themselves. For stone monuments, the earliest classified collection was the *Chin-shih lu* 金石錄, compiled by Chao Ming-ch'eng (1081-1129), husband of the poetess Li Ch'ing-chao (1084-1147), and published between 1119 and 1125.[38] It catalogued over two thousand inscriptions, and described 702 of these in detail.

As part of the evidential movement of the Ch'ing, epigraphy and archaeology played important roles. For instance, one early expert on epigraphical studies, Ku Yen-wu, acknowledged the importance of the new field pioneered by Ou-yang Hsiu: "When I read Ou-yang Hsiu's *Chi-ku lu*

---

[35]Edward L. Shaughnessy, *Sources of Western Zhou History: Inscribed Bronze Vessels* (Berkeley and Los Angeles: University of California Press, 1991), 8-9. On Chinese epigraphy in general, see Dieter Kuhn, *Annotated Bibliography to the* Shike shiliao xinbian 刻史料新編 *[New Edition of Historical Materials Carved on Stone]* (Heidelberg: Edition Forum, 1991).

[36]On this work, see the entry by Chikusa Masaaki in *A Sung Bibliography (Bibliographie des Sung)*, ed. Etienne Balazs and Yves Hervouet (Hong Kong: Chinese University Press, 1978), 199.

[37]Included in Ni Ssu倪思 (1147-1220), *Pan-Ma i-t'ung*班馬異同 (*Ssu-k'u ch'üan-shu chen-pen* ed.), "t'i-yao," 1b-2a.

[38]See the entry by Katsumura Tetsuya in *A Sung Bibliography*, 201-2.

I realized that many of the events recorded in these inscriptions are verified by works of history so that, far from being merely bits of high-flown rhetoric, they are of actual use in supplementing and correcting the histories."[39] Juan Yüan's collation of the classics, the *Shih-san-ching chu-shu*, made extensive use of the stone classics engraved from the Han to the Sung dynasties.[40] In summation, the noted historian Ch'ien Ta-hsin evaluates the importance of epigraphical studies by describing their special utility and value as follows:

> For the most part, writings on bamboo and silk deteriorated rapidly over time. In the process of recopying [these writings] by hand over and over again, their original appearance was lost. Only bronze and stone inscriptions survive from hundreds and thousands of years ago. In them, we see the real appearance of the ancients. Both the writings [of this type] and the affairs [described in them] are reliable and verifiable. Therefore, they are prized.[41]

Chavannes made particularly significant use of the epigraphical material he collected on T'ai Shan (to be discussed below). His field work in Inner Asia collected valuable inscriptions that supplemented the information contained in the dynastic histories. Particularly significant was Chavannes' trip through north China in 1907 to collect rubbings.[42] And in working on epigraphical evidence collected by others he made equally precious data available. For instance, one victorious campaign against *shan-yü* Hou-yen of the Hsiung-nu, led by P'ei Yen in A.D. 137, appears only in epigraphic evidence presented by Chavannes.[43] But then,

---

[39]Cited in Benjamin A. Elman, *From Philosophy to Philology: Intellectual and Social Aspects of Change in Late Imperial China* (Cambridge, Mass.: Council on East Asian Studies, Harvard University, 1990), 190.

[40]Ibid., 191.

[41]Ibid., 190-91.

[42]See William H. Nienhauser, Jr., "Travels with Édouard—V.M. Alekseev's Account of the Chavannes Mission of 1907 as a Biographical Source," *Asian Culture* 22 (Winter 1994): 81-95.

[43]Included in Chavannes, *Dix inscriptions chinoises de l'Asie Centrale d'après les estampages de M. Ch.-E. Bonin* (Paris, 1902), 17-24, no. 1.

he was always breaking new ground in exploiting new sources, whether in exploring the Taoist or Buddhist canons,[44] or in working on the newly discovered documents found by Aurel Stein at Tun-huang.[45]   And while he published little in terms of bibliographical work in the manner of his pupil Pelliot, his studies were careful to sort out the textual traditions and filiation of editions of the works he was translating.[46]

Le Tai chan

Aside from Chavannes' monumental *Shih-chi* translation, his massive monograph, *Le Tai chan: Essai de monographie d'un culte chinois* (Paris, 1910), is the work perhaps most characteristic of his style—the annotated translation with extended commentary—, his major theme—a combination of historical event and religious rite—, and influence—it inspired later French sinologists to follow suit.[47]

According to Chavannes, this work had two main goals. First, he attempted to recount in general the role played by mountains in the Chinese religion, defined as both the state cult and popular beliefs. Second,

---

[44]As an example, "Le Jet des dragons," *Mémoires concernant l'Asie Orientale* 3 (1919):53-220, published posthumously, was the first direct translation of a text from the Taoist canon by a European sinologist. This work utilizes the riches of the entire canon in translating and explicating numerous inscriptions and literary accounts of the ritual of casting into grottoes, caverns, etc. prayers engraved on stone or metal talismans, decorated with dragons which were charged with delivering the prayers. See the introduction of T. H. Barrett to Henri Maspero, *Taoism and Chinese Religion*, trans. Frank A. Kierman, Jr. (Amherst: University of Massachusetts Press, 1981), xii; and Kristopher Schipper, "The History of Taoist Studies in the West," in *Europe Studies China*, 476-77.

[45]*Les Documents chinois découverts par Aurel Stein dans les sables du Turkestan oriental, publiés et annotated* (Oxford: Oxford University Press, 1913).

[46]See, for instance, "Le Royaume de Wu et de Yue 吳越 ," *TP* 17 (1916):129-264; see pp. 133-42 for extensive bibliographical notes on the works that were relevant to his study of these medieval kingdoms.

[47]For instance, Rolf Stein, "Jardins en miniature d'Extrême-Orient," *BEFEO* 42 (1942): 1-104; English translation in *The World in Miniature: Container Gardens and Dwellings in Far Eastern Religious Thought*, trans. Phyllis Brooks (Stanford: Stanford University Press, 1990), 1-119; and Michel Soymié, "Le Lo-feou chan: étude de géographie religieuse," *BEFEO* 48 (1954): 1-139.

he desired in particular to elucidate the special attributes which made one of these mountains, T'ai Shan, paramount among them.   Chavannes' introductory essays treating the general role of mountains in China, the cult of T'ai Shan, and popular beliefs make up only a small portion of this thick work.   The bulk consists of annotated translations of pertinent historical texts, prayers, and inscriptions. Making such a wide variety and amount of primary sources available allows the work as a whole to transcend a common limitation of many expository treatises, that of quoting only selected passages which confirm the arguments of the author. By translating complete chapters and the entire texts of prayers and inscriptions, plus supplying the Chinese characters for the passages translated in his prose narratives, Chavannes has obviated the danger of any unconscious or unintentional special pleading in his presentation.   And, of course, he has conveniently provided much data—translated, annotated, and supplied in context—which pertain to many other areas besides T'ai Shan and mountain worship.

Chavannes commenced his monograph with a general introduction on the sacred role of mountains in China.   Not only the homes of deities, they were themselves gods. The vague personality of the sacred mountain-gods included the following general attributes: because of sheer size and weight, they helped prevent earthquakes by stabilizing the region and regularizing the natural order; they also formed rain clouds, and could be invoked in time of drought or flood. Mount T'ai shared these attributes, and in the spiritual hierarchy it held a rank analogous to that of Duke (kung 公) in the political order. As a subordinate of Heaven, it often served as intermediary between the Son of Heaven and his celestial parent. This explains why the inscribed text for the *feng* 封 sacrifice was not burned, sending the prayer heavenward. Instead, it was buried, for the mountain was expected to transmit requests to Heaven.

Chavannes next further elaborated the personality of T'ai Shan. As the mountain presiding over the east, it came to be regarded as the master of all life, its source and final destination. Hence, it was considered as heading up a fully staffed administration which was concerned with birth and death.   Later, thanks to Buddhist influence, T'ai Shan came to be regarded as the moral arbiter of mortal action, charged with punishing the guilty. Finally, Chavannes detailed a late addition to the lore of T'ai Shan. The "Princess of the Aurora" was its daughter, and was supplicated by expectant mothers on behalf of their children.

In showing the development of the nature and powers of this holy mountain, Chavannes translated many passages from early, medieval, and pre-modern literature. Besides utilizing the standard histories and classics, he culled relevant observations from T'ang, Sung, and Ming miscellanies, including comments and passages collected by Chu Hsi and Ku Yen-wu. Standard encyclopedias were also consulted for the texts of prayers relating to T'ai Shan. But a major source of data for this study was collected by Chavannes himself in the form of rubbings taken from inscriptions located in temples on or near the mountain. Selecting from hundreds of relevant inscriptions, Chavannes translated eleven major ones.

The translations of these inscriptions, which date from the Han to the Ch'ing periods, were as carefully annotated as the three translations of extracts from the dynastic histories filling chapter three of Le T'ai chan. These latter translations were of the historical accounts of the feng and shan 禪 sacrifices performed during Han, T'ang, and Sung times. They supplement the ten-page explanation of the ceremonies of feng and shan which took place at the summit and foot of Mount T'ai. These, as well as all of Chavannes' translations, were based upon broad familiarity with early Chinese texts, and were particularly fortified by Chavannes' specific erudition in the field of early state ritual, for his earliest published translation was a rendition of the chapter on the feng and shan sacrifices of Ssu-ma Ch'ien. And, as he had already finished his monumental work on the Shih-chi, his understanding of the diverse source materials for this study of T'ai Shan was exceptionally comprehensive and his handling of them particularly skillful.

During his trip to T'ai Shan, Chavannes toured and inspected each building and noteworthy site on the mount. Hence his second chapter, covering 113 pages, described in detail 252 temples, belvederes, halls, hermitages, shrines, pagodas, arches, stelae, bridges, peaks, rockeries, and other sacred man-made or natural spots. Deeming the two native Chinese maps as badly graved and occasionally indistinct, Chavannes felt compelled to supply his own hand-drawn map, distinctly showing topographical contours and the 252 numbered sites with their Chinese names.

For the section on popular beliefs relative to T'ai Shan, Chavannes first gathered many incidental references to the mount which exposed the attitude of the common people. Again, this could not have been carried off so successfully in an age before comprehensive indices were available were it not for Chavannes' thorough familiarity with the Chinese literature of many periods. His personal tour of the mount yielded further data on popular beliefs in the form of rubbings taken from mirrors, the seal of T'ai Shan, and a Taoist "Illustration of the True Form of the Five Peaks," all translated and annotated. For these and the rubbings of the inscriptions mentioned above, Chavannes produced photographs of the originals.

A hundred-page appendix on the god of the soil was attached. Its penetrating treatment of many aspects of the familial, provincial, national, and royal soil gods is admirable for many reasons. One footnote (p. 438, n. 1) dealing with the *chung-liu* 中霤, *fu* 覆, and *hsüeh* 穴, anticipated—and probably inspired—a later article by an emigrant to France, R.A. Stein.[48] All in all, this work was a pioneering *tour-de-force* which remains a remarkable methodological example and the best repository of data on the topic even today.

Chavannes was physically very active, as evinced by his expeditions to China, Manchuria, and Mongolia to gather epigraphical evidence and to study sculpture. But he was no less energetic in his studies. Alas, this hard work, combined with the trauma of the Great War, hastened his demise: he died at age 53 on January 29, 1918, a month after the devastating emotional blow to France of the armistice signed between the Central Powers and Russia. He was universally lauded as the foremost sinologist of his time, and lamented as much for his character of discretion and modesty as for the loss to sinology caused by his relatively early death.

His career, the spirit of his approach, and influence were perhaps best evaluated by his teacher Cordier in the thirty-three page necrology published in *T'oung Pao*; the concluding remarks in high-flung phrases follow:

---

[48]"L'habitate, le mond et le corps humain en extrême-orient et en haute Asie," *JA* 245 (1957): 37-74; English translation in *The World in Miniature*, 121-74.

Many sinologues, prisoners of their specialties, lack a sufficient cultural base, and—gifted with a paucity of scientific curiosity—they are deficient in points of comparison; as a consequence they exhibit a tendency to restrain the breadth of their research. Chavannes, thanks initially to the strength of his training and to a classical education which is indispensable for attempting any serious scientific study, was able to give his studies the amplitude they required even while remaining in the field of Chinese, in which he was without rival. Save for linguistics, he cultivated all the diverse branches of the field; but it was above all in history and archaeology that he left profound traces. The reputation of Chavannes, already great both abroad and in France, will yet increase in time and bequeath the lasting fame of being the premier sinologue of his era.[49]

---

[49] *TP* 18 (1917): 131.

2.   PAUL PELLIOT (1878-1945): THE "MARCO POLO OF THE SPIRIT"

"If you wish to mature your thought, attach yourself to the scrupulous study of a great master; inquire into a system until you reach its most secret workings. "
—Emile Durkheim[1]

"The Sinology that means control of texts is a wonderful means but a weak end. "
—Joseph R. Levenson[2]

Paul Pelliot was in all likelihood the greatest philologist among modern Western sinologists. Because of his extraordinary ability to deal with verbal and textual matters—at the heart of research in any aspect of sinology—he was in the forefront of virtually all traditional fields. Bibliography, linguistics, textual criticism, paleography, archaeology, historical research—including the history of art, geography, religions, and material culture—he was an undisputed master in them all. Multiply this astonishing erudition three or four times to include his equally brilliant command of the languages, history, art and archaeology of Central and Inner Asian peoples, and something of the breadth, if not the depth, of his learning can be measured.[3] The "thought" and "system" alluded to in the first epigraph, as applied by Pelliot, were less an intellectual framework than a methodology: the discipline of philology. Many disciples called him their master, and attempted to follow his path, which has been called by some not injustly a "philological positivism;" yet, as the other epigraph foreshadows, his philological approach came to represent for some all that was regarded as intellectually parochial and methodologically constricted in pre-war sinology.

---

[1] Cited in Dominick LaCapra, *Emile Durkheim: Sociologist and Philosopher* (Ithaca: Cornell University Press, 1972), 1.

[2] Joseph R. Levenson, "The Humanistic Disciplines: Will Sinologie Do?" *JAS* 23 (1964):507.

[3] Cf. Franke, *Sinologie*, 21: "Paul Pelliot...mit bestürzender Vielseitigkeit von der Sinologie ausgehend in fast allen Gebieten der asiatischen Philologie heimisch gemacht hatte."

Born in Paris on May 28, 1878, Pelliot conceived of a career in foreign diplomacy.[4] To this end, after his secondary education in English at the Sorbonne he studied Chinese at the Ecole des Langues Orientales Vivantes. His progress was so rapid that he finished the three year course in only two years, and attracted the attention of Edouard Chavannes and Sylvain Lévi. They directed him towards a more scholarly future. In 1900 he arrived in Hanoi as a research scholar of the Ecole Française d'Extrême-Orient. In February he was sent to Peking to purchase books for the school. Caught in the middle of the siege of the legations (July 15-August 15) during the Boxer Rebellion, he distinguished himself in a brave but impetuous one-man sally to the enemy headquarters during a cease-fire. His fluency in Chinese must have been as impressive as his boldness, for he persuaded the besiegers to provide fresh fruit for his comrades which he carried back triumphantly in his arms.[5] After returning to Hanoi in 1901, he was decorated with the Cross of the Legion of Honor for his conduct during the siege—not for the escapade just mentioned but for capturing an enemy flag during the fighting. He was made professor at the Ecole while still only twenty-three years of age, and passed the next few years in China collecting books and in Hanoi studying and teaching.

---

[4]For his life and works, see Paul Demiéville, "La Carrière scientific de Paul Pelliot, son oeuvre relative à l'Extrême-Orient," in *Paul Pelliot* (Paris: Société Asiatique, 1946), 29-54; J.J.L. Duyvendak, *TP* 38 (1947): 1-15; Robert des Rotours, *Mélanges chinois et bouddhiques* 8 (1946-47): 227-34; Serge Elisséef, "Paul Pelliot 1878-1945," *Archives of the Chinese Art Society of America* 1 (1945-46): 11-13; and Li Huang, *Fa-kuo Han-hsüeh lun-chi*, 47-72.

[5]An eyewitness of the siege, Lionel Giles (1878-1934), son of H.R. Giles, recorded the following about Pelliot in his journal: "A Frenchman, name Pelliot, went up to the Chinese barricade in Legation Street and had some tea with the soldiers. The Chinese asked him to go over to their barricade and see their Colonel, one Ma. This he did....There he had a talk with some blue-buttoned officials, who gave him food, and tried to 'pump' him as to the state of our defenses and amount of provisions. He seems to have lied beautifully, making us out to be in a splendid way altogether." Giles, *The Siege of the Peking Legations: A Diary*, ed. L.R. Marchant (Nedlands, Australia: University of Western Australia Press, 1970), 157.

Early Works: Book Reviews, Bibliography, and Historical Geography

Meanwhile he had begun to publish. His first offerings, appearing in the *BEFEO*, were book reviews characterized by a critical and uncompromising spirit which decried the lack of scientific approach, the haphazardness, or the sloppiness of the authors. But besides criticism, he would summarize what he thought were the correct views, often going to great lengths. He frequently ended his remarks with an appendix of works, both primary and secondary, which should have been consulted by the author under review. Because of his magisterial manner of reviewing, his reviews were often more valuable than the works in question.[6] Even some of his most prominent works originated out of this concern. For instance, "Les mots à *h* initial, aujourd'hui amuie, dans le mongol des xiie et xive siècles," takes its point of departure from reviewing four separate works.[7]

His first few original publications were in fields that were to dominate his research interests throughout his entire life: Chinese bibliography and Chinese sources for the cultural, religious, and art history of China and other Asian countries. They all evince the scholarly traits of the mature Pelliot: thorough command of all sources, detailed annotations, clear and imaginative commentary.

The earliest original scholarly contributions of the young Pelliot (24 years) are an annotated translation[8] and one piece representative of his utter command of Chinese bibliography: "Notes de bibliographie chinoise."[9] In

---

[6]For an example of a review more instructive and important than the original book, see "Michael Boym," *TP* 31 (1934): 95-151. Among representative reviews which supplement the original works are "A propos du 'Chinese Biographical Dictionary' de M.H. Giles," *AM* 4 (1927): 377-89; and "Notes sur le 'Turkestan' de M.W. Barthold," *TP* 27 (1930): 12-56.

[7]*JA* 206 (1925): 193-263. "A propos Des Comans," *JA* ser. 11, 15 (1920): 125-85, is another example of this trend.

[8]"Mémoires sur les coutumes du Cambodge, par Tcheou Ta-kouan," *BEFEO* 2 (1902): 123-77; posthumous rev. ed. *Mémoires sur les coutumes du Cambodge de Tcheou Ta-kouan* (Paris: Librairie d'Amérique et d'Orient, 1951).

[9]*BEFEO* 2.4 (1902): 315-40. Among his many contributions on Chinese bibliography must also be mentioned the following: "Les documents chinois trouvés par la mission Kozlov à Khara-Khoto," *JA* ser. 11, 3 (1914): 503-18; "Trois manuscrits de l'époque des T'ang récemment publiés au Japon," *TP* 13 (1912): 482-507; "Manuscrits

this latter ensemble of notices he describes many valuable Chinese works which had disappeared in China only to survive in varying states of preservation in Japan. This article is structured around an analysis of the contents of the *Ku i ts'ung-shu* 古逸叢書 (KITS), a collection of copies of ancient manuscripts, incunabula, and printed works which had been lost in China for centuries. The "Collectaena of Books Lost Anciently" was collected by Yang Shou-ching (1839-1915) and Li Shu-ch'ang (1837-97), two Chinese diplomats stationed in Japan in the late nineteenth century.[10]

The value of this collection is shown by Pelliot in his analysis and evaluation of each entry. First, he translates each title, a practice not usually followed even today. Then follows an analysis of the work, elucidating such pertinent aspects as the author, number of *chüan*, date and place of publication, identity of any commentator, history of transmission until lost, and any references to the text appearing in traditional Chinese bibliographies. Finally, Pelliot text-critically evaluates each work in relation to its value to modern sinology by establishing the text as a) the only extant version; b) the best or earliest edition; c) an edition with significant value as a witness against the received version; d) being valuable for reference; or e) having no real utility other than to confirm problematic readings in the received text. Finally, Pelliot gives practical examples of

---

chinois au Japan," *TP* 23 (1924): 15-30; "Les publications du Tōyō Bunko," *TP* 26 (1928-29): 357-566; "Notes sur quelques livres ou documents conservés en Espange," *TP* 26 (1928-29): 43-50; "Sur quelques manuscrits sinologiques conservés en Russie," *TP* 29 (1932): 104-09; and a valuable unpublished manuscript compiled in 1922, "Inventaire sommaire des manuscrits et imprimés chinois de la Bibliothèque Vaticane." Two studies still indispensable today are "Quelques remarques sur le Chouo Fou," *TP* 23 (1924): 163-220; and "L'édition collective des oeuvres de Wang Kouo-wei," *TP* 26 (1929): 113-82. His collection of disparate notes on early incunabula and the development of printing, inspired by what he felt were major *lacunae* in the work of Carter, is *Les Débuts de l'imprimérie en Chine*, ed. Robert des Rotours, with additional notes and appendix by Paul Demiéville (Paris, 1953).

[10]For Li Shu-ch'ang and the KITS, see Arthur W. Hummel, ed. *Eminent Chinese of the Ch'ing Period (1644-1912)*, 2 vols. (Washington: United States Government Printing Office, 1943), 1:483-84. For Yang Shou-ching and a more penetrating analysis of the KITS, see Wendy Larson, "Yang Shou-ching: His Life and Work," *Phi Theta Papers* 14 (1977): 60-69.

how these works can change or modify established opinion or support an unpopular theory.

Pelliot's pervasive scholarship at least doubles the bibliographic coverage of these notes, for his extended comments on books related to the entries in the KITS are sometimes as extensive as the notes on the KITS works themselves. For instance, because the *Erh-ya*, a work printed in the KITS, is most prominently included in the *Shih-san-ching chu-shu* 十三經 注疏, he briefly describes the three different editions of this collection. This type of digression is not likely to be considered worthwhile by scholars with little respect for bibliographical detail or less well-endowed for this exacting if sometimes onerous work. Nor will such readers appreciate the instances when a particular catalogue is cited as mentioning a work in the KITS and Pelliot goes on to give a lengthy account of the catalogue in a footnote. All in all, Pelliot was the first Western sinologist to command traditional Chinese bibliography as extensively and pervasively as Chinese or Japanese scholars, and the first to show, by constant and convincing example, the method for textual criticism of traditional Chinese sources.[11]

Representative of his historical studies on Chinese border regions is "Deux itinéraires de Chine en Inde à la fin de vii siècle."[12] One of Pelliot's earliest, longest, and, according to Duyvendak, most famous works,[13] this lengthy study on a host of problems relating to the history and geography of Southeast Asia is a model of thorough and imaginative

---

[11]The discipline of textual criticism is discussed at length in chapter six below in relation to the career of Gustav Haloun.

[12]*BEFEO* 4 (1904): 131-413. Pelliot returned to the subject of historical itineraries frequently throughout his career, either with original contributions or through lengthy reviews, culminating with his great work on Marco Polo. Among the former, see "Note sur les anciens itinéraires chinois dans l'orient romain," *JA* ser. 11, 17 (1921): 139-45, and his series of studies of the voyages of Cheng Ho at *TP* 30 (1932): 237-452, *TP* 31 (1935): 274-314, and *TP* 32 (1936): 210-22. Among the latter, see his review of Gabriel Ferrand, *Voyage du marchand arabe Sulaymán en Inde et en Chine*, *TP* 21 (1922): 399-413; review of Arthur Waley, *The Travels of an Alchemist*, *TP* 28 (1931): 413-28; and review of Hirth and Rockhill, *Chau Ju-kua: His Work on the Chinese and Arab Trade in the Twelfth and Thirteenth Centuries*, *TP* 13 (1912): 446-81.

[13]At *TP* 38 (1947): 6.

scholarship. His focal point is two short itineraries on different routes from China to India, one by land and one by sea, both written by Chia Tan 賈耽, preserved in the *Hsin T'ang-shu*. These routes, although historically important, had been studied neither with accuracy nor thoroughness, hence the value of Pelliot's work. But in addition to identifying the names along the way, major contributions to scholarship are his numerous excursuses and appendices which deal with various important questions. Among these are the origin of the name "China," the ethnic identity of the kingdom of Nan-chao, the identity of certain statelets and kingdoms of South Asia, and the location of the capital of Champa.

His methodology is worth detailing. It lay not only upon a foundation of exploiting a wide range of Chinese and other language sources, but also in accurately interpreting these texts, often with the help of the then novel approach of using phonetic reconstructions of transcriptions.

Structurally, Pelliot proceeded by first reviewing earlier work and then criticizing weak hypotheses. His main method of disposing of weak thinking was to use simple logic: he reexamined the evidence and the sources to see if an hypothesis was historically plausible. For example, it was thought by some that the name China derived from the name of a port, *jih-nan* 日南, which was supposedly the place where the "embassy" sent from Marcus Aurelius had disembarked. But Pelliot's reading of the sources proved that the embassy only crossed the Chinese border. Besides, the contemporary ports along the Red River were much more important at the time. Therefore, the hypothesis that the name of this minor port was noised abroad and came to represent all of the Middle Kingdom was shown to be very weak from an historical standpoint. Furthermore, linguistic analysis, the second method of disposing of erroneous or weak hypotheses, indicated that the word "China" could not have been derived from *jih-nan*.[14] Even though phonetic reconstruction was a novel tool at

---

[14]In 1912 Pelliot returned to the name China and supported his previous derivation from the state name of Ch'in, against the views of Berthold Laufer, in "L'origine du nom de 'China,'" *TP* 13 (1912): 727-42.

the time,[15] Pelliot not only used it often in dealing with Chinese transcriptions of foreign words but also compared Persian and Arabic transcriptions of the same native names and terms in striving for accuracy of reconstruction.

Yet another method was Pelliot's careful use of sources. He knew that geographical names could sometimes shift around, thus his comparison of different itineraries such as those in the *Chu-fan chih* 諸藩志 or the dynastic histories was a needed check. This same care, this time applied to the words represented by the graphs enabled him to identify Chinese loan words in other tongues, such as Burmese *udi* (Chinese *wu-ti* 武帝).

In summation, this work from an early stage in his career represents the best in Pelliot: minute attention to or reexamination of many facts laboriously culled and confirmed from a very wide variety of sources, all accurately analyzed and skillfully combined to answer specific historical questions.

Tun-huang and the "Terre d'election"

Although Pelliot's early publications were diverse, his field of research would be greatly expanded by the events he was about to initiate. In 1904 he returned home in order to represent the Ecole des Hautes Etudes Chinoises at the 14th International Congress of Orientalists to be held in Algiers in 1905. While in France he was chosen to direct an archaeological mission to Chinese Turkestan. After a year of preparation, he left Paris on June 15, 1906 together with a specialist in natural history and geography, and a photographer. Although the group did significant archaeological work at several sites, this mission is most famous for the large horde of medieval manuscripts recovered from the caves of Tun-huang and purchased from the Taoist caretaker-priest Wang Yüan-lu in April of 1908. Aurel Stein had visited the hidden library one year earlier, and had also made substantial purchases. But he could not be selective, for he knew no Chinese. On the other hand, Pelliot spent three weeks crouched in the cave examining at break-neck speed every manuscript, and

---

[15]The discipline of historical linguistics is treated at length in chapter three below.

chose what he felt were the cream of the crop.[16]

Another of Pelliot's remarkable gifts was to prove invaluable in this task: his prodigious memory. He drew upon all of his knowledge of bibliography and Asian religions to select the most important among thousands of manuscripts. A famous letter written from Tun-huang, which describes some of the choicer finds in detail all from memory, including precise dates, biographical and textual data, even textual filiation, was an amazing intellectual feat. Those who did not realize the strength of Pelliot's memory, when they later read this letter in the *BEFEO*, could only explain such details by claiming that he faked the manuscripts and wrote up his report from the comfort of a well-stocked library filled with reference works.[17] Many of these detractors were the same persons who were attacking the integrity of the Ecole and the competency of Chavannes. Hence, when he returned home, Pelliot received a hero's welcome only from some quarters; he became the object of much jealous vituperation from others. The attack never really died down until Stein published his own narration of his explorations, taking care to substantiate Pelliot's account of the library, and to praise his qualifications as a scholar.

This journey to Central Asia, the place he came to call his "terre d'election," introduced Pelliot to the Central Asian languages and cultures, and it was not long before he added documents in Mongolian, Turkic, Arabic, Persian, Tibetan, Sanskrit and others to his storehouse of primary sources.[18] He, of course, had great facility in all of the important secondary

---

[16]An engaging entrée into Pelliot's escapades at Tun-huang for the general reader, put in the context of other explorers, is Peter Hopkirk, *Foreign Devils on the Silk Road* (London: John Murray, 1982), 177-89. On Pelliot's importance in developing Tun-huang studies, consult Jean-Pierre Drège, "Tun-huang Studies in Europe," in *Europe Studies China*, 513-32.

[17]Published in part as "Une bibliothèque médiévale retrouvée au Kan-su," *BEFEO* 8 (1908): 501-29. A similar *tour de force* was made when he wrote "Le *Chou king* en charactères anciens et le *Chang chou che wen*," *Mémoires concernant l'asie Orientale* 2 (Paris, 1916): 123-177, which he wrote in comparative academic isolation with the aid of just a few books sent to him by Chavannes.

[18]On the Central Asian and Altaic aspects of Pelliot's scholarship, consult J. Deny, "Paul Pelliot et les études altaiques," in *Paul Pelliot*, 54-68, and L. Hambis, "Paul Pelliot et le études mongoles," in *Paul Pelliot*, 69-77.

languages, including Russian. It is unclear the extent of his command of Japanese. His student and colleague Paul Demiéville claimed that he could not read it. But, older Japanese sinologists remember Pelliot as appropriating their scholarship without citation. According to Enoki Kazuo, Pelliot merely pretended ignorance of Japanese.[19] However he managed to access Japanese, he not only mined it and all these other linguistic sources for data on Sino-Central Asian problems, but made original contributions in textual explication or phonological reconstruction in these languages.[20] The unique erudition of Pelliot, a veritable "Marco Polo of the spirit,"[21] was recognized by the creation of a special chair for him at the Collège de France in 1911 when he was 33 years old: the Chair of the Languages, History, and Archaeology of Central Asia. Like an Alexander the Great, his academic empire did not survive his death—he created it and was its sole potentate.

Among the most valuable finds at the grottoes of Tun-huang was a certain lengthy religious manuscript in the form of a Buddhist sutra. When it was published in the *Tun-huang shih-shih i-shu* 敦煌石室遺書 (Peking, 1909), the Chinese editor Lo Chen-yü could only approximate an identification, for the title was lacking and was not mentioned in the body of the manuscript. In a lengthy study, "Un traité manichéen retrouvé en Chine,"[22] Pelliot and his former teacher Chavannes confirmed this document as Manichaean (already provisionally identified as such by

---

[19]Yoshikawa Kojirō, *Tōyōgaku no sōshisha-tachi* (Tokyo: Kōdansha, 1976), 40-41; 253. This reference was kindly supplied by Prof. Timothy Wixted.

[20]Among many, see "Autour d'une traduction sanscrite du Tao Tö King," *TP* 13 (1912): 351-430; "Quelques transcriptions chinois de noms tibétains," *TP* 16 (1915): 1-26; "Les Mots mongols dans le *Korye Sa*," *JA* 217 (1930): 253-66; "Sur le légende d'Uγuz-khan en écriture Ouigoure," *TP* 27 (1930): 247-358; "Les Formes turques et mongoles dans la nomenclature zoologique du *Nuzhatu-'l-kulub*," *BSOS* 6 (1930): 555-80; and "A propos de 'tokharien,'" *TP* 32 (1936): 259-84.

[21]Characterization of J.J.L. Duyvendak, *TP* 38 (1947): 11.

[22]Part One; *JA* ser. 10, 18 (1911): 499-617; Part Two; ser. 11, 1 (1913): 99-199, 261-394.

Pelliot when he first found it[23]), translated, and annotated it.[24] But, belying the simple scope suggested by the title of their collaborative work, they translated an additional fifty-three documents or passages relating to or mentioning Manichaeism, laboriously culled from many Chinese sources. Also included were discussions on the *Hua-hu ching* 化胡經 and two Manichaean canonical works, the *Erh-tsung ching* 二宗經 and *San-chi ching* 三際經.

The translation of this document made an important contribution to Manichaean studies not surpassed even today, and technically speaking, was an impressive feat. First of all, Pelliot and Chavannes had to decide on the particular meaning of ambiguous graphs. For example, they usually interpreted *hsiang* 相 "form," as "thought" 想 . They based this interpretation on the fact that it seemed to designate an operation of the spirit, a sense found in comparative Christian and Moslem sources. Besides, in this MS 相 most often parallels 思, 念, 心, 意 . Furthermore, their sensitivity to parallelism and rhythm enabled them to render accurately compounds such as *kuang-ming* 光明 as "light," rather than as an inappropriate (in this context) pleonastic "light and brilliance;" it also enabled them to show that the religious sense in a phrase such as *wu fen-ming-shen* 五分明身, demands that *fen* modify *shen*, a conclusion reached after consulting parallel passages and also by comparing this passage with a similar phrase from a Chinese Nestorian text.

The expertise of Pelliot and Chavannes in Buddhist and Taoist technical vocabularies was also useful in comparing the Manichaean usages. But they were quick to point out where there were differences or obscure passages. All of this expertise came as a result of a complete grasp of Chinese religious literature, especially Chinese Manichaean and *contra*-Manichaean sources, including relevant Manichaean texts in Greek, Latin,

---

[23]"Une bibliotheque médiévale retrouvée au Kan-su," 518.

[24]For the history of scholarly treatment of this fragment, now catalogued as Pelliot 3884, and its place in the Manichaean corpus, see Gunner B. Mikkelsen, "Skilfully (sic) Planting the Trees of Light: The Chinese Manichaica, Their Central Asian Counterparts, and Some Observations on the Translation of Manichaeism into Chinese," in *Cultural Encounters: China, Japan, and the West*, Søren Clausen, et al. eds. (Aarhus, Denmark: Aarhus University Press, 1995), 83-108.

Persian, and Sogdian. Much imagination was also displayed in proposing solutions to knotty textual or doctrinal questions. But they were usually on the right path, for in Part Two of this study they utilized newly published documents to fortify or confirm the plausible but still hypothetical solutions posed in Part One. All in all, this monograph is deserving of Berthold Laufer's praise as "perhaps the most brilliant achievement of modern sinology."[25]

The Commentarial Tradition

Although Pelliot published an enormous amount, hardly documented in this survey so far, he never wrote a book in the traditional sense. Many of his monographs, although of book-length such as "Le Hoja et le Sayyid Husain de l'Histoire des Ming,"[26] his Mongolian reconstruction of the *Secret History of the Mongols*,[27] or his notes on the Golden Horde,[28] were nevertheless concerned usually with a single concrete historical problem, or the translation and explication of a major text. His approach most often involved the exploitation of numerous sources in various languages, including establishing textual filiation and priority. The accurate assessment of Duyvendak was that analysis, not synthesis, was his forte.[29] He also liked to address a number of problems, which related closely or loosely to the subject at hand, so that his publications were mines of varied but valuable information.[30] In his own contributions he

---

[25] *JAOS* 22 (1922): 204.

[26] *TP* 38 (1947): 81-292.

[27] *Histoire secrete des Mongols: Restitution du texte mongol et traduction française des chapitres I-VI* (Paris, 1949). Because it was unfinished (the MS was published posthumously), Nicholas Poppe ranked it as "slightly inferior" to the transcription and translation by E. Haenisch; see Poppe, *Introduction to Altaic Linguistics* (Wiesbaden: Otto Harrassowitz, 1965), 90.

[28] *Notes sur l'histoire de la Horde d'Or* (Paris, 1950).

[29] Cf. the following statement: "Probably his mind was more analytic than synthetic, more critical than creative, and the host of facts on any given subject which he could marshal at any time was never coordinated in a more permanent form," *TP* 38 (1947), 13.

[30] Witness, for instance, "Neuf notes sur des questions d'Asie Centrale," *TP* 26 (1929): 201-65.

often helped the progress of sinology by either dispensing new information or suggesting fruitful but heretofore neglected fields or sources that should be investigated;[31] many short notes, comments, or queries were published with the same goal in mind. This fashion of publication is reminiscent of the medieval humanists and their "notebook" approach to glossing a text. It stands squarely in the commentarial tradition of the learned exegetes who revealed and expounded the truths to be found in the classics.

Oral commentaries on Homer, such as that of Zenodotus, the first librarian of the great library at Alexander, existed long before they became recorded. The first written commentary has traditionally been credited to Aristarchus, who in 180 B.C. published his edition of Homer, dividing for the first time the texts of the *Iliad* and the *Odyssey* into twenty-four books each, the basis of the modern text.[32] Yet a fourth-century B.C. commentary on an early Orphic poem was discovered among the papyri at Derveni (west of Belgrade). Hence, the science of exegesis predated the Alexandrian grammarians. Rudolph Pfeiffer insists that the early rhapsodes produced a form of commentary when they "add[ed] elucidating words, half-lines, lines to ambiguous expressions, or to proper names" in the course of their oral compositions.[33] The Sophists of the fifth century also interpreted the epic, again according to Pfeiffer, as they "explained epic and archaic poetry, combining their interpretations with linguistic observations, definitions, and classifications on the lines laid down by previous philosophers."[34] The Alexandrian grammarians worked full-time on elucidating the textual heritage deposited in their famous library. They were branded as busy-

---

[31]A notable example of this is his *Notes sur l'histoire de la Horde d'Or*. Of this work, Denis Sinor stated that "This is a book that one must constantly have at hand, because it not only contains precise data on subjects rarely or badly treated, but also because it suggests new avenues for research;" Sinor, *Introduction à l'étude de l'Eurasie Centrale* (Wiesbaden: Otto Harrassowitz, 1963), 312.

[32]Pfeiffer, *History of Classical Scholarship*, 2:54.

[33]Ibid., 1:4. This practice of self-conscious glossing can also be seen in early Chinese literature, for example in *Shih-chi* 84 where Ssu-ma Ch'ien includes a short internal gloss on the meaning of the title of "Li-sao," or *Lao-tzu* 13, where the text explains itself in a discursive fashion.

[34]Pfeiffer, *History of Classical Scholarship*, 1:16.

body scribblers by one philologically minded poet who advised his friends to ignore the "latest correct editions" of Homer and to consult only "old copies."[35]   They were strongly motivated by their rivalry with the librarians of Pergamum.   As for the Pergamums, according to Luciano Canfora,

> What interested them was the "hidden" meaning, the meaning that lay "behind" the classical and especially the Homeric, texts—the "allegory," as they called it, concealed within these poems.   The Alexandrians, by contrast, patiently found line-by-line and word-by-word explanations, halting wherever the sense was not plain to them.[36]

The competition for the best manuscripts was fierce, even leading to the Alexandrians cutting off the flow of Egyptian papyrus to the Pergamums. Forced to rely on their own resources, they in turn refined the technique of treating animal skins into parchment, which word is a derivative of Pergamum (by way of medieval Latin *pergamena*).   (This led to the invention of the codex, a bound book of double-sided pages that superseded the rolled manuscript).

In general, both allegorical and philological commentaries were written as separate works.   Critical signs such as the *obelos*, the *diple*, the dotted *diple*, the *asteriskos*, and the *antisigma* were used to mark certain passages as spurious, noteworthy, interpolations, etc. and to refer the reader to the appropriate place in the separate commentary.   It was only in the tenth century that commentaries were incorporated as interlinear or separate notes within the text.   These marginal notes, then, called "scholia," were associated with medieval manuscripts.[37]

Despite these tentative steps toward textual exegesis, it is not until

---

[35]Luciano Canfora, *The Vanished Library: A Wonder of the Ancient World*, trans. Martin Ryle (Berkeley and Los Angeles: University of California Press, 1989), 37.

[36]Ibid., 49.

[37]For the commentarial tradition and its technical apparatus, see L.D. Reynolds and N.G. Wilson, *Scribes and Scholars: A Guide to the Transmission of Greek and Latin Literature*, 3rd edition (Oxford: Clarendon Press, 1991), 9-16.

the 15th century and the rise of classical studies that we see most clearly the three major stages in the development of a comprehensive commentarial strategy. First, wealthy princes and prelates began to assemble manuscript collections, inviting the perusal of humanists. Second, the invention of printing made possible a new level of precision in textual scholarship as the humanists vied to edit and publish these manuscripts. They then provided uniform copies of most classical texts, plus the traditional commentaries. These printed texts formed a standard for collation, and such standardized texts attracted the attention of widely-scattered humanists to the same textual problems.   Third, such close attention to textual problems reoriented the direction of scholarship from grammar and rhetoric to the texts themselves. And as Latin was relatively easy to master, the challenge of Latin grammar and rhetoric made this study of less interest to the Humanists. Hence, a new generation of scholars appeared, who served as editors of printed texts.   Such editions gave rise to the line-by-line commentary as the dominant literary form. The disadvantage of this form was that it forced commentators to deal with every problem, and hence made it impossible for creativity to shine through, for originality lay buried among a "mass of trivial glosses"—a phrase reminiscent of the criticism made of some of Pelliot's denser notes. Furthermore, there were no criteria for helping to choose between competing glosses, which were presented without a preference stated. Hence, after the mid-1470s several humanists moved away from the commentary as a literary form, most prominently Poliziano. His 1489 *Miscellanea* was representative of two new types of scholarship, one the collection of annotations on selective passages of interest, and one the collection of short chapters on various topics, sometimes devoted to *ad hominem* attack. His work also provided technical criteria for deciding on the priority of textual variora and scholia. This breakthrough allowed for the development of the first class of professional philologists.[38]

In China, the rise of the commentarial tradition is traced by John Henderson back to the interpretation of omens, oracles, and dreams. "The association between divination," asserts Henderson, "is most obvious with

---

[38]This quick synopsis is based on Grafton, *Joseph Scaliger*, 1:14-90.

the *Classic of Changes*."[39] Both the line statements and interpretive "wings" are early commentary that have been incorporated within the classic itself. Hence the diviner, not the poet as in Greece, laid claim to the keys of interpreting literature. But of course, the classics in ancient China were considered sacred repositories of the wisdom of the sages, not merely belletristic literary works. Hence Confucius''s mission was to preserve and transmit the wisdom of the classics, rather than to compose anything original himself. Indeed, according to Tai Chen (1724-1777), Confucius' mission was that of a commentator: to clarify the teaching of the classics: "Since Confucius did not achieve the status of a ruler and was not in a position to carry on their institutions, ceremonies, and music, he undertook to clarify their basis and to trace them to their source in order that men for a thousand generations might know the causes of peace and disorder and whether it would be appropriate to follow or to change certain institutions and regulations...."[40]

Many early commentaries became part of the classics they elucidated. For instance, since the "Little Preface" 小序 to the *Book of Poems* was, until the Sung dynasty, usually considered as stemming from the teaching of Confucius as transmitted by his disciple Tzu Hsia, it has been regarded as part of the classic itself. The *Ssu-k'u* editors give it an individual entry in their great bibliography because some editions of it, known as the *Shih-hsü*, had been included in different *ts'ung-shu* after Chu Hsi first dislodged it from the head of the *Poems*. Hence some scholars came to regard it as an exegetical work on *the Poems*, rather than as an integral part of the poetical canon itself.[41]

If it took a sage to compose a classic, then it took at least a "worthy" scholar, concerned as much with self-cultivation as with scholarship, to compose a commentary. Hence, if the progression in the West was

---

[39]John B. Henderson, *Scripture, Canon, and Commentary: A Comparison of Confucian and Western Exegesis* (Princeton: Princeton University Press, 1991), 67.

[40]Ann-ping Chin and Mansfield Freeman, *Tai Chen on Mencius* (New Haven: Yale University Press, 1990), 65.

[41]See, *inter alia*, *Lü-t'ing chih-chien ch'uan-pen shu-mu* (Shanghai, 1918), 2.1a; and *Tseng-ting Ssu-k'u chien-ming mu-lu piao-chu* (Shanghai, 1979), 56.

rhapsode, sophist, grammarian, humanist, and classicist, then in China it was diviner, sage, worthy, and scholiast/sinologist. After the closure of the Confucian canon during the Han, commentaries circulated separately. It was not until the Latter Han that commentaries began to be printed interlinearly in the text of the classics, anticipating the same practice in the West by some 800 years.

The primary impulse behind the composition of a commentary was, again quoting Henderson, to "resolve difficult or doubtful points in the classics, to make fully manifest the meanings of the ancient sages. The clarification of such obscurities was necessary not so much because the sages themselves were unclear or incomplete in their teachings, but because of such historical developments as lexical change, the loss or fragmentation of texts, alternations in the forms of the written characters, and changes in culture and institutions."[42]   In the Six Dynasties, the convention of composing commentaries on the commentaries, or epexegetical works called shu 疏 , became vehicles for displaying virtuosic command of knowledge. By late imperial times, notation-style books *(cha-chi* 箚記 , *lu* 錄 , *tsa-chi* 雜記 etc.) in China paralleled the *miscellany* of the humanist in propounding a personal agenda, promoting a specific school of interpretation, or launching a personal attack. Examples include Yen Jo-chü 閻若璩 (1636-1704), *Ch'ien-ch'iu cha-chi* 潛邱箚記 ; Ch'ien Ta-hsin 錢大昕 (1728-1804), *Shih-chia-chai yang-hsin-lu* 十駕齋養新錄; Wang Nien-sun 王念孫 (1744-1832), *Tu-shu tsa-chi* 讀書雜記 ; and the earliest and perhaps greatest, Ku Yen-wu 顧炎武 (1613-1682), *Jih-chih lu* 日知錄 .

Pelliot as Textual Commentator

Pelliot was always a philologist and generally an elucidator of specific texts or textual problems. His publications were characterized by Demiéville as "rough-hewn jewels": "Dragged along by the demon of philological research which always possessed him, pressed as well by the exigencies of an ecumenical memory, Pelliot produced for us his scientific

---

[42]Henderson, *Scripture, Canon, and Commentary*, 75.

works like a littering of rough-hewn jewels."[43] The phrase "pressed...by the exigencies of an ecumenical memory" should give us pause, for it seems to hint at the single factor that inhibited Pelliot from developing the ability to reach provisional historical conclusions, that of a memory that could not forget anything, reminiscent of the "abnormal, even monstrous memory" of the English classical scholar Richard Porson (1759-1808).[44] Pelliot's memory, utilized for many good purposes, as we have seen, nevertheless prevented that procedure so necessary to synthetic work, that of the ruthless discarding of the unessential. Porson may be adduced for another parallel to Pelliot: "This devoted man of learning lacked another essential quality for a scholar who wants to make his mark; I mean the ability to delimit a vast subject sufficiently for appropriate conclusions."[45] Pelliot, of course, made his mark, and made it brilliantly, in many fields of sinology, but his gifts were naturally best served by the discipline of philology rather than of history.

Pelliot's methodology, apart from the working example his publications provide for us, is clearly enunciated at several points. Early in his career he commented on one aspect of his approach by stating that, in a review of his work on Fu-nan,[46] Chavannes approved of his method of commencing by translating all texts and passages that pertain to the question at hand, a "necessary condition for scientific work."[47] Besides this thorough treatment of a broad number of related sources, each was individually analyzed with equal thoroughness. At the end of Pelliot's career he summarized the need for copious annotation, the ancillary of translation, because, "if we simply translate (the texts) in a more or less conventional form, no results are achieved. It is necessary to go to the bottom, to trace the origin of every sentence with due annotation and then

---

[43]Demiéville, "La Carrière scientific de Paul Pelliot, son oeuvre relative à l'Extrême-Orient," in *Paul Pelliot*, 29-30.

[44]For this memory and the emotional and intellectual hardship it caused for Porson, see Brink, *English Classical Scholarship*, 108-09.

[45]Ibid., 131-32.

[46]*BEFEO* 3 (1903): 248-303.

[47]"Deux itineraires," 363.

we shall go forward."[48] His massive work, *Notes on Marco Polo*, published posthumously, crowned a life of achievement and represents the epitome of this approach of exhaustively elucidating a text through annotation.[49]

The views of two modern historians of traditional China may be elicited to illustrate opposing sentiments on the importance of the translation-annotation approach perfected by Pelliot. Hans Bielenstein allowed that the first level on which a good historian must work is the sources: "His first step is to deal with the sources, and the further he goes back in time the more arduous this task becomes. He must attempt, where necessary, to reconstruct the texts in their original form, compare different versions, and recognize corruptions, copyists' errors, and later additions. In short, he must engage in text criticism."[50] A professional philologist provides such first-level spadework in the form of annotated translation à la Pelliot. Herbert Franke comments on the usefulness of presenting translated texts in such detail:

> Whatever we may think of the much-maligned "commentarial tradition," it cannot be denied that also today critical annotated translations of basic Chinese texts do not represent an obsolete approach to Chinese civilization and history. Translation still has or should have its merits. To use premodern Chinese texts, particularly those in literary language, merely as a quarry from which odds and ends are mined in order to illustrate some hypothesis is of course tempting because it allows us to gloss over passages that are incompletely understood by the western scholar.[51]

---

[48]"Orientalists in France During the War," address delivered at a meeting of the Chinese Art Society of America, January 25, 1945, *Archives of the Chinese Art Society of America* 1 (1945-48): 14-25; quote on 24. David B. Honey, "The Sinologist and Chinese Sources on Asia," *Phi Theta Papers* 17 (1987): 21-27, attempts to place both the importance and the limitations of the translation/annotation approach within the general context of the aims of sinological studies.

[49]*Notes on Marco Polo*, 3 vols. (Paris: Imprimérie National, 1959-73).

[50]Bielenstein, "Chinese Historiography in Europe," in *Europe Studies China*, 240.

[51]Franke, "In Search of China," 18. See further Franke, "Sinologie im 19. Jahrhundert," in *August Pfizmaier (1808-1887) und seine Bedeutung für die Ostasienwissenschaften*, ed. Otto Ladstatter Otto and Sepp Linhart (Vienna, 1990), 40.

Yet Bielenstein goes on to make the unwarranted conclusion that, since historians are able to perform their own philological work, annotated translations such as Chavannes' version of the *Shih-chi* or Dubs' rendering of the *Han-shu* are now "out of fashion for the simple reason that knowledge of classical Chinese has improved with each new generation of students." He concludes that "we no longer need the help of a Chavannes or a Dubs, because we are able to read the texts ourselves."[52] He forgets, of course, that other scholars besides historians may be interested in what a text has to say, and may be less philologically gifted at accessing whatever data are desired. The task of presenting a text on its own terms, in the context of its own textual tradition--something most scholars are unwilling to do, however competent they may be—is an honorable endeavor in itself. Erich Haenisch (1880-1966) even went so far as to regard an annotated translation, which he termed "Extenso-Übersetzung," as the necessary qualification for graduation into the ranks of professional sinologists.[53] This approach, made famous by Pelliot, even if long-since superseded in the discipline of history, remains valid and necessary in the separate discipline of philology.

Editorial *Verwaltungsordnung*, Duyvendak, and the *T'oung Pao*

As a scholar, professor, and especially as editor of *T'oung Pao* from 1920 to 1942, Pelliot served almost by common consent as the arbiter of last resort on sinological and Central Asian matters.[54] This was a role he developed for himself, for earlier editors of this journal had not been in a position to survey the entire field of sinology with the confident mastery

---

[52]Bielenstein, "Chinese Historiography in Europe," 241; Burton Watson suggests the same thing in his essay "Chinese History," in *An Encyclopaedia of Translation: Chinese-English, English-Chinese*, ed. Chan Sin-wai and David E. Pollard (Hong Kong: Chinese University of Hong Kong Press, 1995), 349.

[53]Franke, "In Search of China," 19.

[54]His former student, James Ware, expressed it well in a burst of emotion on the occasion of Pelliot's death: "Seldom in the field of philological studies has it been the opportunity and privilege of one man to become a veritable pillar of strength and refuge. Paul Pelliot was such a man." *HJAS* 9 (1946): 187.

of Pelliot, although one tried unsuccessfully to do so.

T'oung Pao was founded by Henri Cordier. He had previously established the *Revue de l'Extrême-Orient*, which, however, proved unsatisfactory because it was unable to print Chinese characters. Searching around, he discovered that the publishing house of E.J. Brill of Leiden possessed a font of Chinese characters and was amenable to publishing a journal dedicated to the Far East.[55] Gustav Schlegel, professor of Chinese at the University of Leiden from 1875 to 1903, joined with Cordier in editing the new journal.[56] It started in 1890, publishing five issues per year. After ten years, a second series was initiated; this series has run annually up to the present, with one short interregnum during World War II, with again five issues per year (printed, however, as numbers 1-2, and 3-5).

From its inception, the scope of the journal was intended to encompass the whole of the Far East—witness the introductory subtitle on the cover: "Archives pour servir à l'étude de l'histoire, des languages, de la géographie et de l'ethnographie de l'Asie Oriental (Chine, Japon, Corée, Indo-Chine, Asie Central et Malaisie)." The first few issues published contributions from many eminent English, German, French, Dutch, and Asian sinologists. And as this tradition continued, it seems that the success of T'oung Pao was assured. But it was not so. "Schlegel was a somewhat pugnacious man," opines Duyvendak in a generous understatement, "and the unusually early age at which he had acquired his knowledge of Chinese made him quite sure that he knew this language far better than anybody else."[57] According to Cordier, the "aggressive" and "authoritative" personality of Schlegel had "eloigné du T'oung Pao tous ses collaborateurs, pendent quelques mois le labeur fut incessant, mais, à force de travail et de

---

[55]The matrices for Brill's characters had been drawn and cut by Johann Joseph Hoffmann (b. 1805), professor of Japanese at the University of Leiden, in 1860; see Duyvendak, *Holland's Contribution to Chinese Studies*, 22.

[56]For notices on Schlegel, see Duyvendak, *Holland's Contribution to Chinese Studies*, 22-23; Wilt L. Idema, "Dutch Sinology: Past, Present, and Future," in *Europe Studies China*, 89-91; and Henri Cordier, "Nécrologie: Le Dr. Gustave Schlegel," *TP* 4 (1903): 407-15.

[57]Duyvendak, *Holland's Contribution to Chinese Studies*, 22.

persévérance, nous avons surmonté les difficulties de la premier heur."[58]

After serving as co-editor from 1890 to 1903, Gustav Schlegel died. Cordier continued on alone as editor for a year until Chavannes offered to replace Schlegel. Cordier gladly welcomed him, and considered his offer as very magnanimous, since Schlegel had attacked Chavannes very bitterly. (Apparently Chavannes had beaten Schlegel to the punch in publishing some transcriptions from Central Asia that Schlegel also had been working on). It was with the editorship of Cordier and Chavannes that the journal truly developed into one of distinction. Along with the *BEFEO*, it had become the most important organ for disseminating information in the form of articles, reviews, notes, notices, news of the field, and bibliographies on the Far East.

Chavannes retired from his position in 1916, two years before his death. Enduring another solo editorialship, this time of two years' duration, Cordier was joined by Pelliot as co-editor in 1920. After four years of teamwork, Cordier died, and Pelliot carried on singly until 1932, when another professor from Leiden, J.J.L. Duyvendak, joined him.

Duyvendak (1889-1954) was born in Harlingen, entered Leiden in 1908 and studied Dutch philology; later he learned Chinese from de Groot.[59] From 1910 to 1911 he studied with Chavannes and Cordier in Paris. From 1912 to 1918 he served his country as an interpreter in the diplomatic service. In 1919 he began his career at Leiden as lecturer in Chinese. In 1930 he was named professor of Chinese, filling the Chair of Chinese Language and Literature that had been left vacant since de Groot's departure for Berlin in 1912; late that same year he founded the Sinological

---

[58]*TP* 18 (1917): 125.

[59]Paul Demiéville, "J.J.L. Duyvendak (1889-1954)," *TP* 43 (1955): 1-22; pp. 22-33 contain a complete biography; Piet van der Loon, "In Memoriam J.J.L. Duyvendak 1889-1954," *AM* n.s. 5 (1955): 1-4; and Wilt L. Idema, "Dutch Sinology: Past, Present, and Future," 92-95. Harriet T. Zurndorfer, "Sociology, Social Science, and Sinology in the Netherlands Before World War II: With Special Reference to the Work of Frederik Van Heek," *Revue européenne des sciences sociales* 27 (1989): 19-32, contains an interesting subsection entitled "A Brief History of Chinese Studies in the Netherlands" (27-31); it culminates with the career of Duyvendak and presents an overview on how Dutch sinology became "philologized."

Institute at Leiden, with indirect funding from the Boxer Indemnity. Two years later he joined Pelliot on the editorial board of *T'oung Pao*.

Duyvendak seemed a perfect match for Pelliot, for he was as ruthless a critic against slipshod work as Pelliot, even if his criticisms were more temperately expressed. Nor did he demand less of his students, who included Derk Bodde, Erik Zürcher, A.F.P. Hulsewé, and Piet van der Loon: he expected the same rigorous attention to the details of philological analysis, with careful consideration of the textual tradition. To him, integral translation of the primary sources was the best defense against dilettantism. According to Piet van der Loon, "'Back to the Scriptures' was his watchword to the students whom he guided, impressing on them the need to exert themselves to understand even apparently insignificant passages, and to confront all the available evidence, before hasty generalization spoke its arrogant Q.E.D. This influence on his students was perhaps the most enduring side of his life as a scholar."[60] His most important works include *The Book of Lord Shang* (Leiden, 1928), which was a translation and study of the *Shang-chün shu* 商君書; and a translation and commentary of the *Tao-te ching*, the Dutch version of which was published in 1950, with French (1953) and English (1954) editions appearing afterwards. Many works in Dutch on contemporary Chinese history, politics, and literature may also be mentioned. Articles and reviews on philosophy, the maritime trade of the Chinese, early Dutch sinology, and Chinese literature maintained Duyvendak's lofty reputation as one of the leading figures in sinology of the first half of the twentieth century. Duyvendak's presence at Leiden established a center of classical Chinese philology that rivaled Paris, and attracted several American sinologists to work with him on their translations, at least at far remove: these include Homer Dubs and his translation of the *Han-shu*, C. Martin Wilbur's study of slavery during the Han, and Arthur Hummel's rendering of the autobiography of Ku Chieh-kang.

Pelliot continued to participate with Duyvendak in editing the journal until 1942, when it closed operation for the remainder of WWII. He died before it resumed publication in 1947.

---

[60]van der Loon, "In Memoriam J.J.L. Duyvendak," 4.

Pelliot's tenure brought *T'oung Pao* to its apex. With his great erudition and reputation, the journal, almost as his personal organ, became the virtual arbiter of Asiatic scholarly standards. Not only did his own numerous productions, sometimes as many as seven per year, set the mark of excellence in the field, his reviews were equally detailed and searching. He even reviewed the contents of journals, especially German, Chinese, and—perhaps at second hand—Japanese ones. And starting in 1931 Pelliot would go so far as to summarize briefly the contents, and add either a yea or nay, to the long list of books received by the journal.

Although very scrupulous and exacting as an editor, Pelliot would publish works with which he did not necessarily agree.[61] But he refused to consider anything that was not constructive. Hence, he endured many personal insults from the pen of the harsh and intolerable von Zach when the latter would correct errors—most often imagined ones—of Pelliot and others. But when von Zach's corrosive reviews became nothing more than unending enfilade from the flanks, Pelliot finally had to act the part of the dictatorial editor and to disassociate von Zach from the journal entirely. After all, the fearless and sometimes less than diplomatic critic of second-rate scholarship was the same bold and brash Pelliot of the Boxer Rebellion. At any rate, in this case he was entirely justified.[62]

Perhaps in some regards Pelliot was overly critical, for, methodologically speaking, he seldom approved anything that did not meet his own lofty standards. Because of this, Wolfram Eberhard considered him as having impeded the development of French sinology, and—ignoring the enlightened precedent of many renaissance humanists—as not playing fair with his European colleagues, especially Mongolists, in sharing some

---

[61]For instance, Creel on ideography, treated in chapter eleven below.

[62]In a short article where he discussed von Zach's manners and methods, Pelliot stated that "M. E. von Zach s'est déconsidéré comme savant par ses balourdises. M. E. von Zach s'est disqualifié comme homme par ses grossieretées. Il ne sera plus question de M. E. von Zach dans le *T'oung Pao*." *TP* 26 (1928-29): 378. This was a strong but necessary move. Eric Haenisch, an editor of *Asia Major*, himself denounced in retrospect the effect the "oft masslose Forme siener [von Zach's] Kritik" had on impeding the development of *Asia Major*. *Oriens Extremus* 12 (1965): 9.

of his rare manuscripts with them.[63] Yet Pelliot's criticisms derived out of intellectual conviction and superior erudition, not from any inbred eristic inclination like that of von Zach. Whether the effect of making his students rise to his standards should be considered as impeding the level of French scholarship, maintaining, or ultimately improving it by producing more exacting researchers, there is no doubt that his pioneering, exhaustive, and almost inimitable scholarship set the standard for a generation of like-minded philologists who considered him their master. And his professional positions institutionalized the influence he was able to exert: at forty-three he was accepted into the French Academy of Inscriptions and Letters as its youngest member, and upon the death of Sylvain Lévi he became the president of the Asiatic Society at Paris. Thus, according to R. Grousset, for a quarter of a century, "Pelliot guided French Oriental studies, bringing great prestige to France by his personality."[64]

As the virtual arbiter of sinological matters before the war Pelliot enjoyed a position of eminence and authority comparable to the *Verwaltungsordnung* of the Berlin Philharmonic, Wilhelm Furtwängler. Naturally enough—and like Furtwängler—he became the focus of a widespread academic polemic after sinology regained its collective feet after the war, a controversy that concerned much more than bruised egos and *ad hominem* antipathy. For both the philological approach and the research agenda of so-called "traditional sinology" came under attack by a rising generation of social and economic historians who, intellectually, knew neither Joseph nor Pelliot, and who defined themselves more by discipline and their fondness for the modern period than by their command of classical Chinese.[65]

---

[63]Personal communication; 12 March 1983.

[64]Elisséef, *Archives of the Chinese Art Society of America*, 1 (1945-46): 13.

[65]Criticism directed against traditional sinology includes its exclusive attention to pre-modern China, its literary and humane focus, and especially its philological approach for the "accumulation of knowledge rather than developing a discipline;" Jerome Ch'en, *China and the West: Society and Culture 1815-1937* (London: Hutchinson, 1979), 121. Arthur Wright, "The Study of Chinese Civilization," *Journal of the History of Ideas* 21 (1960): 233-55, presents the most articulate and theoretically grounded case against traditional sinology. His views will be addressed in the Envoi that concludes this work.

The Marginalization of Philology

The criticism directed against the philological approach by social historians, encapsulated by the epigraph of Levenson at the head of this chapter, may be epitomized by the attitude of Etienne Balasz, himself an admirable philologist:

> Though he admired the great French scholars of China—Marcel Granet, Paul Pelliot, Henri Maspero, and his friend Paul Demiéville—he was sharply critical of many aspects of traditional Sinology; its concentration on antiquity and the Classics, its lack of concern for basic problems of social and cultural history, its penchant for marginalia, which he described as 'disquisitions on philological trifles, expensive trips in abstruse provinces, bickerings about the restitutions of the names of unknown persons and other delightfully antiquated occupations.'[66]

The post-war antipathy to Pelliot and all he represented is understandable from one point of view, that of the desire to explore hitherto neglected areas of Chinese culture and society. Such areas, say, the social history of the lower classes, economic and institutional history, or even popular religions, do not readily lend themselves to the translation *cum* annotation approach, since few traditional Chinese sources are devoted to such topics. And of course some trivial subjects and their technical presentations seemed divorced both from reality and relevancy to the modern world. Historically, philology has had its own periods of excess, as with the romantic gushings of the original Orientalists in the early nineteenth century (called "florists" by their adversaries in the Société

---

[66]Arthur Wright, in Etienne Balazs, *Chinese Civilization and Bureaucracy*, trans. H.M. Wright, ed. Arthur F. Wright (New Haven: Yale University Press, 1964), xiii. Skinner's own caricature of sinology, which he contrasts to the bold advances of "modern Chinese studies," includes other common strictures; see G. William Skinner, "What the Study of China Can Do for Social Science," *JAS* 23 (1964): 517. John K. Fairbank is most concise of all: "Sinology is in itself rather beautiful but in its relation to anything else rather devastating;" Paul M. Evans, *John Fairbank and the American Understanding of Modern China* (New York: Basil Blackwell, 1988), 38.

Asiatique),[67] the mechanical dryness, obsessive specialization, and detached lifelessness of German classical scholarship at the end of the same century,[68] or the rapprochement between philology and both imperialist attitudes and colonial agendas typical of many former scholars and officials alike.[69] But the successful application of the methods and models of either the sociologists or historians is predicated, at least on one level, on the skillful handling of texts.[70] The question is, of course, not a matter of superiority of one discipline over another but of timing and appropriateness to the task at hand.

Herbert Franke, doyen of sino-mongolian studies, once lamented the unreasonable bias against philological studies in sinology:

> The modern contempt of philological work in favor of synthesis and interpretation is, of course, very one-sided. After the war I studied as a minor for my Ph.D. European medieval and modern history and tried to learn about Latin sources (I developed a love for medieval Latin, including poetry). Any historian, regardless of which school he belongs to, has to rely on the patient editorial work done by the Monumenta Germaniae Historica and others. Their philological and

---

[67]And philologists have their own professional jealousies. Witness the competition between Julien and Pauthier. A contemporary witticism directed against these stereotypically cranky sinologists was: "These erudite antagonists have enriched learning with two important discoveries: Julien, the noted sinologist, has discovered that Pauthier does not know Chinese, and Pauthier, the great Indianist, has discovered that Julien does not know Sanskrit;" Schwab, *The Oriental Renaissance*, 326.

[68]As the then professor of philology, Nietzsche, pointed out, such failings were the natural outcome of German historicism; Nietzsche's critique was ably rebutted by the young Wilamowitz, who suggested that the philologist Nietzsche should devote himself full-time to philosophy. See the discussion in Hugh Lloyd-Jones, *Blood for the Ghosts: Classical Influences in the Nineteenth and Twentieth Centuries* (Baltimore: Johns Hopkins University Press, 1982), 172-78. For a concise, yet to my mind overly acerbic, critique of the worst features of classical philology in both Germany and England, consult Gilbert Highet, *The Classical Tradition: Greek and Roman Influences on Western Literature* (1949; rpt. Oxford: Oxford University Press, 1985), 498-500.

[69]As attacked in Edward W. Said, *Orientalism* (New York: Vintage Books, 1979).

[70]See the discussion below on Edward Schafer and the Envoi for more on the foundational role of philology in any approach to Chinese studies.

text-critical spade-work is indispensable and never questioned about its usefulness. Why should it be different for Chinese sources?[71]

But, quite apart from the antipathy directed towards the philological approach, what is equally troubling about the attack against Pelliot is the fundamental error it betrays concerning the purpose of the historical method and what it can accomplish. The weaning of modern historiographic inquiry away from the composition of narratives, general surveys, and syntheses to the investigation of specific, synchronic problems was due to the efforts of French contemporaries of Pelliot: Lucien Febvre, Marc Bloch, and their *annales* group—anticipated, without much effect, by Frederick Teggart.[72] This movement made possible the flourishing of a new historiographic paradigm—the functional/structural—and many types of history—economic, technological, social, and the like—as different investigative techniques were developed to answer newly posited questions.[73] While Pelliot never attempted to orchestrate the results of his studies into a cohesive if merely transient synthesis, the spirit of his work was very modern: it concerned the solving of specific problems, whether

---

[71]Personal communication, letter dated Feb. 28, 1987. For the anti-philological viewpoint, see the various contributions to the "Symposium on Chinese Studies and Their Disciplines." *JAS* 23 (1964). Denis Twitchett, "A Lone Cheer for Sinology," *JAS* 24 (1964): 109-12, places in perspective the importance of philological training for any approach to Chinese studies.

[72]See his *Prolegomena to History* (Berkeley: University of California Press, 1916), 14-15 and *Rome and China: A Study of Correlations in Historical Events* (Berkeley: University of California Press, 1939), vi.

[73]For the French historians, see Peter Burke, ed. *A New Kind of History: From the Writings of Febvre*, trans. K. Folca (London: Kegan Paul, 1973); Marc Bloch, *The Historian's Craft*, trans. Peter Putnam (New York: Vintage Books, 1953); Peter Burke, *The French Historical Revolution: The Annales School 1929-89* (Cambridge: Cambridge University Press, 1990); and Traian Strianovich, *French Historical Method: "Annales" Paradigm* (Ithaca: Cornell University Press, 1976). For the problem-solving orientation of modern historiographical inquiry and the approaches this orientation has spawned, consult William Todd, *History as Applied Science: A Philosophical Study* (Detroit: Wayne State University Press, 1972), and Theodore K. Robb and Robert I. Rotberg, eds., *The New History: Studies in Interdisciplinary History* (Princeton: Princeton University Press, 1982).

textual, linguistic, or historical.[74] The fact that the problems he chose to solve seemed irredeemably backwards to the forward-looking social historians is irrelevant to the question of the validity of his scholarly approach.

Today, if sinology is to be regarded as a science and not as an impressionistic aesthetic exercise, Pelliot's philological studies are still the best examples to follow in setting the textual stage for an investigation and in culling relevant data from the sources. And as the sole occupant of his chair of the Languages, History and Archaeology of Central Asia, he well deserved the praise of his former student and assistant, the current doyen of Inner Asian studies, Denis Sinor, who regards him as "perhaps the greatest scholar who has ever worked in this field."[75]

---

[74]As Serge Elisséef summarized in his necrology, "Pelliot's interest was directed not so much to the publication of general books on Chinese subjects but rather to the thorough investigation of particular problems." See his "Paul Pelliot 1878-1945," 13.

[75]"Central Eurasia," in *Orientalism and History*, ed. Denis Sinor (1954; rpt. Bloomington: Indiana University Press, 1970), 118. Sinor's reminiscences of his early association with Pelliot commencing with the outbreak of WWII are presented in "Remembering Paul Pelliot, 1878-1945," *JAOS* 119 (1999): 467-72.

3. HENRI MASPERO (1883-1945): "L'HOMME DE LA CHINE ANTIQUE"

"Les Historiens sont ma droite balle: ils sont plaisants et aisés, et quant l'homme en général, de qui je cherche la connaissance, y paraît plus vif et plus entier qu'en nul autre lieu: la diversité et vérité de ses conditions internes, en gros et en détail, la variété des moyens de son assemblage et des accidents qui la menacent."

—Montaigne, *Essais*, II.10

Henri Maspero was dubbed at his passing "l'homme de la Chine antique" by his colleague Paul Pelliot. Although capable of brilliant philological feats, tossed off as effortlessly as the encores of a virtuoso violinist to close out a recital, Maspero was essentially an historian. Today the esteem he enjoys as a founding figure of modern sinology results rather for his pioneering explorations of the Taoist canon and penetrating histories of social and religious Taoism. In addition to the fields of Taoism and of ancient Chinese history, he made valuable contributions to the study of ancient Indo-China, Chinese Buddhism, linguistics, literature, law, astronomy, economics, philosophy, and popular religions.[1]

Born in Paris on December 15, 1883, Maspero first studied history and literature. After a year of military service, he joined his father, the eminent Egyptologist Gaston Maspero, in Egypt. His first work, entitled *Les Finances de l'Egypt sous les Lagides* (1905), secured for him the "diplome d'études superieures d'histoire et géographie," and exhibited many of the scholarly qualities which later were to distinguish his sinological work.

---

[1] Maspero's contributions to many of these scholarly fields were surveyed in the conference convened in Paris on the centennial celebration of his birth, jointly sponsored by l'Académie des Inscriptions et Belles-Lettres, le Collège de France, la Société asiatique, and l'Ecole française d'Extrême-Orient, printed in *Hommage à Henri Maspero 1883-1945* (Paris: Fondation Singer-Polignac, 1983). For more on his life, see Jacques Gernet, "La vie et l'oeuvre," in *Hommage à Henri Maspero*, 15-24; Robert des Rotours, "Henri Maspero (15 décembre 1883 - 17 mars 1945)," *Mélanges chinois et bouddhiques* 8 (1946-47): 235-40; Paul Demiéville, "Nécrologie: Henri Maspero (1883-1945)," *JA* 234 (1943-45, 1947): 245-80, with complete bibliography; Li Huang, *Fa-kuo Han-hsüeh lun-chi*, 73-93; and Jacques Gernet, "Henri Maspero and Paul Demiéville: Two Great Masters of French Sinology," in *Europe Studies China*, 45-47.

Returning to Paris, Maspero obtained a license to practice law in 1907, which was to facilitate later work on Chinese jurisprudence. At the same time he had begun to study Chinese, graduating from the Ecole de Langues orientales vivantes, also in 1907. His teachers were Chavannes and Sylvain Lévi.

Attracted by both the opportunities presented by the Ecole française d'Extrême-Orient and the presence of his half-brother Georges Maspero there, he went to Hanoi in 1908. This institution had been founded in 1898 by the Indianists Auguste Barth and Michel Bréal, and a specialist in Southeast Asia, Emile Senart. The first director, Louis Finot, arrived in Saigon in 1899 with funding from the government of French Indo-China. The school came to be supported by both the office of the governor-general of Indo-China and the Académie des Inscriptions et Belles-Lettres. Its purpose was to further the historical understanding of the region, including India and China, through both archaeological investigation and the philological study of texts. The *Bulletin de l'Ecole française d'Extrême-Orient* reflects this two-fold aim. The introductory issue of 1901 announced that comparative studies of India and China, through the approach of philology, would be stressed; specific fields to be covered included political history, institutional history, religion, literature, archaeology, linguistics, and ethnography. In 1902 the school moved to Hanoi; in 1956 it relocated to France.[2] Characteristic of the brilliant personnel at the Ecole, including the young Pelliot, was Eduard Huber (1879-1914). Huber arrived at the school in 1900 at age 21, remaining until his untimely death fourteen years later. Above all a sinologist and indianist, Huber also mastered Arabic, Persian, Turkish, Cham, Khmer, Siamese (Thai), Mon, Burmese, Javanese, Annamese, and Malay, and was cherished for the amity of his personality.[3]

At first a research fellow of that distinguished institute, Maspero became professor in 1911. He stayed in its heady atmosphere until 1920,

---

[2] For the early history of this institution and bulletin, see "L'Ecole française d'Extrême-Orient depuis son origine jusque'en 1920," *BEFEO* 21 (1921).

[3] Casimir Schnyder, *Eduard Huber, ein schweizerischer Sprachengelehrter, Sinolog und Indochinaforscher* (Zurich: Art. Institut Orell Füssli, 1920).

studying both Chinese and Indo-Chinese languages. In spite of a delicate constitution, he undertook several extended journeys during his twelve years in the Orient. Eight months after he first arrived in Hanoi he was sent on a mission to Peking, remaining for almost a year. Later, in 1914, he went on an archaeological expedition in Chekiang province, the results of which were published that same year.[4] He also traveled extensively in French Indo-China, collecting at first hand valuable data on the languages, customs, folklore and history, religion and mythology of the various ethnic groups there, and recorded much useful geographic information as well. His knowledge of the living traditions of the Indo-Chinese added valuable perspective to his outlook on the society of ancient China, a society he regarded as being part of the same cultural welter.

After the death of Chavannes in 1918, Maspero was named to succeed him in the Chaire de Langue et Littérature Chinoise at the Collège de France. His departure from Hanoi unfortunately brought an end to his fertile Indo-Chinese studies. In this broad field he had been the first to produce truly scientific works on the languages of Southeast Asia. Chief among these were "Contribution à l'étude du systeme phonétique des langues Thai," and "Etudes sur le phonetique historique de la langue annamite."[5] He also had made important contributions to the history, society, and culture of this little-known region.[6]

As professor at the Collège de France, Maspero assumed a full load of courses. But far from distracting him from his own research, these courses were organized around various related themes so that class preparation advanced Maspero's current research interests.[7]   This

---

[4]"Rapport sommaire sur une mission archéologique au Tchö-kiang," *BEFEO* 14 (1914): 1-75, with 35 figures; see the tribute to the methodology employed in this article, with some bibliographical updating, by Madeleine David, "Note d'archéologie a la mémoire d'Henri Maspero," in *Hommage à Henri Maspero*, 31-35.

[5]*BEFEO* 11 (1911): 153-69; and 12 (1912): 1-127.

[6]For his scholarship in this field, see Pierre-Bernard Lafont, "Henri Maspero et les études indochinoises," in *Hommage à Henri Maspero*, 25-30.

[7]The courses he offered at the Collège de France, Ecole de Louvre, Ecole pratique des Hautes Etudes, etc. from 1920 until 1944 are listed by Demiéville, "Necrologie: Henri Maspero," 275-79.

culminated in an important book, *La Chine antique*.[8] This work, without the benefit of modern archaeological finds such as those at Hsiao-t'un or Ma-wang tui, is understandably attenuated in many respects with regard to pre-Han China. Jeffrey Riegel, in a review of the 1978 English translation, singles out certain sections as somewhat dated due to the lack of philological tools that were still being developed: Maspero's treatment of the Shang, despite his sporadic use of oracle-bones, and his discussion of Western Chou, because of the paucity of bronze inscriptions available for use. More dated yet are the last three essays in book 5, "Ancient Literature and Philosophy.[9] Even Denis Twitchett, who authored the introduction, concedes that this last section is the most antiquated, due once again to the many analytic studies and translations that have, in many cases, "revolutionized our understanding of the texts themselves."[10] However, the later advancement of philological tools and studies does not impugn Maspero's handling of the means at his disposal. *La Chine antique* remains the single most useful introduction to ancient China in its broad political and cultural outlines.[11]

Marcel Granet: The Man of Primitive China

We shall return to Maspero and his work presently. But here we may consider the contributions of his close contemporary and countryman Marcel Granet (1884-1940), who also emphasized ancient China, rarely encroaching on imperial times, but who was more narrow in his scope of coverage.[12] Granet was trained in the Ecole Normale supérieure at Paris

---

[8](Paris: P.U.F., 1927); English translation based on a revised version produced by Paul Demiéville in 1955, incorporating Maspero's marginal notations: *China in Antiquity*, trans. Frank. A. Kierman, Jr. (Amherst: University of Massachusetts Press, 1978).

[9]Riegel, *JAS* 39 (1980): 789-92.

[10]Twitchett, in *China in Antiquity*, xxv.

[11]Denis Twitchett, "Introduction," *China in Antiquity*, ix-xxx, sets Maspero's contributions to the study of ancient China within the context of the field at the time and its current progress. Maspero's bibliography is given on 498-511.

[12]For instance, Granet's *La Civilisation chinoise: La Vie publique et la vie privée* (Paris: La Renaissance du Livre, 1929; rpt. 1994), English version *Chinese Civilization: A Political, Social, and Religious History of Ancient China*, ed. Kathleen E. Inners and Michael

as an historian, and studied also under Emile Durkheim (1858-1917), the pioneer of modern institutional sociology and the founding editor of *L'Anée sociologique*. Later, at the Fondation Thiers in 1908, Marc Bloch was a classmate. Granet learned Chinese at the Ecole des Langues orientales vivantes, where his studies were supervised by Chavannes. His dual mentors reflect the two major disciplines of his scholarship, Chavannes in sinology and Durkheim in sociology.[13] Indeed, his famous study of the *Shih-ching*, *Fêtes et chansons* (1919), was dedicated to both of them.[14]

Two years study in Peking from 1911 to1913 produced Granet's "Coutumes matrimoniales de la Chine antique," an important piece that anticipated the arguments for *Fêtes et chansons* and the parameters of Granet's last work.[15] Upon returning home Granet taught history in secondary school for a few months before replacing Chavannes as the Director d'études pour les religions d'Extrême-Orient at the Ecole Pratique des Haute Etudes. He was called up for military duty from 1914 to 1918, then transferred first to a general's staff in Siberia and later to China. He returned to France in 1919, married, and passed his doctoral exams in 1920.

R. Brailsford (London: Kegan Paul, 1930), devoted two-thirds of its coverage to ancient Chinese society and only one-third to history. For Granet's life and works, see the introductory essay by Maurice Freedman, "Marcel Granet, 1884-1940, Sociologist," in Granet, *The Religion of the Chinese People*, trans. Maurice Freedman (New York: Harper and Row, 1975), 1-29, the sources cited on p. 7 n. 14, and the complete bibliography on pp. 178-81; the postface by Rémi Mathieu to Marcel Granet, *La Civilisation chinoise* (1929; Paris: Albin Michel, 1994), 522-71, which evaluates Granet's contribution to scholarship and provides supplemental bibliographical notes to update *La Civilisation chinoise*; Rolf A. Stein, "In Memory of Marcel Granet, 1884-1940," in *The World in Miniature*, 1-3; Li Huang, *Fa-kuo Han-hsüeh lun-chi*, 94-100; and the M.A. thesis of Yves Goudineau, "Introduction à la sociologie de Marcel Granet," Université de Paris X, 1982.

[13]Rémi Mathieu would prefer to stress his historical training as helping to form his scholarly approach, which he characterizes as a triple combination of historian, sociologist, and sinologist; see "Postface," *La Civilisation chinoise*, 525.

[14]*Fêtes et chanson anciennes de la Chine* (Paris: Leroux, 1919); English translation by E.D. Edwards, *Festivals and Songs of Ancient China* (London: Routledge, 1932).

[15]*TP* 13 (1912): 516-58. His last work was *Catégories matrimoniales et relations de proximité dans la Chine ancienne* (Paris: Alcan, 1939).

He taught at the Ecole Pratique des Haute Etudes for the rest of his life, with stints at the Sorbonne from 1920 to 1926 and, commencing in 1926, in the Chair of Geography, History, and Institutions of the Far East at the Ecole Nationale des Langues orientales vivantes.

Granet read through a great deal of the textual tradition of ancient China, including the Han. These texts formed his data base for all of his subsequent research. For instance, in the preface to *Chinese Civilization*, he made explicit the philological underpinning of his theoretical conceptions: "All that I have said in this work comes from direct analysis of the documents."[16] His many notable publications exploit this wealth of literature and offer penetrating insights into the nature of ancient society, kinship, and feudalism.

Durkheimian Dances: *Fêtes et chansons*

Granet's sinological methodology was summed up by his student of eight years, Rolf Stein, as follows:

> No single detail of any civilization can be understood and explained except in the context of the entire civilization, just as in a jigsaw puzzle the meaning of a piece can be seen only when it is put into its place in the larger picture. Any interpretation from outside, based on *a priori* principles, was immediately rejected.[17]

Yet Granet's first major work, *Fêtes et chansons*, which was an entirely new interpretation of the *Shih-ching* corpus, today is criticized on the basis of just such an *a priori* approach. For instance, Karlgren offers the following critical appraisal:

> He has construed all the odes he translates to suit a preconceived idea of his own: that they are popular songs, not originating in the class of the gentry but in that of the peasants, that they are stanzas improvised by youths and maidens at the time of the great seasonal festivals, and sung antithetically. Granet's sole support for this is the

---

[16]*Chinese Civilization*, 7.
[17]Stein, *The World in Miniature*, 2.

parallelism of certain modern T'ai (*sic*) people customs, and his whole elaborate structure is for the rest built entirely in the air.[18]

This theoretical thin air criticized by Karlgren is, of course, Granet's basic grounding in Durkheimian sociology, which posits that, just as "religion was the matrix of civilization,"[19] mankind's fundamental religious instincts are most profoundly manifested in communal gatherings. This "sociology of religion," then, provided Granet's overall interpretive framework, and the case of the Black Thai merely illustrated such a framework, but did not generate it. "Worship and beliefs will be studied in their principal forms in order to prefigure their future, and also to show their relations with the social organization in the period when they formed the basis of religious life," explains Granet in the preface to *The Religion of the Chinese People*. "They were above all," clarifies Granet, "the cults and beliefs of urban settings, or better put, the cults and beliefs of the courts as established in the towns of the various domains."[20]

Granet's purpose in *Fêtes et chansons* was first to provide "literary explications" of approximately seventy poems, and then to reconstruct their "symbolic interpretations" to uncover the original sense, all based on his unique approach through ancient Chinese sociology and religion.[21] These song-poems were grouped thematically into "Rustic Themes," "Love in the Villages," and finally "Promenades among the Forests and Streams."

---

[18]Bernhard Karlgren, *Glosses on the Book of Odes* (Stockholm: Museum of Far Eastern Antiquities, 1964), 75. Mathieu, "Postface," 532 ff., addresses the tension between abstract theory and textual source in Granet's work.

[19]Dominick LaCapra, *Emile Durkheim: Sociologist and Philosopher* (Ithaca: Cornell University Press, 1972), 246. For Durkeim's work *The Elementary Forms of the Religious Life* (1912) and his philosophy on the sociology of religion, see LaCapra, 245-91; Ian Hamnett, "Durkheim and the Study of Religion," in Steve Fenton et al., *Durkheim and Modern Sociology* (Cambridge: Cambridge University Press, 1984), 202-18 is good for a quick entré; consult W.S.F. Pickering, *Durkhiem's Sociology of Religion* (London and Boston: Routledge and Kegan Paul, 1984), for the most in-depth treatment. Granet's adoption of Durkheimian thought and terminology—and some of his own concerns—are touched on briefly throughout Pickering's work.

[20]*The Religion of the Chinese People*, 34.

[21]*Fêtes et chansons*, 18.

From these themes, Granet isolated the great spring and autumn festivals of ancient China. He chose to concentrate on four local celebrations, those of Cheng, Lu, Ch'en, and the royal festival in the spring.

In a lengthy review, Maspero saw no reason to reject Granet's reconstruction of either these particular feasts or the attribution to "peasant improvisation" of the origin of these songs.[22] What concerned him was the attempt to link every song that had sexual overtones with the ritual of matrimony. The denotation of marriage, according to Maspero, derived from the moralizing interpretations of later Confucian exegetes. A transcription and translation of a song of the Black Thai people that Maspero had published earlier in the *BEFEO* illustrated this point. Furthermore, there is no textual proof to assign prominence in the state cult to those festivals isolated by Granet, and to diminish the importance of those he ignored. Finally, Maspero preferred to view ancient Chinese society more in the context of the society of indigenous peoples of the entire region, including the modern Thai and aborigines still in China. Reconstructing ancient Chinese society, therefore, stressed Maspero, called not so much for dependence on sociological models of primitive societies with data drawn from the texts as for a comparative anthropological approach.[23]   Nevertheless, as his *Danses et légends* was later to demonstrate,[24] Granet's sociological and religious insights on the ancient peasant population and its culture were to inform many practices and institutions that came to be co-opted by the state cult.

Granet and Textual Sociology

What makes Granet less visible than Maspero as "L'homme de la Chine antique," despite the forceful championing of his cause by his students,[25] and the existence of his notable general surveys of ancient

---

[22]*BEFEO* 19 (1919): 65-75.

[23]On Granet's hesitation to use modern ethnographic fieldwork, see Freedman, "Marcel Granet, Sociologist," 24-27.

[24]*Danses et légends de la Chine ancienne*, 2 vols. (Paris: Alcan, 1926), reprinted by the Presses Universitaires de France in 1994.

[25]For instance, Stein and Rémieu. The latter claims that, "along with *La Pensée chinoise, La Civilisation chinoise* is without a doubt the most celebrated French sinological

Chinese civilization, religion, and philosophy,[26] was his concentration on two major multi-dimensional themes throughout the body of his work, those of feudalism and state ritual, and of kinship and marriage customs, and the resultant division of his audience into two camps, either sinological or sociological.[27]   Thus even his surveys tended to emphasize key sociological topics, down-playing if not always ignoring cultural, historical, or political elements.   Nor did he approach literary or historical texts philologically as did Pelliot and Maspero to present them as independent works worthy of interest in themselves.   Instead, he mined them in a careful way for their sociological or religious data.

Stein emphasizes Granet's meticulous approach to each text, paying special attention to getting the translation of a particular word or phrase just right to avoid bringing in outside associations.   Sometimes Granet's translations, with the original etymology and history of usage in mind, seemed off the mark to those used to the bland generalizations of out-dated dictionaries.   Therefore, "Simpleminded souls have been misled by Granet's translations," explains Stein, "going so far as to claim that he did not know Chinese very well."[28]   The opposite was true; in him Pelliot's insistence on the *mot juste* found full expression.   But, despite his philological acumen, his overall approach--the use to which he put his philological skill, asserts Freedman, was "textual sociology,"[29] and he wrote for fellow sociologists even more than for his sinologist colleagues: "I don't give a damn about China.   What interests me is man."[30]   Freedman concludes,

---

work of the twentieth century;" "Postface," *La Civilisation chinoise*, 522.

[26]*La Religion des chinois* (Paris: Gauthier-Villars, 1922); trans. by Freedman, as noted above; *La Civilisation chinoise*; and *La Pensée chinoise* (Paris: La Renaissance du Livre, 1934).

[27]Examples of these studies include *La Polygynie sororale et les sororat dans la Chine féodale: Etude sur les formes anciennes de la polygamie chinois* (Paris: Leroux, 1920); "Le Dépot de l'enfant sur le sol: Rites anciens et ordalies mythiques," *Revue Archéologique* 14 (1922): 305-61; and *Catégories matrimoniales*.

[28]Stein, *The World in Miniature*, 3.

[29]Freedman, "Marcel Granet, Sociologist," 24.

[30]Ibid., 29.

Partly no doubt because of the nature of his teaching and his apparent
failure to explain to his sinological audiences the precise character of
his sociological premises and reasoning, he has had no true successors
in his combination of the roles of sinologue and sociologist. French
sinology is now less sociological than when he lived, French
sociology only half-aware of the significance of his labors.[31]

This last point, sadly, is underscored by his lack of coverage in a recent
book devoted to the development of sociology in China: it considered his
contributions merely the concrete extension of the thought of Durkheim.[32]
Ultimately, according to Demiéville, he mediated between the tendencies
of nineteenth-century historicism and the excesses of philology, in
introducing the methodology of structuralism into sinology.[33]

The last word on Granet belongs to the man of ancient China.
Maspero evaluated Granet's original scholarship as "marking a happy
alliance of the sociological method with sinological erudition for an exact
interpretation of the ideas and customs of primitive China."[34] To Maspero,
then, Granet was the "Man of Primitive China."

Maspero: Textual Filiation and The Myths of Ancient China

Maspero was never self-stamped as a sociologist like Granet, and
moved easily from theme to theme, discipline to discipline, field to field.
He also moved beyond Granet in the temporal aspect of his studies,
ranging over imperial times with ease. This was especially true in Taoist
studies, of which, as mentioned above, he was the leading pioneer: he was
the first to exploit systematically and widely the heretofore neglected
Taoist canon. His research introduced little-known aspects of Taoism to
scholar and layman alike, and set models of textual explication for all

---

[31]Freedman, "Marcel Granet, Sociologist," 3. The title of the reprinting of his
major essays is also revealing: *Etudes sociologiques sur la Chine* (Paris: Presse Universitaires
de France, 1953).

[32]See Georges-Marie Schmutz, *La Sociologie de la Chine: Matériaux pour une
histoire 1748-1989* (Berne: Peter Lang, 1993), 8-9.

[33]Paul Demiéville, "Aperçu historique des études sinologiques en France," 106.

[34]Maspero, "La Sinologie," 279.

students of sinology.   His Taoist studies uncovered Taoism's earliest antecedents in ancient China and revealed its pervasive influence throughout medieval times.   He made Taoism a socially acceptable subject within sinological circles and placed its study on a firm methodological, historical, and bibliographical foundation.[35]   In doing so, he made it almost exclusively a preserve of French sinology.

One impressive side of his scholarship was the breadth of vision which allowed him to see each text in relationship to a corpus.   His first article, "Le Songe et l'ambassade de l'empereur Ming," is an especially fine example of dealing with textual filiation.[36]

Pious tradition accorded the introduction of Buddhism in China to heavenly intervention: Emperor Ming (r. 58-75) dreamed of a shining god of gold; after one inspired minister revealed the deity to be the Buddha, an envoy was went to Greater Yüeh-chih.   There the Chinese obtained the *Ssu-shih-er chang ching* 四十二章經 (Sutra in Forty-Two Articles), and returned with various icons to found temples and spread the word.

Thirteen early works record this traditional account.   In an attempt to evaluate the historicity of this tradition, Maspero critically examined each work—hence the subtitle of this article: "Etude critique des sources." After a careful comparison, he discovered that nine of these accounts were but copies of the two earliest ones.   These nine centos, then, cannot be used to substantiate the tradition.   The two remaining works, the *Ssu-shih-erh chang-ching* and the *Mou-tzu li-huo* 牟子理惑 seem to be independent sources, for they differ in their literal wording.   But the correspondence of phrases and ideas was striking enough to alert Maspero to their possible relationship.   He determined that relevant passages in the *Mou-tzu li-huo* were embellishments of the parallel passages in the preface to the sutra, the latter being the common and ultimate source for this tradition.   But the early provenance of this sutra does not necessarily establish the veracity of

---

[35]Evaluated by Max Kaltenmark, "Henri Maspero et les études taoistes," in *Hommage à Henri Maspero*, 45-48; Kristopher Schipper, "The History of Taoist Studies in the West," in *Europe Studies China*, 479-81; and T.H. Barrett, "Introduction" to Maspero, *Taoism and Chinese Religion*, vii-xxiii.
[36]*BEFEO* 10 (1910): 95-130.

the tradition, for Maspero showed by internal evidence that this preface could not have been written earlier than the end of the second century, long after the reign of Emperor Ming. He concluded that the traditional account of the introduction of Buddhism in China rested entirely on pious legends current during the last part of the second century.

Besides his detailed study of the sources to establish their filiation, Maspero provided another example of model research in the imaginative reasoning he used to resolve conflicting elements in the sources which tended to disparage the filiation posited. For example, he showed that one reason for different dates being given for the dream of Emperor Ming in the various versions was the desire of some authors to coordinate the introduction of Buddhism with the start of a new sexagenary cycle.[37]

All aspects of his exemplary methodology are apparent in an important work from 1924, the "Légendes mythologiques dans le *Chou king*": textual studies, comparative anthropology, bibliography, graphology, epigraphy, and reconstructed phonology.[38] What is especially impressive about this set of now standard research methodologies is the fact that four of the six were either pioneered, first utilized, or greatly influenced by Maspero. Let us take a close look at this pioneering piece.

In this article, a veritable monograph that followed closely on the heels of a similar work by Gustav Haloun,[39] Maspero attempted to recover many of the now lost Chinese myths. The Chinese have usually considered the legends and myths in their history to have been based on factual events: the ancient flood myth was the remembrance of a past inundation of the Yellow River, the titanic struggle between Huang-ti and Ch'ih-yu was the embellishment of a former rebellion of a minister against

---

[37]Maspero developed a few of the ideas only briefly touched on in his footnotes in a short article that appeared in the same issue of the *BEFEO*, his "Communautés et moines bouddhistes chinois au IIe et IIIe siècles," 222-32. Also of interest is his review on pp. 629-36 of Otto Franke's *Zur Frage der Einfürung des Buddhismus in China*. For an evaluation of his contributions to the study of Buddhism, see Paul Magnin, "L'Apport de Maspero à l'histoire du Bouddhisme chinois," in *Hommage à Henri Maspero*, 49-53.

[38]*JA* Ser. 11, 204 (1924): 1-100.

[39]"Die Rekonstruktion der chinesischen Urgeschichte durch die Chinesen," *Japanisch-deutsche Zeitschrift für Wissenschaft und Technik* 3 (Berlin, 1925): 243-70.

his lord, and the like. In their euhemeristic approach to their heritage, the Chinese misread, misconstrued, and even misprinted the textual evidence for their mythology. In their preference for agnostic historicizing over pious acceptance of the myths, the scribes and historians, even as early as the compiler of the "Yao-tien" chapter of the *Shu-ching*, paralleled the rational and atheistic attitude of the sober scholars of the classical world in the West—after the third century, that is.[40] However, as the scribes at the royal court had limited recourse other than the myths for fabricating their early history, this "history" preserves much of the ancient mythology, albeit in altered form. Recovering the myths from the guise of historical fact, then, was Maspero's goal. His approach was centered on the main cultural heroes and historical worthies whose true mythological natures had been obscured by the dignifying pall of euhemerization: "toute ce que nous savons de positif de l'ancienne mythologie se rapporte a des personages, dieux, ou héros, dont le cult avait un centre bien déterminé."[41] Although this study incorporated many primary sources, it was structured around the *Shu-ching* and the mythological accounts contained therein, illustrated by the case of Hsi-ho 羲和.

Maspero first examined the legend of Hsi and Ho, two functionaries of Yü charged with meteorological duties, at least according to the traditional reading of the *Shu-ching*. However, as Maspero's careful study shows, they were originally but a single figure, the mother of the sun. Through an analysis of the many texts in which Hsi-ho appears, a general idea of her nature and role became apparent. Maspero's annotated translation of the relevant *Shu-ching* passage showed that much more was involved in their supposed duties than mere meteorological observation. He demonstrated the importance of first seeing what the text says, grammatically and linguistically, and only then venturing an

---

[40]Cf. the conclusion of Jean Seznec, *The Survival of the Pagan Gods* (Princeton: Princeton University Press, 1953), 12: "The euhemeristic thesis set at rest for a time the disquiet that the traditional mythology had always inspired in the minds of educated men, who, though unable to accord it their literal belief, had nevertheless hesitated to reject as a mass of outright falsehood the time-honored tales for which Homer himself stood guarantor."

[41]"Légendes mythologiques dans le *Chou king*," 81.

interpretation.[42]   Added to this fundamental philological treatment was Chavannes' "broadside" approach in translating text after text or inscription after inscription of relevant sources. Thus Maspero marshalled many passages about Hsi-ho from texts such as the *Kuei-tsang*, *Shan-hai ching*, *Shih-tzu*, *Huai-nan tzu*, "Li-sao", and "T'ien-wen."

Another manifestation of his superior methodology was in his concern for thorough bibliographic control over the editions of the texts he consulted. For example, the *Shan-hai ching* passage concerning Hsi-ho was later copied into the medieval encyclopedias *Ch'u-hsüeh chi* and *T'ai-p'ing yü-lan*. This extracted passage contained more information on Hsi-ho than the original reading in the extant version of the *Shan-hai ching*, and had apparently been copied from an edition superior to the received version. Another example concerns a reading from the *Huai-nan tzu* that again is more accurately preserved in an encyclopedia, this time the seventh-century *Pei-t'ang shu-ch'ao*. In quoting the relevant passage, Maspero relied on the T'ang period encyclopedia, for in post-T'ang editions of the *Huai-nan tzu*, the name Hsi-ho had been expurgated, and replaced by the words "his/the daughter" *(ch'i nü)*. If Maspero had stopped with the most convenient edition at hand, he would have missed this important passage concerning Hsi-ho.

Since this legend had been expunged from the historical record, leaving little clear indication in later literature, Maspero drew on several different types of early sources, including graphologic evidence such as the etymologies of 旭 , 東 , and 杲 , and textual evidence embedded in ancient texts such as the *Shu-ching*, and the rituals preserved in the *Chou-li*. And to help elucidate and interpret his findings, Maspero drew from the oral traditions of several Thai tribes and other ethnic peoples of south China to show that the myth of Hsi-ho and the sun was part of the cultural heritage

---

[42]Bernhard Karlgren demonstrated this principle very simply in his "On the Authenticity and Nature of the Tso Chuan," *Göteborgs Högskolas Arsskrift* 32.3 (1926): 17, where a crucial argument hinged solely upon the correct reading of a paragraph in the *Han-shu*, a paragraph that was free of any obscure graphs, alternate readings, or interpolations. All that was needed was to punctuate the text accurately and to read the text grammatically. He did, Otto Franke did not.

of many of the early inhabitants of the region.

This same careful and thorough methodology was continued by Maspero in studying the legends and myths of Yü the Great, T'ai-t'ai, Nü-kua, Kung-kung, and Ch'ih-yu as they related to the deluge myth. He showed that contrary to the general belief among Westerners in China, especially missionaries eager to find Hermetic connections, this myth was not the Chinese version of the biblical flood, nor an historical inundation of the Yellow River; rather it was a creation myth where the land was made habitable for man only after draining away the water. A final section of the article is devoted to the myth of Chung-li, who was commanded by deity to break off the lines of communication between Heaven and Earth.

In his study of these myths, Maspero demonstrated how many of them had originated as local legends or myths, and had changed as they spread from place to place. He revealed both the traditional attitude toward the heroes, as well as those heroes' true guises as mythological figures. Finally, he suggested that the euhemerization of these cultural heroes had already taken place before the compilation of the short treatises which came to make up the *Shu-ching*.

The last method adroitly employed in this important article, reconstructed phonology, was a particular interest of Maspero.

The Discipline of Historical Phonology

The development of specialized studies in historical phonology in the West may be traced to a teacher of Greek in Germany, Johannes Reuchlin (1455-1522). He learned Greek from Greek immigrants in Paris, and taught his students the modern pronunciation. His friend and admirer Erasmus reacted against this in a 1528 publication entitled *De recta Latini et Graeci sermonis pronuntiatione*, as summarized here by Pfeiffer:

> Comparing the deformed pronunciation of Latin in modern national languages, he [Erasmus] explained that the simplified system of vowels in modern Greek could not be the original one. He showed how Latin had adapted the Greek vowels as well as consonnts in ancient times, and thus demonstrated the original difference of vowels like η ι υ and so on. Characteristically Erasmus did not do this in a dry article; on the contrary, he chose the form of a witty

dialogue between a lion and a bear in which it is shown how the lion's whelp should learn to read Greek properly with amusing examples of how badly Greek was read by Dutch, Scotch, German, or French people....The so-called Erasmian pronunciation was generally adopted in Western Europe, but in Protestant as well as in the Catholic part of Germany and in Italy the Reuchlinian practice prevailed until the time of German New Humanism.[43]

Hebrew biblical scholars borrowed this aesthetic and critical philology that the Renaissance Humanists had applied to Greek and Latin classics as part of their exegetical *cum* polemical work. In Spinoza's (1632-77) *Short Treatise on Hebrew Grammar* (published posthumously in his collected works of 1677), he called the Hebrew vowels the "soul" of the consonant letters, thus centering the debate primarily on phonological concerns. "Comprehension of the Hebrew Bible," explains Maurice Olender, "depends on the vowels. Represented by diacritical marks below or above the letters of the text, the vowels set the text in motion and bestow sound and meaning."[44] Richard Simon (1638-1712), one of the founders of modern exegesis, turned to an examination of the markings of vowels, among other textual manipulations, to forestall claims by the early Christian Fathers that the Jews had distorted the text to show that the Messiah had not come.[45] Although Simon's *magnum opus, Critical History of the Old Testament* (1678) was declared heretical and banned by the King's council the same year it appeared, it did set in motion a critical spirit of exegesis that was concerned with bypassing the rabbinical tradition of vowel pointing to recovering the sacred sounds of the original Hebrew in order both to emend the textual tradition and serve as an aid to exegesis. The most noteworthy examples of this spirit include Robert Lowth, *Lectures on the Sacred Poetry of the Hebrews* (1753), and Johann Gotfried Herder (1744-1803), *Treatise On the Origins of Language* (1782-83).[46]

---

[43]Pfeiffer, *The History of Classical Scholarship*, 2:88-89.

[44]Olender, *The Languages of Paradise*, 24.

[45]Ibid., 22-23.

[46]Ibid., 28-36. A broad intellectual context of the beginnings of linguistics is provided by Schwab, *The Oriental Renaissance*, 168-89.

Critical work in Sanskrit initiated by William Jones and other comparative philologists of the nineteenth century sought to replace the biblical Eden with an Aryan paradise. In other words, the debate shifted from the search for a universal language to the lost civilization of the Indo-Europeans.[47]   Friedrich von Schlegel's (1772-1829) *Essay on the Language and Wisdom of the Indians* (1808), and Franz Bopp's (1791-1867) *Comparative Grammar* (1833-49) influenced such theorists as Hegel and Humboldt.[48]

In China, the discipline of historical linguistics may be traced to Hsü Shen and his great etymological dictionary *Shuo-wen chieh-tzu*, or "Explanations of Simple Graphs and Analyses of Complex Characters." In it he treated 9,353 different Chinese characters, arranging them under 530 classifiers. As evaluated by Wang Nien-sun, "The *Shuo-wen*, as a document, is an exegetical work on etymology and phonology."[49]   A thousand years after the *Shuo-wen*, Sung scholars went too far afield in concentrating on the written representation of the characters, ignoring their phonetic elements. The Ch'ing philologists, starting with Ku Yen-wu, Ch'ien Ta-hsin, and most importantly, Tuan Yü-ts'ai, restored the primacy of pronunciation as a guide to understanding both historical etymologies and current usages. The modern fallacy among Western sinologists and lay-students of Chinese alike, that Chinese characters are *ideographs*, representing meaning without recourse to their pronunciation, is the direct heritage of Sung paleographers such as Wang An-shih (1021-1086) and his *Tzu-shuo*. His arbitrary etymologies, arrived at by dissecting each graphic element that made up the character, out-do the rash conjectures even of Ernest Fenollosa, Ezra Pound, or Florence Aiscough. Yet the key to ancient pronunciation was evident both in the rhyme schemes of the ancient *Book of Poetry* as well as in the phonetic elements so artfully isolated by Hsü Shen.

The inherent element of tones in the Chinese language provided

---

[47]Maurice Olender, "Europe, or How to Escape Babel," *History and Theory* 33 (1994): 5-25.

[48]Ibid., 6-11.

[49]*Shuo-wen chieh-tzu chu* (Taipei: Han-ching wen-hua, 1983), preface.

another key to interpreting meaning. During the Yung-ming period (483-493), Shen Yüeh (441-513), inspired by the rules for chanting Sanskrit sutras, decided to codify rules of prosody for Chinese that took into account the nature of the four tones and prescribed how to balance them out in poetry. Known as the "four tones and eight afflictions" (*ssu-sheng pa-ping* 四聲八病) these rules of versification have caused more emotional trauma to poets over the ages than the scansion of metric feet or the writing of Greek accentation ever did. T'ang scholars such as Lu Te-ming, in his *Ching-tien shih-wen*, and Yen Shih-ku, in his *K'uang-miu cheng-su* 匡謬正俗 , payed close attention to phonology as is clearly evident in the early manuscripts of their works recovered at Tun-huang. For they often indicated variant tones with red-ink marks, placed sometimes in the center of a character, sometimes on one of its four corners, depending on the system employed.[50] The use of tones in determining either an unusual grammatical form or a loan-word was discussed by another T'ang scholar, the famous annotator of the *Shih-chi*, Chang Shou-chieh. Prefacing his listing of thirty-nine characters in the *Shih-chi* that represent more than one word, depending on the tone, he stated: "In ancient writings the characters are few; there are hence many borrowed forms. Each character can have several tones, so I have observed the meaning and added [tone-indicator] marks, all according to whether the tones are level, rising, departing, or entering."[51]

The emphasis on isolating the sound and tone of a character, regardless of its graphic spelling, is the key to being able to read the word behind the graph. This is one of the greatest methodological legacies of the Ch'ing philologists. As stated by perhaps the most accomplished of them, Wang Yin-chih (1766-1834), "If the student can look for the meaning through the sound and see the appropriate character behind its loan form, then difficulties will dissolve of themselves. If, however, he insists on taking the loan character at its face value, then in his search for meaning he

---

[50]Ishizuka Harumichi, "The Origins of the *Ssu-sheng* Marks," *Acta Asiatica: Bulletin of the Institute of Eastern Culture* 65 (1993): 30-50; 43.
[51]Ibid.

will be hindered by obstacles."[52]

Sinology and Historical Phonology

Accessing the sound of a word at various points in time is, of course, the burden of historical phonology. The Swedish scholar Bernhard Karlgren (1889-1978) was the first Western sinologist to systematize the study of Chinese historical phonology through the methods of the school of historical linguistics current in Europe.[53] "Bernhard Karlgren [was] the pioneer of the modern scientific study of Chinese historical phonology," states Pulleyblank. "He brought a rigour to the subject that was not found among his predecessors and that has all too often been lacking among his would-be followers."[54] Pulleyblank even suggests that the field be divided into two periods, "BK (before Karlgren) and AK (after Karlgren)."[55] Yet Maspero had anticipated Karlgren's efforts, as we will see.

Ch'ing philologists had harnessed the discipline of historical phonology to the study of the classics, concentrating especially on the rhyming categories of the *Shih-ching*.[56] When Karlgren began his labors, therefore, both a conceptual framework and a large body of traditional scholarship was available for his research. His predecessors in the West, however, had been hopelessly derailed in the effort to elucidate ancient

---

[52]*Kuang-ya shu-cheng*, ed. D.C. Lau (Hong Kong: Chinese University Press, 1978), 1:4. A modern illustration of the use such phonetic attention should be put to in philological research is N.G.D. Malmqvist, *Han Phonology and Textual Criticism* (Canberra, 1963).

[53]On his life and works, see Søren Egerod, "Bernhard Karlgren," *Annual Newsletter of the Scandinavian Institute of Asian Studies* 13 (1979): 3-24; Elsie Glahn, "A List of Works by Bernhard Karlgren," *BMFEA* 28 (1956); and Göran Malmqvist, "On the History of Swedish Sinology," in *Europe Studies China*, 167-74.

[54]E.G. Pulleyblank, *Middle Chinese: A Study in Historical Phonology* (Vancouver: University of British Columbia Press, 1984), 1.

[55]Pulleyblank, "European Studies on Chinese Phonology: The First Phase," in *Europe Studies China*, 339.

[56]See Benjamin Elman, "From Value to Fact: The Emergence of Phonology as a Precise Discipline in Late Imperial China," *JAOS* 102 (1982): 493-500; and William H. Baxter, *A Handbook of Old Chinese Phonology* (Berlin: Mouton de Gruyter, 1992), pp. 139-74.

Chinese through comparison with so-called cognate languages in the Semitic or Indo-European language families.[57]

Joseph Edkins (1823-1905) published a section on the history of Chinese pronunciation in his 1853 grammar, and contributed the "Old Sounds" that appeared in Samuel Wells Williams' 1874 *Syllabic Dictionary of the Chinese Language*.[58] He seems to have had a very good grasp of traditional Chinese sources on historical phonology, without, however, hazarding any reconstructions. In 1871 he published *China's Place in Philology* to draw China into the comparative matrix of Indo-European languages.[59] The *Sino-Aryaca* of Gustav Schlegel published one year later in 1872 was just as untenable as Edkins' opus.

Eugenio Zanoni Volpicelli (1856-1936), *Chinese Phonology* (Shanghai, 1896), at least saw the need to approach ancient Chinese through modern dialects. He utilized both Edkins' earlier work and the dialect materials provided by E.H. Parker to Giles' dictionary. In 1890 Franz Kühnert published a piece on the rime tables of the *K'ang-hsi tzu-tien* that

---

[57]These predecessors are discussed by Karlgren in *Etudes sur la phonologie chinoise* (Leiden, 1915-1926), 5-9. The following discussion is based both on this work by Karlgren and Pulleyblank, "European Studies on Chinese Phonology: The First Phase," 340-46, who goes into admirable detail.

[58]Joseph Edkins, born in Glouchestershire, was an evangelist for the London Missionary Society who lived in China for fifty-seven years; after retirement as a missionary he worked for the Maritime Customs in Peking for the last twenty-five years of his life. Always active as a writer, he produced most notably *A Grammar of the Chinese Colloquial Language Dialect* (Shanghai: London Mission Press, 1857); *A Grammar of the Shanghai Dialect* (Shanghai: Presbyterian Mission Press, 1868?); and *Chinese Buddhism: A Volume of Sketches, Historical, Descriptive, Critical* (London, Kegan Paul, n.d.) (published ca. 1880). A partial bibliography is supplied by Alexander Wylie, *Memorials of Protestant Missionaries to the Chinese* (1867; rpt. Taipei: Ch'eng-wen, 1967), 187-91. A brief biography is included in *The Blackwell Dictionary of Evangelical Bioigraphy 1730-1860*, 2 vols., ed. Donald M. Lewis (Oxford: Blackwell, 1995), 1:343. Samuel Wells Williams is discussed in chapter nine below.

[59]*China's Place in Philology: An Attempt to Show that the Languages of Europe and Asia Have a Common Origin* (1871; rpt. Taipei: Ch'eng-wen, 1971). A short encapsulation of work in comparative philology in Europe relevant to sinology ("Accadian" and Sanskrit were in, Hebrew was out) is presented in Edkins' "Present Aspects of Chinese Philology," *China Review* 3 (1874): 125-27.

provided some fruitful suggestions later adopted by Karlgren.[60] S. H. Schaank (1897-1902), in a series of articles in *T'oung Pao* called "Ancient Chinese Phonetics," again analyzed the rime tables of the K'ang-hsi dictionary, positing the first reconstruction of an earlier stage of the language, and influenced both Pelliot and Maspero—and through them—Karlgren.[61]

Yet, of all the work accomplished on Chinese dialectology before Karlgren, only Maspero's "Etudes sur le phonetique historique de la langue annamite," grasped the essential differences in the dialects and proceeded with a "rigorous method." In this work, Maspero also proposed a provisional reconstruction of the language of the Sung period rime tables, which he considered to be the same as the *Ch'ieh-yün*. Pelliot had also put forward such a system in a series of articles published from 1911 to 1914.[62] Hence, when Karlgren began his work, he was reacting to the proposals of Maspero and Pelliot.

Bernhard Karlgren and the Refinement of the Discipline

In 1915 appeared the first of Karlgren's *Etudes sur la phonologie chinoise*, his doctoral dissertation from the University of Upsala.[63] It was awarded the Prix Julien for 1916. Karlgren summarized his methods and the main sources for reconstructing Chinese historical phonology in several places, most conveniently, in "Compendium of Phonetics in Ancient and Archaic Chinese."[64] As the title indicates, Karlgren had all along divided the language into that of the *Shih-ching* rhymes, which he called "ancient" Chinese (now usually called Old Chinese) and that of the *Ch'ieh-yün* and

---

[60]Franz Kühnert, "Zur Kenntniss der alteren Lautwerthe des Chinesischen," *Sitzungsberichte der Kaiserl. Akademie der Wissenschaften in Wien, phil.-hist. Klasse* 122 (1990).

[61]*TP* 8 (1890): 361-67, 457-86; 9 (1891): 28-57; n.s. 3 (1902): 106.

[62]See Karlgren, "The Reconstruction of Ancient Chinese," *TP* 21 (1922): 1.

[63]Reviewed by Maspero in *BEFEO* 16 (1916): 61-73.

[64]*BMFEA* 26 (1954): 211-367. A good overview of this methodology with new approaches suggested, is Paul L-M.Serruys, *The Chinese Dialects of Han Time According to the Fang Yen* (Berkeley: University of California Press, 1959), "Part One: The Problem of Reconstruction," 3-70.

Sung period rime tables, termed "archaic" Chinese (now Middle Chinese).

Maspero returned to Middle Chinese phonology in 1920, responding to Karlgren's *Etudes sur la phonologie chinoise* with his own detailed study of the *Ch'ieh-yün*, "Le Dialecte de Tch'ang-an sous les T'ang."[65] In turn, Karlgren incorporated some of the suggestions made by Maspero and refuted others in a 1922 publication, "The Reconstruction of Ancient Chinese."[66] In his conclusion Karlgren sums up his debt to Maspero as follows: "My reconstructive system of 1919 (*Phonologie chinoise*, III) thus holds good with the exception of three important points, where Maspero has introduced or at least shown the way to valuable emendations."[67] In this final form, Karlgren's reconstruction of Middle Chinese held sway over the field for many years, with minor modifications of certain points occasionally suggested,[68] until a totally new approach was

---

[65]*BEFEO* 20 (1920):1-124, which won the Prix Ordinaire from l'Académie des Inscriptions et Belles-Lettres in 1921. Later works along linguistic lines include "Préfixes et dérivation en chinois archaique," *MSLP* 23 (1930): 313-27; and "La langue chinoise," *Conférences de l'Institut de Linguistique de l'Université de paris, année 1933* (Paris, 1934): 33-70.

[66]*TP* 21 (1922): 1-42.

[67]"The Reconstruction of Ancient Chinese," 38. In *Philology and Ancient China* (Oslo, 1926), 78, Karlgren gives even more credit to Maspero. Pulleyblank adds that Karlgren, although emerging as the clear winner in their debate, rejected some of Maspero's suggestions with more vehemence than was justified. But Maspero's suggestions have been recently resurrected by linguists with profit; see Pulleyblank, "European Studies on Chinese Phonology: The First Phase," 347. The bulk of the remainder of Pulleyblank's study consists of reevaluating Karlgren's system, and to a minor extent, detailing Maspero's contributions to the modern views of the field. Egerod, "Bernhard Karlgren," touches on the various debates over the decades between Karlgren and Maspero, and not just in the field of historical phonology.

[68]For phonological features, e.g. "Yuen Ren Chao, "Distinctions Within Ancient Chinese," *HJAS* 5 (1940-41): 203-33; and Lo Ch'ang-p'ei, "Evidence for Amending B. Karlgren's Ancient Chinese j- to γj-," *HJAS* 14 (1951): 285-90; for orthography, see Peter A. Boodberg, "Ancient and Archaic Chinese in the Grammatonomic Perspective," in *Studia Serica Bernhard Karlgren Dedicata*, ed. Søren Egerod and Else Glahn (Copenhagen: Ejnar Munksgaard, 1959), 212-22. Other suggested publications revising or altering Karlgren's framework are listed in Egerod, "Bernhard Karlgren," 14-17.

suggested by E.G. Pulleyblank.[69] Karlgren's system of reconstruction of Old Chinese, anticipated by Walter Simon in 1927-28,[70] has been itself rendered obsolete with the appearance of William H. Baxter's *A Handbook of Old Chinese Phonology*, which supersedes the Ch'ing philologists and proposes new rhyming categories for the *Shih-ching*.[71]

Two of Karlgren's most important works, called by Boodberg "towering monuments to scholarship,"[72] are summarized by fellow sinologist, George A. Kennedy:

> The publication by Professor Bernhard Karlgren of the *Analytic Dictionary of Chinese* in 1923 was an event of the first importance because it put into the hands of sinologists too busy to wrestle with Chinese compendia like the *Kuang-yün* a quick and easy guide to the reading of written symbols at a particular period. The publication of *Grammatica Serica* in 1940 enlarged the field of knowledge.[73]

---

[69]*Middle Chinese: A Study in Historical Phonology.* Pulleyblank regarded Karlgren's system as fatally flawed since he did not distinguish between the language of the *Ch'ieh-yün/Kuang-yün* and the Sung rime tables, which he considered to be a later stage of the language. Pulleyblank therefore posited the separate divisions of Early Middle Chinese and Late Middle Chinese. Detailed criticisms directed against Karlgren's ancient Chinese reconstruction are also reviewed in Baxter, *A Handbook of Old Chinese Phonology*, 27-30, and most recently by Pulleyblank, "European Studies on Chinese Phonology: The First Phase."

[70]Simon, "Zur Rekonstruktion der altchinesischen Endkonsonanten," *Mitteilungen des Instituts für Orientforschung* 30 (1927) and 31 (1928), published as appendices to the regular issues. Apparently Maspero had devised his own reconstruction of Old Chinese around 1920, but felt that sufficient documentation for publication was lacking. However, one result of this work was the 1930 article "Préfixation et dérivation en chinoise archaique."

[71]For recent movement of the field away from the "neo-Karlgrenian" or "Karlgren/Pulleyblank" model of reconstructing abstract phonological systems to the living languages of China at various stages of history, see Jerry Norman and W. South Coblin, "A New Approach to Chinese Historical Linguistics," *JAOS* 115 (1995): 576-84.

[72]Boodberg, "Ancient and Archaic Chinese in the Grammatonomic Perspective," 213.

[73]"A Note on Ode 220,"in *Studia Serica Bernhard Karlgren Dedicata* (Copenhagen, 1959), 190-98; rpt. in *Selected Works of George A. Kennedy*, ed. Li Tien-yi (New Haven: Far Eastern Publications, 1964), 463-76; quote on 463.

The *Analytic Dictionary*, dedicated to the memory of Edouard Chavannes, had as its purpose the facilitation of "a systematic study...of the Chinese script" (some 6,000 characters)—not only through graphic forms but also through phonetics.[74] Therefore, while often including such data as the ancestral bronze form of a graph, more often Karlgren combined both approaches by presenting lists of words felt to be related both graphically—"co-signific" words that shared the same radical—and phonetically, or words in the same phonetic compound series (*hsieh-sheng*).

Since Karlgren treated not just words but entire word families for etymological study (anticipating his much fuller treatment in *Grammatica Serica*), Walter Simon appreciated the utility of this dictionary for Sino-Tibetan lingusitics, calling it a "work tool for comparativists."[75] The entries are arranged, therefore, not by one of the 214 traditional K'ang-hsi "radicals" but under the phonetic values of Karlgren's reconstruction of Middle Chinese.

Grammatica Serica: Script and Phonetics in Chinese and Sino-Japanese was arranged under the phonetic series of Old Chinese, based on the rhyming categories of the *Shih-ching*, and had as its purpose "to verify which sound variations are possible within the series of one Phonetic of the script, such as it was created in Archaic times, and built on the Archaic language."[76] Indeed, the index is keyed to the phonetic element of each character. A 1957 revision, the *Grammatica Serica Recensa*,[77] presented new definitions based on Karlgren's philological studies of the *Shih-ching* and *Shang-shu*, together with the results of the best Ch'ing scholarship. This new edition for the first time provided the ancient tones.

Karlgren as Sinological Linguist

Karlgren was, of course, much more than an historical phonologist.

---

[74]*Analytic Dictionary of Chinese and Sino-Japanese* (1940; rpt. New York: Dover Publications, 1974), 1.

[75]See Simon's review in *Deutsche Literaturzeitung* 1924, cols. 1905-1910.

[76]*Grammatica Serica* (1940; rpt. Taipei: Ch'eng-Wen Publishing House, 1966), 11.

[77]*BMFEA* 29 (1957).

He produced an astonishingly wide variety of pioneering contributions, including several volumes of translations and philological glosses on the *Shih-ching* and *Shang-shu*, studies of the *Tso-chuan* and the *Lao-tzu*, analyses of bronze mirrors, bronze inscriptions, and other art objects, grammatical, epigraphical, and lexicographical works—most published in the *Bulletin of the Museum of Far Eastern Antiquities*.[78] Particularly innovative was his statistical analysis of the distribution of grammatical particles to determine authorship.[79] Another novel approach was his division of ancient texts into "systematizing" and non-systematizing" categories, i.e. texts that deliberately focused on ancient customs (and hence were suspect and likely anachronistic, probably normative, or at least idealistic) and those which gave such information nonchalantly, almost in passing.[80] His important work on codifying the practice of loan characters cannot be overlooked.[81] Yet it was his reconstruction of the various stages of Old and Middle Chinese that defined his overall contribution to the field of sinology—he liked to style himself a "sinological linguist."[82] Nevertheless, while the merit for codifying the early results of historical phonology lies at the feet of Karlgren, and his important dictionaries and handbooks made this crucial tool widely available to sinologists lacking a linguistic background or bent, the field had been systematically initiated in this century and

---

[78]Egerod isolates Karlgren's work in bronze inscriptions as his second main specialization. His most important contributions to this and other fields are introduced and evaluated by Egerod, "Bernhard Karlgren."

[79]"On the Authenticity and Nature of the Tso Chuan," *Göteborgs Högskolas Arsskrift* 32 (1926); and "The Authenticity of Ancient Chinese Texts," *BMFEA* 1 (1929). Of course, Karlgren based his distribution analysis on standard texts of early works. Dr. Sin Chow-yiu has called attention to the fact that pre-Han classics, as attested in newly discovered manuscripts, were written in a script different from the standard editions used by Karlgren. This totally changes the data base for Karlgren's conclusions (see *Journal of Oriental Studies* 29 [1991]: 207-36). Nevertheless, Karlgren's innovative methodology was sound, even if a new data base now needs to be analyzed.

[80]"Legends and Cults in Ancient China," *BMFEA* 18 (1946); and "Some Sacrifices in Chou China," *BMFEA* 40 (1968).

[81]"Loan Characters in Pre-Han Texts," I-IV, *BMFEA* 35 (1963); 36 (1964); 37 (1965); and 38 (1966).

[82]*BMFEA* 35 (1963): 7.

modestly refined by Maspero.[83]

Maspero, Chronology, and the Oral Language

Another article by Maspero, "Le Roman historique dans la littérature chinoise de l'antique," is a methodological bagatelle for the importance of keeping chronology straight.[84] It demonstrates the value of alert reading, and painstaking comparison of related texts, to establish correct dating, even if the labor involved seems unnecessarily tedious. In the case of this article, the dates discussed by Maspero defined a particular text as literary fiction rather than as a factual historical account.

The anonymous political romance *Su-tzu* Ä⌐ ⌐l , in a common enough genre, provided the matter out of which Ssu-ma Ch'ien constructed a biography of Su Ch'in, the famous architect of the *tsung* alliance against Ch'in during the Warring States period. Maspero was first alerted to the possibility that the exploits of Su Ch'in were fictional by the fact that the chronology of events given in the *Shih-chi* was not congruent with chronologies preserved elsewhere. Maspero showed that not only were many of the events of Su's biography anachronistic, but contradictory as well, since several of the participating kings were not even contemporaries.

In order to resolve these various difficulties, Maspero compared the

---

[83]The general use of historical phonology in sinological studies is introduced by Karlgren, *Philology and Ancient China*. Of a more technical nature is Paul Serruys, "Philologie et linguistique dans les études sinologiques," *MS* 8 (1943): 167-219. Serruys' goal was to 1) describe the present state of historical linguistics, including historical phonology; 2) expose the limitations of this school; 3) propose a new linguistic methodology (linguistic geography); and 4) demonstrate this methodology. Jerry Norman, *Chinese*, 23-57 traces the development of historical phonology; Pulleyblank, "How Do We Reconstruct Old Chinese?" *JAOS* 112 (1992): 365-382 sums up the latest theories and offers new directions; see also Pulleyblank, "*Qieyun* and *Yunjing*: The Essential Foundation for Chinese Historical Linguistics," *JAOS* 118 (1998): 200-16.

[84]*Mélanges posthumes*, vol. 3 (Paris, 1950), 53-62. Pelliot, "Le *Chou King* en characteres anciens et le *Chang Chou Che Wen*," 134, provides, in one paragraph, the same methodological example. Charles S. Gardner, *Chinese Traditional Historiography* (1938; rpt. Cambridge, Mass.: Harvard University Press, 1970), 25 discusses the problems of anachronism and interpolation in Chinese textual criticism, happily illustrated through the work of Maspero.

dates in the *Shih-chi* with dates taken from a reliable chronology, the *Chu-shu chi-nien*. A harder step was to compare accounts of the same or related events in other historical works. The chronologies constructed by Chavannes, Maspero himself, and a group of Japanese scholars give the actual historical events their true sequence.

The recent discovery of a silk manuscript associated with Su Ch'in demonstrates that he was an historical figure.[85] But this does not overturn Maspero's conclusion that Ssu-ma Ch'ien's account is literary fiction, not sober historical narrative.[86] An equally impressive study of chronology that has not been successfully challenged is found in *La Chine antique*, where Maspero discusses the possiblity of changing Confucius' traditional dates. Riegel analyzes the validity of this argument as follows:

> His conclusion that there is "no insurmountable difficulty in making the traditional dates later by about a quarter of a century" is still well supported and important because it solves numerous difficulties involving the dates of Confucius's disciples and descendants. No subsequent scholarship, including the grand titrations of calendrical records concocted by Ch'ien Mu, has added to or overturned it.[87]

A methodology of a different bent, having to do with uncovering the ancient oral language, was illustrated by a 1914 offering, "Sur quelques textes anciens de chinois parle."[88] Before the Chinese literary revolution of the early twentieth century had "vulgarized" the written language, it differed considerably from the spoken language, changing only gradually and almost imperceptibly over the centuries from the stiff but stately styles established by the great classicists of the past. Monuments dating from the Yüan dynasty, recording official pronouncements in the vernacular, as well as colloquial drama, attest to the wide divergence between oral and written

---

[85]See Riegel, *JAS* 39 (1980): 791.

[86]See the comments of Stephen Durrant, *The Cloudy Mirror: Tension and Conflict in the Writings of Sima Qian* (Albany: State University of New York Press, 1995), 187, n. 25.

[87]Riegel, op cit.

[88]*BEFEO* 14 (1914): 1-36.

Chinese. A few Sung texts closely approach the vernacular, but are less reliable than the Yüan sources. At any rate, the farthest sinology could go toward reconstructing tentative outlines of the grammar, style, and vocabulary of ancient spoken Chinese before Henri Maspero published this article—well before the vernacular texts from Tun-huang were made available—was to the twelfth century.

The monks of the Dhyāna school (*ch'an-tsung*) had the pious practice of recording the discourses, sermons, and simple conversations of celebrated masters of their sect for the edification of the faithful. With the recent publication at Kyoto of a supplement to the Tripitaka, a number of these rare texts were made available to sinologists. In his 1914 article, Maspero utilized five of the most ancient works of this kind published in the supplement, all dating from the ninth century, that contain vernacular materials.[89]

For these works, Maspero gave as detailed an account of their textual histories as possible: date of compilation, history of transmission until first publication, dates of various printed witnesses and editions, and their different inclusions as chapters of larger miscellanies. All of this bibliographical spade-work was necessary to insure the integrity of the vernacular accounts contained within, for some works of this genre had had their vulgar passages reworked into the more refined style of the written language by later editors. Maspero was thus careful to see whether his sources had been subjected to any modification or revision. And as each master was shown to have come from a different part of China, Maspero insured that the spoken language recorded was not the peculiar dialect nor even the mother tongue of a particular master, but represented the acquired *lingua franca* of the educated Chinese world, the *kuan-hua*.

---

[89]One of the earliest scholars to appreciate Maspero's work in vernacular language was James Crump. He lists five sources for medieval vernacular, namely Tun-huang literature, Buddhist *yü-lu*, early illustrated *p'ing-hua* texts, *p'ing-hua* texts of the Five Dynasties period, and Yüan plays; see Crump, "On Chinese Medieval Vernacular," *Wennti* 5 (1953): 65-74. The importance of the vernacular language and vernacular culture is addressed in masterful brevity by Glen Dudbridge, *China's Vernacular Cultures: An Inaugural Lecture Delivered Before the University of Oxford on 1 June 1995* (Oxford: Clarendon Press, 1996).

Thus, this article attempts to elucidate the vernacular language of the court as spoken in the first half of the ninth century.

The grammatical headings under which Maspero listed particular words, compounds, and usages with illustrative examples culled from these texts are Substantives, Nouns of Number, Numerals, Demonstratives, Verbs (including the copula, passive and potential constructions, and an auxiliary verb), Verb Objects, Particles and Final Particles, and Interrogative Pronouns. Under each heading are examples which closely, sometimes even exactly, parallel modern usage. Maspero pointed out the close affinity between ancient and modern vernacular usage in these cases, and dismissed false parallels through etymological and phonological evidence.

Another valuable contribution of this article in presenting so many incontrovertible vernacular elements is to allow the philologist to identify them even when they are found embedded within literary texts. This identification again helps in both the interpretation of meaning as well as in the more difficult appreciation of tone and mood. For example, Maspero shows that shih 是 was the vernacular copula, thus anticipating Boodberg in his thesis that Tu Fu used it intentionally for its colloquial flavor.[90] Other examples support another thesis developed later by Boodberg, that shih evolved from a classical demonstrative, "this," to the vernacular copula "[this] is": 是 這 個 言 語 and 是 這 個 眼 目 . As Maspero's interest lay in identifying the ancient spoken language, he avoided applying his data toward solving stylistic questions of tone and mood. Rather, he concentrated on isolating colloquialisms in otherwise strictly literary contexts. He accordingly offered several examples taken from Six Dynasties literature such as the songs of Tzu Yeh, early Buddhist writings, and T'ang hsiao-shuo. He further showed how some of the words classical commentators such as Yen Shih-ku had trouble defining were often merely adoptions of common colloquial forms.

---

[90]See Peter A. Boodberg, "On Colloquialisms in Tu Fu's Poetry," in Selected Works of Peter A. Boodberg, compiled by Alvin P. Cohen (Berkeley: University of California Press, 1979), 194-95.

Maspero was named a member of the Académie des Inscriptions et Belles-Lettres in 1936. In 1942, besides his normal teaching at the Collège de France, he began to teach the history of the Far East at l'Ecole Nationale de la France d'Outre-mer. And, at the same time he succeeded to Granet's chair of Chinese Civilization at l'Institut des Hautes Etudes chinoise at the Sorbonne. To this fatiguing schedule was added the stress of a week of incarceration by the Germans in April of 1942. For the next two years Maspero worked on the economic history of early China. But on July 28, 1944 he was again arrested by the Germans due to the underground activities of his 19-year-old son Jean. He endured the inhuman conditions of Buchenwald for almost a year. While there, he sometimes took a turn leading discussions with a group of fellow intellectuals. But his health, always delicate at best, succumbed at last on March 17, 1945, less than a month before the Americans liberated the camp.

Maspero and Granet in Retrospect

The importance of Maspero to sinology today goes far beyond the factual contributions of his publications, many of them first printed posthumously.[91] His research into Taoism and economics opened up new fields. His methodology, and especially his insight in being able to discern ritual, religious, or mythological implications where traditional interpreters have seen only bureaucratic or moral metaphors, without being overly iconoclastic, is a major source of inspiration for the modern need to reexamine the traditional classics.

Nevertheless, his work on pre-Ch'in China needs widespread revision. Historical constructs, to the extent that they are built from individual bits of data, become obsolete in the face of the advance of knowledge. "To the college undergraduate," as a classicist reminds us, "it is always a surprise to learn that it is the *early* chapters of ancient history that have to be most frequently re-written." Continues Narka Nelson,

---

[91]Paul Demiéville, "Complements à la bibliographie des oeuvres d'Henri Maspero," *Hommage à Henri Maspero*, 69, lists most of these posthumous publications.

It is a startling revelation made by Bury in the Preface to the second edition of his *History of Greece* that the revision was imperative because the Trojan War, in the first edition treated as only a myth, must now, in view of archaeological investigation, take its place in the pages of history. The spade of the archaeologist is daily causing history to be re-written. [92]

The factual basis of ancient Chinese history has changed more than any other period through the progress of archaeology: new sources of documentary materials, including oracle bones, bronze inscriptions, wooden or bamboo strips, and silk manuscripts, together with a deluge of material remains, especially grave goods, have all changed the data base for the writing of the history of ancient China. And the traditional documentary sources have continued to undergo translation and reinterpretation from a variety of perspectives. It is therefore not surprising that Maspero's studies of the earliest periods have not endured the test of time as well as those of Granet, who worked in a much narrower field. For example, reprinting a pre-World War II manuscript of Maspero on the institutions of ancient China and the Ch'in/Han era, Demiéville often found it necessary to correct and supplement the text by making generous use of bracketed comments. After all, opined Demiéville, "For a long time Chinese studies have had an accelerated development. And the history of China is much better known, thanks to the work of philologists and archaeologists, than it was fifteen or twenty years ago."[93] Granet largely avoided historical constructs, concerning himself instead with comparative models of understanding that relied more on structures of relationships—ritual complexes, social institutions, feudal hierarchies, etc. His portrayal of social processes of long duration, then, remain on the whole as persuasive—and in some circles, as controversial—today as when

---

[92]Narka Nelson, *The Classical Journal* 37 (1942): 281.

[93]Henri Maspero et Etienne Balazs, *Histoire et institutions de la Chine antique des origines au XIe siècle après J.-C.*, ed. Paul Demiéville (Paris: Presses Universitaires de France, 1967), vi.

first articulated.[94]

In this regard, Maspero's work is like that of Karlgren in historical phonology: path-breaking in terms of pioneering new approaches, exploiting new sources, and in synthesizing the entire field at the time, yet now in need of extensive revision. Yet, in many other areas, especially Taoism, Maspero has been superseded neither by the march of time nor by the advance of the field. If Maspero's studies of ancient China have been dated by the progress of archaeology, he remains, methodologically speaking at least, as the philologist of ancient China who provided the most persuasive, humane, and comprehensive histories of his generation, and, more importantly, still spiritually presides over the field as the grand patriarch of Taoist studies.

---

[94]Of course, when Granet focused on the history rather than sociology of primitive and ancient China, he was much less persuasive than Maspero, but that is another issue.

PART THREE: GERMAN SINOLOGY: CLASSICAL PHILOLOGY AND NATIONAL HISTORIOGRAPHY[1]

"Habe nun, ach! Philosophie,
Juristerei und Medizin
Und leider auch Theologie
Durchaus studiert, mit heißem Bemühn.
Da steh ich nun, ich armer Tor!
Und bin so klug als wie zuvor;
Heiße Magister, heiße Doktor gar,
Und ziehe schon an die zehen Jahr
Herauf, herab und quer und krumm
Meine Schüler an der Nase herum—
Und sehe, daß wir nichts wissen können!"

—Goethe, *Faust*[2]

4. THE FOUNDING FATHERS: ALTERTUMSWISSENSCHAFT AND HUMANISTIC BILDUNG

If Goethe—through Faust—despaired of learning anything after a lifetime of effort, it was more a question of his mortality than his methodology. He could not blame his cultural heritage, for, after Italian humanists had inaugurated the first revival of learning, which roused the French to scholarly action in the sixteenth century, the second revival was ushered in by fellow Germans. Each revival had pioneered a different philological agenda, Latin texts in the first, Greek classics with the second. Impelled by the new science of *Altertumswissenschaft*, Germans led the

---

[1]A rudimentary version of parts of this chapter appeared as "The Foundation of Modern German Sinology," *Phi Theta Papers* 16 (1984): 82-101.

[2]Johann Wolfgang Goethe, *Faust: Der Tragödie erster und zweiter Teil* (Berlin: Verlag Neues Leben, 1966), 27.

intellectual world of the West from the late seventeenth century until the Great War began in 1914.

In the realm of the fine arts, German Neo-Hellenism held powerful sway. The seventeenth century, described by Pfeiffer as "the age of humanistic revolution" (in contrast to the age of the scientific revolution of the previous century), was when "the masterpieces of classical literature once again produced a miraculous quickening of the spirit." Continues Pfeiffer:

> The new humanistic approach, first inspired by the study of Greek poetry, and then applied to art, became fruitful again for literature....In Germany, but nowhere else, there grew up a sort of evangelistic humanism which was both warmly espoused and bitterly attacked for several generations. It was a powerful movement, which, headed by Winckelmann, took its place beside the systems of the leading philosophers from Kant to Hegel; and it was this power that renewed classical scholarship in Germany.[3]

Specifically, as Pfeiffer has written, Winckelmann reoriented the artistic sensibilities of the public away from the baroque and the rococo to classical ideals; Lessing broke the French monopoly on dramatic theory through his studies of ancient drama and his own compositions; Goethe infused German aesthetics with paganism, mythology, and the classical concept of the Gods as natural forces; and Wagner's massive musical dramas gave rebirth to Greek tragedy.

In the field of scholarship, Humboldt reorganized higher education by separating vocational training from humanistic *Bildung* in the gymnasium, and founded the University of Berlin—which immediately served as a model for European universities. The historians Herder and Ranke developed both critical methods and a national school of objective if somewhat idealistic historiography. Marx founded a school of economic theory and more, but had first written a doctoral dissertation on Epicurus. Finally, the great sociologist Max Weber was a student of Mommsen, the

---

[3]*History of Classical Scholarship*, 2:171.

most distinguished ancient historian of his age. New investigative techniques and modes of presentation—critical analysis, textual criticism, the seminar, doctoral degrees awarded for dissertations that made "original contributions to scholarship," etc.—were pioneered, institutionalized, and epitomized by German scholarship of the eighteenth and nineteenth centuries. And, perhaps of less relevance if not interest, it was a German, Friedrich August Wolf (1759-1824), who was the first modern man to claim the august title of "studiosus philologiae" (at his noisy entrance into the University of Göttingen on April 8, 1777).[4] Such heights of artistic, intellectual, and academic achievement were the heritage of the German sinologist, whose labor depended more on this honorable tradition of creativity and scholarship than a lengthy missionary presence in China.

Julius Klaproth, Karl Gützlaff, and Wilhelm Schott

Julius Klaproth (1783-35) is probably the earliest German Orientalist to surface who did more than dabble in Chinese.[5] It is true that Andreas Müller (1630-1694) played an enormous part in the intellectual life of the times through the influence exerted by the premise of his unfinished

---

[4]Anciently, Eratosthenes was the first to call himself a philologist (*philolo yos*); he actually coined the title, which referred to "persons familiar with the various branches of knowledge or even with the whole of the *lo yos*." See Pfeiffer, *History of Classical Scholarship*, 2:101; 1:156-59 discusses the earliest use of the term which, I am pained to admit, meant for Plato "a man fond of talk, dispute, dialectic in a wide and rather vague or ironical sense." Of course, Plato never learned to appreciate poets either.

[5]Henri Cordier, "Un Orientaliste allemand: Jules Klaproth," *Comptes rendus de l'Académie des Inscriptions et Belles-Lettres* (1917), 297-308; Samuel Couling, *The Encyclopaedia Sinica* (Shanghai: Kelly and Walsh, 1917), 275-76. For the earliest attempts in German sinology, see Otto Franke, "Die sinologischen Studien in Deutschland," *Ostasiatische Neubildungen* (Hamburg, 1911): 357-77; Herbert Franke, *Sinology at German Universities* (Wiesbaden: Franz Steiner Verlag, 1968), 4-9; Rainer Schwartz, "Heinrich Heines 'chinesische Prinzessin' und seine beiden 'chinesischen Gelehrten' sowie deren Bedeutung für die Anfäng der deutschen Sinologie," *Nachrichten der Gesellschaft für natur- und Völkerkunde ostasiens/Hamburg* 144 (1988): 71-94; and, most recently, Helmut Martin and Christiane Hammer, eds., *Chinawissenschaften: Deutschsprachige Entwicklungen—Geschichte, Personen, Perspektiven* (Hamburg: Institut für Asienkunde, 1998).

Clavis sinica. Müller even corresponded with Leibniz (1646-1716), one of the founders of comparative linguistics and author of *Discourse on the Natural Theology of the Chinese* (1716), at the latter's initiative.[6] Yet Müller knew no grammar and very few Chinese characters, only enough to handle individual phrases or titles, scarcely a sufficient linguistic base from which to translate an entire text.[7] This leaves the field of early sinology in Germany to Klaproth.

Born in Berlin, Klaproth started to study Chinese with the help of Bayer's *Museum Sinicum*, Mentzel's vocabulary, and Diaz' Chinese-Spanish dictionary. He studied at Halle and Dresden, and at age nineteen published two volumes of *Asiatisches Magasin* in 1802. In 1804 he was summoned to Russia to work in the service of the Tsar, and accompanied the 1805 Golowkin embassy to China as interpreter; afterwards he traveled extensively, learning Mongolian, Manchu, and more Chinese. Upon his return to Europe, he joined the Academy of St. Petersburg, and was sent to Berlin to supervise the printing of a catalogue of the Chinese and Manchu books held by the academy.[8] He later became an unaffiliated professor of Oriental Languages in Paris. This came about in the following manner: a year after his arrival in Paris, at the request of Humboldt, the

---

[6]See David E. Mungello, *Leibniz and Confucianism: The Search for Accord*, p. 6. For their correspondence, see the translation in Donald F. Lach, "The Chinese Studies of Andreas Müller," *JAOS* 60 (1940): 564-75. On the various works of Leibniz on China, including his famous "Discourse on the Natural Theology of the Chinese," consult Julia Ching and Willard G. Oxtoby, *Moral Enlightenment: Leibniz and Wolff on China* (Sankt Augustin: Institut Monumenta Serica, 1992), 63-141.

[7]David E. Mungello, *Curious Land: Jesuit Accommodation and the Origins of Sinology*, 209-36. For his ability in Chinese, see Eva S. Kraft, "Frühe chinesische Studien in Berlin," *Medizinhistorisches Journal* 11 (1976): 92-128, and Lach, "The Chinese Studies of Andreas Müller," both utilized by Mungello. Christopher Harbsmeier would rather emphasize a later "key" to Chinese, J. Marshman's "well organized and thoughtful survey" entitled *Elements of Chinese Grammar: Clavis Sinica* (1814); see Harbsmeier, "John Webb and the Early History of the Study of the Classical Language in the West," in *Europe Studies China*, 331.

[8]*Julius von Klaproth. Katalog der chinesischen und mandjurischen Bücher: der Bibliothek der Akademie der Wissenschaften in St. Petersburg*, ed. Harmut Walravens (Berlin: C. Bell Verlag, 1988).

Emperor of Prussia gave Klaproth the title of Professor of the Languages and Literature of Asia in 1816 with a generous salary, and funds for publishing the results of his own research.   Although he had no institutional affiliation, his "intolerable behavior" at the Société Asiatique "badly repaid the hospitality he received" in Paris.[9] Except for a visit in 1834 back to Berlin, Klaproth remained in Paris until his death on August 27, 1835. Among his notable publications were *Inscription de Yu* (Paris, 1811); *Supplement au dictionaire chinois du Basile de Glemona* (Paris, 1819); and *Chrestomathie mandchou* (Paris, 1828).

Unfortunately, like Müller, Klaproth had his own set of shortcomings, albeit of a moral rather than intellectual nature. Despite his knowledge of Oriental tongues, his reputation was gained more by the library he had acquired and the methods he used to acquire it. "Already as a young man," according to van der Loon, "Klaproth coveted other men's dictionaries and later he became notorious for taking manuscripts from public collections."[10] As he held a professorial chair in Paris, German sinology would perhaps prefer to seek its founding father elsewhere, even while paying homage to the bibliographic basis Klaproth established for the Royal Berlin Library in his self-appointed role as "Quellenfinder."[11]

Germany, like England and the United States, did have an early missionary presence. However, Karl Friedrich Gützlaff (1803-51) seems to have been the only German missionary of note to have aroused interest regarding China back on the home front equal to that spurred by Richard

---

[9]Schwab, *The Oriental Renaissance*, 184.

[10]Piet van der Loon, *AM* 2nd ser., 13 (1968): 107. An example of a specific text, a 200-year- old work in Chinese composed by Fr. Intorcetta et al., called the *Hai-p'ien*, is mentioned by Mungello, *Curious Land*, 217-18.

[11]The establishment and development of the Berlin Chinese holdings are reviewed in Abel Rémusat, *Mélanges Asiatiques*, 2:352-71; and Martin Gimm, "Zu Klaproths erstem Katalog chinesischer Bücher, Weimar 1804," in *Das andere China: Festschrift für Wolfgang Bauer zum 65. Geburtstag*, ed. Helwig Schmidt-Glintzer (Wiesbaden: Harrassowitz, 1995), 560-99. See also *Catalogue des livres imprimés, des manuscrits et des ouvrages chinois, tartares, japonais, etc., composant la bibliothèque de feu M. Klaproth* (Paris, 1839). The term "Quellenfinder," or "source-locater," was applied to Klaproth by Georg von der Gabelentz; see Gimm, "Zu Klaproths erstem Katalog chinesischer Bücher," 561.

Wilhelm later, at the turn of the twentieth century.[12] Gützlaff had studied Chinese in Batavia and Singapore before arriving in China. He was very successful in converting native Chinese, and, though eventually based in Hong Kong, organized Christian cells in each province except far-flung Kansu. Such was his knowledge of Chinese that he eventually succeeded Morrison as Chinese secretary to the British diplomatic presence in Canton. He also helped negotiate the treaty of Nanking. His reports on China to Germany excited much interest, and inspired the founding of a monthly periodical called *Morgenrot in China's Nacht*.[13] Yet, since the first professional scholars of China in Germany were contemporary with the resident German missionaries, the foundation of German sinology derived from profane, not lay, circles.

---

[12]It is true that Ernest John Eitel (1838-1908), German-born missionary of the Basel-Missionary Society, served many years in Hong Kong, publishing several important works on Buddhism and the Cantonese language. But he soon began to identify more with British interests in Hong Kong than German interests back home. He broke with the Basel Missionary Society in 1865 and transferred his allegiance to the London Missionary Society, married an English teacher in Hong Kong, and served the Hong Kong government in a voluntary capacity as Acting Inspector of Schools, among other positions. He became a naturalized British citizen in 1880. All of his major publications were in English, chiefly *Handbook for the Student of Chinese Buddhism* (1870; 2nd ed., revised and enlarged, Tokyo: Sanshuha, 1904); *Fengshui: The Science of Sacred Landscape in Old China* (London: Trubner and Co., 1873); and *A Chinese-English Dictionary in the Cantonese Dialect*, revised and enlarged by Immanuel Gottlieb Genahr (Hong Kong: Kelly and Walsh, 1910). For a penetrating study of Eitel's many contributions to missionary work, sinology, and public service in Hong Kong, see Wong Man-kong, "Christian Missions, Chinese Culture, and Colonial Administration: A Study of the Activities of James Legge and Ernest John Eitel in Nineteenth Century Hong Kong," Ph.D. diss., Chinese University of Hong Kong, 1996, pp. 199-212; 217-28.

[13]For Gützlaff, see J.G. Lutz, "Karl F.A. Gützlaff: Missionary Entrepreneur," in *Christianity in China*, ed. Suzanne W. B. Barnett and J.K. Fairbank (Cambridge, Mass.: Harvard University Press, 1985), 61-88; Lutz in *The Blackwell Dictionary of Evangelical Biography, 1730-1860)*, 2 vols, ed. Donald M. Lewis (Oxford: Blackwell Publishers, 1995), 1:495-96; Herman Schlyter, *Karl Gützlaff als Missionar in China* (Lund: Gleerup, 1946) and *Der China Missionar Karl Gützlaff und seine Heimatbasis* (Sweden: WK Gleerup, 1976). More of Gützlaff's personal qualities, including some dubious distinctions, are narrated from original sources in Arthur Waley, "Gutzlaff and his Traitors: Mamo," in *The Opium War Through Chinese Eyes* (1958; rpt. Stanford: Stanford University Press, 1968), 222-44.

Wilhelm Schott (1807-89), a former theologian, taught Chinese at the University of Berlin for fifty years (commencing in 1838), and produced the first German translation of the *Lun-yü*, among other writings on China. But Cordier once again advises caution, characterizing Schott's work as being more remarkable for its quantity than its quality.[14]

Berlin I: Georg von der Gabelentz

The first truly scientific and systematic study of Chinese, without any French *post factum* opprobrium, began with the career of Georg von der Gabelentz.[15] Hans Georg Conon von der Gabelentz (1840-93), son of the great scholar of Manchu, Hans Conon von der Gabelentz, taught himself Dutch, Italian, and Chinese during his years at the gymnasium in Altenburg. Following his father's wishes, he went to Leipzig to study languages, concentrating on Oriental tongues, especially Chinese, Japanese, and Manchu. He earned his doctoral degree with a translation of the *T'ai-chi t'u* 太極圖 in 1876 from Dresden. In 1878 he was appointed to a chair of general linguistics (i.e., philology) at the University of Leipzig. In 1889, he replaced Schott at Berlin.

Today he is known for his large compendium, *Chinesische Grammatik* (Leipzig 1881). According to a modern sinologist,

> His *Grammatik* remains until today recognized as probably the finest overall grammatical survey of the language to date. Interestingly enough, those who disagree with this assessment do not feel that any of the newer grammars is superior, but they tend to feel that Stanislas Julien is perhaps to be preferred, though he was not as great a linguist as Georg von der Gabelentz.[16]

---

[14]*TP* 9 supplement, 46. According to Franke, *Sinology at German Universities*, pp. 9-10, the most noteworthy of Schott's strictly sinological publications are *Entwurf einer Beschreibung der chinesischen Literatur* (1854), *Chinesische Sprachlehre* (1857), and *Das Reich Karachitai oder Si-Liao* (1849).

[15]Gustav Schlegel, "Hans Georg Conon von der Gabelentz," *TP* 5 (1894): 75-78.

[16]Christopher Harbsmeier, "John Webb and the Early History of the Study of the Classical Language in the West," in *Europe Studies China*, 333.

It is made more accessible by a reprinting in 1960 with an introduction by Eduard Erkes.[17] Among the many other scholarly works of Gabelentz, noteworthy are his pioneering analysis of the complicated grammar of the *Chuang-tzu*,[18] an introduction to the methods and principles of linguistic (i.e., philological) research,[19] and a history of Chinese grammar, the first of its kind.[20]

At his death in 1893, he was not succeeded by a traditional sinologist trained in the old school. There were qualified replacements, including Friedrich Hirth and Gabelentz's own assistant in Berlin, Wilhelm Grube. But since the establishment in Berlin of the Seminar für orientalische Sprachen in 1887, modeled after l'Ecole des Languages orientales vivantes of Paris, the emphasis at the University of Berlin had shifted from classical research to training in modern languages for diplomatic service. The newly inaugurated chair in modern Chinese at the Seminar was occupied by Carl Arendt, formerly chief interpreter at the German legation in Peking.[21] Von der Gabelentz's responsibilities in Berlin were, however, effectively if not officially assumed by Wilhelm Grube.

---

[17] *Chinesische Grammatik: Mit Ausschluss des niederen Stiles und der heutigen Umgangssprache* (rpt. Halle: Max Niemeyer Verlag, 1960). The introduction is dated 1953. In 1956 appeared Erkes' supplement, *Chinesische Grammatik: Nachtrag zur Chinesischen von G. v. d. Gabelentz* (Berlin: VEB Deutcher Verlag der Wissenschaften, 1956), which drew on the grammatical studies of Conrady, Grube, Karlgren, Simon, Unger, von Zach, and the work of Erkes himself.

[18] "Beiträge zur Chinesischen Grammatik: Die Sprache des Cuang-tsï," *Abhand. d. Phil.-Hist. Cl. D. Königl. Sächsischen Ges. d. Wissen....* Bd. 10 (1888): 579-638.

[19] *"Die Sprachwissenschaft, ihre Aufgaben, Methoden und bisherigen Ergebnisse* (Leipzig: Weigel, 1891).

[20] "Beitrag zur Geschichte der Chinesischen Grammatiken und zur Lehre von der grammatischen Behandlung der chinesischen Sprache," *ZDMG* 32: 601-64.

[21] Arendt had a thorough command of modern Chinese, and authored, according to Cordier, a "remarkable" grammar, his *Handbuch der Nordchinesischen Umgangsprache mit Einschluss der Angangsgründe des Neuchinesischen Officielden un Briefstils* (Berlin, 1891).

Berlin II: Wilhelm Grube

Born in St. Petersburg, Grube (1855-1908) began to study Oriental languages there.[22] He received advanced training under von der Gabelentz at Leipzig, obtaining his doctorate in 1881. He was named an assistant in the Berlin Ethnological Museum in 1883 and concurrently served as a lecturer at the university. In 1892 he became assistant professor, and in this capacity continued von der Gabelentz's courses. From 1897 to 1899 he and his wife lived in China, and he brought back a rich collection of artifacts for the museum. Because of this extended first-hand experience in China, Grube became the first German scholar of the classical language to have command also of the modern tongue.

Grube made valuable contributions to many fields. His *Geschichte der chinesischen Literatur* (Leipzig, 1902) was highly praised by Cordier;[23] Karlgren recommended that it be translated into English.[24] Chavannes admitted that he learned much from Grube's *Religion und Kultur der Chinesischen* (Leipzig, 1910) and expressed regret that Grube had not published more on Chinese religions.[25] Grube translated much of the *Feng-shen yen-i*, and published several articles on the Chinese "philosophy of nature," *li-ch'i*, and the theological philosophy of Chu Hsi.

The works mentioned above show the extent of his explorations among original Chinese sources, and, anticipating the genius of Otto Franke, a gift for summary and synthesis. But Grube was equally gifted in linguistic research and reconstruction. His *Die sprachgeschichtliche Stellung der Chinesischen* (Leipzig, 1884) presents an astonishingly sophisticated view of the nature of ancient Chinese. This brief pamphlet throws light on many hitherto unsuspected linguistic features of the archaic language: initial consonant clusters and the decay of these initial and final consonants, the role of monosyllabism and binominal expressions, word

---

[22]Edouard Chavannes, "Le Professor Wilhelm Grube, "*TP* 9 (1908): 593-94; Nicholas Poppe, *Introduction to Altaic Linguistics* (Wiesbaden: Otto Harrassowitz, 1965), 96.

[23]He remarked that is was "Un des ouvrages plus remarquables parus dans les dernieres annés," *TP* 124 (1903): 327.

[24]"On the Authenticity and Nature of the Tso Chuan," 33.

[25]*TP* 12 (1911): 747-48.

families, and other features. Yet despite all of Grube's many valuable contributions to sinology, it is the Altaicists who now appreciate him most. His work on Tungusic dialects is noteworthy; of singular importance is his glossary of Nanai (Goldi), compiled on the basis of materials collected by Maxinowicz and others in the Amur region from 1855 to 1860; his *Die Sprache und Schrift der Jucen* (Leipzig, 1896; rpt. Tientsin, 1941), "is still the principal source of our knowledge of Jurchen."[26]

In addition to his brilliance as a scholar, Grube was honored for his "elevated character" and his "superior spirit" (Chavannes). His early death at the age of fifty-three was all the more regrettable in that most of his remarkable works were completed after he was forty; hence, his creative period was tragically short.

AWOL from Berlin: Friedrich Hirth

The Seminar for Oriental Languages had trained students of law and other disciplines in various Asiatic languages since 1887, but, with the lack of a classical sinologist at the University of Berlin after the passing of von der Gabelentz, scientific research had lagged behind. When the Turfan expeditions of Albert Grünwedel and Albert von le Coq returned with their artistic treasures and manuscript remains, the need for scientifically trained specialists in Asiatic studies, including Chinese, was acute. "It was therefore decided in 1912," reminisces Fritz Jäger, "to establish a professorship for sinology in the University of Berlin. Germany's leading sinologist, Friedrich Hirth, was then on the staff of Columbia University, New York, and it became necessary to appoint a foreigner, J.J.M. de Groot, a Dutchman, to that post."[27]

The unavailability of Hirth for the new chair leads to a closer look at the politics of sinological circles in Germany at the time. Hirth was

---

[26]Poppe, *Introduction to Altaic Linguistics*, 96.

[27]Fritz Jäger, "The Present State of Sinological Studies in Germany," *Research and Progress* 3 (1937): 96.

born in Grafentonna, Thüringen in 1845.[28]   He was a classicist turned sinologist, who published in the fields of Chinese art—including painting, bronzes, mirrors—and the history of the commerce and traffic between China and the West.   His main contributions were in this last field, including his pioneering *China and the Roman Orient* (Shanghai, 1885), and an equally important work done in collaboration with W.W. Rockhill, *Chau Ju-kua: His Work on the Chinese and Arab Trade in the Twelfth and Thirteenth Centuries, entitled Chu-fan-chi* (St. Petersburg, 1911).[29]   Despite the scope of these wide-ranging works, Hirth exhibited a certain amount of insularity in maintaining a methodological maxim that one must concentrate solely on Chinese, and leave the other languages alone.[30]

From 1870 until 1895 Hirth worked in various official capacities, including   Commissioner of Customs, in Canton, Amoy, Formosa, Shanghai, and Chungking.   In each location he met with local scholars and studied with them.   Besides his official title, he also carried the German title of *Professor*, owing to his distinguished contributions to scholarship through his own publications and through his service in collecting and sending to Berlin a large library in 1890. (Among the finds was the *Hua-I i-lu* 華夷譯錄 , which Grube later mined for his Jurchen studies.) In 1897 Hirth was elected as Outside Member of the Bavarian Academy of

---

[28]Friedrich Hirth, "Biographisches nach eigenen Aufzeichnungen," *Asia Major* 1 (1922): ix-xxxxviii; Eduard Erkes, "Friedrich Hirth," *Artibus Asiae* 2 (1927): 218-21; Bruno Schindler and F. Hommel, "List of Books and Papers of Friedrich Hirth," *AM* 1 (1922): xxxxix-lvii; and Henri Cordier, "Les Etudes chinoises (1895-1898)," *TP* 9 supplement (1908): 98-101.

[29]This was a very valuable study, despite some highly dubious identifications based on a faulty grasp of historical linguistics. For an instance of the latter, see Paul Wheatley, "Geographical Notes on Some Commodities Involved in Sung maritime Trade," *Journal of the Malayan Branch of the Royal Asiatic Society* 32 (1959): 13.

[30]Otto Franke argued that self-respecting sinologists should study as a minimum Sanskrit, Tibetan, Mongolian, and Manchu to be qualified to place the study of China within its entire continental context, the so-called geographical approach of Teggart. For the debate between Hirth and Franke, et al., see *TP* 6 (1895): 364-68; *TP* 7 (1896): 241-50, 397-407.

Sciences, becoming a full member in 1901,[31] and was considered to be the doyen of German sinologists.

His first opportunity at a chair in Germany was to succeed von der Gabelentz. But, as Hirth was far from being able to lecture on either Chinese or general linguistics, he was not a suitable replacement. But by the time the powers-that-be considered constituting a chair in sinology, Hirth's public reputation had suffered, owing to his vocal stand against the dilettantish dabbling in sinology of the popular geologist and geographer Baron Ferdinand de Richthofen.[32] Cordier sums up the crux of the issue by lamenting that Richthofen's "influence on the sinological studies so flourishing in Germany today certainly had been nefast during several years in discouraging the ambition of men of true knowledge such as Friedrich Hirth."[33] Hence it was that after a short period of activity in St. Petersburg, Hirth accepted a professorship at Columbia, where he remained until 1917. He retired from academia and active research after returning to Germany that same year. Therefore, the senior German sinologist did not contribute directly to the development of German sinology, other than to leave an inspirational model of scholarship, and to purchase books for the Berlin university library.

Berlin III. Dutchman as Deutscher: J.J.M. de Groot

The first occupant of the new Berlin chair in Chinese, established in 1912 (in 1909 the Hamburg chair had gained the merit of becoming the first academic chair of sinology in Germany), was a Dutchman, J.J.M. de Groot.[34] A former diplomat who had served in the Far East, de Groot was

---

[31]The original diploma of 1897 is now in the possession of Herbert Franke, who obtained it from Erich Haenisch. It is beautifully printed with the elegant epitaph of "Academia Litterarum et Scientiarum Regia Boica Te Fridericum Hirth propter egregia de litteris et historia Sinensium illustrandis merita socium extraordinarium in concessu die XIV. mensis Iulii habito cooptavit."

[32]Eduard Erkes, *Artibus Asia* 2 (1927): 220.

[33]Cordier, *TP* 6 (1905): 646.

[34]For his life, see Wilt L. Idema, "Dutch Sinology: Past, Present and Future," in *Europe Studies China*, 91-92; and J.J.L. Duyvendak, *Holland's Contribution to Chinese Studies*, 24.

appointed to the Chair of Ethnology of the Dutch East Indies at Leiden, where he had earlier studied with Schlegel. After the death of Schlegel, de Groot moved over to the chair of Chinese Language and Literature in 1904. Unfortunately, German sinology stagnated under the direction of this diplomat-turned-scholar.[35]   For although he knew Chinese well enough, he did not possess all the tools for critical scholarship.[36] Particularly embarrassing was his attack on the systematic study of Chinese phonology.[37]   His reputation was salvaged, at least partly, by Erich Haenisch. Always the gentleman, Haenisch explained that the First World War had hindered the development of de Groot's work, and that by the end of the conflict he was mentally and physically broken.[38] Nevertheless, de Groot's main contribution to scholarship, *The Religious System of China*, 6 vols. (Leiden: E.J. Brill, 1892-1910), is credited by Kristofer Schipper as having inaugurated the sociological method in the study of Chinese religion.[39]

The successor to de Groot in 1923 was Otto Franke, the senior German sinologist during the first half of the twentieth century. As he will be treated in detail below, we will now turn instead to Franke's own successor.

Erich Haenisch

Erich Haenisch (1880-1966) replaced the distinguished Professor Franke in 1932.[40] Born in Berlin, Haenisch studied East Asian languages with Grube, and obtained his degree with a dissertation on the Chinese redaction of the *Erdeni-yin tobči*, a Mongolian chronicle by Saghang Sechen. Haenisch lived, taught, and traveled in China and Tibet before

---

[35]Paul Pelliot, *TP* 24 (1928-29): 130.

[36]Piet van der Loon, *AM* n.s.5 (1955): 1.

[37]For an instance of the results of this neglect, see Karlgren, *TP* 21 (1922): 41-42.

[38]*OE* 12 (1965): 7.

[39]Schipper, "The History of Taoist Studies in Europe," in *Europe Studies China*, 472.

[40]Oscar Benl, et al., "Eric Haenisch in memoriam," *OE* 15 (1968): 121-22; Herbert Franke, "Erich Haenisch zum 80. Geburtstag," in *Studia Sino-Altaic: Festschrift für Erich Haenisch zum 80. Geburtstag* (Wiesbaden, 1961), 1-3.

returning to lecture in Chinese at Berlin under de Groot and Franke. He also taught Mongolian and Manchu under Eric Hauer. From 1925 to 1932 he occupied the chair that had been Conrady's at Leipzig. His work in Berlin as Franke's replacement was soon hindered by the Nazi regime, which he despised. After the war he founded in 1946 a new seminar at the University of Munich, where he worked until his retirement in 1952.

Most of the Chinese scholarship by this good man centered around Chou and Han-period biographies, but an introductory article on the *Ch'ing-shih kao* (1930) should at least be mentioned. Haenisch is better known for his still useful graded introduction to Classical Chinese, the *Lehrgang der chinesischen Schriftsprache*, 3 vols. (Leipzig, 1929-33). This grew out of his conviction that the sinologist must be fully functional as a philologist and at home in the texts. This basic competency was, in his view, best demonstrated by producing an annotated translation in the mode of Pelliot. In the words of Herbert Franke, "He regarded an integral and annotated translation ("Extenso-Übersetzung") as the necessary prerequisite for qualification as a sinologist, and always stressed the importance of 'Texterfahrung' (reading experience)."[41] Such a methodological mind-set was inspired less by the mechanics of research than his impassioned vision of Chinese civilization, as recalled by his former student Wolfgang Franke: "For Haenisch, China was a completely classical culture, just like Greek and Roman antiquity, and sinology was purely the philological study of antiquity ('philologische Alturtumwissenschaft'), which had no connection with the present."[42]

Haenisch also contributed to Altaic studies, including Manchu. But his well-deserved academic reputation rests on his pioneering Mongolian research. He was the father not only of *Erdeni-yin tobči* studies, but also of *Secret History* scholarship: he published the first complete transcription of the text, which according to Nicholas Poppe was superior to Pelliot's

---

[41]Herbert Franke, "In Search of China," in *Europe Studies China*, 19.

[42]Wolfgang Franke, *Im Banne Chinas: Autobiographie eines Sinologen 1912-1950* (Dortmund: Projekt Verlag, 1995), 39. Franke adds the sensitive observation that it was just this attitude, a studious avoidance of present realities, that allowed the Nazis to take advantage of his scholarship for their own purposes.

version;[43] the first complete translation (1935; 2nd ed. 1948), which according to Cleaves was generally more accurate than the translation of Pelliot;[44] a dictionary of the vocabulary in the text; and also a preliminary study of the grammar of its language.[45] For these and other important works—studies on the *Hua-I i-lu* and various hP'ags-pa texts, for instance—Haenisch was honored at his death as the Nestor of Mongolian studies.

Leipzig: August Conrady and Eduard Erkes

While German sinology stagnated in Berlin under de Groot, it flourished in Leipzig under the leadership of the brilliant Conrady.[46] August Conrady (1864-1925) was born in Wiesbaden, and studied classical and Indian philology. From Sanskrit he turned to Tibetan, and eventually to Chinese. In 1891 he became a lecturer at Leipzig, assistant professor in 1897, and finally professor in 1920.

All of his work was marked by ingenious ideas, sometimes too advanced to be appreciated or confirmed. He was especially gifted in linguistic reconstruction. He presented as a general rule the double role played by the "phonetic" element of a graph: it carried both the sound and the sense of the word.[47] His *Eine indo-chinesische* (i.e., Sino-Tibetan) *Causativ-Denominativ-Bildung und ihr Zusammenhang mit den Tonaccenten* (Leipzig, 1896), posited the existence of initial sonants in archaic Chinese. He showed the relationship between the surd or sonant initial and the level of the tone. He also demonstrated, as part of his theory, that the alternation of surd and sonant initial in the same series was due to the presence of ancient prefixes, a theory taken up later by Maspero. Pelliot regretted that the state of linguistic knowledge among sinologists at the

---

[43]Poppe, *Introduction to Altaic Linguistics*, 89.

[44]Cleaves' comments comparing the Haenisch and Pelliot versions are scattered throughout his extensive review of the former's second edition; Cleaves prefaces his review by including a complete bibliography of all scholarly work done by Haenisch on the *Secret History* up to 1948; see *HJAS* 12 (1949): 497-534.

[45]Poppe, *Mongolian Society Bulletin* 5 (1966), 7.

[46]Pelliot, "Auguste Conrady," *TP* 24 (1928-29): 130-32.

[47]See Pelliot, *TP* 22 (1923): 359.

time was too primitive to take advantage of Conrady's theories or to question intelligently some of his specific findings.[48]

A year of residence at Peking University helped initiate Conrady into the society and customs of the people. His studies on ancient China profited from this first-hand knowledge. Pelliot praised his firm handling of early texts, as he went beyond paraphrasing the traditional commentaries to infuse his accurate translations with original insights from sociology and religion. Only twenty-five items found their way into print, for Conrady's high standards precluded easy or rapid publication: at his death 390 manuscripts were found, on a broad variety of topics, including linguistics, grammar, literature, paleography, religion, art, history, and culture. In the opinion of an expert, almost half were ready for publication.[49]

After Conrady's death in 1925, Erich Haenisch assumed his chair. But, although von der Gabelentz had lectured at Leipzig in 1878-79, and Haenisch was based there, teaching from 1925 until 1932, the school of sinology at Leipzig was founded, formed, and made famous by the methods and personality of Conrady. He trained, among others, Gustav Haloun, Otto Maenchen-Helfen, Lin Yutang, Bruno Schindler, and Eduard Erkes.

Eduard Erkes (1891-1958), nephew of August Conrady, was born in Geneva.[50] He studied Chinese at Leipzig under Conrady, and obtained his degree with a translation of Sung Yü's "Chao-hun." Like Laufer, Erkes worked in a museum, the Leipzig Ethnological Museum from 1913, eventually becoming Commissioner-Director, until his retirement in 1947. Unlike Laufer, however, he also doubled as a lecturer, and later as professor in Chinese, at the university.

Erkes published widely in ancient history, literature, religion, archaeology, and natural history. Already mentioned is the introduction

----

[48]*TP* 24 (1928-29): 130.

[49]Bruno Schindler, "Der wissenschaftliche Nachlass August Conradys," *AM* 3 (1926): 104-15.

[50]Kate Finsterbusch, "In Memoriam Eduard Erkes 23. Juli 1891-2 April 1958," *AA* 21 (1936): 167-70; J. Schubert, ed. *Eduard Erkes In Memoriam 1891-1958* (Leipzig, 1962), is rather a *Festschrift* dedicated to his memory. However, at least his personal bibliography, in five pages of double columns, is included as an appendix.

to the grammar of von der Gabelentz. Perhaps today his most important contributions are a series of articles on related themes, the history of different animals in the Chinese world: the horse, the bird, the dog, the sheep, the pig, and the bee, published mostly in *T'oung Pao*. While falling short of the technical virtuosity of a Laufer or the humanistic insights of a Schafer, these are all competent and comprehensive presentations of their subjects. His translation of the Ho-shang Kung commentary to the *Lao-tzu* is informed by first-hand observations he made on Taoist meditation practices during a stay in China.

Hamburg: Alfred Forke and Fritz Jäger

Sinological studies at the University of Hamburg (formerly the Hamburg Colonial Institute) began at the end of 1909 with the appointment of Otto Franke as Professor of East Asian Languages and History. After he was called to Berlin in 1923, he was replaced by the venerable master of Chinese philosophy, Alfred Forke.[51]   Alfred Forke (1867-1944) was born in Bad Schöningen at Braunschwieg. He studied law, Sanskrit, Arabic, and Chinese at the seminar in Berlin, and then worked in China as translator at the German embassy in Peking, and for the Consul General in Shanghai from 1890 to 1903. He then lectured at the seminar in Berlin until 1913, when he was invited to the University of California at Berkeley as Agassiz Professor; there he served from 1914 until 1917. After Otto Franke left Hamburg in 1923, Forke replaced him as professor, retiring in 1935.

Although he published widely on a variety of sinological subjects, including comparative linguistics and poetry, Forke's renown as an interpreter and translator of Chinese philosophy overshadows all other aspects of his scholarship. His many articles and translations of the works of Yang Chu, Wang Ch'ung, Mo Ti, Mencius, Yen Ying, Confucius, Shang Yang, and others culminated in three monumental volumes: *Geschichte der alten chinesischen Philosophie* (Hamburg, 1927), *Geschichte der*

---

[51]Eduard Erkes, "Alfred Forke," *AM* 9 (1946): 148-49; Erich Haenisch, "Alfred Forke." *ZDMG* 99 (1945-49): 4-6; Fritz Jäger and Erwin Rousselle, "Herrn Professor Dr. Jur. et Phil. h.c. Alfred Forke zu seinem 70. Geburtstag gewidmet," *Sinica* 12 (1937): 1-14.

mittelalterlichen chinesischen Philosophie (Hamburg, 1934), and *Geschichte der neuren chinesischen Philosophie* (Hamburg, 1938).   Probably the foremost modern interpreter of ancient Chinese philosophy, A.C. Graham, praised Forke's work as being more comprehensive than Fung Yu-lan's *History of Chinese Philosophy*. In reviewing the 1964 reprinting of Forke's *Geschichte*, Graham comments that "for orthodox as well as heterodox thinkers Forke's history remains the most comprehensive yet written, and a modern reader still has frequent occasion to consult its convenient summaries and brief but well-chosen Chinese quotations."[52]

Forke's successor at Hamburg was a local product. Fritz Jäger (1896-1957) was born in Munich, and, like Hirth, came to sinology with a strong background in the classics.[53] He began Chinese with Franke at Hamburg, and continued on as a teaching assistant. He became a lecturer in 1925. After a two-year residence in China, he returned to Hamburg. In 1935 he succeeded Forke, and remained in residence until his death in 1957.

Jäger's oeuvre includes several interesting works on the *Shih-chi* and an important article entitled "Leben und Werk des P'ei Kü: Ein Kapitel aus der chinesischen kolonialgeschichte."[54]

Richard Wilhelm

The University of Frankfurt started offering Chinese with the arrival of Richard Wilhelm and the establishment of his China Institute in 1924.[55] Richard Wilhelm (1873-1930), was born in Stuttgart and studied art, philosophy, music (violin), and theology. From 1899 to 1924 he lived in China and worked as missionary, academic advisor to the German embassy in Peking, and Professor of German Literature at Peking University. He made a number of significant translations (in collaboration

---

[52]*AM* 12 (1966): 120.

[53]Wolfgang Franke, "Fritz Jäger in memoriam," *OE* 4 (1957): 1-4.

[54]*Ostasiatischen Zeitschrift* 9.

[55]Salome Wilhelm, *Richard Wilhelm, der geistige Mittler zwischen China und Europa* (Düsseldorf, 1956);   W.F. Otto, "Richard Wilhelm: Ein Bild seiner personalischkeit," *Sinica* 5 (1930): 49-57; Wilhelm Schüler, "Richard Wilhelms wissenschaftliche Arbeit," *Sinica* 5 (1930): 57-71; anonymous, "Umschau: Übersicht über die Schriften Richard Wilhelms," *Sinica* 5 (1930): 100-11.

with native scholars) during his residence in China, including the *Lun-yü* (1910), *Lao-tzu* (1911), *Meng-tzu* (1914), and most significantly, the *I-ching* (1924). Frederick Mote characterized Wilhelm's eventual move back home as also being in the spirit of missionary work, this time as a cultural ambassador (or spiritual mediator, as the title of his biography reads) between the two civilizations: Wilhelm had decided to "discontinue his teaching work for the German church mission in Shantung, and to return after WWI with his family to Germany, where he could promote the study of China in Europe."[56] His translations and publications on many aspects of China, in the journal of the China Institute *Sinica* (running from 1925 to 1942), began to interest the German people in the culture of China, and soon popularized its study. In this role, he became the Arthur Waley of Germany, although he operated in the realm of Chinese philosophy, not poetry.

---

[56]Mote, *MS* 29 (1970-71): iii.

5. THE SENIOR SINOLOGIST: OTTO FRANKE (1863-1946)

"Only a philologist can translate a Greek poem.... We the philologists, dry as dust, who stick to the letter and analyze grammatical subtleties, we also happen to be perverse enough to love the ideals we serve with all our heart. Servants we are indeed, but servants of immortal spirits to whom we lend our mortal mouths: is it surprising that our masters are stronger than we are?"
—Wilamowitz-Moellendorff, "Was ist Übersetzen?"[1]

Otto Franke was the senior German sinologist during the first half of the twentieth century.[2] His numerous works, especially the monumental *Geschichte des chinesischen Reiches*, are still valuable, and in some cases remain indispensable, today. His Berlin seminar trained most of the great German sinologists of the 1920s and 1930s, including W. Eberhard, W. Fuchs, and W. Simon, and also the American George A. Kennedy. Although not capable either by training or temperament of performing the same textual acrobatics of a Pelliot or a Haloun, Franke's genius was in historical synthesis: the "immortal spirit" he served with humble dedication was Cleo, not the literary muses. And his scholarship and teaching greatly contributed to the growth and sophistication of modern sinology.

Otto Franke was born on September 27, 1863 in Gernrode (in modern Halle District, formerly in East Germany). After graduating from Freiburg University, he attended college in Berlin, where he was attracted to history and comparative linguistics. The lectures of Johannes Schmidt

---

[1]Trans. by Andre Lefevere, *Translating Literature: The German Tradition from Luther to Rosenzweig* (Amsterdan: Van Gorcum, 1977), 103.

[2]Otto Franke, *Erinnerungen aus zwei Welten: Randglossen zur eigenen Lebensgeschichte* (Berlin: Walter de Gruyter, 1954); Wolfgang Franke, "Otto Franke und sein Sinologisches Werk," *Sinologica* 1 (1948): 352-54; Fritz Jäger, "Otto Franke (1863-1946)," *ZDMG* 100 (1950): 19-36; Bruno Schindler, "Otto Franke," *AM* 9 (1933): 1-20 (contains partial bibliography up to 1933 by F. Jäger); and Beatus Theunissen, O.F.M., "Otto Franke In Memoriam," *MS* 12 (1947): 277-81. The autobiography of his sinologist son Wolfgang Franke contains brief remarks concerning his father, see *Im Banne Chinas: Autobiographie eines Sinologen 1912-1950*.

introduced him to the importance of Sanskrit for comparative linguistics. After a year of compulsory military duty, he began the study of Sanskrit in 1884 at Göttingen. He obtained his degree by translating and annotating a short work on phonetics. Franke had originally signed up for the proseminar in Greek philology with Wilamowitz, but later changed his mind since Greek textual criticism, especially of the tragedians, was rather far removed from his long-range goal of studying history. Instead, he studied German history up to the reformation. He thus missed his chance to study with the greatest classical philologist of the turn of the century.[3]

Upon the advice of some friends in the foreign service, Franke applied for work as an interpreter. He studied law and Chinese, before being accepted as interpreter for the German Embassy in Peking. He arrived in China in 1888, one year earlier than Chavannes, and worked and traveled in China, including excursions to Mongolia, Siberia, Manchuria, Korea, and Japan until 1901. During this time, Franke gained his command of Mandarin, and became an expert on current Chinese affairs, both through study and personal involvement. Hence, after his return to Germany he was able to make a living from 1902 to 1907 by contributing articles to the *Kölnischen Zeitung*, commenting on political and cultural events of East Asia. He also served as an advisor to the Chinese Embassy in Berlin during this period.

His academic career began in 1910, when he was named to the newly created Chair for the Language and Culture of China, at Hamburg University. In 1923 he succeeded de Groot at the University of Berlin and became a member of the Preussische Akademie der Wissenschaften. He was granted emeritus status in 1931, but continued working until his death on August 5, 1946.

Historian as Philologist

Franke's scholarship was characterized by a curious blend of brilliant historical synthesis marred in some specifics by the occasional philological lapse. Trained in Sanskrit, he was schooled in the details and methods of philological work. German philology of the time, justly

---

[3]Franke, *Erinnerungen aus zwei Welten*, 30.

famous if somewhat dry and technical after years of ascendancy, had developed from the triple towers of Indology, Classics (especially Greek), and German dialectology. That brilliant pair, Conrady and Grube, had added sinology to the jewels of German humanistic scholarship. But, unfortunately for Franke, he had to transfer his working principles over to classical Chinese without advanced training. His *Studien zur Geschichte des konfuzianischen Dogmas und der chinesischen Staatsreligion: Das Problem des Tsch'un-ts'iu und Tung Tschung-sch'us Tsch'un-ts'iu fan lu* (1920) is a case in point. Karlgren praised Franke as an historian for offering a balanced and thorough presentation of all sides of an issue—here, on the nature of the *Ch'un-ch'iu*—and for giving clear and cautious opinions. He also appreciated Franke's talent for conveniently summing up the fundamental points of reasoning and arguments. But, as mentioned earlier, in examining Franke's own version of an important passage, Karlgren showed where a correct translation would have led Franke to settle the issue instead of merely summarizing it.[4] This does not mean that Franke was not capable of wielding the standard set of philological tools; it is just that he was interested in applying them to historical tasks, not literary ones. Nor did he contribute either to developing new methodologies or to refining existing ones. Franke once described the relative importance he placed on both philological and historical studies. He stated that, while his work would be in the fields of Chinese language and culture, and would be based on a philological foundation, his intellectual constructions would be built in the "higher" realm of cultural (i.e., historical) studies.[5]

Nationalist Historiography: *Geschichte des chinesischen Reiches*

Franke's most lasting contribution to sinology is in this latter realm. In five volumes of his *Geschichte des chinesischen Reiches: Eine Darstellung seiner Entstehung, seines Wesens und seiner Entwicklung bis zur*

---

[4]Karlgren, "On the Authenticity and Nature of Tso Chuan," 7-18.

[5]Franke, *Erinnerungen aus zwei Welten*, 131. In "Die sinologischen Studien in Deutschland," *Ostasiatische Neubildungen* (Hamburg, 1911), 363, Franke further betrays his intellectual leanings by letting his historian's sense of order boil over in outrage against the "outdated and intolerant philology" that he felt beset some sinological circles.

neuesten Zeit, Franke attempted to relate the history not of the Chinese people or empire, but of the Chinese state. His fixation on the "Universalist Idea" and its embodiment in political institutions was the main factor in leading him to concentrate on the surface phenomena of Chinese history, i.e., the military campaigns, court intrigues and rebellions, and to ignore social or cultural externalities such as religion and economics, literature or art. In this, he was merely working within the unconscious set of assumptions that guided the classical national tradition of German historiography since the Wars of Liberation. That his chief intellectual exemplars were the historians Humboldt and Ranke instead of the classicists Wilamowitz and Fränkel led to some understandable philological lapses and, equally expected, a total neglect of non-political factors. "History, at least until Meinecke," asserts George Iggers of the German approach, "...was mostly history in a narrow political sense, relating the actions of statesmen, of generals, and of diplomats, and leaving almost entirely out of account the institutional and material framework in which these decisions were made."[6] Nevertheless, as a history of Chinese political events, *Geschichte des chinesischen Reiches* remains the best work of its kind.

Otto Van der Sprenkel summarizes its strengths in the following general terms:

> He was...successful, within the bounds of the somewhat narrow interpretation he himself gave to politics, in producing a political narrative of permanent value; and his carefully worked out, detailed, and accurate account of the surface phenomena of Chinese history will long remain indispensable reading for the Western student....It is quite permissible to question or reject his general interpretations of the flow of Chinese history while at the same time gratefully accepting the results of the painstaking labour he devoted to establishing the facts of his story.[7]

---

[6] George C. Iggers, *The German Conception of History: The National Tradition of Historical Thought from Herder to the Present* (Middletown, Conn.: Wesleyan University Press, 1983), 15.

[7] O. Berkelbach Van der Sprenkel, "Franke's *Geschichte des chinesischen Reiches*," *BSOAS* 18 (1956): 312-321; quote on 321.

This work appears even greater when viewed within the context of the traditional European attitude towards Chinese history. Because, according to Van der Sprenkel, Franke portrayed China as "a development, an unfolding drama," he freed it from the stultifying dogmas that it had no real history (since it never changed), and that its story was therefore unimportant for understanding the nature and course of universal history. Marianne Bastid-Bruguière characterized the *Geschichte* as a "monumental undertaking" that was a "milestone in European historiography on China." This is because, she asserts, "it conveyed a sense of nobility, significance and dignity that could be equated to those great works on the history of the ancient world and medieval Europe." In essence, it was the first historical work of Western sinology to find a happy medium between interpretive translation and general description, and consequently "set new standards and orientations for further research."[8]   In contrast to her generous endorsement is the negative evaluation of Hans Bielenstein. He called the *Geschichte* a "noble failure," and lamented that Franke wasted decades of his life writing it: "His work can be compared to *The Golden Bough* by Sir James George Frazer (1854-1941), where the facts are basically right and the conclusions usually wrong."[9] (Then again, Bielenstein does not endorse any general history even at the present moment because, he feels, enough is not known).

Another contribution of this work was its wide use of primary sources. Franke criticized previous general histories of China as being limited to Chu Hsi's *T'ung-chien kang-mu* and its "arbitrary text-interpretation and arrogant intolerance." His was the first major history (Cordier's *Histoire générale de la Chine* of 1921 was much reduced in scope) to break away from this narrow source and to utilize the standard histories and other sources on a large scale. Nevertheless, Maspero claimed that Franke utilized these sources only to verify the *Kang-mu* rather than to supplement and complement it: "Mais en dépit de cet effort méritoire, le

---

[8]Marianne Bastid-Bruguière, "Some Themes of 19th and 20th Century Historiography on China," in *Europe Studies China*, 235.

[9]See Bielenstein, "Chinese Historiography in Europe," in *Europe Studies China*, 242.

cadre rest toujours celui de Tschu Hi."[10]

Franke also made several important contributions to Chinese philosophy and historiography. Among them are the previously mentioned *Studien zur Geschichte des konfuzianischen Dogmas und der chinesischen Staatsreligion* (1920), "Der Ursprung der chinesische Geschichtschreibung" (1928), "Das Tse tschi t'ung kien und das T'ung kien kang mu, ihr Wesen, ihr Verhaltnis zueinander und ihr Quellenwart" (1930), and "Der konfuzianismus zwischen Han- und Sui-Zeit" (1934). Two legal studies helped pioneer the field in Germany: "Die Rechtsverhältnisse am Grundeigentum in China" (1903) and "Zur Geschichte der Extraterritorialität in China" (1935).

Historian as Philological Theoretician

Despite the occasional philological mistake, Franke was well informed in theory; he even composed two very valuable articles on methodology, which almost by themselves justify the amount of treatment accorded him in a survey focused on philologists.

The second of these articles, dating from 1934, is entitled "Wiedergabe fremder Länder- und Völkernamen im Chinesischen."[11] It deals with problems in the transcription of names of foreign countries and peoples in Chinese, and was recommended by Otto Maenchen-Helfen as required reading for linguists who might otherwise ignore cultural and contextual factors in blind adherence to strict linguistic reconstruction.[12]

The other article is quite a sophisticated statement, for the times, called "China and Comparative Philology."[13] In it Franke tried to damp out the current vogue among business and consular men resident in China who delighted in comparing Chinese with every language imaginable. For example, some related Chinese with Celtic, or declared the Greek system of accentuation to be related to the Chinese tones. To offset this ignorant

---

[10]*Orientalistiche Literaturzeitung* 1942, no. 5/6, column 261. Franke responded to Maspero's criticisms in *ZDMG* (1942): 495-506.

[11]*SBAW* XV (1934).

[12]See Maenchen-Helfen, "History in Linguistics," *JAOS* 68 (1948): 123.

[13]*The China Review* 20 (1892-93): 310-27.

and amateurish speculation, Franke stated some of the tenets of Indo-Germanic comparative linguistics. He discussed the necessity of reconstructing the oldest forms of a language and only comparing these, of establishing word families and using the vernacular tongues (foreshadowing the "linguistic geography" of Grootaers and P. Serruys), and of going beyond surface similarities. He presented some of the features of archaic Chinese such as consonantal clusters, the decay of initial and final consonants, and the role of monosyllabism. Finally, for all who use the "global approach" to China, and work in sources besides Chinese, he stated the following principle:

> These examples, I think, will suffice to show, how necessary it is first *to know* a language, before we can undertake to compare it with another tongue. When I studied comparative philology at home, our academic instructors insisted upon our being enabled to understand a written text in each of the chief languages of the Indogermanic family. Sanskrit and Greek of course having always to play the leading part.[14]

The support of Boodberg and Maenchen-Helfen for this view is, of course, well known; they both argued against the deadly comparison of words from dictionaries instead of words from the living contexts of texts.

Besides his large corpus of publications,[15] Franke contributed to the growth of sinology through teaching and training an entire generation of sinologists. Among them were Stefan (Etienne) Balazs, Rolf Stein (before he went to Paris), K. Bünger, W. Eberhard, W. Fuchs, A. von Gabain (later turned Turcologist), E.H. von Tscharner, Walter Simon, and most likely George A. Kennedy. This sinologist, historian, and teacher, then, was largely responsible for the maturation of modern German sinology and, through the efforts of some of his emigré and exchange students, a portion of English and American sinology as well.

---

[14]"China and Comparative Philology," 323

[15]His many articles on contemporary Chinese politics deserve honorable mention; they are favorably reviewed by L. Arrousseau in *BEFEO* 11 (1911): 436-39.

End of the National Ideal

Like many patriotic German intellectuals and artists, Franke did not survive the trauma of the war.[16] The national idealism that had always underscored German historiography made the final humiliation of the state and the bankruptcy of traditional values all the more poignant to the historically minded Franke. The conclusion of Franke's life, as epitomized by Ferdinand Lessing, makes a fitting if sober end of our treatment of the senior German sinologist:

> Franke's last years, as may be imagined of a man so instinct with love and pride of his country, were poisoned by a bitterness which ended in despair. Perhaps he could have been spared a little if he had accepted the invitation extended to him in 1934 by the University of California to accept the chair of Agassiz Professor of Oriental Languages. This full life, replete with happy and sorrowful experiences which were interwoven with the background of momentous historical events, came to its close as the curtain fell on the last act of that tragedy which sealed the fate of his beloved homeland.[17]

---

[16]A tragic parallel is the famous author, librettist and poet Stefan Zweig, collaborator with Richard Strauss in his later vocal works. Although leaving Germany in 1935, he was unable to endure the twin emotional onslaughts of writing in exile and the atrocities of the war; he committed suicide in Brazil in 1942. His memories of a Germany lost forever, *The World of Yesterday* (New York, 1943), recall at least the happier moments of one of Franke's *zwei Welten*.

[17]Ferdinand Lessing, review of *Erinnerungen aus zwei Welten*, FEQ 14 (1955): 577.

6. THE EXPATRIATES[1]

The exile holds an honored place in the history of Western civilization. Dante and Grotius and Bayle, Rousseau and Heine and Marx, did their greatest work in enforced residence on alien soil, looking back with loathing and longing to the country, their own, that had rejected them.[2]

I cannot close this letter without expressing my deep regret at the conditions that keep me separated for the moment from Germany. And nothing would make me happier than observing a change outside the realm of concert life which would free me from the compulsion of conscience striking at my very heartstrings to renounce Germany.
     —Letter from the violinist Bronislaw Hubermann to Wilhelm Furtwängler, 31 August, 1933[3]

    The English classicist Hugh Lloyd-Jones in 1976, with a witty tongue in his learned cheek, once commented that "Hitler did more for classical studies in this country than for most branches of education."[4] Chinese studies also greatly benefitted from the exodus of professionals from National Socialism, the "learned refugees" of Gilbert Murray, as sinologists as well as classicists, historians, not to mention musicians, artists, and writers, fled abroad seeking refuge and outlet for their professional talents. While their contributions to scholarship were often ignored, sometimes even concealed, back home, many fine Germans belonged to this class of expatriate sinologist, that of the scholar whose publications honor his heritage and the great tradition of German *Altertumswissenschaft*, but who did not live or teach in Germany, and hence

---

    [1]A rudimentary version of parts of this chapter appeared as "The Foundation of Modern German Sinology," *Phi Theta Papers* 16 (1984): 82-101.
    [2]Peter Gay, *Weimar Culture: The Outsider as Insider* (New York: Harper and Row, 1968), xiii.
    [3]Quoted in Sam H. Shirakawa, *The Devil's Music Master: The Controversial Life and Career of Wilhelm Furtwängler* (Oxford: Oxford University Press, 1992), 163.
    [4]*Classical Survivals: The Classics in the Modern World* (London: Duckworth, 1982), 17.

did not directly influence the development of sinology in the fatherland.[5] Among the sinologists who fled from the religious and ethnic purges were some who were targeted for their political connections—Eberhard, for instance. Regardless of the reason for taking flight, among the most prominent of this group of refugee sinologists were Walter Simon, William Cohn, Etienne Balasz, Gustav Haloun, Bruno Schindler, and Wolfram Eberhard.[6] The stature in contemporary German sinology of some of these names and the loss to sinology their absence caused may be imagined, qualitatively, by linking them with refugees in other fields, such as conductors Bruno Walter and Otto Klemperer, composers Arnold Schönberg and Paul Hindemith, theater directors Max Reinhardt and Leopold Jessner, the writer Thomas Mann, or Edward Teller, father of the atomic bomb. Quantitatively, it is sobering to realize that before 1938 some 2,500 writers fled abroad, impoverishing the field of German literature.[7]

Boutefeu from Batavia: Erwin von Zach

Perhaps the most visible expatriate sinologist was not even German. This was the Austrian Erwin Ritter von Zach (1872-1942), mentioned above in connection with Pelliot.[8] Zach had a remarkable command of both modern and literary Chinese.[9] Of his numerous publications, he is

---

[5]For the story of this hegira of German sinologists and Asian art historians and its impact on modern global sinology, see Martin Kern, "The Emigration of German Sinologists 1933-1945: Notes on the History and Historiography of Chinese Studies," *JAOS*, 118 (1998): 507-29.

[6]Herbert Franke, *Sinologie an deutschen universitaten* (Wiesbaden, 1968), 32. This new batch of German sinologists, including many who remained behind in their homeland, had been introduced in Wolfgang Franke, "The Younger Generation of German Sinologists," *MS* 5 (1940): 437-46.

[7]See J. C. Jacmann and C. M. Borden, eds. *The Muses Flee Hitler: Cultural Transfer and Adaptation 1930-1945* (Washington, D.C., 1983).

[8]Alfred Hoffman, "Dr. Erwin Ritter von Zach (1872-1942) in memoriam: Verzeichnis seiner Veröffentlichungen," *OE* 10 (1963): 1-60.

[9]Witness his many word studies, *Lexicographische Beiträge*, 4 vols. (Peking, 1902-6), and *Zum Ausbau der gabelentzschen Grammatik* (Peking: Deutschland-Institut, 1944).

most respected for having translated the poetry of Tu Fu and Han Yü,[10] and much of the *Wen-hsüan*.[11] The greatest translator of this anthology, David R. Knechtges, summarizes the life and career of Dr. Zach as follows:

> Zach had been a member of the Austro-Hungarian consular service from 1901 to 1919, and during most of this time he served in China. He had a profound knowledge of Chinese as well as Manchu and Tibetan. Although he studied briefly at Leiden under Gustav Schlegel (in 1897), Zach seems, like Waley, to have been self-trained....
>
> After the dissolution of the Austro-Hungarian empire in 1919, Zach worked for the Dutch consular service in the East Indies until 1924, when he resigned to devote full time to his scholarly pursuits. Until his death in 1942 aboard a ship that was torpedoed by the Japanese, Zach devoted himself mainly to the translation of Chinese literature. He translated virtually all of the poetry of Du Fu, Han Yu, and Li Bo, and at the time of his death was still working on a complete rendition of the *Wenxuan*....
>
> Zach's irascible personality and penchant for acerbic criticism of other Sinologists' work eventually made it difficult for him to publish in established sinological journals. Virtually all of his translations were published in obscure Batavian journals. His *Wenxuan* translations mostly appeared in the *Deutsche Wacht*, a monthly magazine intended for the German community in the Dutch East Indies. After 1933, when the *Deutsche Wacht* was no longer available to him, Zach published his translations at his own expense in a series he called *Sinologische Beiträge*....
>
> Zach viewed himself as a "scientific" scholar who had no time for what he called "theoretical rigamarole." His style has been called "flat and philological," a remark that Zach would have taken as a compliment, for he intended his translations as a student's trot....In spite of Zach's desire for "literalness" and "conformity to meaning,"

---

[10]*Tu Fu's Gedichte*, 2 vols. (Cambridge, Mass.: Harvard University Press, 1952); *Han Yü poetisch Werke*, ed. James R. Hightower (Cambridge, Mass.: Harvard University Press, 1952).

[11]*Die Chinesische Anthologie: Übersetzungen aus dem Wen Hsüan*, 2 vols., ed. Ilse Martin Fang (Cambridge, Mass.: Harvard University Press, 1958).

his translations are not always philologically exact.[12]...Any defects that Zach's translations might have are offset by the overall excellence of his work. He was obviously working under a severe handicap. He had few reference materials....

   Zach had an astounding knowledge of Chinese, and few Western scholars, given the same resources available to Zach, could have done as well.[13]

Despite his admitted philological gifts, von Zach qualifies as an interloper among the Germans treated in this section not only because of his nationality, but because he interloped in the social circles of sinology, including public debate in the journals. That he was eventually ostracized, like his teacher Schlegel, had nothing to due with his Austrian citizenship: scholarly discourse was made impossible by the tone of his distemper.

Austrian Orientalist: August Pfizmaier

   Another, earlier Austrian was even more prolific than von Zach if hardly as competent. The sinological Orientalist August Pfizmaier (1808-87) probably translated more from the Chinese—and Japanese, Ainu, Russian, etc.—than any other sinologist. He was self-taught in French, Italian, English, Latin, Greek, Turkish, Russian, Dutch, Persian, Egyptian, Chinese, Japanese, Manchu, and various Scandinavian tongues.[14]

   Pfizmaier's Chinese translations, although they were extensive and often exploited unusual material—for example, obscure Taoist texts—were uncritical and seldom annotated. Perhaps he spread himself too thin. As it was, his works were characterized by their quantity rather than their quality: "The death of Pfizmaier has left vacant a place easy to fill, for this

---

[12]Compare Waley's evaluation of his merit as a translator in *BSOAS* 22 (1959): 383-84.

[13]David R. Knechtges, *Wen xuan, or Selections of Refined Literature*, vol. 1 (Princeton: Princeton University Press, 1982), 66-68.

[14]See Richard Walker, "August Pfizmaier's Translations from the Chinese," *JAOS* 69 (1949): 215-23, and the individual contributions in Otto Ladstatter and Sepp Linhart, eds., *August Pfizmaier (1808-1887) und seine Bedeutung für die Ostasienwissenschaften* (Vienna: Austrian Academy of Sciences, 1990).

scholar was more remarkable for the number than for the value of his publications," was the blunt assessment of Cordier.[15] He was, at least, instrumental in purchasing a font of Chinese and Japanese type which, unfortunately, was seldom used in Austria except by himself.

Ferdinand Lessing

Ferdinand Lessing (1882-1961) is the first true German expatriate sinologist to be treated here.[16] He studied both law and oriental languages at the University of Berlin under F.W.K. Müller, and worked at the ethnological museum in Berlin until he was twenty-five. In 1907 he went to China and stayed for seventeen years. After teaching at the Peking School of Interpreters, he became professor at the German-Chinese College in Tsingtao, later moving to Peking University and then to the Igaku shoin in Mukden. Along with Wilhelm Othmer he authored the most widely utilized primer of Chinese for German speakers.[17] Back in Germany, he taught at the Berlin seminar before returning to China to pursue research on Buddhist iconography and Lamaism. In 1926 he earned his doctorate from Friedrich-Wilhelms-Universität in Berlin with a thesis called *Vergleich der wichtigsten Formwörter der chinesischen Umgangssprache und der Schriftsprache.* From 1930 to 1933 he participated in Sven Hedin's Sino-Swedish Expedition. After a short visit to Germany, he accepted an invitation to come to the University of California at Berkeley in 1935 as Agassiz Professor of Oriental Languages.

Lessing's most important works include *Yung-Ho-Kung: An Iconography of the Lamaist Cathedral in Peking* (Stockholm, 1942), and the

---

[15] *TP* 3 (1892): 561; cf. *TP* 6 (1895): iii.

[16] For his life and work, see Richard Rudolph, "Ferdinand Lessing in memoriam," *OE* 9 (1962):1-5; Alexander Wayman, "Ferdinand Diederich Lessing, 26 February 1882 - 31 December 1961," *AA* 25 (1962):194-97; Hartmut Walravens, "Ergänzungen zum Schriftenverzeichnis von Prof. Ferdinand Lessing," *OE* 22 (1975):49-58 and Walravens, "Ferdinand Lessing (1882-1961)–Vom Museum für Völkerkunde zu Sven Hedin aus den Reiseberichten und dem Briefwechsel," *Jahrbuch Prussischer Kulturbesitz* 1992: 175-98. Dr. Walravens kindly supplied me with copies of his works on Lessing.

[17] *Lehrgang der nordchinesischen Umgangssprache* (Tsingtao: Deutsch-Chinesische Druckerei und Verlagsanstalt, 1912).

unique *Mongolian-English Dictionary* (Berkeley: University of California Press, 1961), which had taken nineteen years of research and collaboration. *Yung-Ho-Kung* was informed not only by his pervasive scholarship but by his rich personal experiences performing the actual duties of a lama in the temple on Wu-t'ai-shan. Unfortunately, the second volume did not make it past the manuscript stage, and four projected volumes never were composed.

Walter Simon

An equally interesting émigré, and much more influential, though in the field of linguistics and pedagogy rather than Buddhology or Mongolian, was Ernst Julius Walter Simon (1893-1981).[18] He was trained in Romance and Classical Philology at the University of Berlin, and received his doctorate with a dissertation on the Judaeo-Spanish dialect of Salonika in 1919. In 1920 he passed the "Higher Library Examination" and became a bibliographer at his alma mater. Before his departure from Berlin in 1936, he had become an established librarian with the rank of *Bibliotheksrat*. But beginning in 1932 he started the study of Chinese with Otto Franke, and would eventually gain expertise in Tibetan and Manchu, and a working ability in Mongolian. He became a coeditor of the *Orientalische Literaturzeitung*, and was made professor in 1932 (*Nichtbeamteter ausserordentlicher Universitätsprofessor*) and took the whole range of Asian philology and linguistics as his field.

Simon was dismissed from his post because of his race in 1935, and left Germany the following year. In 1937 Simon was invited to join the School of Oriental Studies in London as a part-time lecturer, and soon occupied a Readership in his own right. In 1947 he was elected to a Chair of Chinese, and became Acting Head of the Department of the Far East in 1950; he took over leadership of the department in 1952. He retired from

---

[18]For his life and works, see the appreciation by C.R. Bawden, "Ernst Julius Walter Simon," *Proceedings of the British Academy* 67 (1981): 459-77; B. Schindler, "List of Publications by Professor Simon," *AM* 10 (1963): 1-8; and *The Dictionary of National Biography, 1931-1940*, ed. l.G. Wickham Legg (1949; rev ed. Oxford: Oxford University Press, 1975), 338-39.

his Chair of Chinese in 1960, and died in 1981. Despite the invitation to assume the Chair of Sinology at the University of Berlin in 1946 and the chance to succeed Gustav Haloun in the Chinese Chair at Cambridge around the same time, Simon loyally remained in the employ of the School that had given him refuge, and in which he had served the war effort by training intelligence officers in Chinese.

His chief publication outlet was *Asia Major*, which he helped edit as member of the board, serving as chief editor from 1964 to 1975, and in which he published a series of grammatical and lexicographical studies.[19] His endless patter about the particle *erh* 而 at dinner parties, spelled in the *Gwoyeu Romatzyh* system that he championed as *erl*, earned him the sobriquet of "Erlkönig" among his friends.

His pupil Denis Twitchett places Simon's studies of the early stages of the Chinese language second only to those of Karlgren.[20] Maspero lent his work qualified endorsement: "Simon…has published interesting works on ancient Chinese which always contain remarks of value, even when the general conclusions are not acceptable."[21] Maspero regarded Simon's monograph on Sino-Tibetan linguistics, *Tibetische-Chinesische Wortlgleichungen, ein Versuch* (Berlin-Leipzig, 1930), as embodying pathfinding research with, alas, premature conclusions. Nevertheless, he concludes his review with the encouraging words that, "Even if one does not accept the majority of the results, it is impossible to render justice to the considerable effort this article represents."[22] Manchu, Tibetan, and pedagogy were additional fields to profit from this same enthusiastic and assiduous research.[23] His main contributions to the growth of British

---

[19]Representative are "Bih 比 ' = Wei 為 '?", *BSOAS* 12 (1947-48): 789-802; "Der Erl Jiann 得 而 見 and Der Jiann 得見 in *Luenyeu* 論語 VII,25," *AM* 2 (1951): 46-67; "Functions and Meanings of *Erl* 而, 1: *Erl* in Conditional Sentences," *AM* 2 (1951): 179-202; "Functions and Meanings of Erl 而, Part IV," *AM* 4 (1954): 20-35.

[20]Denis Twitchett, *Land Tenure and the Social Order in T'ang and Sung China* (London: Oxford University Press, 1962), 13.

[21]Maspero, *Journal Asiatique* 13th ser. 1 (1933-42): 74.

[22]Ibid., 79.

[23]See, *inter alia*, *Manchu Books in London: A Union Catalogue* (London: British Museum Publications, 1977) (with Howard G. H. Nelson); and *Tibetische-Chinesische*

sinology came less from his numerous but unsystematized publications than from his assiduous and unremitting effort to build up the Chinese language program at the School of Oriental Studies, both during the war and afterwards. His many publications of Chinese textbooks and teaching materials fulfilled an early interest in pedagogy, and were widely used at the time; still useful is his *A Beginner's Chinese-English Dictionary* (London: Lund Humphrics and Co., 1947). He is especially honored for his vision as Department Head in expanding the scope of areas studied to include Korea, Mongolia, and Tibet. "Indeed," concludes Bowden, "The Department of the Far East at the School of Oriental and African Studies, as it exists today, over twenty years after Simon's retirement, is essentially his creation, even if its shape has been modified in detail and it has sustained some unrepaired loss."[24]

Gustav Haloun

One final German scholar to take refuge in England matched his counterparts in classics with the same fortunate combination of technique and humanism. This brilliant man was Gustav Haloun (1898-1951).[25] Born in what was then part of Austria, Haloun trained under von Rosthorn at Vienna and Conrady at Leipzig. After teaching in Halle and Göttingen, where he conducted a sinological seminar and built up an impressive library, he emigrated to England, replacing the retired A.C. Moule at Cambridge.

His command of classical Chinese was impressively broad. He was among the few Western sinologists of the times to gain a wide acquaintance with bronze inscriptions, which, together with his grasp of paleography and historical phonology, lent tremendous weight to his interpretations of early texts. The hundreds of etymological suggestions and corrections

---

Wortgleichungen: Ein Versuch (1929), Abt. 1 (Berlin and Leipzig, 1930), 72 pages.

[24]Bowden, "Ernst Julius Walter Simon," 471.

[25]For a brief biography, critical appraisal, and bibliography, see Herbert Franke, "Gustav Haloun (1898-1951) In Memoriam," *ZDMG* 102 (1952): 1-9; see also E.B. Ceadel, "Published Works of the Late Professor Gustav Haloun (12 Jan. 1898-24 Dec. 1951)," *AM*, n.s. 11.1 (1952): 107-08.

scribbled on the pages of his copy of Karlgren's *Analytical Dictionary* would be a distinct service to sinology were they made widely accessible.[26]

His expertise in traditional bibliography was matched only by Pelliot, and his technical sophistication in textual criticism even surpassed that of the French master. It is in his handling of the science of textual criticism that Haloun made his most enduring contribution to sinology and its methodologies. But the long neglect by Western sinologists of textual criticism warrants a closer look into its history and use.[27]

The Discipline of Textual Criticism

The importance of textual criticism has long been appreciated among classical scholars of ancient Greek and Latin, who have worked assiduously to produce critical editions to form the foundation of the analytical studies of other disciplines. Textual recension began in the third century B.C. with the Greek scholars in the great library at Alexandria. Of more than antiquarian interest, the techniques of textual criticism that were developed there helped them win out in their intense rivalry with the librarians of Pergamom, who had somehow obtained superb editions of previously lost works; only textual studies by the sober Alexandrian scholars enabled them to expose the fraudulent productions of the Pergamoms.[28] In Byzantium, apart from the classical tradition, textual criticism preserved the veracity of sacred writings against interpolations

---

[26]See Pulleyblank, *Studia Serica Bernhard Karlgren Dedicata*, 184, n. 1, for another example of the value of Haloun's marginalia, this time on a copy of von der Gabelentz's grammar.

[27]The following section is based in part on David B. Honey, "Philology, Filiation, and Bibliography in the Textual Criticism of the *Huainanzi* (review article)," *Early China* 19 (1994): 161-92.

[28]Canfora, *The Vanished Library: A Wonder of the Ancient World*, 45-50, presents a very learned though disconnected discussion, in a popular format, of the rivalry between the centers of textual criticism and allegorical interpretation that seems very similar, in certain aspects, to the Han debate between the Old Text and New Text schools or the later methodological competition between Han versus Song learning. The rise and development of textual scholarship in Alexandria is treated in depth by Pfeiffer, *History of Classical Scholarship*, vol. I, Part Two, "The Hellenistic Age."

and even forgeries supporting theological deviation or heresy.[29]

The rise of textual criticism in modern times can be traced to Franciscus Petrarch (1304-1374), who began collating manuscripts, recording variant readings, and suggesting emendations.[30] Lorenzo Valla (1407-57) was probably the first professional philologist, even if Angelo Poliziano (1454-94) was most likely the first professional textual critic.[31] An early articulation of the principles at work is the *Ars critica* (1697) of Jean Le Clerc (Clericus, 1657-1736). Among his various "laws" of textual criticism is the famous Law V: *difficilior lectio potior.*[32] The English classicist Richard Bentley (1662-1742) led the way to a new scientific approach to textual criticism;[33] the Bentleian school spread to both Holland and Germany, opening the way for Karl Lachmann (1793-1851). For the terms "recension" and "emendation," and to a large part the entire stemmatic method in its maturest manifestation, are themselves due to Lachmann's working example; his critical edition of Lucretius was, according to Wilamowitz, "the book from which we all have learnt critical method and which every student is required to ponder."[34]

In China, the tradition of textual criticism, defined as the effort to authenticate, establish, and present texts, arose in China after the burning

---

[29]See N.G. Wilson, *Scholars of Byzantium* (Baltimore: Johns Hopkins University Press, 1983), 68.

[30]On Petrarch's work as a textual critic, consult Pfeiffer, *History of Classical Scholarship*, 2:3-16.

[31]Grafton, *Joseph Scaliger, vol. 1: Textual Criticism and Exegesis*, 9-44; see the individual treatments of Valla and Poliziano at Pfeiffer, *History of Classical Scholarship*, 2:35-41; 42-46.

[32]E.J. Kenney, *The Classical Text: Aspects of Editing in the Age of the Printed Book* (Berkeley and Los Angeles: University of California Press, 1974), 43.

[33]Brink, *English Classical Scholarship*, 21-83.

[34]Wilamowitz-Moellendorff, *History of Classical Scholarship*, 131. This work is centered on surveying the producers and products of medieval textual criticism directed towards the sources of the classical world. Lachmann's scientific contributions are treated most thoroughly in Harald Weigel, *Carl Lachmann und die Entstehung der wissenschaftlichen Edition* (Freiburg: Verlag Rombach, 1989). For a superlative study of a textual critic seminal in the development of the method, see the work of Grafton on Joseph Scaliger noted above.

of the books by Ch'in Shih Huang-ti in 213 B.C. . Indeed, according to Charles S. Gardner, "it may be claimed without exaggeration that textual criticism has absorbed much of the attention of the best Chinese scholars from the second century before Christ to our own day."[35] This traditional occupation with texts culminated in Ch'ing *chiao-k'an-hsüeh* 校勘學 , which, at base, was the study of collating manuscripts to produce authoritative editions.[36] A branch of the *k'ao-cheng* 考証 movement that was often closely associated with the revival of Han Learning that emerged most maturely in the Ch'ien-lung period, *chiao-k'an-hsüeh* saw the beginnings of the closest thing to critical editions in Chinese scholarship.

The collation of manuscripts had been undertaken early in imperial China, beginning most notably with the work of Liu Hsiang 劉向 (c. 79-c. 6 B.C.) and his son Liu Hsin 歆 (c. 50 B.C.-A.D. 23) during the Han.[37] Colophons of books published from the Sung period on frequently mention, as a matter of course, the care taken to collate various editions of the work being published, regardless of whether this was so or not.[38] But, despite this heritage and the pioneering work of the Southern Sung polymath Wang Ying-lin 王應麟 (1223-1296),[39] it was the emergence of

---

[35]Gardner, *Chinese Traditional Historiography*, 18. Chapter Three of this excellent monograph is entirely devoted to textual criticism.

[36]For recent surveys of this discipline, see Chiang Po-ch'ien, *Chiao-ch'ou mu-lu-hsüeh tsuan-yao* (1946; rpt. Taipei: Cheng-chung shu-chü, 1957) and Tai Nan-ai, *Chiao-k'an-hsüeh kai-lun* (Sian: Shansi jen-min ch'u-pan-she, 1986).

[37]For the bibliographical and collation activities of the two Lius, see the entries by Jeffrey Riegel and Timoteus Pokora in *The Indiana Companion to Traditional Chinese Literature*, ed. William H. Nienhauser, Jr., et al. (Bloomington: Indiana University Press, 1986), 583-86; P. van der Loon, "On the Transmission of the Kuan-Tzu," *TP* 41 (1952): 358-366; and Ch'ien Mu, "Liu Hsiang/Hsin fu-tzu nien-p'u," *Ku-shih pien* (rpt. Shanghai: Shanghai ku-chi ch'u-pan-she, 1982), 5:101-248; this last work has been republished in *Liang-Han ching-hsüeh ku-chin-wen p'ing-i* (Taipei: San-min shu-chü, 1971).

[38]See Ming-Sun Poon, "The Printer's Colophon in Sung China, 960-1279," *Library Quarterly* 43 (1973): 39-52.

[39]Credit is given to Wang as the pioneer whose works paved the way for later Ch'ing textual critics by Jeffrey K. Riegel, "Some Notes on the Ch'ing Reconstruction of Lost Pre-Han Philosophical Works," *Selected Papers in Asian Studies 1* (Albuquerque, 1976), 180, n. 1. For an introduction to Wang Ying-lin and a list of relevant studies, see the entry by C. Bradford Langley in *The Indiana Companion to Traditional Chinese*

Ch'ing dynasty scholars such as Sun Hsing-yen 孫星衍 (1753-1818) and Lu Wen-ch'ao 盧文弨 (1717-96) and their concern to provide the best textual basis for the new learning that harnessed collation and textual reconstruction to the traditional endeavors of Confucian classical exegetes.[40] Among nineteenth-century collators of lost texts, mention must be made of Ma Kuo-han 馬國翰 (1794-1857) and Yen K'o-chün 嚴可均 (1765-1837).[41] And, of course, textual criticism continued among scholars who were concerned to establish the best documentary foundation for existing works by carefully re-editing received versions, through collating other editions such as incunabula or rare and manuscript editions, as well as fragmentary passages preserved in encyclopedias and other compendia.[42]

Critical editions of a sort are produced by modern Chinese and Japanese scholars for various Chinese texts, especially philosophical ones. These usually consist of the printing of a standard "base" text, with an exhaustive listing and discussion of variora and textual commentary, and are called *chi-shih* 集釋 , *chi-chieh* * 解 "collected explanations" or

---

Literature, 882-84. See further K.T. Wu, "Chinese Printing Under Four Alien Dynasties," *HJAS* 13 (1950): 470-71, for the complicated history of the printing of Wang Ying-lin's major works, the *Yü-hai* 玉海 and the *K'un-hsüeh chi-wen* 困學紀聞 .

[40]See Benjamin A. Elman, *From Philosophy to Philology: Intellectual and Social Aspects of Change in Late Imperial China*, (Cambridge, Mass.: Council on East Asian Studies, Harvard Univ., 1984), 37-85, for the rise of *k'ao-cheng-hsüeh*; see 68-70 for textual reconstruction and collation.

[41]For the work of these scholars and their confreres on reconstructing philosophical texts, see Riegel, "Some Notes on the Ch'ing Reconstruction of Lost Pre-Han Philosophical Works," and Arthur Hummel, ed. *Eminent Chinese of the Ch'ing (Period 1644-1912)*, 2 vols. (Washington: United States Government Printing Office, 1943), 1:557-58; 2:910-12.

[42]An excellent example of textual treatment of this sort is provided by Hu Shih, "A Note on Ch'üan Tsu-Wang, Chao I-Ch'ing and Tai Chen: A Study of Independent Convergence in Research as Illustrated in Their Works on the *Shui-Ching Chu*," in *Eminent Chinese of the Ch'ing Period*, 2:970-982. The history and methodology of textual criticism on historical documents is treated by Gardner, "Textual Criticism," in *Chinese Traditional Historiography*, 18-63, and Chang Shun-hui, *Chung-kuo ku-tai shih-chi chiao-tu-fa* (1962; rpt. Shanghai: Shanghai ku-chi, 1980).

something similar.[43]   Some historical texts have been treated in this manner, most notably the monumental edition of the *Shih-chi* by Takigawa Kametarō 瀧川龜太 , and the well-known work of Wang Hsien-ch'ien 王先謙 on the *Han-shu* and *Hou Han-shu*. Probably the closest China came to producing modern critical editions are the texts established for the Harvard-Yenching Institute Sinological Index Series from 1932 to 1951. Out of sixty-four titles in history, literature, philosophy, historical geography, and bibliography, twenty-three of them had new texts established, punctuated, and variora noted.[44] Sinology in this strict sense, according to Denis Twitchett, "is in the last analysis the traditional discipline of textual criticism and 'philology' applied to Chinese literature....This discipline is the irreducible essential in the training of a scholar who is to deal professionally with China's past."[45]

This enterprise has not, however, save for occasional exceptions, caught on in the still nascent tradition of Western sinology, which seems to have skipped a stage in the evolution of scholarship. According to Paul Thompson, "we show rather signs of affecting the luxury of anti-philological attitudes, to which we, unlike our Europeanist colleagues, have not earned the right. Until we have mended our texts and trimmed them well, no amount of aesthetic intuition or statistical method will move the study of Chinese antiquity out of the doldrums in which it has languished so long."[46]

---

[43]On the use of this base-text among modern Chinese textual critics, consult Kuan Pu-hsün, "Chiao-k'an ti-pen tsa-t'an," *Ku-chi cheng-li yen-chiu t'ung-hsün* 10 (1994): 18-20.

[44]For this series, inspired and directed by William Hung, see Susan Chan Egan, *A Latter-day Confucian: Reminiscences of William Hung (1893-1980)* (Cambridge, Mass.: Council on East Asian Studies, Harvard University, 1987), 140-45.

[45]Twitchett, "A Lone Cheer for Sinology," 110.

[46]Paul Thompson, *The Shen Tzu Fragments* (Oxford: 1979), xvii. For textual criticism by occidental sinologists, see Gardner, "Textual Criticism," in *Chinese Traditional Historiography*, 18-68; Thompson, *The Shen Tzu Fragments*; William G. Boltz, "Textual Criticism and the Ma Wang tui *Lao tzu* (review article)," *HJAS* 44 (1984): 185-224; Boltz, "Textual Criticism *More Sinico*," *Early China* 20 (1995): 393-405; and Harold David Roth, *The Textual History of the "Huai-nan Tzu"* (Ann Arbor: Association for Asian Studies, 1992).

Haloun and The Critical Edition

Haloun's mature command of this discipline, characterized by Denis Twitchett as "a most rigorous conception of textual criticism,"[47] set it upon a firm methodological foundation, even if his example has seldom been followed. His skill is manifested in the main by a series of articles in *Asia Major* devoted to reconstituting the texts of scattered philosophical fragments; in these articles he supplied the first examples in sinological circles, East or West, of a critical apparatus for such reconstructions.[48] Haloun developed an original format, with subdivisions of reconstituted text, parallel passages, and critical apparatus including rhymes, all on a single page, placing the translation and commentary on the facing page. He even included a *stemma* or genealogical tree diagram positing the filiation of editions, and anticipated Boodberg by six years in the use of colometry in parsing classical Chinese passages. But of course he was merely drawing on his classical education, for the format he adopted recalls the work of another German refugee scholar then at Oxford, namely Rudolf Pfeiffer's great edition of *Callimachus*.

Haloun's papers are on deposit at the Cambridge University Library. Perhaps the most important item is a nineteen-page manuscript entitled "Chinese Textual Criticism" (see Appendix A, #6). It is the script of a lecture written in a very small hand in German. The miniature hand and the use of an idiosyncratic system of romanization make difficult reading, even for native speakers. In general, it is concerned with setting forth the main principles of Chinese textual criticism, teaching reverence for the text, and the need to establish principles of procedures for the systematic authentication of texts. To this end, after a lengthy preamble,

---

[47]Twitchett, *Land Tenure and the Social Order in T'ang and Sung China*, 12. Cf. Herbert Franke, *Sinology at German Universities*, 18: "The editions of early Confucian texts by Gustav Haloun..., in which for the first time, one may say, the methods of philological textual criticism and editorship were applied by a Western scholar to an old Chinese text, bear witness to great exactitude of textual criticism."

[48]"Fragmente des Fu-Tsi und des Ts'in-tsi," *AM* 8 (1932): 437-518; "Das Ti-Tsi-Ts'i: Frühkonfucianische Fragmente II," *AM* 9 (1933): 467-502; "Einige Berichtigungen und Nachträge zum Ti-Tsi-Tsi und zum Fu-Tsi," *AM* 10 (1935): 247-50; and "Legalist Fragments, Part I: Kuan-tsi 55 and Related Texts," *AM* n.s. 2 (1951): 85-120.

Haloun isolates nine principles that must be observed, concrete steps that must be followed in conducting textual criticism in Chinese sources. These include the importance of the phonological shape of suspected words, including rhyming patterns; the graphological derivation of variants from earlier forms, including the cursive styles which obtain in handwritten manuscripts; grammatical considerations; metrical analysis, and the like.

Item #13, Lecture Course 3: "*Li-chi*, 'Ju-hsing' chapter," is Haloun's attempt to present a maximum of textual information in a compact apparatus and translation meant for his students, for all of his work with texts was designed to assist readers of the text. It consists of two facing pages. The first page includes the text of two editions written out in parallel lines, one below the other, to isolate more easily the variants. Such variants are discussed in the margins. The facing page contains three parallel horizontal lines: the reconstituted text is above; below is a transcription in Mandarin; last comes a translation in German. Roughly the same format is followed by all of the lecture courses listed in Appendix A. Such an apparatus would, inevitably in the course of holding class, teach the basics of working closely with texts.

Item #18, "*Shih-chi* Book Seven," presents a translation of the biography of Hsiang Yü. Of note, however, is the fact that Haloun marks all instances where the text of the *Han-shu* differs from the *Shih-chi*. He generally give the reason for adopting one reading over the other; examples are one reading "sounds wrong," or "seems better;" one reading "corrects" another reading, or is a "stylistic correction," or "corrects the orthography;" it may even be judged to be a "superfluous" reading. On the basis of comparing all variants between the texts of the *Shih-chi* and *Han-shu* versions of this biography, Haloun comes down firmly on the side of the *Han-shu* as preserving the best text. He even goes so far as to make the following bold statement: "All *Shih-chi* additions [are] obvious glosses (p. 5)." In fact, after preparing Item # 49, "The Biography of Chang Ch'ien," Haloun makes the reasonable suggestion that perhaps this portion of the *Han-shu* version of the "Memoir on the Western Regions" preserves an early draft of the *Shih-chi*.[49]

Item # 51, "The Life of Huan Kung," demonstrates that, even when preparing a text for his own research interests rather than for teaching purposes, Haloun would go to the trouble of undertaking a two-stage study of any passage or text. First, he would lay out the text in parallel lines, one above the other, then note all of the variora in the right-hand margin. Second, he would prepare a critical edition, that is, a reconstituted text with accompanying apparatus that incorporated and commented on all of the data isolated in the first stage. The same careful philological preparation was behind the assertions of the priority of the present-day text of the *Han-shu*. Even when he was examining texts from the parallel traditions, Haloun would take the same philological trouble. For instance, in Item #49 mentioned above, when Haloun examined the text of the *Han-chi* he provided a full textual apparatus of variants to buttress his translation.

Haloun's text-critical work went far beyond his own published or manuscript offerings, however, as he contributed fundamentally to the research of other Orientalists such as Waley, Maenchen-Helfen, Bailey, and Minorsky, by preparing reconstituted texts of selected chapters of canonical and philosophical sources for their use. The gratitude of Arthur Waley may be taken as emblematic of all who benefitted from Haloun's generosity: "I am deeply indebted to Professor Gustav Haloun...who not only put at my disposal the resources of the splendid Chinese library which has been formed at Göttingen under his care, but also directed my studies...." Waley in fact dedicated his translation of the *Shih-ching* to Haloun, and renewed it in the preface to the second edition with a generous admission of indebtedness: "In the preface to the first edition I spoke of my deep debt of gratitude to Gustav Haloun, who shortly afterwards became Professor of Chinese at Cambridge and died there in 1951. The book was (and still is) dedicated to him. In a sense it is his book

---

[49]My own work has supported the general textual priority of the *Han-shu* over the *Shih-chi* in the case of Han-period accounts; see "Ssu-ma Ch'ien's Hsiung-nu *logos*: A Textcritical Study," *Chinese Literature: Essays, Articles, Reviews* 21 (1999): 67-97.

as well as mine."[50] (Haloun, like Sir Walter Scott, died of overwork, but from teaching rather than writing.)

Based on such a philological foundation, Haloun's more humanistic studies attained an authority rarely acknowledged in the field, and included a variety of wide-ranging historical, anthropological, and religious syntheses. Chief among them are works on the Chinese knowledge of the early Indo-Europeans,[51] ancient clan-settlements,[52] Manicheanism,[53] and Later Han history.[54] His success in analyzing early Chinese clans elicited the following endorsement from Wolfram Eberhard: "Haloun's work on clan settlement was perhaps the most original and promising of all these studies, but after his emigration to England he could not continue his work and found no successors."[55]   An early offering in 1925, "Die Rekonstruktion der chinesischen Urgeschichte durch die Chinesen,"[56] perhaps best epitomizes Haloun's blend of philological analysis and historical synthesis by combining a linguistic approach for an historiographic *cum* ethnological aim: how the Chinese "reconstructed" their early history from earlier myths, legends, and folk-tales. The ouevre of this great man, the first professionally trained sinologist to take a chair in England, would honor any up-to-date social historian, and therefore belies the controversy between old-fashioned philology, so called, and the

---

[50]Arthur Waley, *The Book of Songs* (1937; rpt. New York: Grove Press, 1960), prefaces. Cf. Franke, "Gustav Haloun," 7, for Haloun's collaboration with other scholars.

[51]*Seit wann kannten die Chinesen die Tocharer oder Indogermanen überhaupt* (Leipzig, 1926). Franke, *Sinology at German Universities*, 23, characterizes this work as a "compendium of ancient Chinese ideas about geography, difficult to read, but rewarding the patient reader with countless ideas and hints." And of course, it also contains much text-critical work.

[52]"Beiträge zur Siedlungsgeschichte chinesischer Clans, I: Der Clan Feng," *Asia Major* (1923): 165-81; "Contributions to the History of Clan Settlements in Ancient China, I," *AM* 1 (1924): 76-101; 587-623.

[53]"The Compendium of the Doctrines and Styles of the Teaching of Mani, the Buddha of Light," *AM* n.s. 3 (1952): 184-212 (with W.B. Henning).

[54]"The Liang-Chou Rebellion, 184-221.A.D," *AM* n.s. 1 (1950): 119-32.

[55]*JAOS* 95 (1975): 522.

[56]*Japanisch-deutsche Zeitschrift für Wissenschaft und Technik* 3 (Berlin, 1925): 243-70. Cf. the review by Henri Maspero, *JA* 11th ser. (1927): 142-44.

new-fangled opportunism, again so called, of the social sciences.

With the careers of these two expatriates, we have sketched the development of German philology from its first fumbling steps in the nineteenth century, through the heady days of the Weimar Republic, and during the rise of National Socialism. The unhappy rise of Hitler created the existence of the refugee sinologist. And in Great Britain, all of these refugee scholars, most prominently Walter Simon and Gustav Haloun, created the "first breath of new life" in sinology in Great Britain, a wave of German influence on scholarship that paralleled an earlier scholarly wave of Germanic classical scholarship. "Their arrival was shortly followed by the outbreak of war, which necessitated the rapid improvisation of programmes for teaching modern Chinese and Japanese intensively on an unprecedented scale," concludes Denis Twitchett.[57] C.R. Bawden regards Simon and Haloun as the first professional British sinologists. His reasons are worth revealing at length:

> It is no exaggeration to evaluate Simon, along with Gustav Haloun, as one of the founders of modern, professional British sinology. To do so is not to denigrate his predecessors at the three great universities, Cambridge, Oxford, and London....Right up to the time of the Second World War, British sinology had remained, broadly speaking, the preserve of distinguished amateurs, the province of men who, after retiring from active life, and often brilliant careers in the East as government servants or missionaries, occupied their latter years in the pursuit of what remained exotic studies, outside the mainstream of university life. There was no academic tradition, in the sense of a continuing line of masters and pupils....Brilliant scholars there were indeed....But for one reason or another, personal disinclination or the absence of a supportive climate of opinion, they

---

[57]Twitchett, review of Barrett, *Singular Listlessness*, in *Journal of the Royal Asiatic Society* series 3, 5.2 (1995): 247. For the development of a post-World War II school of British sinology more along the disciplinarial and institutional lines of the Area Studies movement in the U.S., see Michael McWilliam, "Knowledge and Power: Reflections on National Interest and the Study of Asia," *Asian Affairs* 26 (1995): 33-46.

did not, and could not, found schools.   To have done this was Simon's merit.[58]

The story of British sinology that held sway before this flurry of war-inspired effort that led to the schools founded by Simon and Haloun, is the theme of the next two chapters.

---

[58]Bawden, "Ernst Julius Walter Simon," 475.

APPENDIX A: HALOUN PAPERS, CAMBRIDGE UNIVERSITY LIBRARY
ADD 7575 (B)

Box 1: Lectures 1-10; Lecture Courses 1-7

1. Lecture 1: "Chinese Script." Given to Oriental Ceramic Society, 2 February, 1944.
2. Lecture 2: "The Beginnings of Chinese History."
3. Lecture 3: "Some Early Relations of China with the West."
4. Lecture 4: "Entwicklung Des Gottesdankens im alten China." 19 pp.
5. Lecture 5: "The Chinese Language." In German.
6. Lecture 6: "Chinese Textual Criticism." In German.
7. Lecture 7: "Die Rassen Ostturkestans." In German. Ethnographic Institute at Leipzig.
8. Lecture 8: "Das Tocharerproblem." In German.
9. Lecture 9: "Chinese and Indo-Europeans." In German. Halle, 1927.
10. Lecture 10:"Early Relations Between East and West Asia." In German.
11. Lecture Course 1: "Chinese Grammar Particles."
12. Lecture Course 2: "*Chung-Yung*."
13. Lecture Course 3: "*Li-chi*, 'Ju-hsing' chapter."
15. Lecture Course 4: "*Hsün-Tzu*, Chapter 23."
16. Lecture Course 5: "*Chuang-Tzu*" Chapters 1, 17, and 2."
17. Lecture Course 6: "*Lun-Yü*, Books III to VII."
18. Lecture Course 7: "*Shih-chi*, Book 7."

Box 2: Lecture Courses (cont.)

19. Lecture Course 8: "*Meng-Tzu*, IA, IIIA, VIA and Misc."
20. Lecture Course 9: "*Mo-Tzu*, 14, 15, and 16."
21. Lecture Course 10: "Li-Sao."
22. Lecture Course 11: "Chinese Religion." In German.
23. Lecture Course 12: "Early Chinese History." In German.
24. Lecture Course 13: "The Earliest Period in Chinese History."
25. Lecture Course 14: "Chinese Institutions." In German.
26. Lecture Course 15: "Historical Development of the Chinese Language."
27. Lecture Course 16: "Chinese Grammar."

28. Lecture Course 17: "Miscellaneous Notes." [on grammar; appended to item #27 above, but separately (mis-)numbered]

Box 3
28. 1. "Sven Hedin Documents, 15, 16."
29. 2. "Materials For Prof. Minorsky's Book 'Marvazī.'"
30. 3. "Notes for Prof. Henning's Article 'Date of the Early Sogdian Letter.'"
31. Lecture Course 17: "Word Formation in Chinese" [numbered 17 despite existence of lecture course 17 listed above]
32. Lecture Course 18: "Sino-Tibetan Language Group."
33. Lecture Course 15: "Stress in Chinese" [misnumbered]
34. Lecture Course 14: "Chinese Tones." [misnumbered]
35. Lecture Course 21: "History of Chinese Phonetics."
36. Lecture Course 22a: "Handbooks on Chinese."
37. Lecture Course 22b: "Handbooks on Chinese Phonetic System."
38. Lecture Course 23: "Chinese Script."

Box 4: Articles, Notes, Etc.
39. 4A: "*Kuan-Tzu*, 49"
40. 4B: "*Kuan-Tzu*, 49"
41. 4C. "*Kuan-Tzu*, 49"
42. 5: "Legalist Fragments, 2 and 3: Shen Pu-Hai and Shen Tao."
43. 6: "*Hua-I I-Yü*."
44. 6 (cont.): "Letters to and by Haloun concerning *Hua-I I-Yü*
45. Letter from Gordon H. Luce, 6 Feb., 1945." It thanks Haloun for photostats and a "useful letter" concerning Chinese texts on Old Burma.
46. 7A: "*I-Chou-Shu*."
47. 7B: "Notes on Yü Yüeh."
48. 8: "Legends of the Great Yü (the Flood Legend)."
49. 9: "The Biography of Chang Ch'ien."

Box 5: Articles, Notes, Etc.
50. "Articles, Notes, Etc. II: The Blondies." [Wu-sun]
51. "Articles, Notes, Etc. 10: The Life of Huan Kung."

Box 6

52. List of eighty-three names to send copies to of "Zur Üe-tsï-Frage," *ZDMG* 91 (1937):243-318. All of the big names of sinology in UK, Europe, China, Japan, and Russia are included. Only forty-nine names are checked-off, though. A shorter list is found with a bound copy of "Das Ti-Tsi-Ts'i: Frühkonfucianische Fragmente II," *AM* 9 (1933): 467-502.

PART FOUR. ENGLISH-SPEAKING SCHOLARS: FROM CHINA COAST SINOLOGY TO CHINESE STUDIES

"The study of the Chinese language is a matter eminently suited to one of the world's greatest universities, where there have been cultivated the highest standards of scholarship. At such an institution and in such an atmosphere there can be truly appreciated the scholarly culture of a country such as China. A great university would indeed be incomplete unless it offers the opportunity for the study of the world's greatest cultures in their own languages. Chinese scholarly productions must, moreover, be made available to the rest of the world."
—Homer H. Dubs, *China: The Land of Humanistic Scholarship*[1]

7. THE BRITISH TRIUMVIRATE: MORRISON, WYLIE, AND GILES

British sinology developed during the nineteenth century out of the efforts of a pair of Scottish Protestant missionaries, James Legge and Alexander Wylie, both born in 1815, as distinguished in their spheres of spiritual and intellectual action as were an earlier pair of Scots in mercantilism, William Jardine and James Matheson. Legge and Wylie were also both highly esteemed for their personal qualities. Robert Morrison, himself born of Scottish parents in Northumberland, was the pioneer of British Protestant missionaries; he set Chinese lexicography on firm ground for the nineteenth century. American sinology had a similar missionary heritage and a successor to Morrison in Chinese lexicography in the person of Samuel Wells Williams.[2] But both camps were equally indebted to the mercantile and diplomatic corps resident abroad, who had established official ties and who had built up the Western presence in the treaty ports. Of all these competing interest groups, initially only the

---

[1]*China, The Land of Humanistic Scholarship: An Inaugural Lecture Delivered before the University of Oxford on 23 February 1948* (Oxford: Clarendon Press, 1949), 23.

[2]A convenient entre into the progress of British and American missionary efforts in China is *Comparative Chronology of Protestantism in Asia 1792-1945* (Tokyo: Institute of Asian Cultural Studies, International Christian University, 1984).

167

missionaries sought to learn the language in order to communicate with the Chinese and to proselytize among them. Diplomats with both expertise in Chinese and the inclination for research, such as Herbert Giles and W.W. Rockhill, came later.[3]

Early British Missionaries and Diplomats

"By the law of China it was forbidden that any Chinese should teach 'barbarians' the language of the Flowery Land. Thus it happened that from the earliest times the English traders were at the mercy of those Chinese who professed to have a sufficient knowledge of some Foreign language to enable them to act as interpreters. This class...was known as the linguists.*"*
—Eames, *The English in China*.[4]

English contacts with China commenced in the seventeenth century. Inspired by the success of the Dutch trading ventures in the Indies, the London merchants successfully petitioned the Crown for exclusive rights to trade with India and the East. They were granted a fifteen-year charter in December of 1600, and in 1609 King James I renewed the grant in perpetuity. This mercantile association, originally called "The Governor and Company of Merchants of London trading into the East Indies," incorporated itself in 1612, and became known as the East India Company. It retained its monopoly on trade in the East until 1833, in name if not always in practice. For instance, the first English trade mission to China, an expedition organized by Sir William Courteenes under the direction of Captain John Weddell, was made by a rival association. Embarking on April 14, 1636, the flotilla of four vessels arrived off Canton at Lantao on June 25, 1637.[5] We are fortunate that among its crew was one Peter Mundy, a merchant with a keen eye and a

---

[3]For nineteenth-century developments that fostered sinological studies in the West by the English and Americans, see Kenneth Scott Latourette, *A History of Christian Missions in China* (New York: Macmillan, 1929); and Jerome Ch'en, *China and the West: Society and Culture 1815-1937* (London: Hutchinson, 1979).

[4]James Bromley Eames, *The English in China* (London: Curzon Press, 1909), 82.

[5]Eames, *The English in China*, 12-13; for the historical background to the East India company, see 1-44; and Chang I-tung, "The Earliest Contacts Between China and England," *Chinese Studies in History and Philosophy* 1 (1968): 53-78.

sense of history; his diary is a valuable account of the English contact with the East at this time.[6]   Political maneuvering behind the scenes by rival merchants, civil war in England and China, and the hostility of the Dutch and Portuguese caused a hiatus of several decades in English attempts to establish trade with China.   Then in 1673 a squadron of merchant vessels reached Formosa, off the coast of China, and initiated trade with Koxinga both on his island bastion and in his port of Amoy on the mainland.   But this ended with the conquest of Taiwan by the Ch'ing in 1683.   In 1684 trade was commenced at Amoy, which was now back in the control of Ch'ing authorities.   In 1689, four years after the opening of the port of Canton, the English began sending trading missions there, and in 1699 the Ch'ing court granted them permanent trading privileges.   After 1757, all foreign trade with China, except by the Russians, was limited to Canton until the establishment of the treaty ports in 1842.[7]

England's first diplomatic efforts to establish official relations with China came in a more detached, characteristically lethargic, fashion: both Queen Elizabeth and King James addressed epistles to the Emperor of China.   The English letters of the King did not seem to be any more effective than the Latin missives of the Queen, if they even reached China.[8] The linguistic context of commerce with China in the seventeenth and eighteenth centuries maintained the same misdirected course:

> One of the most striking features of the commercial intercourse between the nations of Europe and the Chinese is, that for more than two centuries it was carried on without any adequate means of communication in the nature of a written or spoken language. In the earliest times the English traders had to use Portuguese in order to

[6]See Sir Richard Carnac Temple, ed., *The Travels of Peter Mundy 1608-1667* (London, 1919).

[7]Eames, *The English in China*, 23-40. Rich documentation of early British trade with China is included in Hosea B. Morse, *The Chronicles of the East India Company Trading to China: 1635-1834*, 5 vols. (London: Oxford University Press, 1924-1929). See also Michael Greenberg, *British Trade and the Opening of China, 1800-1842* (Cambridge: Cambridge University Press, 1951); and William Conrad Costin, *Great Britain and China, 1833-1860* (London: Oxford University Press, 1937).

[8]Eames, *The English in China*, 11; Timothy Barrett, *Singular Listlessness*, 30-32.

make themselves understood, that being the only foreign tongue with which the Chinese could claim any kind of acquaintance.[9]

This reliance on Latin and English instead of Chinese is characteristic of historical English attitudes. It is true that Latin was the learned language of the Jesuits who often acted as interpreters or translators at court. Witness the brief interlude when Ferdinand Verbiest served as translator between the Manchu court and a Russian embassy, when, according to the terms of the Treaty of Nerchinsk, the official languages of exchange were Russian, Manchu, and Latin.[10] But the occasional use of priestly middlemen was symptomatic of English arrogance towards foreign languages in general, and Chinese in particular—the British never saw the need to learn Chinese themselves until the mid-nineteenth century, and then only for the narrow purpose of diplomatic, and occasionally commercial, intercourse. Such a narrow vision of the utility of foreign languages has continued into the twentieth century and affects both the funding and recruiting of Chinese language teaching today in England. This attitude toward practical linguistic competence contrasts strangely with the historical English eagerness to embrace Latin as the language of scholarship and French as the language of culture. Apparently, an urbane knowledge of foreign languages for the sake of sophistication was acceptable in refined circles. China, alas, was not part of this cultural heritage. "China is now one of the most important members of the world community; that it should remain so poorly covered in the British educational system seems highly inadvisable," laments Barrett. "But the roots of the neglect lie very deep."[11] So deep, in fact, that the first large-

---

[9]Eames, *The English in China*, 82. Another early translation medium was Malay; cf. Barrett, *Singular Listlessness*, 33.

[10]For Jesuit mediation at this treaty, see the inside story presented at first-hand in Joseph Sebes, S.J., *The Jesuits and the Sino-Russian Treaty of Nerchinsk (1689): The Diary of Thomas Pereira, S.J.* (Rome: Institutum Historicum S.I., 1961).

[11]Barrett, *Singular Listlessness*, 14. Cf. David Hawkes, *Classical, Modern and Humane*, 3: "To be sure it may seem strange...that a language spoken by nearly a quarter of the world's inhabitants should be studied by only a score or so of people in one of the world's great universities [Oxford]. Such, however, is the case....It is studied by only one-

scale publication on the Chinese language in the West was authored by an Englishman who knew no Chinese![12] It was not until the arrival of the first missionaries on the scene that the imperative need for learning Chinese was realized.

Because of the early neglect of Chinese studies by merchants and diplomats, and the difference between mastering Chinese for interpretation and the study of Chinese for its own sake, the history of British and American sinology, like the earlier Portuguese, Spanish and French, is best told through the story of pioneering missionaries and their language studies.

Robert Morrison and the Scottish Connection

Robert Morrison (1782-1834) was born in Northumberland on January 5, 1782.[13] He was the son of a Scottish Presbyterian elder and shoemaker from Dumferline, Scotland who had been raised as a Scottish

---

fifth of 1 per cent of the undergraduates of this university."

[12]John Webb (1611-72), basing himself on European authorities such as Martino Martini and Nicolas Trigault, composed *An Historical Essay Endeavoring a Probability That the Language of the Empire of China is the Primitive Language* (London, 1669). See Christopher Harbsmeier, "John Webb," in *Europe Studies China*, 297-338.

[13]Sources for the life of Robert Morrison are very numerous. See, *inter alia*, E. Armstrong Morrison, *Memoirs of the Life and Labours of Robert Morrison* (London, 1839); Marshall Broomhill, *Robert Morrison: A Master Builder* (New York: Dolan and Co., 1924); Floyd L. Carr, *Robert Morrison, Protestant Missionary* (New York: Baptist Board of Education, 1925); Lindsay Ride, *Robert Morrison: The Scholar and the Man* (Hong Kong: Hong Kong University Press, 1957); and Phyliss Matthewman, *Robert Morrison* (Grand Rapids: Zondervan House Publishers, 1958). A much abridged survey of his accomplishments is Latourette, *A History of Christian Missions in China*, 210-15. Donald W. Treadgold, *The West in Russia and China: Religious and Secular Thought in Modern Times*, vol. 2: *China 1582-1949* (Cambridge: Cambridge University Press, 1973), 38-41, gives him his due for his institutional and translation work without concealing his antipathy for the Chinese as a people. The most recent treatment includes Murray A. Rubinstein, *The Origins of the Anglo-American Missionary Enterprise in China, 1807-1840* (Lanham, Maryland: The Scarecrow Press, 1996), Part One; and Donald M. Lewis, ed., *The Blackwell Dictionary of Evangelical Biography 1730-1860*, 2:795-96. Dr. Barton Starr and Dr. Stephanie Chung, Hong Kong Baptist University, are currently editing the papers of Robert Morrison.

Presbyterian. Robert Morrison experienced a religious conversion still in his youth, and determined to become a minister. Consequently, he studied for two years at the Hoxton Academy before deciding upon the path of a missionary; he then applied to the Missionary Society, the forerunner of the London Missionary Society.[14] In preparation for his mission to China, for which he had the explicit assignment of compiling a dictionary and translating the Bible, he began to study Chinese in London in 1805 with the help of some dictionaries and a Cantonese informant. Upon arrival in Canton in September 1807 he became the first proselytizer for British Protestantism to China, living in Malacca and Canton. Timothy Barrett marks the true beginning of British sinology with Morrison's arrival in Canton.[15] In 1809 Morrison became the Chinese Secretary and Translator to the British East India Company factory.

In 1813 he was joined by a fellow Scotsman, William Milne, who soon began to collaborate with him in his translation work. William Milne (1785-1822) was born near Huntly, Aberdeenshire, the same locale that produced James Legge. His letters and Chinese tracts sent home to the Legge family helped the young James develop an interest in the China mission.[16] Milne's own conversion occurred in 1804. The record of his searching interview upon his ordination reveals the same intense commitment to missionary work and zealous service through translation as Morrison. To the question "How do you purpose to exercise your ministry among the Heathen?" he answered:

> I resolve...to prosecute my studies, in order to attain a greater
> knowledge of the word of God—to pay particular attention to the

---

[14]For the London Missionary Society, see Rubinstein, *The Origins of the Anglo-American Missionary Enterprise in China.*

[15]Barrett, *Singular Listlessness*, 63. Another candidate for the father of English sinology is Sir George Staunton, put forward by Twitchett, *Land Tenure and the Social Order in T'ang and Sung China*, 4. For comparative treatment, see J.L. Cranmer-Byng, "The First English Sinologists, Sir George Staunton and the Reverend Robert Morrison," in *Symposium on Historical Archaeology and Linguistic Studies on Southern China, South-East Asia and The Hong Kong Region* (Hong Kong: Hong Kong University Press, 1967), 247-60.

[16]Wong, *James Legge*, 8-9.

language of heathen....Should it please God to spare me to acquire the language with sufficient accuracy, I purpose to go from house to house, from village to village, from town to town, and from country to country, where access may be gained, in order to preach the Gospel to all who will not turn away their ear from it.

He next turns to a practical bent, perhaps realizing that oral preaching in a country governed by bookish Confucian mandarins was impractical:

As, however, the translation and distribution of the Scriptures forms one great object of the Chinese Mission, to which I am destined by the Directors, I resolve to use every means to attain a more full and critical knowledge of them....[17]

One subsection of Milne's history of the early years of the Chinese mission bears out this focus: section IV contains the heading "Oral instruction not the immediate object of the Chinese Mission."[18]

Milne arrived in Macao in July, 1813, bringing a young wife and infant son in tow. He left after only eight days for Canton on order of the government. Milne rapidly acquired command of the language; after only three months tutoring with Morrison he was on his own;[19] and soon he was able to assist Morrison in translating the Bible. They produced, in fact, the second complete translation of the Bible into Chinese, finished in 1819 but not published until 1823, the year after Milne died. The first translation was by Joshua Marshman in 1822.[20] For this second version

---

[17]*Ordination of The Rev. William Milne, As a Missionary to China, on Thursday, July 16th, 1812. At the Rev. Mr. Griffin's, Portsea* (London, 1812), 16.

[18]William Milne, *A Retrospect of the First Ten Years of the Protestant Mission to China...Accompanied with Miscellaneous Remarks on the Literature, History, and Mythology of China* (Malacca: Anglo-Chinese Mission Press, 1820), 50.

[19]Ibid., 105-7 details Morrison's pedagogical approach, which Milne accepted with alacrity.

[20]Joshua Marshman (1768-1837) was a Baptist missionary who first learned Chinese in Bengal. Along with his Chinese instructor, Joannes Lassar from Macao, he published the first complete translation of the Bible into Chinese at Serampore in 1822. For Marshman and Lassar, see Barrett, *Singular Listlessness*, 61-62. The life of Marshman

Morrison translated thirty-nine books, and Milne supplied the remaining ones. As for most of the New Testament, Morrison revised a manuscript translation that had been found in the British Museum by a Jesuit identified by Jost Oliver Zetzsche as Jean Basset (ca. 1662-1707);[21] Milne describes it as a "Harmony of the Gospels."[22] Alas, posterity, taking a lead from George Chinnery's portrait "Dr. Robert Morrison Translating the Bible," has forgotten Milne's contribution to this collaborative translation.[23]

Milne's short-lived mission was packed with productivity: he published a monthly periodical, the *Indo-Chinese Gleaner*, wrote book reviews, ran the mission press in Penang, was the first principal of Morrison's Anglo-Chinese College, and authored many tracts. The most important one was the notable "Two Friends" pamphlet, which eventually enjoyed a circulation of one million copies.[24] (A copy of this tract was in the Legge family library in Huntley; Legge knew of its existence but apparently did not read it.) Upon Milne's untimely death, Morrison mourned his loss as dearly as he had mourned his wife, for in Milne he lost a kindred spirit: Milne too, had lost his wife in the mission field, had learned Chinese and labored in the mission with the same intense passion as had Morrison.[25]

---

is sketched in Alexander Wylie, *Memorials of Protestant Missionaries to the Chinese* (Shanghai: The Presbyterian Press, 1867), 1-3.

[21]"The Bible in China: History of the *Union Version* or the Culmination of Protestant Missionary Bible Translation in Chinese," Ph.D. diss., University of Hamburg, 1996), 9-10. I wish to thank Dr. Zetzsche for providing me with a copy of his dissertation.

[22]Milne, *A Retrospect of the First Ten Years of the Protestant Mission to China*, 56.

[23]For more background, see I-Jin Loh, "Chinese Translations of the Bible," in *An Encyclopedia of Translation: Chinese-English, English-Chinese*, ed. Chan Sin-wai and David E. Pollard (Hong Kong: Chinese University Press, 1995), 54-69; Marshall Broomhall, *The Bible in China* (San Francisco: Chinese Materials Center, Inc., 1977); and Zetzsche, "The Bible in China," 11-27.

[24]See Daniel H. Bays, "Christian Tracts: The Two Friends," in *Christianity in China: Early Protestant Missionary Writings*, ed. Suzanne W. Barnett and John King Fairbank (Cambridge: Cambridge University Press, 1985), 19-34.

[25]For the life and career of Milne, see Robert Morrison, *Memoirs of the Rev. William Milne, D.D.: Late Missionary to China and Principal of the Anglo-Chinese College*,

After Milne's death, Morrison threw himself into his translation work with even more intensity. Ride encapsulates Morrison's vision of the task of the translator as the dual effort both to understand, with sympathy and accuracy, and to translate, idiomatically as well as elegantly. In Morrison's own words:

> In my translations, I have studied fidelity, perspicuity, and simplicity; I have preferred common words to rare and classical ones; I have avoided technical terms, which occur in the pagan philosophy and religion. I would rather be deemed inelegant, than hard to be understood. In difficult passages I have taken the sense given by the general consensus of the gravest, most pious, and least eccentric divines, to whom I had access....[26]

The Infant Cause of Chinese Philology

Based on his fundamental grasp of the classical language, Morrison was able to produce a number of pioneering pedagogical and lexicographical works, including a grammar in 1811,[27] a primer in 1816,[28] a vocabulary of Cantonese,[29] and *A Dictionary of the Chinese Language in Three Parts* (Macao: East India Company's Press, 1815-23). This last work, according to Twitchett, "remained unsurpassed in Europe until the eve of the twentieth century."[30] James Legge later commended the Honorable

---

Compiled from Documents Written by the Deceased; to Which are Added Occasional Remarks by Robert Morrison, D.D. (Malacca: Mission Press, 1824); Wylie, *Memorials of Protestant Missionaries to the Chinese*, 12-25; and *The Blackwell Dictionary of Evangelical Biography*, 2:774-75.

[26]Ride, *Robert Morrison*, 21.

[27]Not printed until later: *A Grammar of the Chinese Language* (Serampore: Mission Press, 1815).

[28]*Dialogues and detached sentences in the Chinese language; with free and verbal translation in English; Collected from Various Sources. Designed as an initiatory work for the use of students of Chinese* (Macao: East India Company's Press, 1816).

[29]*Vocabulary of the Canton Dialect* (Macao: East India Company's Press, 1828).

[30]*Land Tenure and Social Order in T'ang and Sung China*, 3. Wu Jingrong notes one serious defect of this dictionary in the critical matter of pronunciation: it fails to distinguish between aspirated and unaspirated stops; see Wu, "Chinese-English Dictionaries," in *An Encyclopaedia of Translation*, 519.

East India Company for underwriting two of Morrison's main publications, the grammar and dictionary, thus having "contributed £15,000 to the infant cause of Chinese philology."[31]

The major innovations of Morrison's dictionary were highlighted in an advertisement, in contrast with the nature of its predecessors:

> The Manuscript Dictionaries (by the Jesuits) contain from ten to thirteen thousand characters; the late printed French copy contains thirteen thousand, three hundred and sixteen. Neither the Manuscript Dictionaries, nor printed copies, insert the Chinese characters in the examples; and the omission of these leaves the learner in great uncertainty. In the present Work, this material defect is [corrected].[32]

Morrison further added the seal-script and cursive forms of each entry. The dictionary was expressly based on a variety of sources, including unpublished Jesuit manuscripts: "Kang-he's Tsze-tëen forms the ground work....The definitions and Examples are derived chiefly from it, from Personal knowledge of the use of the character; from the Manuscript Dictionaries of the Romish Church; from Native Scholars; and from Miscellaneous Works Perused on Purpose."[33] A convenient handbook was extracted from the dictionary proper before publication because it was considered useful enough to enjoy separate circulation, called *A View of China for Philological Purposes; Containing a Sketch of Chinese Chronology, Geography, Government, Religions, and Customs. Designed for the Use of Persons Who Study the Chinese Language* (Macao: East India Company's Press, 1817). It was the first of many such handbooks, cresting with H. Giles' *A Glossary of References on Subjects Connected with the Far East.*[34]

In 1816 Morrison's linguistic expertise was called upon when he

---

[31]*Inaugural Lecture on the Constituting of a Chinese Chair in the University of Oxford. Delivered in the Sheldonian Theatre, October 27, 1876* (Oxford: James Parker and Co., 1876), 4.

[32]Advertisement blurb inserted between pp. 15 and 16 of Ride, *Robert Morrison*; it was extracted from the preface to Morrison's dictionary, x.

[33]"Preface," ix.

[34]2nd ed. (Hong Kong, Shanghai, and London, 1886).

traveled to Peking as interpreter for the luckless Amherst mission. In 1817, his pre-eminence as translator and China specialist was recognized with the conferral of the degree of Doctor of Divinity by the University of Glasgow. He received an additional honor in 1825 when he was elected fellow of the Royal Asiatic Society as well as a member of the Board of Directors of the London Missionary Society. He died in Canton on August 1, 1834.[35]

The Anglo-Chinese College Morrison founded in Malacca in 1818 had the purpose of training young Chinese men in English sufficient for them to read and preach from the scriptures.[36] This educational program was an important component of Morrison's overall conception of his mission: to educate the Chinese in Christianity and to educate the British about China.[37] This explains why, on a journey home to England in 1824, he brought 10,000 volumes of Chinese books from his personal library, intending to donate them to a university with the proviso that a chair in Chinese language be endowed. Alas, his plan failed; and the Language Institute he founded as a philological society for the study of Chinese did not last more than a few years (1825-28). But the new principal of the Anglo-Chinese College, fellow Scots James Legge, inherited both Milne's and Morrison's missionary zeal and dedication to educating the English-speaking world about China and the Chinese language.

Alexander Wylie

The life and career of the next important British missionary, James Legge, especially his monumental translation of the Confucian classics, will

---

[35]The memorial inscriptions for both Morrison and his wife Mary, with short biographical notices, are reproduced in Lindsay and May Ride, *An East India Company Cemetery: Protestant Burials in Macao*, abridged and edited by Bernard Mellor (Hong Kong: Hong Kong University Press, 1996), 229-35.

[36]See Brian Harrison, *Waiting for China: The Anglo-Chinese College at Malacca, 1818-1843, And Early Nineteenth-Century Missions* (Hong Kong: Hong Kong University Press, 1979).

[37]As amply illustrated in his sermons and speeches; see Morrison, *A parting memorial; consisting of miscellaneous discourses, written and preached in China; at Singapore; on board ship at sea; in the Indian Ocean; at the Cape of Good Hope; and in England. With remarks on missions, &c. &c* (N.p., n.d.).

be dealt with separately in the next chapter. Here we will treat Legge's contemporary and fellow Scotsman, Alexander Wylie (1815-1887). Wylie also translated much of the Confucian canon, but his versions remained in manuscript form. Wylie made a name for himself in different spheres, that of bibliography, history, and the sciences of mathematics and astronomy.

Wylie was born to Scottish parents in London on April 6, 1815, the same year as Legge; he died on February 6th, 1887, a decade before Legge's demise.[38] Wylie was educated in Drumlithe, Scotland, and in London. After graduation he was apprenticed as a cabinet maker. He had always been fascinated with China, and had the discipline to teach himself Chinese with the aid of Prémare's *Notitia linguae sinicae* and the New Testament in Chinese translation. When Legge returned on home leave in 1846 he was immediately impressed with Wylie's ability to read the Gospels in Chinese, and recruited him to work for the London Missionary Society's printing establishment in Shanghai. After specialized training in the printing trade and studies in Chinese with Legge, Wylie sailed for Shanghai, arriving in 1847.

Wylie worked successfully as a printer at the Mission Press in Shanghai until 1860, when he returned to England. Back in China in 1863, he became the agent for the British and Foreign Bible Society, and traveled extensively throughout China. He retired to England in 1877, suffering from poor eyesight. He later endured a debilitating two-year illness, accompanied by blindness, and died in 1887.

Wylie early on harbored the ambition of translating the Confucian classics, for the same reason that had impelled Legge. Cordier sums this up as follows:

> Knowing well the enormous influence the Classics have in the mind of the natives, and how necessary it is for the missionary to penetrate into the inner thought of the individual, he undertook to translate for himself the whole of the *King*. This wonderful labour he successfully

---

[38]The major biographical sources on Wylie are printed in Wylie, *Chinese Researches*, and include J. Edkins, "The Value of Mr. Wylie's Chinese Researches" (3 pages); James Thomas, "Biographical Sketch of Alexander Wylie" (6 pages); and Cordier, "The Life and Labours of Alexander Wylie" (12 pages).

accomplished, and I well remember the six or seven half-bound volumes containing his manuscript on the topshelf of one of his book-cases.   However, Wylie considered these translations too imperfect to be printed, so they have remained unpublished.[39]

Riccian Acculturation Through the Sciences

Most of Wylie's specialized research is included in *Chinese Researches.* This work is divided into four parts, "Literary," "Historical," "Scientific," and "Philological." Among the most important offerings in part one are "Lecture on Prester John" (pp. 19-43) and "Buddhist Relics" (pp. 44-80). In part two pride of place belongs to "The Nestorian Tablet in Si-Ngan-Foo" (pp. 24-77). Part three contains perhaps the most valuable entries, including such indispensable works as "The Mongol Astronomical Instruments in Peking" (pp. 1-15), "Eclipses Recorded in Chinese Works" (pp. 29-105), and "Jottings of the Science of Chinese Arithmetic" (pp. 159-94). Wylie also translated eight works into Chinese, among them books 7-15 of Euclid that were left undone by Ricci and his collaborator Hsü Kuang-ch'i (1562-1633). All of these works on the Chinese sciences remain valuable today, according to the assessment of Joseph Needham. And while Wylie is grouped with other Protestant missionaries such as Joseph Edkins and John Fryer as among those missionary-scholars who helped spread the Copernican view of astronomy in China, only his contributions retain their worth today. In the field of mathematics Needham proclaimed Wylie as the unique figure of the age.[40]

Wylie did not view the study of the sciences as foreign to the work of the missionary: besides cultivating the intellect, the study of astronomy "may lead to juster and more exalted conceptions of 'Him who hath created these orbs....'" Like Legge, all Wylie endeavored and accomplished was dedicated to the service of his God. In this work Wylie was merely

---

[39]Cordier, "Life and Labours," 9.

[40]Joseph Needham and Wang Ling, *Science and Civilisation in China,* vol. 3: *Mathematics and the Sciences of the Heavens and the Earth* (Cambridge: Cambridge University Press, 1959), 2. Consult Wang Ping, "Alexander Wylie's Influence on Chinese Mathematics," in *International Association of Historians of Asia, Second Biennial Conference Proceedings* (Taipei: Taiwan Provincial Museum, 1962), 777-86.

following in the path first blazed by Ricci. And, as mentioned above, he even finished Ricci's incomplete Chinese translation of Euclid's *Elements*. He stated in the English preface that

> Truth is one, and while we seek to promote its advancement in science, we are but preparing the way for its development in that loftier knowledge, which as Christian men and missionaries, it is our chief desire to see consummated.[41]

As noted by Cordier, Wylie was ever after associated with Ricci, especially since Tseng Kuo-fan had their translations of Euclid published together at Nanking in 1865.[42]

Part four of *Chinese Researches*, "Philology," contains a lengthy essay on the "Chinese Language and Literature" (pp. 195-237), written most likely by Cordier, and "A Discussion of the Origin of the Manchus, and Their Written Character" (pp. 239-71), tracing the historical development of both the Manchu people and their script.

Wylie as Bibliographer

Wylie made an equally great contribution to the field of bibliography. Whereas Rémusat had failed to establish traditional bibliography on a firm footing, leaving at his demise an unpublished survey of the classics based on the *Wen-hsien t'ung-k'ao*,[43] Alexander Wylie produced his still useful *Notes on Chinese Literature*, utilizing in the main the superior bibliographical researches of the *Ssu-k'u ch'üan-shu tsung-mu*.[44] According to a recent evaluation by David Helliwell of the Bodleian library, Wylie additionally made much use of his personal library for composing *Notes on Chinese Literature*, especially for those works which

---

[41]Cited in Cordier, "Life and Labours of Alexander Wylie," 12.

[42]Ibid.

[43]Abel Rémusat, *Mélanges Asiatiques*, 2:373-426, prefaces his survey of Chinese books in the royal library with an overview of earlier sinological catalogues in Europe.

[44]*Notes on Chinese Literature: With Introductory Remarks on the Progressive Advancement of the Art and A List of Translations from the Chinese Into Various European Languages* (Shanghai, 1867; rpt. New York: Paragon Books, 1964).

had not been covered in the *Ssu-k'u ch'üan-shu* catalogue. This library, counted second in China only to that of the diplomat Sir Thomas Wade, was acquired by the Bodleian from Wylie in two stages.[45]   Four hundred twenty-nine items had been purchased from Wylie in 1881 for £5 pounds, including four hundred and five printed books and twenty-four MSS; in 1882, a further five hundred eighty-one items were acquired, including five hundred twenty-six printed books and fifty-five MSS, for £110. Apparently Wylie did not desire to profit from the sale of his books, and only charged what they had cost him. This body of books is described by Helliwell as follows: "Inevitably, as one of the pioneers of serious Chinese bibliographical study in Europe, Wylie has described in the *Notes* a number of works in his collection which are of little consequence, but through judicious purchasing with modest resources he formed a collection which is generally well balanced, includes a number of items of considerable rarity, and now constitutes an important part of the library's [the Bodleian] holdings of old Chinese books."[46]

Wylie's *Notes on Chinese Literature* describes over 2,000 works, many treated to entries of several pages or more. Needham frequently depended on Wylie's evaluations of traditional Chinese scientific works on astronomy, mathematics, and mineralogy. Not surprisingly, there are sections devoted to such unusual topics, at least from the point of view of traditional Chinese bibliography, as swords, coin collections, inks, perfumes, teas, liquor, diet, and food.[47] In his own introduction Wylie surveys the various historical and contemporary European bibliographies, mainly library catalogues—French, German, Russian, Latin, and English—but this work superseded them all.   Nevertheless, it is acknowledged to be far from exhaustive: "The books named are but a small selection from the mass....By far the greater number have been described

---

[45]According to Helen Legge, the presence at Oxford of James Legge induced Wylie to arrange for his books to be sold there rather than to the British Museum; see Helen Edith Legge, *James Legge* (London, 1905), 64-65.

[46]David Helliwell, *A Catalogue of the Old Chinese Books in the Bodleian Library*, vol. II: *Alexander Wylie's Books* (Oxford: The Bodleian Library, 1985), xiii.

[47]See the assessment of Howard S. Levy, in his introduction to the 1964 reprinting.

from actual examination; but a number of important works which were not accessible to me, have been notified, from records in other Chinese publications."[48] *Notes on Chinese Literature* does for traditional sources what Cordier's *Bibliotheca Sinica* does for secondary studies; indeed, Cordier termed it "the *vade mecum* of those who seek to orient themselves in the labyrinth of the literature of China."[49]

In addition, another equally significant dimension of Wylie's bibliographical studies is in this same field of secondary scholarship. Indeed, Wylie's personal library of Chinese books and works on China was the "very foundation" of Cordier's bibliography. For it was while Cordier was engaged to compile the catalogue of the Library of the North China Branch of the Royal Asiatic Society, a library based largely on Wylie's personal holdings, that Cordier conceived the idea for his great bibliography. "I drew much of the necessary materials from the N.C.B. Asiatic Society's Library," explains Cordier, "a great deal more from the new collection made by Wylie during his visit to Europe in 1860."[50] An earlier catalogue of the London Missionary Library at Shanghai published by Wylie in 1857 was, according to Cordier, a "very brilliant prelude to his greater undertaking."[51]

Another work of this kind, part biographical, part bibliographical, is *Memorials of the Protestant Missionaries to the Chinese: Giving a List of Their Publications, and Obituary Notices of the Deceased, with Copious Indexes* (Shanghai, 1867). This work details the published works in both English and Chinese of all Protestant missionaries who worked in China from 1807 to the early 1860s.[52] Wylie also supplied much bibliographical data for the researches of his contemporaries, including Sir Emerson Tennent and his

---

[48]*Notes on Chinese Literature*, vi.

[49]Cordier, *Bibliotheca sinica*, 1:xiii-iv.

[50]Cordier, "Life and Labours," 7. According to Cordier, *Catalogue of the Library of the North China Branch of the Royal Asiatic Society* (Shanghai, 1872), 718 volumes in western languages located in the North China Branch library were Wylie's, as were forty Chinese titles, in 1,023 *chüan*.

[51]Ibid., 15.

[52]Ralph R. Covell, in *The Blackwell Dictionary of Evangelical Biography, 1730-1860*, 2:1220-21.

history of Ceylon, Sir Henry Yule and his work on Marco Polo, and Sir Henry Howorth and his research on the Mongols. On occasion he helped proof-read the work of others, and prepared the indices.[53] Late in his career in China he edited several journals, including the *Journal of the N.C.B.R. Asiatic Society* and the *Chinese Recorder*. All in all, methodologically speaking, Wylie was the first English sinologist to conduct historical research by going directly to the original sources.

Herbert Giles

"Sinologue. An advanced scholar of the Chinese language, literature, etc. From the Latin *Sinæ....*It has recently been objected that the word S. wears a French dress, and that to preserve uniformity, English people should say 'Sinologist;' but it is highly improbable that such a change will ever be successfully introduced."
—Giles, *A Glossary of Reference Subjects Connected With the Far East*[54]

Herbert A. Giles (1845-1935) functions as a transitional figure, a China hand who turned to academics later in life; in his case, he was a translator and consular official turned professor of Chinese.[55] His former superior in the service, Thomas Wade, was probably the first English diplomat to attain command of Chinese,[56] even if a young George Staunton

---

[53]E.g. Joseph Edkins, *Chinese Buddhism* (London, n.d.); it includes a very generous note of acknowledgment.

[54]Giles, *A Glossary of Reference Subjects Connected With the Far East*, 2nd ed. (Hong Kong: Lane, Crawford and Co., 1886), 222.

[55]For a short biography and bibliography of Giles, see *Who Was Who*, vol. 3 1929-1940, 2nd ed. (London: A. and C. Block, 1967), 512-13; Ishida Mikinosuke, *Ō-Bei ni okeru Shina kenkyū* (Tokyo, 1942), 396-406; and the necrologies of A.C. Moule, *Journal of the Royal Asiatic Society* (1935), 577-79, and John Ferguson, *Journal of the North China Branch of the Royal Asiatic Society* 66 (1935), 134-36. See further Charles Aylmer, ed., "The Memoirs of H.A. Giles," *East Asian History* 13-14 (1997): 1-90.

[56]Sir Thomas Wade (1818-1895) matriculated from Trinity College, Cambridge; but his father, sensing the unsuitability of his son for academic enterprises, bought him a military commission. As an army lieutenant Wade fell in love with the language while stationed in south China; he worked as Cantonese interpreter to the Hong Kong garrison in 1843 and to the Hong Kong Supreme Court in 1846. He participated in both of Lord Elgin's embassies, 1857 and 1859. His career in the consular service was punctuated by

had mastered it earlier.[57]   But even if the names of Wade and Giles are forever linked as the first two occupants of the Cambridge Chinese chair, and even more egregiously as the co-conspirators of the "Wade-Giles" system of romanization, they seemed to despise each other.

The transition in sinological attitudes and attainments that took place between the generations of Wade and Giles marked the beginnings of the professionalization of British sinology. Before Giles, and with many of his contemporaries, sinology was the part-time hobby of busy professional men. Denis Twitchett, with charity and insight, sums up the state of nineteenth-century English sinology in the following terms:

> Our nineteenth-century scholars...were almost without exception part-time scholars, often holding responsible and time-consuming posts as officials or missionaries....They had comparatively little time for their studies. They rarely had access to first-class Chinese scholars or to really good libraries. Those who entered academic life did so only after their retirement, and when they did the universities did little for them....Considering the difficulties under which they

---

bouts with malaria and the frustrated effort to retire as soon as possible in order to devote himself to study and to publishing language textbooks for missionaries and interpreters. Although he never realized this ambition, he did revise the teaching of Chinese to new student interpreters, making it for the first time a relatively effective pedagogical program. He served, among various posts, as Chinese secretary in 1856 and retired at age 64 as Chinese Minister (1871-1882). By the time he assumed the new Cambridge chair of Chinese in 1888, he was, according to P.D. Coates, "mentally exhausted": "Leisure for scholarship had in the end come too late, he published nothing more, and he had no pupils;" P.D. Coates, *The China Consuls: British Consular Officers, 1843-1943* (Hong Kong: Oxford University Press, 1988), 85. For his life, see Sidney Lee, ed., *The Dictionary of National Biography* (London: Smith, Elder and Co., 1899), 58:420; and J.C. Cooley, *T.F. Wade in China: Pioneer in Global Diplomacy 1842-1882* (Leiden, 1981).

[57]Sir George Staunton (1781-1859) technically was the earliest English diplomat to speak Chinese; but he was only eleven years old when he accompanied his father, the secretary to Lord Macartney, on the latter's celebrated mission; at the time young George was the only member of the delegation conversant in Chinese. He is well known for his translation of the Ch'ing code (London, 1810), but made his mark in the East India Company, rather than in diplomacy. For his life, see Twitchett, *Land Tenure and the Social Order in T'ang and Sung China*, 4-6.

worked, men like Beal[58] and Douglas[59] were probably little worse than their contemporaries elsewhere, and it is remarkable that they achieved as much as they did.[60]

Wade donated his collection of Chinese books to Cambridge in 1886, two years before taking up the newly created chair in Chinese.[61]

H.A. Giles was the fourth son of the Reverend J.A. Giles, a very prolific author of works on history, the classics, and religion (Giles' privately produced catalogue of the holdings of his personal library, on deposit in the Cambridge University Library, contains a listing of sixty-six of his father's publications). One son, Lionel Giles (1875-1958), joined him as a professional sinologist in his work at the British Museum on the Tun-

---

[58]Rev. Samuel Beal (1825-89), a former naval chaplain and the pioneer of Buddhist studies in England, translated the travelogue of Hsüan-tsang, *Buddhist Records of the Western World*, 2 vols. (London, 1884) and produced a biography of his hero, *Life of Hsüan-tsang* (London, 1911). He held the chair in Chinese at University College, London, from 1877 to 1889.

[59]Robert Kennaway Douglas (1838-1913), former consular officer in Tientsin, came to the library of the British Museum in 1865, and held the chair of Chinese at King's College until his retirement in 1905. In his *The Language and Literature of China: Two Lectures* (London, Trubner and Co., 1875), 7-8, Douglas touches on the economic impetus of sinology in the England of his day: "And with the exception of two or three scholars, among whom Dr. Birch of the British Museum, and Mr. Beal, the learned translator of several works on Chinese Buddhism, are chief, the study of Chinese has been with us entirely confined to those who by the nature of their professional duties are compelled to grapple with the language."

[60]Twitchett, *Land Tenure and the Social Order in T'ang and Sung China*, 10-11. The academic mission of A.C. Moule was to abolish the British amateur sinologist–"may I be the last of them!" See his "British Sinology," *The Asiatic Review* 44 (1948): 189. Otto Franke was even less kindly disposed towards the "Dilettantismus" of the "Amateur-Sinologie;" consult Franke, "Die sinologischen Studien in Deutschland," *Ostasiatische Neubildungen* (Hamburg, 1911), 357-58, 366-67.

[61]See Herbert A. Giles, *A Catalogue of the Wade Collection of Chinese and Manchu Books in the Library of the University of Cambridge* (Cambridge, 1898); *Supplementary Catalogue of the Wade Collection of Chinese and Manchu Books* (Cambridge, 1915) for the collection; for the historical background, see Charles Aylmer, "Sir Thomas Wade and the Centenary of Chinese Studies at Cambridge (1888-1988)," *Han-hsüeh yen-chiu* 7 (1989): 405-20; and Barrett, *Singular Listlessness*, 77-79.

huang manuscripts, a career that culminated with an appointment as Keeper of the Department of Oriental Printed Books and Manuscripts.[62]

Giles joined the consular service in 1867 at age twenty-two, and remained for twenty-five years. He served in a succession of posts, including Vice-Consul in Pagoda Island (1881-83) and Shanghai (1883-85), and Consul in Tamsui (1885-91) and Ningbo (1891-1893). His career is summarized by P.D. Coates as checkered by internal bickering with his Western confrères both within and without the consular service: "Giles was a quarrelsome man. His career was littered with silly official quarrels, and in private life he broke off relations with three of his own sons. At Amoy he ran true to form. He quarreled with the Customs commissioner and with his United States colleague, and Wade had to make excuses to the admiral for Giles' correspondence with the navy."[63] The details of his feud with his son Lancelot Giles (1878-1934), who followed him into the consular service in China, confirm the characterization of Coates.[64] Sir Robert Scott, with more sympathy, merely states that as he was "too much of an individualist to settle easily into a civil service mould, his career as a consular official was not outstanding."[65] Giles resigned from the service in 1893, and returned to Great Britain. He was living in Aberdeen when he was elected to the Cambridge chair late in 1897; he held it until his retirement in 1932.[66] His successor, the Rev. A.C. Moule (1873-1957), already residing in convenient proximity at Trumpington Vicarage in Cambridge, occupied the chair from 1933 until 1938.[67] It was only with

---

[62]Lionel Giles' work at the British Museum resulted, after the labor of many years, in *Catalogue of Tun-huang Manuscripts in the British Museum* (London: British Museum, 1957). See J.L. Cranmer-Byng, "Lionel Giles 1875-1958)," *Journal of Oriental Studies* 4 (1957-58): 249-52.

[63]Coates, *The China Consuls*, 206.

[64]Lancelot Giles, *The Siege of The Peking Legations: A Diary*, ed. L. R. Marchant (Nedlands, Australia: University of Western Australia Press, 1970), xxiv-xxv.

[65]Scott, from his forward to Giles, *The Siege of The Peking Legations*, xix.

[66]According to Denis Twitchett, the fact that Giles held on to his chair longer than he was effectively able to function led Cambridge to impose a mandatory retirement age; private conversation, April 2, 1997, Cambridge, England.

[67]He was a member of the missionary Moule family: his father George had been bishop in mid-China from 1880 to 1908; brother Henry Moule was also a missionary in

Gustav Haloun's assumption of the chair in 1938, replacing Moule, that the first professional sinologist held a professorship of Chinese in England. Giles hence was one of the last self-trained sinologists with long residence in China to take up full-time scholarship as a second career.

From Diplomacy to Sinology

Giles, then, was a professional foreign-service officer turned sinologist. But when he made the transition, he brought a wealth of experience, a keen mind nurtured on the Greek and Latin classics, and an energetic capacity for wide-ranging reading. His career at Cambridge is encapsulated by Sir Richard Scott as follows:

> Punctual, methodical, hardworking, fond of controversy, Giles set out to transform current European ideas about China....When he went to Cambridge, the university did not rate Chinese studies highly, nor was the subject popular with undergraduates. But, if the stipend was small, the teaching load was light. With abundant energy, ample leisure, and the facilities of the university at his disposal, Giles pursued his chosen task of revealing and explaining China to the West.[68]

He composed almost thirty works relative to China, including *A Chinese-English Dictionary*, *Chinese Biographical Dictionary*, *Strange Stories from a Chinese Studio*, *Chinese Poetry in English Verse*, *The Travels of Fa-hsien*, *A History of Chinese Verse*, *An Introduction to the History of Chinese*

China, and donated two hundred fifty vols. of books to the Cambridge University Library in 1920. Arthur Christopher Moule published the notable *Christians in China* (rpt. Taipei: Cheng Wen, 1972), and several articles on minor Friars in China in the pages of the *Journal of the Royal Asiatic Society*. Still convenient to consult is his *The Rulers of China, 221 B.C. -A.D. 1949* (London: Routledge and K. Paul, 1957), with an appended chronology of pre-Ch'in rulers by W. Perceval Yetts. Two works concern Marco Polo: an English translation of *The Travels of Marco Polo*, nominally done in collaboration with Pelliot, but entirely Moule's effort (rpt. New York: AMS Press, 1976) and *Quinsay: with other Notes on Marco Polo* (Cambridge; Cambridge University Press, 1957). He was a fellow of Trinity College during his tenure as professor of Chinese at Cambridge.

[68]Scott, *The Siege of The Peking Legations*, xx.

Pictorial Art, Religions of Ancient China, and various other general histories, surveys, travelogues, handbooks, and especially translations. He produced numerous translations of original literary and philosophical works because, despite the number of his general works on China, he felt that "the acid test of Chinese scholarship is published translation from the Chinese of works which have never been translated before, or at the least new renderings of works which have been put on the market in the form of mistranslations. Mere literature about Chinese books is of little or no value."[69]

His collection of minor works, *Adversaria Sinica,*[70] is in the main a reprinting of essays and book reviews, including several by his son Lionel Giles, and was devoted to matters of philology in the broadest sense: "The pages...of *Adversaria Sinica* are not intended for book-reviews in the ordinary sense of the term, but they are rather for the discussion of linguistic and other questions arising out of the interpretation of Chinese texts."[71]   Examples include such backwater oddities as "Ventriloquism in China" (pp. 81-82), "Psychic Phenomena in China" (pp. 145-62), and "Phrenology, Physiognomy, and Palmistry" (pp. 178-84).   Despite his relative command of classical Chinese, the failings of the nineteenth-century mind-set are revealed in "Who Was *Si Wang Mu?*" (pp. 1-19, 298-99), which attempts to equate the storied Queen Mother of the West with the Greek goddess Hera. Even historical linguistics plays its part, however flawed:

> Further, it is possible that the *Si* of Si Wang Mu, probably pronounced in the second century B.C. more like *sei* (=say), may simply be the first syllable of Hera, taken in concordance with Chinese monosyllabic custom to represent the whole name....Also, that the portrait of the grave old gentleman given in the *San Ts'ai T'u Hui* as the portrait of the King-Father of the East may possibly be a

---

[69]"The Memoirs of H.A. Giles," 39.
[70]*Adversaria Sinica* (Shanghai: Kelley and Walsh, 1914).
[71]Ibid., 163.

far-off semblance of some presentation of Olympian Jove.[72]

If his comparative approach was hopelessly outdated, his attitude towards textual criticism was far in advance of his contemporaries, drawing as it did on his command of Greek and Latin. His short note on "Textual Criticism" (pp. 208-14), should be required reading in graduate school:

> If a paragraph in the Chinese Classics cannot be made, even with the help of many native commentators, to yield sense, the resources of a translator are not necessarily exhausted. He may set aside all previous interpretations and substitute one of his own....Or he may have recourse to the more dangerous expedient of textual emendation; but this is only to be tolerated when everything else has failed; and further, the recognized conditions of sound emendation, as applied to the Greek and Roman classics, should always be stringently observed.

His example is *Lunyu* XIV, 39, where he emends *se* 色 to *yi* 邑 , and *yan* 言 to *fu* 阜 , yielding the following: "The master said, Perfectly virtuous men retire from the world; The next (in virtue), from their country; The next, from their district; The next, from their village."[73] Although his textual adjustments may seem (to some) to exemplify Paul Maas' famous dictum ("It is better to make a wrong conjecture than to ignore a difficulty"), he nevertheless resolves, in this case, the problem of translation much more adroitly than Waley's forced reading of the received text: "The Master said, Best of all, to withdraw from one's generation; next to withdraw to another land; next to leave because of a look; next best to leave because of a word."[74]

---

[72]Giles, *Adversaria Sinica*, 18. Another example of his Sino-Greek comparative studies is lecture #4, "China and Ancient Greece," in *China and the Chinese: Lecture (1902) on the Dean Lung Foundation in Columbia University* ([New York: Columbia University Press,1902]), 109-40; incidentally, this set of lectures in 1902 inaugurated the annual Dean Lung lecture at Columbia.

[73]*Adversaria Sinica*, 213.

[74]Arthur Waley, *The Analects of Confucius* (New York: Vintage Books, 1938), 190.

Rhymed versus Free Translation

Giles demonstrated a curious blend of confident intellectual independence and abject cultural dependency, for he felt that, except for an experienced student of Chinese, one "who has devoted himself chiefly to the linguistic side of the question," all translation should be undertaken with the aid of a native informant: "Outside China it is impossible to have that ready recourse to a well-primed native scholar which makes translation an affair of minutes instead of hours; and it is beyond doubt that no one who has not served a long apprenticeship is capable of succeeding when left to his own resources."[75] Once he qualified his own translation with the apology that he lacked such an expert informant.[76] Yet Giles was very capable in classical Chinese, as his review of Laufer, *Chinese Pottery of the Han Dynasty*, proves at some length. In it he focuses on some questionable translations, and demonstrates his overall linguistic ability in classical prose.[77] Nevertheless, he did not understand that classical Chinese, like any other language, had its own system of grammar, claiming that the Chinese language was "guiltless" of it.[78] In poetry, what ultimately trips him up is his approach to translation and his misguided effort to render the overall spirit of the original in an equally poetic if loose English paraphrase, adorned with rhymes, that "troublesome and modern bondage" abjured by Milton.

Giles justifies rendering Chinese poetry into rhymed English verse for three reasons: first, those who denounce it do so because they couldn't produce it even if they wanted to; second, the English general reader likes it; and third, Chinese poetry is almost all rhymed.[79]

---

[75] *Adversaria Sinica*, 304.

[76] "Hence the attempt in the following pages...may in turn be capable of improvement at the hands of students resident in China who can enlist, as I cannot, the services of a well-educated native scholar;" quoted in Ivan Morris, ed., *Madly Singing in the Mountains: An Appreciation and Anthology of Arthur Waley* (New York: Walker, 1970), 300-301, n. 1.

[77] *Adversaria Sinica*, 304-11. On his strengths as a translator of prose, see David Pollard, "H.A. Giles and His Translations," in *Europe Studies China*, 492-512.

[78] "The Memoirs of H.A. Giles," 14; see pp. 24, 29 for his ignorance of the causative construction.

[79] "The Memoirs of H.A. Giles," 40.

A good case in point against Giles' use of rhyme is his rendering of the two verses written on the blackboard of the Chinese division of the Cambridge library for the benefit of a distinguished Chinese visitor on May 24, 1906, preserved in photographs on pp. 205 and 207 of *Adversaria Sinica*. Wang Ts'an's famous couplet *Ching-Man fei wu hsiang,/ho wei chiu chih-yin* 荊蠻非吾鄉, / 何爲久滯淫 comes off as "A lovely land I could not bear,/If not mine own, to linger there." Another couplet, by Hsüeh Tao-heng 薛道衡 (540-609) is more successful, even if the sense is stretched to provide a rhyme: "If home, with the wild geese of autumn we're going,/Our hearts will be off ere the spring flowers are blowing" (*Jen kuei lo yen hou,/ssu fa tsai hua ch'ien* 人歸落雁後 ,/ 思發在花前). Waley's dismissal of such rhymed translation was due to the paucity of English rhymes: "But rhymes are so scarce in English (as compared to Chinese) that a rhymed translation can only be a paraphrase and is apt to fall back on feeble padding."[80] Legge's renderings of the entire corpus of the *Book of Poetry* confirms this judgement, in my view;[81] yet its celebration at the hands of a recent critic, Lauren Pfister, leads us to take a closer look at one aspect of the poetics of translation in sinology, as illustrated by Giles.

First we must acknowledge the important fact that Giles' translations from the Chinese, regardless of how one views either their accuracy or aesthetics, helped initiate the Pound-Williams era in American Modernist literary circles. Both Ezra Pound (1885-1972) and William Carlos Williams (1883-1963) were indebted to Giles' *A History of Chinese Literature*, for they actively mined it for inspiration as well as matter in their own orientalizing poetic productions (commencing in 1913 for Pound, and 1916 for Williams).[82] It is true that Pound first had been attracted to Chinese and Japanese art through the lectures of the assistant

---

[80]*Madly Singing in the Mountains*, 137. For Waley's critique of Giles' approach centered on a specific case, see his "Notes on the 'Lute-Girl's Song," in *Madly Singing in the Mountains*, 297-302; for David Hawke's expansion on Waley's concerns, see "Chinese Poetry and the English Reader," in *The Legacy of China*, ed. Raymond Dawson (Oxford: Oxford University Press, 1971), 98-101.

[81]See the discussion in chapter eight below.

[82]See Zhaoming Qian, *Orientalism and Modernism: The Legacy of China in Pound and Williams* (Durham: Duke University Press, 1995).

keeper in the British Museum's Department of Prints and Drawings, Laurence Binyon (1869-1943);[83] this made him receptive to the invitation of Mary Fenollosa, widow of the American Orientalist Ernest Fenollosa (1853-1908), to edit her late husband's manuscripts on Chinese poetry and Japanese *Noh* drama.[84]   Later on, the translations of the young Arthur Waley, working under Binyon in the British Museum, provided further stimulation.   "It was through Ernest Fenollosa, H.A. Giles, and Arthur Waley that Modernists like Pound and Williams had dialogues with the great Chinese poets," concludes Zhaoming Qian.[85]

Giles' *A History of Chinese Literature* provided a broad panoply of Chinese poets for Pounds and others to draw from.[86] But the sparse, exotic imagery Giles used, not his rhymed translation strategy, is what influenced the modernists.   The concern at present is rather with his practice of producing metrical, rhymed renderings of Chinese poems in the attempt to capture the poetic spirit of the originals.   Giles' purpose was to supply the "soul" of the poetry, as he himself explained, Victorian enough, in a prefatory poetic dedication to an anthology of verse translations:

---

[83]Laurence Robert Binyon was born in Lancaster; he studied classics and composed poetry at Trinity College, Oxford, before joining the Dept. of Printed Books at the British Museum in 1893. Two years later he transferred to the Dept. of Prints and Drawings, becoming assistant keeper in 1909.   He loved to combine the visual presentation of art with the auditory effects of poetry in his exhibitions. By 1913 a special sub-department of oriental prints and drawings was created and put under his care. His publications (e.g., *Painting in the Far East*, 1908) and lectures (e.g., "The Spirit of Man in Asian Art" lecture series at Harvard, 1933-34) did more than any other contemporary to spread the appreciation of Oriental Art, including Chinese, Japanese, Persian, and Indian. Later influences on Arthur Waley include both Waley's professional and personal interests in Oriental poetry and art as well as his creative utilization of the natural stress-accents of speech borrowed from the poetry of Gerard Manley Hopkins (via Binyon's own verses) for his own poetic compositions. For his life, see John Hatcher, *Laurence Binyon: Poet, Scholar of East and West* (Oxford: Clarendon Press, 1996); and *Dictionary of National Biography, 1941-1950*, ed. L.G. Wickham Legg and E.T. William (Oxford: Oxford University Press, 1959), 79-81.

[84]For Fenollosa, see Lawrence W. Chisolm, *Fenollosa, The Far East and American Culture* (New Haven: Yale University Press, 1963).

[85]Qian, *Orientalism and Modernism*, 1.

[86]*A History of Chinese Literature* (New York: D. Appleton, 1901).

Dear Land of Flowers, forgive me!—that I took
    These   snatches   from   thy
    glittering wealth of song,
And twisted to the uses of a book,
    Strains that to alien harps can
    ne'er belong.
Thy gems shine purer in their native bed
    Concealed beyond the pry of
    vulgar eyes;
And there, through labyrinths of language led,
    The patient student grasps the
    glowing prize.
Yet many, in their race toward other goals,
    May joy to feel, albeit at second-
    hand,
Some far faint heart-throb of poetic souls,
    Whose breath makes incense in
    the Flowery Land.[87]

An example from Giles' translations that seems to be "twisted to the uses of a book" is his version of Mao #76, "Chiang Chung-tzu" (Mr. Chung) entitled by Giles' "To A Young Gentleman":

Don't come in, sir, please!
Don't break my willow-trees!
Not that *that* would very much grieve me;
But alack-a-day! What would my parents say?
    And love you as I may,
I cannot bear to think what that would be.

Don't cross my wall, sir, please!
Don't spoil my mulberry-trees!
Not that *that* would very much grieve me;
But alack-a-day! What would my brother say?
    And love you as I may,
I cannot bear to think what that would be.

---

[87] *Chinese Poetry in English Verse* (n.p., n.d.), preface Cambridge, October 1898.

> Keep outside, sir, please!
> Don't spoil my sandal-trees!
> Not that *that* would very much grieve me;
> But alack-a-day! What would the world say?
> And love you as I may,
> I cannot bear to think what that would be.[88]

Pound's version, with intermittent end-rhyme, is even more removed from the original imagery and intent, even if composed in more engaging English:

> Hep-Cat Chung, 'ware my town,
> don't break my willows down.
> The trees don't matter
> but father's tongue, mother's tongue
>   Have a heart, Chung,
>   it's awful.

> Hep-Cat Chung, don't jump my wall
> nor strip my mulberry boughs,
> The boughs don't matter
> But my brother's clatter!
>   Have a heart, Chung,
>   it's awful.

> Hep-Cat Chung, that is *my* garden wall,
> Don't break my sandalwood tree.
> The tree don't matter
> But he subsequent chatter!
>   Have a heart, Chung,
>   it's awful.[89]

James Legge's literal rendering in prose should be contrasted to highlight what was sacrificed in content by Giles for the sake of rhyme and by

---

[88]*Chinese Poetry in English Verse*, #1.
[89]Ezra Pound, *The Confucian Odes: The Classic Anthology Defined By Confucius* (1954; rpt. New York: New Directions, 1959), 37-38.

Pound for the sake of rhyme and proto-beatnik rhythm:

> I pray you, Mr. Chung,
> Do not come leaping into my hamlet;
> Do not break my willow trees.
> Do I care for them?
> But I fear my parents.
> You, O Chung, are to be loved,
> But the words of my parents
> Are also to be feared....[90]

A holdover from the Victorian era, translating into verse is still very current today. Two modern translators of Celtic and Anglo-Saxon poetry in the Penguin series offer contrasting perspectives. Michael Alexander, translator of *The Earliest English Poems*, states unequivocally that "I have never seen the point of translating verse into anything but verse." He continues: "...the first aim in translating a living poem from a language which happens to be unknown into one's own language is to produce something with art in it, something which lives."[91] Opposite to this tack is the approach of Kenneth Hurlstone Jackson, translator of *A Celtic Miscellany*, who provides a broader context for his preferred translation style:

> Eighteenth- and nineteenth-century taste would accept—indeed preferred—renderings which were nothing but the wildest paraphrases, at least if they were made from languages which the readers did not themselves know. The later nineteenth century favoured an artificial semi-Biblical English which might degenerate into pure Wardour Street. Traces of this are still with us. We still sometimes meet the outrageous paraphrase, particularly in translations into English verse, where it is excused on the ground that it "renders the spirit" rather than the word; but it is used primarily of course because it makes it possible to rhyme and scan in English. On the whole, however, a much higher standard of accuracy is usually

---

[90]Legge, *Chinese Classics*, 4:125-26.
[91]*The Earliest English Poems*, 3rd ed. (Middlesex: Penguin Books, 1991), xxiii.

expected, because the reader naturally wishes to feel that he is really getting as near as possible to the original, unhampered by the translator's notions of style or his struggles with a rhyming dictionary.[92]

The end product of a translation of a poem from a foreign language, according to the first view, is another poem; it is thus the result of an act of creation. According to the second view, it is a linguistic means of approaching an understanding and appreciation of the original; it functions, therefore, as a scholarly aid and is hence the task of a scholar. For the sake of creating an effective English poem, then, Pound would often alter uncongenial elements in the original. As an example, Qian cites Pound's treatment of the *Shih-ching*: "It is amazing that Pound, who knew nothing about the debate, should form an opinion so close to twentieth-century *Shi jing* scholarship. But with a more radical attitude, he has to a considerable degree intensified the grievance of the original, and, moreover, modified certain details that appear inappropriate for the anti-war motif."[93] In other words, he writes a different English poem for purposes of his own, in this case, to express an anti-war sentiment. Such an approach underscores much modern criticism of the translations of Arthur Waley. If Waley has been criticized by Chinese philologists for sometimes being too free (to be discussed in chapter nine), he has received equal opprobrium from critics for the lack of adventure in his English. One prominent critic is Hugh Kenner, a disciple of Pound. In his study *The Pound Era*, Kenner dismisses Waley's translations as being uninspired, for they drew upon dry sources. Referring to Waley's version of one of the "19 Old Poems," Kenner claims that "This is a resourceless man's verse; the resourceless man wrote but did not transmute; it's hard alone to wring song from philology." A general aspersion against sinologists in general that could comfortably include Waley reveals the same fixation on translation as independent poem rather than linguistic reflex: "Other translators of Chinese, marveling at Pound's translucency but deploring his want of scholarship, have supposed

---

[92]Kenneth Hurlstone Jackson, *A Celtic Miscellany* (Middlesex: Penguin Books, 1971), 15-16.

[93]Qian, *Orientalism and Modernism*, 75.

themselves to have learned his lesson when they have kept the syntax simple and the line-length irregular, and have composed nothing it is possible to remember."[94]

Waley's version of Mao #76, already translated by Giles, Pound, and Legge above, is presented now. Although perhaps not worth remembering as an independent poem, it does merit repeated study for access to what the Chinese had to say and how it was expressed, prefaced by a scholarly introduction that sets the context of comparative anthropology:

> I beg of you, Chung Tzu,
> Do not climb into our homestead,
> Do not break the willows we have planted.
> Not that I mind about the willows,
> But I am afraid of my father and mother.
> Chung Tzu I dearly love;
> But of what my father and mother say
> Indeed I am afraid.
>
> I beg of you, Chung Tzu,
> Do not climb over our wall,
> Do not break the mulberry-trees we have planted.
> Not that I mind about the mulberry trees,
> But I am afraid of my brothers.
> Chung Tzu I dearly love;
> But of what my brothers say
> Indeed I am afraid.
>
> I beg of you, Chung Tzu,
> Do not climb into our garden,
> Do not break the hard-wood we have planted.
> Not that I mind about the hard-wood,
> But I am afraid of what people say.
> Chung Tzu I dearly love;
> But of all that people will say

---

[94]Hugh Kenner, *The Pound Era* (Berkeley and Los Angeles: University of California Press, 1974), 195, 209.

Indeed I am afraid.[95]

In the final chapter Edward Schafer shall have much to say on translators who attempt to compose poetry instead of to construct linguistic counterparts accompanied by critical explication. But at least one recent practicing translator deserves citing in support of the welcome notion that translation can engage the original text even more closely than a commentary, providing, I may add, that it is a genetically related translation and not an independent poem. Paul Kroll, in discussing the translation of the *Ch'u-tz'u*, concludes that "As scholarship and exegesis improve, so should translation. Indeed, between different languages, the most fully engaged commentary on a text is not annotation but rather translation. I am fond of Walter Benjamin's notion of translation being a posthumous extension of the text into times and tongues beyond its native endowment."[96] When a translation ceases to share with the original either the corporeal connection of linguistic proximity or spiritual identity of common imagery, then it can no longer extend the original into either time or foreign tongues. To the extent that any attempt at accommodating an English rhyme is made at the expense of an image or tone peculiar to the original, such an extension is foreshortened or severed altogether.

Recent theoretical work has been adduced by Lauren Pfister to evaluate the success of James Legge's poetical, rhyming renderings of the *Shih-ching*. Sandwiched between his 1871 *Chinese Classics* version in prose and the 1879 *Sacred Books of the East* edition is a metrical rendering that appeared in 1876 entitled *The She King, or The Book of Ancient Poetry, Translated in English Verse, with Essays and Notes.*[97] Legge had earlier been criticized by one reviewer for not taking the trouble to render his English translations into verse.[98] Perhaps such criticism, coupled with his own fondness for a metrical version of the Psalms that his grandmother used to recite to him, plus his own attempt to render the entirety of Psalms into metrical English verse, led him to this new foray. For this metrical version

---

[95]Waley, *The Book of Songs* (1937; rpt. New York: Grove Press, 1960), 35

[96]Kroll, "On 'Far Roaming,'" *JAOS* 116 (1996): 656.

[97](London: Trübner and Co., 1876).

[98]Eitel, "The She-King," *The China Review* 1 (1872): 5.

he obtained the assistance of his two nephews, the Revs. John Legge and James Legge, and the Rev. Alexander Cran; Legge's friend W.T. Mercer helped revise and polish the poetry.

In evaluating the success of these metrical and rhymed translations, Lauren Pfister adopts a reader response paradigm:

> Moving beyond the literal text, translators were urged to find other locutions which might have only tenuous literal associations with the original idea but which provoked appropriate responses in the audience. This kind of translation has been described as "dynamic equivalence," suggesting that it produces a similar or even the same effect in the audience of the target language that the original phrase has in its own context.[99]

Pfister's theoretical authorities for this approach include Susan Bassnett-McGuire and Peter Newmark.[100] In the context of literary theory and appreciation, this approach may be a workable, even commercially marketable, strategy. And I do not mean to deny the existence of this audience nor demean its viability. But within the context of the scope and purpose of scholarship, a different audience exists, an audience of scholars, not literary aesthetes. To the extent that attention is turned away from the poet and the poem to the response of a reading audience is the focus shifted from demonstrable philological fact to psychological fancy. Notwithstanding many eloquent champions of this approach,[101] the fact that similar emotional responses may be elicited by a walk in the woods, listening to Mahler late at night, or relaxing by the fireplace in a snowstorm should lead us, a very particular and textually conservative

---

[99] Pfister, "James Legge's Metrical *Book of Poetry*," *BSOAS* 60 (1997):64-85, quote on pp. 69-70.

[100] Bassnett-McGuire, *Translation Studies* (New York: Routledge, 1991), and Newmark, *Approaches to Translation* (New York: Pergamon Press, 1988).

[101] For instance, Wai-lim Yip: "It seems quite clear now that although Pound has been sharply limited by his ignorance of Chinese and by much of Fenollosa's text, he possesses a sense of rightness, an intuitive apprehension in poetic organization or, to borrow a term from Eliot, 'the creative eye;'" Yip, *Ezra Pound's Cathay* (Princeton: Princeton University Press, 1969), 92.

audience, to be cautious about abandoning philology for feeling. That Giles' translations were poorly served by Pound and Williams, at least from a philological point of view, should not detract from his importance in setting the stage for Waley and in stimulating the latter to do Giles one better, as best indicated in Waley's response to Giles's criticisms of his translation of the "P'i-p'a hsing" of Po Chü-i.[102]

Lexicography and Biography

Much more than command of classical Chinese is required to make a scholar. Among the most important tools are bibliography, both in traditional sources and in modern secondary studies, and a methodical, scientific approach. It is on just these grounds that Maspero severely castigates Giles' *Adversaria Sinica*.[103] The essays in this work, despite Giles' admirable knowledge of Chinese, betray a uniform lack of critical method—except for rudimentary textual criticism—and an equally artless ignorance of the scholarly accomplishments of either China or Europe: no attempt is made to place any hypothesis or conclusion within the appropriate bibliographic setting. Perhaps this is partly the fault of his genre—general philological notes inspired by particular textual problems randomly encountered. This sort of casual *sui-pi* jottings ultimately is better left to the province of the self-published *samizdat* such as produced by Boodberg, Kennedy, and Schafer, or those that are popular in German circles today. At any rate, Moule's characterization is on target: "Giles was a fairly original sinologist, but did not know what research meant."[104] David Pollard suggests that the overall intention of Giles' work was to help popularize the study of China; his writings, therefore, were not directed towards fellow British sinologists, for no such creatures existed: "Perhaps it was to make up for this lack of help that Giles covered so wide a field

---

[102]"Notes on the 'Lute-Girl's Song," in *Madly Singing in the Mountains*, 297-302.

[103]Maspero, *BEFEO* 10 (1910): 593-600.

[104]Moule, "British Sinology," 189. To see the difference between opinions formed on broad but generalized reading versus disciplined research, one only has to compare Giles' 1901 *A History of Chinese Literature* with the 1902 German countermeasure of Grube, *Geschichte der chinesischen Literatur*.

and wrote such a staggering amount."[105] Giles himself admitted that his purpose in his scholarship was to educate English readers about China, "some knowledge of whose language, literature, philosophy, history and social life I have struggled for many years to convey to British and American readers."[106]

Much more healthy for Giles' modern reputation is his work in lexicography and biography, endeavors of patient tabulation that were better suited to his scholarly temperament.

He once commented on the English tradition of Chinese lexicography, placing himself in an ever-changing continuum:

> On 23 October, 1902, he [Sir Edmund Backhouse (1873-1944)] had written to tell me that he was "trying to write an Anglo-Chinese dictionary;" and I have since learnt that he has been engaged for some years upon a Chinese-English Dictionary, which is of course intended to supersede my own work. Well, dictionaries are like dogs, and have their day; and I should be the last person to whine over the appearance of the dictionary of the future, which it is hoped will come in good time, and will help to an easier acquisition of "the glorious language." Morrison and Medhurst, both Englishmen, between them held the blue ribbon of Chinese lexicography from 1816 to 1874; then it passed to Wells Williams, who held it for America until 1892, when I think I may claim to have recaptured it for my own country, and to have held it now (1925) for thirty-three years. When the day comes to hand over, if still "enjoying the vital air" I shall say of my tenure what Harriet Martineau, at 74, said of life–"I have had a noble share."[107]

The two volumes of *A Chinese-English Dictionary* were first published at Shanghai in 1892 after eighteen years of effort. A second edition appeared in 1912, of which the fourth and fifth fascicles, printed in 1911, won the Julien Prize. It took advantage of native Chinese

---

[105]Pollard, "H.A. Giles and His Translations," 494.
[106]"The Memoirs of H.A. Giles," 19.
[107]Ibid., 38-39.

scholarship that had appeared in the interim, and considerably expanded what was already a voluminous work, treating 10,926 characters in 1711 pages with many tables. For each graph Giles included Edward Parker's dialect transcriptions of Pekinese, Cantonese, Hakka, Foochow, Wenchow, Ningpo, Hankow, Yangchow, and Szechwan dialects along with Korean, Japanese, and Annamese.[108] The rhyming category according to the *P'ei-wen yün-fu* allows each character to be quickly located in that thesaurus. A table on p. vii showing the number of vocabulary entries under twenty-five select Chinese characters illustrates the progressive advance in lexicography made with the appearance of the dictionaries of Morrison (1819), Medhurst (1843), Williams (1874), and Giles' two editions of 1892 and 1912. A comparison of the same select Chinese characters with R.H. Mathews, *Chinese-English Dictionary* (Shanghai: China Inland Mission and Presbyterian Mission Press, 1931), reveals that Mathews made no advance in the number of entries, and treated 3,000 fewer characters. Of course, conciseness was a virtue with Mathews, and his work was consecrated to his fellow missionaries. Giles' dictionary, on the other hand, was dedicated to those who needed the more technical vocabularies of diplomacy and commerce: "To the Members of H.B.M Consular Service in China and Other Students of the Chinese Language This Dictionary is Sympathetically Offered in the Hope that it may Lighten the Burden of what must always be a Toilsome Task." Although it was not infallible—no work ever is—and Berthold Laufer had occasion to differ with some of Giles' conclusions,[109] Laufer nevertheless praised it as "monumental," a work "which is marked by progress and new results on every page, and for which every student of Chinese is largely indebted to [Giles]."[110] In his own work Laufer habitually referred the reader to Giles' *Dictionary* for the

---

[108]For Edward Harper Parker (1849-1926)'s work in dialectology and combative relationship with Giles, see David Prager Branner, "Notes on the Beginnings of Systematic Dialect Description and Comparison in Chinese," forthcoming, and "The Linguistic Ideas of Edward Harper Parker," *JAOS* 119 (1999): 12-34.

[109]See, for example, Laufer's extended discussion on the rhinoceros and Giles' erroneous conclusions in Laufer, *Chinese Clay-Figures. Part 1: Prolegomena on the History of Defensive Armor* (1914; rpt. New York: Krause, 1967), 75-80.

[110]Laufer, *Jade: A Study in Chinese Archaeology and Religion* (1912; rpt. New York: Kraus, 1967), ii.

characters of Chinese words under discussion, and did the same for the next great opus of Giles.

A Chinese Biographical Dictionary was first conceived in 1891, and was produced before the second edition of the dictionary came out (preface dated January 27, 1898) . It was designed in part to supply the biographical data for the biographical entries in the *Chinese-English Dictionary*. A total of 2579 entries include both historical worthies and contemporaries of note; on pp. 981-1018 is the handy "Index to Literary Names, Sobriquets, Canonisations, and Persons Whose Names are only Mentioned in the Body of the Work." The biographical dictionary was reviewed favorably by Pelliot in 1925, who particularly appreciated the fact that precise dates were furnished.[111] It garnered the Julien Prize for 1898.

All in all, Giles was the most accomplished of the consular-men turned academics, and the most influential,[112] who had a number of "firsts": the first general history of Chinese literature, the first anthology literary translations (*Gems of Chinese Literature*), the first introduction to Chinese pictorial art, and the first biographical dictionary. We must not let the fact that his publications, apart from his dictionary and the biographical dictionary, are entirely superannuated today blind us to their usefulness to his contemporaries and to the inspiration they exerted on his readership. He was, in fact, highly decorated in his time, receiving such distinguished awards as an honorary LL.D. from Aberdeen in 1897, an honorary D. Litt. from Oxford in 1924, and the Order of Chia Ho, 2nd Class, with Grand Cordon, from the Chinese government. He was the Hibbert Lecturer in 1914, received the Triennial Gold Medal of the Royal Asiatic Society in 1922, received the Julien Prize twice, and was invited to join the French

---

[111]Paul Pelliot, "A propos du 'Chinese Biographical Dictionary' de M.H. Giles," *AM* 4 (1927): 377-89. His two criticisms are that the biographical data were often compiled at second-hand from unspecified sources, and sometimes dates and facts were faulty. Still, he spends part of his review defending Giles from the unfounded attacks of von Zach, whose critical review had appeared in the previous volume of *Asia Major* ("Einige Verbesserungen zu Giles' Chinese Biographical Dictionary," 3 [1926]:545-68). Besides providing corrections and supplemental information, Pelliot also offered what he hoped would serve as model entries for a revised edition in the future.

[112]Ishida, *Ō-Bei ni okeru Shina kenkyū*, 401, terms his work subtle and elegant, the essence of English scholarship.

Academy in 1924. Herbert Franke regards him as "one of the greatest pioneers of sinology."[113] In many ways he prefigured the career of the incomparable but stay-at-home Arthur Waley, the last of this breed of autodidactic, far-ranging intellects who read widely and published broadly and, usually, authoritatively. Ultimately Waley was reacting to Giles' handling of Chinese poetry as he developed his own translation voice.

At the close of his life, Giles acknowledged two dominating ambitions in his career since 1867, one already mentioned above: "(1) to contribute towards a more easy acquisition and a more correct knowledge of the Chinese language, written and spoken; and (2) to arouse a wider and deeper interest in the literature, history, religions, art, philosophy, and manners and customs of the Chinese people."[114] While claiming success in accomplishing the first with the publication of his two dictionaries, he lamented his failure in the second. It was not for want of trying. It is the merit of his rival among translators, Arthur Waley, that, having inherited this task, he was able to accomplish the popularization of Chinese (and Japanese) literature in the English speaking world.

---

[113]Franke, *Sinologie*, 22.
[114]"The Memoirs of H.A. Giles," 85-86.

8. JAMES LEGGE: ONE THAT DREAMED

"During all the years I was in China, I often wished that there were Chairs for its language and literature in the great universities of this country. That I should myself occupy one of them did not enter into my thoughts. When this was first suggested, about eighteen months ago, I was as one that dreamed."[1]

James Legge (1815-97) did more than any other nineteenth-century sinologist to establish Chinese philology on a professional basis. He was born on December 20th, 1815, in Huntly, Aberdeenshire, home not only to William Milne but to such later luminaries as James Hastings and George MacDonald.[2] As heir to the intellectual heritage of the Scottish

---

[1] Legge, *Inaugural Lecture*, 27.

[2] A biographical sketch by Lindsay Ride is found in Legge, *The Chinese Classics*, 5 vols. (1861-93; rpt. Hong Kong: Hong Kong University Press, 1970), 1:1-25. See also the panegyrics of Helen Edith Legge, *James Legge*; and G. Schlegel, "Necrology: James Legge," *TP* 9 (1898): 59-63. More scholarly is Wong Man-kong, *James Legge: A Pioneer at Crossroads of East and West* (Hong Kong: Hong Kong Educational Pub. Co., 1996). For Legge's religious views regarding Chinese civilization, especially in light of his missionary calling, consult Raymond Dawson, *The Chinese Chameleon: An Analysis of European Conceptions of Chinese Civilization* (London: Oxford University Press, 1967), 138-41. Short appreciations are included in Barrett, *Singular Listlessness*, pp. 75-76; David Hawkes, *Classical, Modern and Humane*, 4-6, and Treadgold, *The West in Russia and China: Religious and Secular Thought in Modern Times*, vol. 2: *China 1582-1949*, 41-45. I have not seen Lau Tze-yui, "James Legge (1815-1897) and Chinese Culture: A Missiological Study in Scholarship, Translation, and Evangelization." Ph.D. diss., University of Edinburgh, 1994.

Norman Girardot and Lauren Pfister have each completed massive works on the life, labors, and transformation of James Legge from missionary translator to Oxford sinologist and student of comparative religions. The title of Girardot's opus is *The Victorian Translation of China: James Legge's Oriental and Oxonian Pilgrimage*. It portrays Legge as a latter-day parallel of Confucius and his self-conception of mission, and as paradigmatic of the process of both acculturation through translating alien texts as well as transforming psychologically and intellectually through such acculturation. Pfister's manuscript is called *In Pursuit of the Whole Duty of Man: James Legge and the Sino-Scottish Encounter in 19th Century China*, and concentrates on Legge's life and labor in Hong Kong. Preliminary findings already published include "The Fruit and Failures of James Legge's Life for China," *Ching Feng* 31 (1988): 246-71; "Some New Dimensions in the Study of the

Enlightenment, and in particular deeply imbibing Scottish realist philosophy as formulated in Aberdeen by Thomas Reid (1710-1794), he won great distinction for his studies at King's College, University of Aberdeen; his association with this university deepened the original Scottish connection with China first established by Morrison and Milne, and started a new trend of Aberdeen men serving in China in various capacities.[3] After serving as a schoolmaster for a year, Legge decided to join the ministry and began divinity college at Highbury Theological College in 1837. In 1839, under the sponsorship of the London Missionary Society, Legge set sail for Malacca with a new bride in tow, arriving on January 10, 1840. He served as the Principal of the Anglo-Chinese College until 1843, when he orchestrated the removal of the college to the nascent colony of Hong Kong. After a lengthy career spent in the service of missionary work and scholarship, punctuated by several trips home to England, Legge finally left Hong Kong for good in 1873. His reputation preceded him, for he had become renowned for his translation of the Chinese classics, and now enjoyed the esteem of the sinological community and its leading light, Stanislas Julien.[4]

Riccian Acculturation Through the Classics

According to Legge's own account, he had "enjoyed the benefit of a few months' instruction in Chinese from the late Professor Kidd at

---

Works of James Legge (1815-1987): Part I," *Sino-Western Cultural Relations Journal* 12 (1990): 29-50; "Part Two," *Sino-Western Cultural Relations Journal* 13 (1991): 33-48; "Clues to the Life and Academic Achievements of One of the Most Famous Nineteenth Century European Sinologists–James Legge (A.D. 1815-1897)," *Journal of the Hong Kong Branch Of the Royal Asiatic Society* 30 (1990): 180-218; and "James Legge," in *Encyclopedia of Translation*, 401-22.

[3]Between 1860 and 1900, forty graduates of the University of Aberdeen worked in China, whether in medicine, missionary endeavors, or as consular officers; see John D. Hargreaves, *Academe and Empire: Some Oversees Connections of Aberdeen University 1860-1970* (Aberdeen: Aberdeen University Press, 1994), 74.

[4]Out of an apparently "massive correspondence" between Julien and Legge in the 1860s, only four letters remain preserved in the Bodleian; see Pfister, "Some New Dimensions, Part Two," 41.

University College, London."[5] A classmate was William Charles Milne, son of William Milne.[6] Legge commenced the study of the Chinese classics while still at Malacca, with the determination to master them as an indispensable aid to his missionary endeavors:

> It seemed to him (i.e., the author, Legge)...that he should not be able to consider himself qualified for the duties of his position, until he had thoroughly mastered the Classical Books of the Chinese, and had investigated for himself the whole field of thought through which the sages of China had ranged, and in which were to be found the foundations of the moral, social, and political life of the people.[7]

The epigraph that introduces Ride's biographical sketch explains this compelling rationale:

> Such a work was necessary in order that the rest of the world should really know this great Empire and also that especially our missionary labours among the people should be conducted with sufficient intelligence and as to secure permanent results. I consider that it will

---

[5]Legge, *Chinese Classics*, 1:vii. The Reverend Samuel Kidd (1797-1843) had been a missionary at the Anglo-Chinese college, but after many years of service returned to England in 1832 due to illness. In 1837 he became the first professor of Chinese in England, teaching at the University College in London. He wrote *China, or Illustrations of the Symbols, Philosophy, Antiquity, Customs, Superstitions, Law, Government, Education, and Literature of Chinese* (London: Taylor and Walton, 1841). Alas, his chair was endowed for only five years--through the largess of Sir George Staunton--and was not renewed. Staunton then drummed up support for a Chinese chair at the rival King's College. Thus it was that in 1845, J. Fearon, a retired interpreter, became first professor of Chinese at King's College. He lasted until the chair lapsed in 1851. In 1852 the Rev. James Summers assumed the reestablished chair; however, his students found that their training by a professor who knew only Cantonese and the Shanghai dialect left them hopelessly at sea upon their arrival in Peking. "Consequently," explains Twitchett, "the initial training of consular and foreign service personnel in London was rapidly abandoned;" Twitchett, *Land Tenure and the Social Order in T'ang and Sung China*, 7. On Kidd and Chinese at London, see Twitchett, 2-7; and Barrett, *Singular Listlessness*, 71-72.

[6]Wong, *James Legge*, 15.

[7]Legge, *Chinese Classics*, 1:vii.

greatly facilitate the labours of future missionaries that the entire books of Confucius should be published with a translation and notes.

As Ride explains, Legge was "going to be a missionary to his own people and race first; he was going to translate and explain the learning of the East to the scholars and the missionaries of the West."[8]   This endeavor was impelled not merely on rational grounds; emotionally, Legge had an abiding capacity for Christ-like empathy for the Chinese.   He demonstrated this at many points while working long hours out among the people, visiting the sick, ministering to members, and seeking converts.[9] Twice he was stoned by Chinese for his efforts.[10]   Yet ethnic stereotypes and cultural mischaracterizations such as occasionally slipped out from the mouths and pens of contemporary missionaries were never evident from Legge.[11]   In this capacity of charitable cultural medium, Legge pioneered the role Richard Wilhelm was later to adopt for himself.

The Chinese Classics
Legge's translation of the Confucian canon was the first to render the entirety of the Four Books and Five Classics in English.[12]   Undergoing

---

[8]Ibid., 10.

[9]This is seen most persuasively in Legge's near-martyrdom in Poklo, an event that made him a folk hero among the missionary community in Hong Kong; see Pfister, "From the Golden Light Within: Reconsideration of James Legge's Account of Ch'ëa Kam-Kwong, The Chinese Protestant 'Proto-Martyr.'" Paper presented at James Legge: The Heritage of China and the West, An International Conference, Aberdeen, Scotland, April 8-12, 1997.

[10]"I have more than once been stoned in a Chinese village" is how he commenced his twenty-two-page manuscript entitled "Reminiscences of Professor James Legge," dated 1858, Bodleian Library, MSS Eng. Misc., C. 812, 1.

[11]An egregious example of this lack of empathetic understanding comes from an early work by Robert Morrison. In his *A View of China for Philological Purposes*, 124-25, the following unfortunate passage occurs: "The Chinese are Specious, but Insincere, Jealous, Envious, are Distrustful to a High Degree....The Chinese are generally selfish, cold-blooded, and inhuman."

[12]David Collie (d. 1828), resident at the Anglo-Chinese College in Malacca from 1822 to 1828 and for part of the time professor of Chinese there, had earlier translated the Four Books, *The Chinese Classical Works Commonly Called the Four Books* (Malacca, 1828).

various permutations and published in multiple editions,[13] they remain classics even today, claims Herbert Franke, because they closely translate the text, enriched by copious annotations.[14] Legge went to such pains to produce exhaustive, densely detailed annotations for the sake of that rare reader who was willing to benefit from it: "I want to do full justice to my work on the Chinese classics. Probably out of 100 readers 99 will not care a bit for the long critical notes; but then the hundredth man will come, who will not find them to be a bit too long. For that hundredth man I ought to write."[15]

According to Herbert Giles, Legge's translation was the greatest single endeavor in sinological studies: "The fashion now is to slight Dr. Legge's great work, this practice dating from the days of Sir Thomas Wade who announced that the translations were 'wooden.' In my opinion, Legge's work is the greatest contribution ever made to the study of Chinese, and will be remembered and studied ages after Sir Thomas Wade's own paltry contribution has gone...to the dust-heap."[16] An opposing view

---

His translation influenced Emerson and Thoreau, according to Barrett, *Singular Listlessness*, 65. See the fascinating evaluation by Pfister, "Serving or Suffocating the Sage? Reviewing the Efforts of Three Nineteenth Century Translators of the Four Books, With Special Emphasis on James Legge (A.D. 1815-1897)," *The Hong Kong Linguist* 7 (Spring and Summer 1990): 25-56. A superficial, hasty, and negative overview is C.Y. Hsü, "James Legge and the Chinese Classics," *Asian Culture Quarterly (Asian-Pacific Culture Quarterly)* 23 (Spring 1995): 43-58.

[13]Legge published three translations of the *Lun-yü, Meng-tzu,* and *Shih-ching;* four translations of the *Chung-yung;* two versions of the *Shang-shu,* and one each for the rest of the classics. See Pfister, "Some New Perspectives on James Legge's Multiform English Translations of the *Chinese Classics* and *Sacred Books of China,*" Lecture presented at Hong Kong Baptist University for the 70th Anniversary of the Department of Chinese of the University of Hong Kong, December 10, 1997. The enduring value of Legge's translations of the Chinese classics is reconfirmed by a recent set of unpublished critical essays by Lauren Pfister, Liu Jiahe, and Shao Dongfang, that seek to place Legge's accomplishments within the context of the achievements of modern sinological study of the classics. The critical apparatus they provide is especially useful.

[14]Herbert Franke, "Sinologie im 19. Jahrhundert," in *August Pfizmaier (1808-1887) und seine Bedeutung für die Ostasienwissenschaften,* 40.

[15]Helen Legge, *James Legge,* 42.

[16]Giles, *Adversaria Sinica,* 346.

is voiced by Raymond Dawson, who characterizes Legge as having been "quite out of touch with the latest Chinese scholarship and accepted the old-fashioned orthodox interpretation...who wrote in an English which now seems extremely antiquated."[17]　In the rest of this section I will endeavor to demonstrate the error of the latter view, stipulating to the inescapable King James' quality of Legge's prose without conceding that it is, in itself, a bad thing.[18]

At first reading, Legge's faults seem to be more in the area of philosophical assumption than technical approach.　Waley attributes Legge's mistakes in *The Works of Mencius* to a dependence on Chu Hsi's theological interpretations rather than Chao Ch'i's 趙岐 (d. A.D. 201) philological glosses—the same error of outlook can be claimed for the entire set of translations.　It is only erroneous, however, if one desires a translation based on the Han exegetical world-view rather than a Neo-Confucian reading that was, after all, both orthodox and normative for most of late imperial China.

In discussing the *Book of Odes*, Legge explained the relative scholastic stances of Mao and Chu as follows:

---

[17]Dawson, *The Chinese Chameleon*, 6.　Ride, "Biographical Note," 20-22 includes quotations of the scholarly appreciations of Legge by his contemporaries and the younger generation of sinologists, including Joseph Edkins, G. Schlegel, and Henri Cordier. Eugene Eoyang offers more searching, theoretical criticism of Legge's translation of the *Analects* in *The Transparent Eye: Reflections on Translation, Chinese Literature, and Comparative Poetics* (Honolulu: University of Hawaii, 1993), 170-77.　That Legge never overcame either the world-view of his times or the mind-set of a missionary is not really a criticism by Eoyang, who instead attempts to illustrate the "horizon of expectations" of translators.

[18]At various places in his massive manuscript *The Victorian Translation of China*, Norman Girardot points out that Legge's archaic style was noticed by his contemporaries; evidently, it was a conscious stylistic choice, not a product of his age.　An instance is E.J. Eitel, who remarked that "we cannot shut our eyes against a certain rigid stateliness, almost amounting to prosy heaviness and quaintness, that characterized Dr. Legge as a translator in his previous publications and comes out more strongly here where he is dealing with quaint poetical effusions which he was not enthusiastic enough to admire very highly;" Eitel, "The She-King," 5.

The traditional interpretation of the odes, which we may suppose is given by Maou, is not to be overlooked; and, where it is supported by historical confirmations, it will often be found helpful. Still it is from the pieces themselves that we must chiefly endeavor to gather their meaning. This was the plan on which Choo He proceeded; and, as he far exceeded his predecessors in the true critical faculty, so China has not since produced another equal to him.[19]

Legge was perplexed that the imperial editors "show an evident leaning to that of the old school," and assumed that modern readers would also wonder at it.[20] When both commentaries agreed, then Legge was content with the consensus view: "So far both schools of interpreters are agreed on this ode, and we need not be long detained with it."[21] Yet he departed more often from Chu Hsi than did Séraphin Couvreur, whose translations from the classics into French and Latin were both elegant and impeccably precise, but who, according to Demiéville, never "essayed any original interpretation or personal criticism."[22] The evaluation of Wong Siu-kit and Li Kar-shu of Legge's *Shih-ching* rendering is based on this same assumption, that Legge was entirely dependent on Chu Hsi, an assumption effectively countered by Lauren Pfister at various points.[23] Legge never hesitated to express his own scholarly assessment. In fact, sometimes he could scarcely restrain his umbrage at the perversity of the traditional interpretation. For instance, after summarizing the tradition attendant on Mao #5, he uttered with more disgust than temper, "Surely this is sad stuff."[24] Mao #3 elicited the invective "no interpretation could be more licentious. It is astonishing that the imperial editors should lean to this

---

[19]Legge, *The Chinese Classics*, 4:5.
[20]Ibid.
[21]Ibid., 4:10.
[22]Paul Demiéville, "Aperçu historique des études sinologiques en France," 465.
[23]Wong and Li, "Three English Translations of the *Shijing*," *Renditions* 25 (Spring 1986): 113-39. Pfister, "James Legge," 408-12, is a general rebuttal of the view of Wong and Li. Part Two of Pfister's "Some New Dimensions," 38-40, reevaluates Legge's independence from Chu Hsi based on specific documentation to Legge's translations of *The Analects* for both pro- and contra-Chu Hsi interpretations.
[24]*The Chinese Classics*, 4:12.

view."[25] Not even Chu Hsi escaped his wrath: "The account of those two names, 天 and 上帝, given by Ch'ing E, and accepted by Choo and all subsequent writers, is absurd....We are as good judges of what is meant by Heaven, as a name for the Supreme Power, as Ch'ing was...."[26] And we must add that Legge only followed Chu when there was compelling reason. For instance, concerning Mao #7, Legge confessed: "Choo makes 肅肅 descriptive of the careful manner in which the nets were set; Maou, of the reverent demeanour of the trapper. It is difficult to choose between them."[27] Sometimes he elected to harmonize both views in his translation, as in Mao #167: Mao took an odd binome as meaning "strong;" Chu rendered it as "unresting;" Legge "united the explanations" to yield "eager and strong."[28] On occasion, he even dumped both of them in preference to another authority.[29]

When Legge did find sufficient grounds for choosing between them, he went with Chu Hsi in the majority of cases. For instance, in the first subsection of eleven poems, the *Chou-nan* 周南, Chu is mentioned twenty-six times positively and ten times negatively, for a positive ratio of 72%; Mao sixteen times positively and nineteen negatively, for a positive ratio of 46%. Whenever Legge cited Chu's exegetical glosses, he agreed with him 70% of the time; Mao, 41%. As for overall interpretation of the odes, when he mentioned Chu he agreed with him 75%; whenever Mao's name came up, it was positive in 63% of the citations. Sometimes, it is true, he cited both views as plausible, but Chu's won out in the end as "much to be preferred."[30] Still, if he was persuaded on linguistic or contextual grounds, he did not hesitate to follow Mao.[31] The overall assessment of Pfister is

---

[25]Ibid., 4:9.

[26]Mao #192; Ibid., 4:316.

[27]Ibid., 4:13.

[28]Ibid., 4:260; cf. Mao #116; 4:178.

[29]As in Mao #s 10 and 240; see ibid., 4:6-17; 447.

[30]See Legge's commentary in ibid., 4:250, Mao # 164.

[31]For instance, at Mao #196: "Choo says the *këw* here is the *pan këw* (班鳩), or pigeon; but the opinion of Maou, who makes it the same as the dove in I.v.IV.3, is preferable. Maou also is the more correct in his definition of 翰, by 高, 'high;'" ibid., 4:333-34.

that Legge, through his copious citation of various authorities, "offered a much wider scope of references submitted to the interpretive judgments of his readers, one much more complex than a simple mirroring of Zhu's position."[32] In the matter of Chu Hsi's reorganization of the text of the *Chung-yung*, however, a text for which Legge published four separate translations, he was harshly critical of the Neo-Confucian master.[33]

In contrast with the assertion of Raymond Dawson that Legge was "quite out of touch with the latest Chinese scholarship and accepted the old-fashioned orthodox interpretation," his broad-minded perusal of the entire commentarial tradition was appreciated by his contemporary expatriates in China,[34] and even more so by his assistant, Wang T'ao (1828-1897). After the publication of volumes one and two, Legge enjoyed the close collaboration of Wang, a learned Chinese scholar who earlier had assisted Medhurst. An admirably eclectic scholar, Wang admired the same quality in Legge. Paul Cohen notes that "As a general rule...[Legge] weighed the materials he took from K'ung [Ying-ta] and Cheng [Hsüan] against the opinions of the Ch'eng brothers [Ch'eng Hao and Ch'eng I] and Chu [Hsi]. His attitude toward the teachings of the Han and Sung schools was one of impartiality."[35] And in rebuttal to the first charge, that he was quite out of touch with contemporary scholarship, he became intimately acquainted with the contents of the Huang-ch'ing ching-chieh 皇清經解 no more than two years after its publication in 1892.[36]

---

[32]Pfister, "Some New Perspectives on James Legge's Multiform English Translations of the *Chinese Classics* and *Sacred Books of China*," 9.

[33]Ibid., 5, n. 14.

[34]Witness E.J. Eitel: "If we examine the long list of native works he daily consulted and which, by the way, form a good-sized library, we find, there is scarcely a Chinese work on the She-king of any importance, that is not constantly being quoted all through the two volumes;" Eitel, "The She-King," 4.

[35]Paul A. Cohen, *Between Tradition and Modernity: Wang T'ao and Reform in Late Ch'ing China* (Cambridge, Mass.: Harvard University Press, 1974), 59.

[36]I ascertain this from the contents of an article Legge published in the *Journal of the Royal Asiatic Society* in 1895; given the lag time in publication, and the time it would take to transship books from China, a period of roughly two years first to access and next assimilate seems more than reasonable. For more on this point, see Helen Legge, *James Legge*, 30-31.

Wang T'ao's role consisted largely of collecting and coordinating the vast commentarial material. According to Cohen, "Wang assembled exhaustive commentaries for each classic, paying special attention to opinions which, being buried in out-of-the-way works, would otherwise have escaped the notice of a foreign scholar. Legge appreciated and gave full recognition to these compilations."[37] After joining Legge with volume three of *The Chinese Classics*, Wang provided in all eight centos of commentaries to the *Shih-ching*, *Ch'un-ch'iu Tso-chuan*, *Li-chi*, and *Chou-i*.[38] Legge once described his debt to Wang as follows: "My own version [of the *Li-chi*] is based on a study of these two imperial collections, and on an extensive compilation, made specially for my use by my Chinese friend and former helper, the graduate Wang Thâo, gathered mostly from more recent writers of the last 250 years."[39] Wang therefore served more as what we would now call a research assistant who performed preliminary bibliographical work than as linguistic informant who nursed his employer along in the language.[40] For Legge had a masterful and independent grasp of both the complexities of the Chinese classical language as well as the breadth of its vocabulary base. More common in those days was the case of Giles, who leaned heavily on native Chinese help. Although Legge himself professed regret that he did not have "the assistance of any Chinese graduate with who I could talk over complicated and perplexing paragraphs" of the *Li-chi*, he nevertheless trusted that the unavoidable mistakes would be very few.[41] Legge was neither emotionally servile nor

---

[37]Ibid., 60.

[38]Robert S. Britton, in *Eminent Chinese of the Ch'ing Period*, 2:837.

[39]*Li Chi Book of Rites*, 1:lxxxii.

[40]See Lee Chi-fang, "Wang T'ao's Contribution to James Legge's Translation of the Chinese Classics," *Tamkang Review* 17/1 (1986): 47-67; Wong, *James Legge*, 114-26; the Chinese and English studies listed in Lam Kwok-fai and Wong Man-kong, "Wang T'ao yen-chiu shu-p'ing," *Hsiang-kang Chung-kuo chin-tai-shih hsüeh-hui hui-k'an* (July 1993): 67-85; and three articles on Wang T'ao's scholarship, baptism, and his unpublished letters to James Legge by Lee Chi-fang, Su Ching, and Wong Man-kang, in *Li-shih yü wen-hua* 1 (January 1998):45-58; 59-67; 69-76. Most complete is Lee Chi-fang, "Wang Tao (1828-1897): His Life, Thought, and Literary Achievement." Ph.D. diss., University of Wisconsin, 1973.

[41]*Li Chi Book of Rites*, 1:lxxxiii-lxxxiv.

linguistically dependant on native Chinese informants. Such intellectual self-confidence was his scholarly right after having spent the better portion of his adult life immersed in the classical Chinese tradition.

Legge the Philologist

On the technical level of philology, Legge had many methodological virtues. For one, he had an enlightened view of the nature of the Chinese script. If on occasion he yielded to the temptation to dismiss a difficult word as an unintelligible particle, consigning it offhand to the dustbin of meaningless sounds, he nevertheless understood the flexible nature of graphic spellings, and recognized that many binomes are mere orthographic variations of the same word. For instance, in Mao #5 we have the phrase *chung-ssu yü, shen-shen hsi* 螽斯羽詵詵兮, rendered by him as "Ye locusts, winged tribes,/How harmoniously you collect together!"[42]   Legge's gloss on *shen-shen* is instructive: "We have the character in the text, the form of the Shwoh-wan [*Shuo-wen*], 辛 with 羽 at the side, 先 with 馬 at the side, and 生 with another 生 at the side;—all in binominal form with the same meaning."[43]   The fact that Legge is probably in error regarding the function of *ssu* as part of the word *chung* instead of a particle,[44] should not lead us to underestimate the advance his grasp of the orthography made over that of his contemporaries. Besides, many words that Legge could only dismiss as unintelligible particles remain as obscure today. For instance, in treating the locution *po-yen* 薄言 in Mao #9, Legge commented that "both of these terms have been noticed, on Ode II., as untranslatable particles. Nothing more can be said of them, when they are found, as here, in combination."[45] Neither Waley's "Here we go" or Schuessler's "there" address the function of the words even if they supply a stop-gap translation. Sometimes Legge can only admit defeat

---

[42]*The Chinese Classics*, 4:11.

[43]This particular example, without reference to Legge's gloss, has been confirmed by Axel Scheussler, *A Dictionary of Early Zhou Chinese* (Honolulu: University of Hawaii Press, 1987), 534a.

[44]See Bernhard Karlgren, *Glosses on the Book of Odes* (rpt. Stockholm: Museum of Far Eastern History, 1964), 91, for the linguistic and contextual evidence *contra* Legge.

[45]*The Chinese Classics*, 4:15.

and appeal to the "particle" defense. An example is Mao #13; after detailing why the views of earlier exegetes are untenable, Legge ruefully concedes that he must agree with Wang T'ao: "Our best plan is to take 于 and 以 together as a compound particle, untranslatable; so Wang T'aou (于以猶薄言，皆發聲語助也) [yu-i is the same as po-yen, they are both expletive particles"].[46]

His treatment of the particle chih 之 , "sign of the genitive," shows a sensitivity to the rhythm of the line not demonstrated until George Kennedy and his famous article on metrical irregularity.[47]   The line in question is the opening couplet of Mao #6: 桃之夭夭，灼灼其華. Taking chih in its normal role as a genetive marker, Legge offered as an alternate translation of the first line the awkward rendering "In the young and beautiful time of the peach tree." Dissatisfied with this reading, Legge noticed that contextually, chih had an alternate function widespread in Shih-ching despite its normal usage: "Still, 之 is so constantly used throughout the She in the middle of lines, where we can only regard it as a particle, eking out the number of feet, that it is, perhaps, not worth while to resolve such lines as this in the above manner."   Thankfully, his sensitivity to Shih-ching metrics overruled his strict sense of grammar and yielded the following more pleasant line: "The peach tree is young and elegant;/Brilliant are its flowers."[48]

Legge's one unavoidable rule of thumb was to stick closely to the syntax. This principle, according to Giles, was "the golden key to the written language of China." It was first widely announced by Marshman, author of Clavis Sinica: "the whole of Chinese grammar depends upon position."[49]   "It is impossible to exhaust the meanings of a Chinese character by definitions," continues Giles, "each word being (to quote from Professor Sonnenschein) 'like a chameleon, which borrows its colour from

[46]Ibid., 4:22.
[47]Kennedy, "Metrical Irregularity in the Shih Ching," HJAS 60 (1939): 284-96.
[48]The Chinese Classics, 4:12.
[49]Quoted in Giles, A Chinese-English Dictionary, 1:xiv.

its environment.'"[50] Legge noticed this virtue when he had first auditioned Wylie: "His pronunciation was not exact, but he had got hold of the principle of relative position by which the meaning of the symbolic characters in their combination is determined."[51] What Legge considered a methodological aid Robert Douglas, the Chinese collection librarian at the British Museum, regarded as a stylistic fault: "No word can be moved out of its determined position without entirely changing its value, or rendering it meaningless. Thus the literature has lost much of its variety and elegance which belongs by nature to that of the polysyllabic languages."[52] Legge also seemed to have a certain feel for the language, "whose instinct," according to George Kennedy, "kept him on the alert even when his analysis lagged."[53]

Finally, Legge the fledgling philologist was at least partially aware of the importance of textual criticism, and, on occasion, even went so far as to supply variant readings of at least one other textual witness to support the base-text he supplied. His motivations for doing so betray an admirable attitude towards completeness in his translations, even if he did not quite grasp the essential point in doing so: "In the notes to the present republication of the Corea [Korean] text...I have taken the trouble to give all the various readings (amounting to more than 300), partly as a curiosity and to make my text complete, and partly to show how, in the transcription of writings in whatever language, such variations are sure to occur...while on the whole they very slightly affect the meaning of the document."[54] It nevertheless speaks highly of his overall grasp of the basis of philology that he paid so much attention to providing a good base-text: since there are so many errors in previous versions of the text, "it seems

---

[50]Ibid., 1:viii. Edward Adolf Sonnenschein (1851-1929) was an Oxford-trained classical scholar. As a professor of Greek and Latin at Birmingham University, he edited the popular parallel grammar series; he reformed teaching by treating all Indo-European languages on the same plan, with a common terminology.

[51]Cordier, "The Life and Labours of Alexander Wylie," 9.

[52]Douglas, *The Language and Literature of China*, 61.

[53]Kennedy, *Selected Works of George A. Kennedy*, ed. Li Tien-yi (New Haven: Far Eastern Publications, 1964), 55.

[54]*A Record of Buddhist Kingdoms*, 4.

desirable that I should annex to my translation a more correct Chinese text than had previously been printed."[55] One last irresistible quotation sums up Legge's philological mind-set:

> All Chinese texts, and Buddhist texts especially, are new to foreign students. One has to do for them what many hundreds of the ablest scholars in Europe have done for the Greek and Latin classics during several hundred years, and what thousands of critics and commentators have been doing for our Sacred Scriptures for nearly eighteen hundred centuries. There are few predecessors in the field of Chinese literature into whose labours translators of the present century can enter. This will be received, I hope, as sufficient apology for the minuteness and length of some of the notes.[56]

In conclusion, Legge's philological approach exhibited certain technical advances over his contemporaries that not only served him well but continue to undergird classical Chinese philology today. In sum, these are the following: 1) his grasp of the logographic nature of Chinese orthography; 2) a sensitivity to metrics; 3) unswerving adherence to the rule of syntax; 4) a literal translation style that eschewed elegance for accuracy; 5) mastery of the commentarial tradition and willingness to follow the best authorities, where based on the evidence from the text itself; and 6) concern for utilizing the best text, even to creating a simple variorum edition.

Better Wooden Than Wooly: Translation Style

A particular strength of Legge's translations, according to David Nivison, is his literal renderings that did not smooth over linguistic or textual problems: difficulties in the English translation merely reflected difficulties in the original:

> Legge will impress many readers as old-fashioned and awkward; this is a consequence, in part, of the fact that this translation was the

---

[55] *The Nestorian Monument*, iii-iv.
[56] *A Record of Buddhist Kingdoms*, xiii.

work of a missionary working more than a century ago. But in large measure it results from an extraordinary conscientiousness that refuses to smooth over a spot in the text where the translator feels the sense to be difficult to ascertain. Legge's awkwardness is therefore actually a virtue, and it is not his only virtue.[57]

Fidelity to both the semantics and stylistics of the text is, of course, the first duty of the philologist, who should not anticipate what the potential readership may desire to extract from the text. The task of the philologist is to present the documents and the raw data they contain, including such overlooked features as linguistic character, grammatical usage, and stylistic nuance. A translation that reads smoothly and effortlessly, such as Burton Watson's renderings of the *Shih-chi*, does not live up to such a lofty commitment, and hence is less broadly serviceable than it could be.[58] While it may be less literally wooden in style, such a reading is irritatingly imprecise in providing a wooly linguistic texture.[59] Legge's literalness was a conscious stylistic choice of the translator, not a result of any lack of taste or skill, for his translations went through three or four independent versions, each set aside for a period of time for later reflection and revision.

Lauren Pfister comments on Legge's process of translation as follows:

> The first complete translation of a text being finished, he would file it away. Returning to the Chinese text a few years later, Legge would do another independent translation without reference to his earlier

---

[57]David S. Nivison, "On Translating Mencius," in *The Ways of Confucianism: Investigations in Chinese Philosophy*, ed. Bryan W. Van Nordern (Chicago: Open Court, 1996), 175-201; quote on 177. Gustav Schlegel also noted Legge's fidelity to the text, never skipping linguistic difficulties; "Necrology: James Legge," 63.

[58]C. S. Goodrich took Watson to task for just this reason (among several important issues) in his review in *JAOS* 82 (1962): 190-202; and again in his surrejoinder to Watson's rejoinder; see *JAOS* 83 (1963): 115.

[59]Watson realized this in retrospect; see his comments in "Some Remarks on Early Chinese Historical Works," in *The Translation of Things Past*, ed. George Kao (Hong Kong: Chinese University, 1982), 36.

draft. Only after completing the whole work would he compare it with his earlier effort, checking to see what had changed, in what ways he had matured, and identifying any further patterns which suggested better ways to handle general problems of ancient grammar or idioms. For any one text, depending on the length, Legge may have done as many as three or four independent versions before preparing the manuscript for publication.[60]

It is for this rigid fidelity, coupled with Legge's command of the language and the commentarial tradition, and his "perceptive treatment of Mencius' philosophy," that Nivison hails his version of the *Meng-tzu* as "one of the best presentations available."[61]

We leave it to Professor Giles to have the last word on Legge's classical studies:

> Students of the 'The Chinese Classics,' as translated and annotated by Dr. Legge, must have frequently been struck by the amazing industry and the extraordinary accuracy of the great Aberdonian....His translation of the Confucian Canon has helped many a weaker brother to a right understanding of a most difficult text,--a point the latter might not have otherwise reached; and it has also enabled other and still weaker brethren to pose as independent interpreters of works which lie in reality beyond their powers.[62]

Legge's masterful accomplishment was recognized by his contemporaries, and in 1875 he won the first Julien Prize ever awarded.

From Missionary Translator to Professional Sinologist

In 1876 Legge was appointed to the first Chair of Chinese established at Oxford in Corpus Christi College, a position he held until his death in 1897.[63] This chair had been endowed by a group of merchants

---

[60]Pfister, "James Legge," 403.

[61]Nivison, "On Translating Mencius," 200.

[62]Giles, *Adversaria Sinica*, 117.

[63]A fellow Scots, the great lexicographer and founding editor of the *Oxford English Dictionary*, James Murray, chose to be buried near his friend Legge in Wolvercote

with the proviso that Legge hold the chair.[64] Although his non-Anglican status as a Nonconformist led to an occasional social difficulty with his associates, Legge enjoyed a close relationship with his great Oxford contemporary Max Müller (1832-1900).[65] A lengthy extract from a letter sent to Legge from Müller reveals the deep respect Legge was accorded by both Müller and Julien; it is dated February 13, 1875, the year before Legge came to Oxford:

> It would be the greatest pleasure to me to make your personal acquaintance. I have long wished for an opportunity of being introduced to you, and being able to tell you how much I admire your magnificent edition of the *Chinese Classics*.
> As to the soundness of your work, I have, of course, no right to express an opinion, but I knew, when I heard my old friend Stanislaus Julien speak of your work in the highest possible terms, that it must, indeed, be of the highest order to extort such praise from a man not very lavish of praise.
> All I can say for myself is that I wish we had such translations as yours of the other sacred writings of the world.[66]

Legge reveals, in an off-handed remark, that Julien came to be most effusive in his praise: "Julien is a most voluminous correspondent. His letters to me bristle with compliments."[67] Among Legge's papers found after his death were several bundles of letters from the French sinologue, "all beautifully written," according to Helen Legge, "full of Chinese quotations and often with delicate slips of Chinese printing gummed in."[68] In addition to Müller and Julien, Legge also corresponded with Schlegel and von der

---

Cemetary. His grave lies at the foot of Legge's.

[64]For the establishment of this chair, see the detailed treatment by Wong, *James Legge*, 80-89.

[65]Treated at great length by Girardot in *The Victorian Translation of China*; see also Pfister, "Some New Dimensions," Part Two, 36-38.

[66]Max Müller, *The Life and Letters of the Right Honorable Friedrich Max Müller, edited by His Wife*, 2 vols. (London: Longmans, Green, and Co., 1902), 1:483.

[67]Helen Legge, *James Legge*, 45.

[68]Ibid.

Gabelentz, among European Orientalists. One final compliment accrues to Legge by way of Müller. In introducing a letter sent to Legge from Müller on March 10, 1876, Mrs. Müller praised Legge as being the only scholar among a great many collaborators on the *Sacred Works of the East* project who never disappointed him; especially in terms of deadlines: even if many others were sometimes years behind in turning in their manuscripts, once Legge promised a date, he invariably made the deadline.[69]

Legge remained active in scholarship for the next twenty-one years, utilizing the resources he had collected over a lifetime in what must of been the most impressive sinological library in the West, public or private.[70] During his Oxford tenure, he translated such seminal works as the *Hsiao-ching* (1979), *I-ching* (1882), *Li-chi* (1885), *Fo-kuo chi* (1886), *Chuang-tzu, Lao-tzu*, and *T'ai-shang kan-ying p'ien* (1891), and "Li-sao" (1895). In 1884, while attending the tercentenary celebration of the University of Edinburgh, he received an honorary degree of LL.D. At his death he was working on the *Ch'u-tz'u*. His translation of Taoist classics, *The Texts of Taoism*, included as volumes 39 and 40 of Müller's *Sacred Books of the East* series, according to one modern authority, constituted "the first important presentation of Taoism as a whole in the West."[71]

Willliam E. Soothill

William Edward Soothill (1861-1935) was the next occupant of Legge's Oxford chair. He was a former missionary who was appointed to succeed Legge in 1920, and served until 1935. That Soothill was not selected until 1920, a hiatus of twenty-three years, indicates the lack of institutional commitment to the chair in Chinese. In 1938, three years after Soothill's retirement, the distinguished Chinese scholar Ch'en Yin-k'o was appointed, but, due to the war, only arrived in England after the end of World War II in 1946, and was prevented from assuming his duties by

---

[69]Müller, *The Life and Letters*, 2:12.

[70]Pfister, "Some New Dimensions," Part Two, 33-35.

[71]Kristopher Schipper, "The History of Taoist Studies in the West," in *Europe Studies China*, 471.

eye problems.[72]   An American, Homer H. Dubs (1892-1969), another former missionary, was elected to the chair in 1947.[73] It was not until the accession of David Hawkes in 1961 that the first professional sinologist to have been trained for his duties in academia, not missionary work, held the Oxford chair. The precedent of drawing upon retired missionaries or, on occasion, foreign service personnel for academic posts, whether at Oxford, Cambridge, or London, so firmly entrenched in English sinological circles for many generations, hence stretched from Dubs directly back through Legge to Kidd.

---

[72]For Ch'en Yin-k'o (pronounced Ch'en Yin-ch'üeh in the PRC), see Howard L. Boorman and Richard C. Howard, eds., *Biographical Dictionary of Republican China*, 5 vols. (New York: Columbia University Press, 1967), 1:259-61.

[73]Dubs is treated among American sinologists in chapter ten below.

9: ARTHUR WALEY: PHILOLOGIST AS POET

"Only in rare combination can philologists double as poets, or poets as philologists. The philologist is concerned with excavating expression from a foreign language, the poet with perfecting expression in his own language. The combination that succeeds is then a combination of both."

—Kennedy, *Selected Works*[1]

"Inspiration of the moment is not enough; it must be supplemented by the long and thoughtful work of the mind, if something useful is to be produced. That, then, is no longer philology, no longer our craft. We cannot do without our philology, in this case, but it is not enough....Necessary though it is, learning is not sufficient, not even to understand the text, and when translation is also something like the writing of poetry, the help of the Muse is most certainly needed."

—Wilamowitz, "Was ist Übersetzen"[2]

Born two years after Wylie's death, Arthur Waley would share more with Wylie than a resting-place in Highgate cemetery, for Waley was the most accomplished of the self-taught Orientalists. Waley combined both rare literary insight and recondite technical erudition, although he declined to put his learning to institutional use: he never held nor desired an academic post. Yet he more than matched any English professional sinologist of the times,[3] and was very supportive of professional activities, attending conferences and reading papers. And if Legge enjoys the reputation of being the greatest nineteenth-century translator from the Chinese, then fellow compatriot Waley assumed his unofficial mantle

---

[1]"Fenollosa, Pound and the Chinese Character," rpt. in *Selected Works of George A. Kennedy*, ed. Li Tien-yi (New Haven: Far Eastern Publications, 1964), 460.

[2]Lefevere, *Translating Literature*, 103.

[3]The sentiments of Hugh Lloyd-Jones apply equally well to Waley as to Western classicists: "Not all of the most learned men teach in universities. Some of the most learned persons I have known have worked in libraries, or in museums, or in great publishing houses," Lloyd-Jones, *Greek in a Cold Climate* (Savage, Maryland: Barnes and Noble, 1991), 70.

during the first half of the twentieth.[4]

"He Remains an Englishman"

Arthur Waley (1889-1966) was born Arthur Schloss in Tunbridge Wells, of part German ancestry, and studied at King's College, Cambridge from 1907-1910 on a scholarship in the classics. Despite the promise he showed at Cambridge, his studies ground to a halt due to eye problems. In 1913, after an abortive effort to please his parents by working in the export business, he was given a position in the Department of Prints and Drawings in the British Museum, in the newly-created Oriental Sub-Department under the Orientalist and poet Laurence Binyon.[5] He left the British Museum in 1929 to devote himself to writing and translation by adopting a time-honored pretext of Chinese officialdom to excuse himself from service: he pled illness. Other than a brief stint during the war as a censor in the Ministry of Information (1939-45) Waley did not hold a full-time job again.

Waley never visited Asia or learned to speak modern Mandarin or Japanese. Of course, other prominent scholars often preferred to remain home, never willing to risk subverting their historical vision by personal observation. The famous Oxford Indologist Max Müller is an example of this. The difference between Waley and Ralph Rackstraw, the sailor hero of Gilbert and Sullivan's lighthearted operatic farce *H.M.S. Pinafore*, is that Waley was not even tempted to "belong," whether emotionally attached or intellectually loyal, to other nations but remained staunchly and steadfastly

---

[4]For his life and works, see David Hawkes, "Obituary of Arthur Waley," *AM* 12 (1966): 143-47; Wong Siu Kit and Chan Man Sing, "Arthur Waley," in *An Encyclopaedia of Translation*, 423-28; Ivan Morris, ed., *Madly Singing in the Mountains: An Appreciation and Anthology of Arthur Waley*; and F.A. Johns, *A Bibliography of Arthur Waley* (New Brunswick, 1968). A reminiscence was written by his on-again, off-again lover, later wife for a month Alison Waley, *A Half of Two Lives: A Personal Memoir* (London: George Weidenfeld and Nicolson, 1982); it sheds little light on the scholarly life of Waley and spotlights some peculiar personality characteristics in perhaps too harsh a glare.

[5]For Waley's career in the British Museum, see Basil Grey, "Arthur Waley at the British Museum," in *Madly Singing in the Mountains*, 37-44. Laurence Binyon has been treated briefly in chapter 7 above.

an Englishman. One would think that both Waley and Müller partook of the same defensive posture as the Greek scholar Ingram Bywater, who is said to have avoided Greece because "the reality might interfere with his imaginative picture of the country in ancient times."[6]

In a very perceptive review of *Madly Singing in the Mountains*, Jonathan Spence muses at length on some of the reasons inhibiting Waley from visiting modern Asia.[7] Chief among them was the very Englishness of his very upper-middle-class education:

> Waley was a classicist; and he was also in King's College at the time when Goldsworthy Lowes Dickinson...still presided over young minds, inculcating the virtues of an aesthetic humanism which are the heart of what people came to know as "Bloomsbury," virtues that were permanently captured in the essays and novels of E.M. Forster. Dickinson was dejected by the ugliness and cruelty and insensitivity of the world that lurked just outside Cambridge; how could the Athenian ideals be preserved in such an appalling environment? Those men who valued decency, honesty, and compassion must state their values clearly lest the new Englishman—"Divorced from Nature but unreclaimed by Art; instructed, but not educated; assimilative, but incapable of thought"—inherit the earth.[8]

Hence he sought to transcend the crude realism and often barbaric realities of modern life—painfully apparent in modern Asia and threatening the very existence of England in the twin forces of imperial Germany of the First World War and the Third Reich of the Second—and commune with those spirits of the past with whom he felt he could share his own sense of aesthetic truth and enlightened compassion. Thus, if Waley's particular views of Asia were entirely the product of an incisive intellect that fed on a wide-ranging array of classical sources in many languages, his choice of authors to translate was itself guided by the force of his moral convictions

---

[6]Lloyd-Jones, *Blood for the Ghosts*, 163.

[7]Reprinted in *China Roundabout: Essays in History and Culture* (New York: W.W. Norton, 1992), 329-36.

[8]*China Roundabout*, 330.

and the leanings of his heart. In return for his personal selection of favorites, we readers received versions of classic works that serve, in the words of Spence, as "oriental benedictions to a way of life" that contains much of merit for our own even if not always reflecting reality. Ultimately, then, Waley's translations "were the product of a...belief that there are certain values that are not transitory, certain attitudes that can never be anachronistic, because they have always (and always will be) true."[9]

Autodidactic Orientalist

Because of this refusal to experience Asia on its own terms, preferring the self-induced vision of China and Japan that was conjured up through philology, perhaps it may be said that Waley reverted to the intellectual imperialism of nineteenth-century Orientalism that sought to impose, as Edward Said would have it, an Occidental value-system through colonial textualism. But of course it was the China of the past, in all its artistic and literary splendor, that concerned Waley. That his epistemology was so persuasive was due both to the inherent attractiveness of his construction of Asian aesthetics as well as the seduction of his prose. Standing forever outside of institutional sinology, he never could have succeeded without the skills his self-acquired methodology afforded him.

It was upon his arrival at the Oriental Department of Prints and Drawings that Waley first began the study of Chinese and Japanese, under the nominal tutelage of his supervisor, Laurence Binyon. According to Waley's successor at the museum, Basil Gray, "he learned by reading the best literary texts on which he could lay his hands, and this accounts for the flow of translations from both languages and from very varied works which he began to publish from 1916 onwards."[10] This flow never stopped, but periodically fresh infusions to the current of publications were made by a number of varied and valuable scholarly works. By 1964 his productivity, according to the tabulation of Ivan Morris, had amounted to "some forty books, more than eighty articles, and about one hundred book

---

[9]*China Roundabout*, 336.
[10]"Arthur Waley at the British Museum," 39.

reviews, his books alone totaling over nine thousand pages."[11]

Waley's official duties included describing the collection of Chinese paintings held in the museum and in compiling an index (printed in 1922). His descriptions were never published, but some of them were reworked in his 1923 publication, *An Introduction to the Study of Chinese Painting*.[12]

All along, Waley had been devoting his attention to Japanese literature, his personal research finally coming after 1923 to parallel his work at the museum on a catalogue of Japanese woodcut books. In 1919 appeared *Japanese Poetry: The 'Uta'*, and in 1921 *No Plays*. In 1925 he published the first volume of *The Tale of Genji*; volumes 2-6 ultimately came out in 1933. In between, he produced *The Pillow Book of Sei Shonagon* (1928). A final reference work that was compiled during this time was the important *A Catalogue of Paintings Recovered from Tun-huang by Sir Aurel Stein Preserved in the British Museum and the Museum of Central Asian Antiquities, Delhi* (London, 1931).

Even earlier than this interest in Japanese literature was a fascination with Chinese poetry, which lasted throughout his life. In 1916 the first of his translations from the Chinese appeared. More widely-known works soon came forth: *A Hundred and Seventy Chinese Poems* (1918); *More Translations from the Chinese* (1919); and *The Temple and Other Poems* (1923).

After his years at the museum and the financial support that his published translations gained him, Waley was able to devote himself full-time to research, increasingly to the classics of Chinese thought and literature, all buttressed by scholarly introductions and evaluations: *The Way and Its Power* (1934); *The Book of Songs* (1937); *The Analects of Confucius* (1938); and *The Nine Songs: A Study of Shamanism in Ancient China* (1955). When he did return to traditional Chinese poetry, it was mainly in the form of book-length studies of individual poets that ran along these same scholarly lines: *The Life and Times of Po Chü-i* (1949); *The Poetry and Career of Li Po* (1950); and *Yüan Mei* (1956).

---

[11]Morris, "The Genius of Arthur Waley," in *Madly Singing in the Mountains*, 76.
[12](London: Ernest Benn, 1923), 262 pp., with 49 plates.

Poet as Philologist

Ivan Morris isolates five general qualities of Waley that undergird all of his writings. First is profound scholarship and an incredibly wide range of knowledge. Second is his remarkable linguistic skill. Third is his sensibility in English prose and poetry. Fourth is his devotion and commitment to literature. Lastly is his power of concentration.[13] To these abstractions I will attempt to add some concrete qualities.

Most importantly, at the base of both his scholarship and wide range of knowledge was his remarkable linguistic skills. He acquired languages as easily as one acquires college credit in night school. His famous off-hand remark about classical Japanese bears repeating: "Since the classical language has an easy grammar and limited vocabulary, a few months should suffice for the mastering of it."[14] He had a reading knowledge of Greek, Latin, Sanskrit, Hebrew, Mongolian, Turkish, Ainu, Italian, Dutch, and Portuguese. He also read and spoke fluent French, German, and Spanish. He used this knowledge to plumb many documentary depths, especially anthropological literature. For instance, his translation of the *Tao te ching* is rife with apt comparisons, from tortoise-divination in Africa and magic ritual in Babylon to omen lore of Alpine peasants and Buddhist and Christian thought.[15]

He also knew what to do with language, especially classical Chinese, handling its intricacies with exceptional skill. A prominent example is his treatment of textual layers in the *Tao te ching*, now revealing embedded scholia (e.g., #XXXI), now ossified axioms (e.g., #'s VI, XII, and XXIV). He is especially sensitive to the interplay of puns and the nuances of onomatopoeia. On the latter, he once remarked that

> Chinese abounds in reduplicative expressions...used in an onomatopoeic or quasi-onomatopoeic way. These words, representing shades of feeling as well as nuances of sound, appearance,

---

[13]"The Genius of Arthur Waley," 69-77.

[14]Waley, *Japanese Poetry: The 'Uta'* (1919; rpt. Honolulu: University of Hawaii Press, 1976), 12.

[15]Waley the comparative anthropologist is perhaps best seen in an important article on the *I-ching*, "The Book of Changes," *BMFEA* 5 (1933): 121-42.

etc., could not of course be rendered pictorially, and are often expressed by phonological equivalents that, taken separately, have a quite different meaning. Thus under the heading 坎 we get the expression 坎坎, a reduplicate which is generally admitted to have a quite different meaning from 坎 by itself.[16]

One crucial aspect of his technical philological skill is his holistic approach to the nature of the logographic writing system that allowed for various graphic "spellings" of the same word, an understanding not reached universally among sinologists in England even today.[17] For instance, concerning the text of Mencius, Waley preferred to regard *cheng* 征 as standing for 爭: "there is every reason to suppose that 征 is a phonetic substitute or mistake for 爭;"[18] or "關 is a phonetic substitute for 彎. No satisfactory sense can be got out of this passage as it stands. Probably something has dropped out of the text."[19] It is true that Karlgren considered such elasticity of interpretation as making too free with graphic forms, substituting at will characters that fit with one's preconceived interpretations, without the immediate defense of textual notes:

> In regard to the philology proper, the interpretation of difficult words and phrases, [Waley] has assiduously studied many of the best Ts'ing time authorities. And yet the student is left somewhat helpless and bewildered, because Waley's book was published as a literary volume without any scholarly apparatus at all (an additional volume of 32 pages containing textual notes offers so little as to be of no practical assistance)....

> Particularly I object to Waley's frequent alterings of the text (scores of important cases) where the transmitted text admits of a perfectly satisfactory interpretation....Our principle must

---

[16]"The Book of Changes," 139-40.
[17]For example, Needham and his coterie of learned colleagues insist on referring to Chinese characters as "ideographs" throughout the various volumes of *Science and Civilisation*.
[18]"Notes on Mencius," in Legge, *The Chinese Classics*, 2:viii, #126.
[19]Ibid., 2:xii, #427.

be a great caution: never to alter the transmitted text unless it is necessary and the emendation is obviously plausible.[20]

Since Karlgren has the reputation in his various exegetical works of dredging up, with admirable effort, a wide variety of opinions without always choosing between them, this attitude is more a reflection of Karlgren's lack of creative insight than a disparagement of Waley's scholarship. Subjective judgement, guided by literary style and a feel for the language, is always necessary in any text-critical work. And of the latter qualities Waley possessed an abundance.

Waley also was extremely careful to define and choose his terminology precisely, even at the expense of lengthy digressions, as in the introduction to *The Way and Its Power*:

> I have still a number of other words to discuss. The reader will perhaps at this point begin to wonder whether I have lost sight of my original purpose in writing this introductory essay and have, owing to a predisposition towards philology, forgotten Chinese thought and slipped into writing a treatise on the Chinese language. I can only say that I see no other way of studying the history of thought except by first studying the history of words, and such a study would seem to me equally necessary if I were dealing with the Greeks, the Romans, the Egyptians, the Hebrews, or any other people.[21]

Thus, belying his reputation as merely a poet-translator, Waley often engaged in the same finely argued philological analysis that occupied his professional colleagues. His famous powers of concentration and commitment to uncovering the meaning of each word often led him to excessive lengths in order to solve solitary linguistic problems, as in some cross-continental jaunts to make use of the rare manuscript or odd edition. For instance, in "Blake the Taoist," Waley considered whether Blake had been influenced by any Taoist text. Consequently, he devoted a full page

---

[20]Karlgren, *Glosses on the Book of Odes*, 76. The same sentiments are expressed in Wong Siu-kit and Li Kar-shu, "Three English Translations of the *Shijing*," 116-17.

[21]*The Way and Its Power* (New York: Grove Press, 1958), 29-30.

detailing the transmission history of the only Taoist text available in England at the time, an early Latin translation of the *Tao te ching* first brought to London in 1788.[22] And, if he was not willing to spend his time on tedious work in textual criticism to uncover strands of filiation, he was at least aware of the problem and admirably cautious where lacking such a study.[23]

Popularizing Poetry

Underlying all of Waley's work was his intention to popularize Oriental literature, whether Chinese poetry, Japanese novels, an Ainu epic, or *The Secret History of the Mongols*. He expressed this intent on more than one occasion. For instance, at the close of his book *Yüan Mei*, he concluded

> Despite their imperfections my translations have in the past done something towards inspiring a number of people with the idea that, for lovers of poetry, Chinese is a language worth learning. I hope that this book may serve the same purpose and in particular do something to dispel the common idea that all good Chinese poetry belongs to a remote antiquity.[24]

Hence his larger works were directed towards the general reader. His non-specialist audience seemed almost to justify his existence at the margins of academia. This also explains his avoidance of most of the technical apparatus of sinology: extensive documentation and annotation, bibliographical digression, learned philological diversions, or the use of arcane technical jargon. Again, from *Yüan Mei*: "This book is meant chiefly for the general reader with no knowledge of pre-Soviet China....I have concentrated...on whatever in his story has a general human interest,

---

[22]"Blake the Taoist," in *The Secret History of the Mongols and Other Pieces* (London: George Allen and Unwin, 1963), 169-75.

[23]See, for example, "Some References to Iranian Temples in the Tun-huang Region," *Bulletin of the Institute of History and Philology* 28 (1956): 123-28.

[24]*Yüan Mei: Eighteenth Century Chinese Poet* (1956; rpt. Stanford: Stanford University Press, 1970), 204.

and on translating such of his poems as can be made intelligible without an undue amount of explanation."[25] In his self-appointed role of popularizer of Chinese and Japanese poetry, he created the most enduring impression on the English literary outlook towards the Orient since the publication in 1879 of Edwin Arnold's epic poem about the life of the Buddha, "The Light of Asia."[26]

When Waley felt compelled to produce notations to document the sources of his studies, to offer explanatory background, or to explain the basis of a conclusion, he preferred to consign them to the appendices, as in *The Way and Its Power* and *The Poetry and Career of Li Po*, or even to publish them entirely separate, as in his "Notes on the Tun-huang Pien-wen chi,"[27] meant to elucidate the translations included in his *Stories and Ballads from Tun-Huang: An Anthology* (1960), as well as his textual notes to his *Shih-ching* edition and his version of the *Meng-tzu*.[28] The most he would generally concede to the niceties of scholarship was a reference list of sources used, or a finding list of poems, as he once wryly explained: "I write chiefly for the general reader. But specialists seem sometimes to read my books as a recreation, and for their benefit I have given references to the Chinese texts used, in the hope that they will check up on some of my translations and tell me of my mistakes."[29]

As this quick survey shows, Waley wrote widely on an impressively diverse array of subjects, some interconnected, some not. Yet despite his breadth, he never merely dabbled as many of his amateur countrymen had in the previous century—the quaint habit of proffering strongly held if uninformed views on a subject, published in journalistic fashion, then moving on to a fresh target. On the contrary, his grounding in the original

---

[25] *Yüan Mei*, preface.

[26] See Philip C. Almond, *The British Discovery of Buddhism* (Cambridge: Cambridge University Press, 1988), 1.

[27] *Studia Serica Bernhard Karlgren Dedicata*, 172-77.

[28] *The Book of Songs: Translated from the Chinese. Supplement Containing Textual Notes* (London: George Allen and Unwin, 1937); "Notes on Mencius," *AM* n.s. 1 (1949): 99-108; rpt. in Legge, *The Chinese Classics*, 2:vii-xiv.

[29] *The Opium War Through Chinese Eyes* (1958; rpt. Stanford: Stanford University Press, 1968), 5.

sources, a certain feel for cultural values, and his unerring sense of taste guided him to those areas he felt competent to evaluate. His explorations, then, not only helped open up new areas, but usually set their investigation upon solid ground.

His salutary restraint and intellectual modesty in the face of unexplored research territory is explained at length in his 1923 offering, *An Introduction to the Study of Chinese Painting*:

> This book is rather a series of essays than a general survey of early Chinese painting. To attempt such a survey at the present time would, I think, be dangerous owing to the lack of those detailed and special studies by which general works are usually preceded....The danger of demanding symmetry and completeness from a historian who has not the necessary material at his command is well illustrated by many Histories of the obscurer literatures. A writer, let us say, undertakes to compile a history of the literature of some remote country. He himself is perhaps interested in fiction, but only moderately in poetry, and not at all in philosophy; there exist no preliminary researches to guide him. He will write sensibly of fiction, perfunctorily of poetry, and ludicrously of thought.
>
> Conscious of this danger, I have confined myself so far as possible to topics of which I have special knowledge. I have tried, moreover, to mention as few rather than as many artists as possible, lest my book should become a mere dictionary.[30]

Waley may have limited the scope of the subjects receiving specialized treatment, but each subject was faithfully and artfully set within the full context of contemporary history, current cultural and literary trends, and artistic achievement. In fact, at times so broad were his background settings that he felt compelled to justify them:

> A considerable part of this book is occupied with the history of Chinese art-tradition, aesthetic, and taste; an attempt is also made to give in the broadest outlines a history of early Chinese civilization in

---

[30]*An Introduction to the Study of Chinese Painting*, 3.

general.   If anyone says that the knowledge of these things is irrelevant to the study of art, I answer that in human beings, as we know them, sensitivity to art is usually accompanied by some degree of intellectual curiosity....Now if, in regard to any age or country, these questions can be answered at all, it will be largely through the study of literature, and principally, of poetry. Hence in writing this book I have sometimes been helped by knowledge gained from the study of Chinese poetry. Moreover, in supplying a certain literary background, I am justified, I think, by the intimate connection between poetry and painting which from early times existed in China.[31]

Translator as Traducer

Nine translations from the *Shih-ching* are included in *An Introduction to the Study of Chinese Painting* as illustrative examples, and are mostly extended extracts of lengthy originals. Excerpts from these 1923 samples in the column on the left below may be compared with the 1937 versions on the right to introduce Waley's general approach to the art of translation.[32]

Mao #167

We pluck the bracken,	We plucked the bracken, plucked the bracken
The new bracken,	
The bracken springing from the earth...	While the young shoots were springing up.
"Home, home," we cry,	Oh, to go back, go back!
For the old year's ending...	The year is ending.
We have no home, no house,	We have no house, no home
Because of the Hsienyün....	Because of the Hsien-yün...

Mao #30

All day the wind blew wild.	Wild and windy was the day;
You looked at me and laughed;	You looked at me and laughed,
But your jest was lewdness and your	But the jest was cruel, and the

---

[31]Ibid., 3-4.
[32]Ibid., 13-16; *The Book of Songs* (1937; rpt. New York: Grove Press, 1960), *infra*.

laughter, mockery.   laughter mocking.
Sick was my heart within.   My heart within is sore.

All day the wind blew with a whirl   There was a great sandstorm that
        of dust.   day;
Kindly you seemed to come,   Kindly you made as though to
Came not, nor went away.   come,
Long, long I think of you.   Yet neither came nor went away.
                                           Long, long my thoughts.

The dark wind will not suffer   A great wind and darkness;
Clean skies to close the day.   Day after day it is dark.
Cloud trails on cloud. Oh, cruel   I lie awake, cannot sleep,
        thoughts!   And gasp with longing.
I lie awake and moan.

The sky is black with clouds;   Dreary, dreary the gloom;
The far-off thunder rolls;   The thunder growls.
I have woken and cannot sleep,   I lie awake, cannot sleep.
        for the thought of you   And I am destroyed with longing.
Fills all my heart with woe.

Mao #115
There grows an elm-tree on the hill;   On the mountain is the thorn-elm;
And by the mere, an alder tree-   On the low ground the white elm-
You have a coat but do not wear it,   tree.
You have a gown, but do not trail   You have long robes,
        it....   But do not sweep or trail them....

In the first version of Mao #167 Waley preserves the repetition of
the noun "bracken," while in the second he opts to reflect the repetition of
the verb "pluck," restating the third instance of the noun as "young
shoots." The second version "Oh, to go back, go back" again more
faithfully reproduces the repetition of the verb in the original.

In Mao #30, the first version follows the surface meaning of the
word *chung* 終 in lines 1 and 5. In the second, Waley has opted for a more
scholarly approach: he adopts a gloss of Wang Yin-chih, already proposed

in Legge, taking *chung* as a marker of completed action, equivalent to *chi* 既 . The alliteration of "Wild and windy" in the second version attempts to duplicate a phonological feature of the original, a rhyming pattern (*chung-feng* 終風). Yet the first version better reflects the repetition of *chung-feng* and its variants in stanzas one through three. All in all, the second version is more economical in expression. Again, the second translation of Mao #115 is more economical, and reflects the original syntax better.

As Waley matured, he not only refined his style, but his English versions increasingly embodied more dimensions than just surface meaning. According to Edward Schafer, the scholarly act of translation encompasses three distinct aspects of language:

> A translation which aims at illuminating the literary craftsmanship, the intellectual riches, and the imaginative resources of a writer in a foreign language, must, to the greatest possible degree compatible with the structure of the translator's language, take into account the semantic subtleties of that writer's lexicon (first of all), and the morphology (secondly) and the syntax (lastly) of his language.[33]

Hence, the mature Waley, as our comparison of *Shih-ching* poems shows, was often able to reflect all three aspects without sacrificing style or taste.

Yet, the two versions represent more than a maturing of style over time; they represent Waley's division of translation into two fundamental approaches, the free versus the literal, the recreative versus the imitative, or the literary versus the scholarly. Hence, the 1937 *Book of Songs* version, on the whole, more closely reflects both the line, the imagery, and the style of the original, with all its terseness and repetition. Yet, since Waley thought that "so much is inevitably lost in translating Oriental literature that one must give a great deal in return,"[34] he therefore concentrated on making each translation, whether from the *Shih-ching*, *Ch'u-tz'u*, ballads,

---

[33]Schafer, "Preliminary Remarks on the Structure and Imagery of the 'Classical Chinese' Language of the Medieval Period," *TP* 50 (1963): 263.
[34]"The Genius of Arthur Waley," 71.

or *shih* poetry, as independent and artistic as possible. And because of the audience he had in mind, he eschewed the use of footnotes to explain the background or expand on the meaning.

Ivan Morris once explained that what Waley was able to give back to readers through his translations was a sense of the artistry of the original:

> What enabled him to do this was a rare mastery of style and a self-assurance that allowed him after he had thoroughly understood a Chinese or Japanese text, to recast it entirely in supple, idiomatic, vibrant English, rather than stick to a phrase-by-phrase or sentence-by-sentence rendering, which might convey the surface meaning but would inevitably mar the artistry of the original.[35]

Waley himself on several occasions expressed the literary aims of his translations, never more comprehensively than in 1958, reproduced in *Madly Singing in the Mountains*: "If one is translating literature, one has to convey feeling as well as grammatical sense."[36] To do this, Waley insists, a translator must command all of the resources of his native language. And as a practicing poet, Waley certainly could claim a supple feel for English.

One special characteristic of his translations of Chinese poetry is the beauty of his English. His practice was to make one English stress equivalent to each Chinese syllable, resulting in what some would call "sprung rhythm."[37] On this verse form, J.M. Cohen remarks as follows:

> To him it is as natural a measure as blank verse, and one that has the advantage of being free from 19th-century associations....Dr. Waley's "sprung rhythms" have the virtue of freshness, and of a conversational ease which aptly renders the very restrained and direct emotion of such a reflective writer as Po Chü-i.[38]

---

[35]Ibid., 71.
[36]Ibid., 152.
[37]Ibid., 158.
[38]Ibid., 33.

If Waley as a stylist is almost always beyond criticism, it is in his choice of translation strategy, specifically the practice of foreshortening extended passages by way of paraphrase or selected ellipses, that have involved him in recent polemics.

The most successful modern translator of *The Tale of Genji*, Edward Seidensticker, himself an admirer of Waley, nevertheless epitomizes Waley's most obvious failings as follows:

> ...The Waley translation is very free. He cuts and expurgates very boldly. He omits one whole chapter, the thirty-eighth, and close scrutiny reveals that the titles of at least two chapters...are meaningless in his translation because he has omitted the passages from which they derive. It may be argued that he tidies things up by cutting, and therefore "improves." In some cases he probably does....On the whole, however, his excisions seem merely arbitrary.
>
> More complex, and perhaps more interesting, is the matter of amplification. Waley embroiders marvelously, sometimes changing the tone of an episode or the psychological attributes of a character. Perhaps here too he sometimes "improves," but the process of amplifying and embroidering is continuous, and one is very reluctant indeed to conclude that Murasaki Shikibu has the worst of it all the way.[39]

Seidensticker's translation also preserves more of the hundreds of poems that appear throughout the work, many of which are expunged by Waley.[40] All in all, those who prefer Waley do so because of the effects of his

---

[39]Edward Seidensticker, *Murasaki Shikibu: The Tale of Genji* (New York: Alfred A. Knopf, 1983), xiv. This work, and the one by Edward Kamens cited below, were kindly drawn to my attention and supplied by my colleague Professor Scott Miller.

[40]A similar tendency is found in Waley's version of *The Travels of an Alchemist* (London, 1931), where some, but not all, of the poems in classical Chinese are removed. Even Waley's version of the *Shih-ching* omits fifteen poems, partly to spare the reader the so-called "banality" of the originals, and partly due to textual problems (see *The Book of Songs*, preface to the first edition).

"beguiling cadences."[41]

Waley adopted a similar approach in his rendering of *Journey to the West*, which he called *Monkey*.[42] In his preface, Dr. Hu Shih noted that Waley only translated thirty of the original one hundred chapters; yet, in spite of some omissions remembered from his boyhood with fondness, Hu agreed with most of what Waley cut, and endorsed his method of "omitting many episodes, but translating those that are retained almost in full."[43] Of course, it is the "almost in full," and the amplifications redolent in *Genji*, that have attracted critical attention. Yet, in comparison with Ezra Pound, Waley the translator was found by a scholar of comparative literature, Eugene Eoyang, to be more faithful to the original structure, sense, and tone of the *Shih-ching* even if more prosaic and less inspiring in his English: "Waley produces contingent translations of unerring if often bland good taste. Pound produces surrogate translations of variable quality, ranging from misjudged exercises in failed rhetoric to superlative re-creations with a life of their own."[44] Of course, only someone more concerned with the emotions engendered by reader response than the authority of the author accessed by philological tools would even pose the question that opens Eoyang's essay: "Who is the better translator? Arthur Waley or Ezra Pound?"[45] According to traditional sinology, philology, not

---

[41]For more on Waley versus Seidensticker, see Edward Kamens, ed., *Approaches to Teaching Murasaki Shikibu's "The Tale of Genji"* (New York: Modern Language Association of America, 1993), 6-11.

[42]*Monkey: Folk Novel of China by Wu Ch'eng-en* (1943; rpt. New York: Grove Press, 1958).

[43]Ibid., 4.

[44]Eugene Chen Eoyang, *The Transparent Eye: Reflections on Translation, Chinese Literature, and Comparative Poetics* (Honolulu: University of Hawaii Press, 1993), 208; see 183-209 for the entire Waley-Pound comparison, and Eoyang's definitions of "contingent" translations (for readers who have some knowledge of the target language but not expertise) and "surrogate" translations (for readers who do not know the target language).

[45]Any fair-minded reader would readily admit that Waley was unfairly outnumbered at the outset, for Pound conceded that a team effort was at his side in making his translations: "Cathay, Translations by Ezra Pound, for the most part from the Chinese of Rihaku, from the Notes of the Late Ernest Fenollosa, and the Decipherings of the Professors Mori and Ariga;" Yip, *Ezra Pound's Cathay*, 3.

phenomenology, should decide the issue. The question of who is a better poet, however, is a matter for aesthetics.[46]

When translating individual poems, Waley would often sacrifice the literal sense for the sake of safe imagery or unruffled diction. Though not as blatant as expunging entire chapters or extended passages, such an effort is intended to accommodate the tastes or expectations of a reader rather than to convey the literary construct of the author.

A case in point is a poem from early in Waley's career, contained in his 1919 publication *Translations from the Chinese.* "Song of the Men of Chin-ling" is not a translation of the title but a description of the poem, originally entitled "Song of Entering the Court" (*Ju-ch'ao ch'ü* 入朝曲) bracketed by Waley as a subtitle, "Marching Back into the Capital."[47] The translation is smooth and pleasant, without any jarring neologisms or awkward locutions:

> Chiang-nan is a glorious and beautiful land,
> And Chin-ling an exalted and kingly province!
> The green canals of the city stretch on and on
> And its high towers stretch up and up.
> Flying gables lean over the bridle-road:
> Drooping willows cover the Royal Aqueduct.
> Shrill flutes sing by the coach's awning,
> And reiterated drums bang near its painted wheels.
> The names of the deserving shall be carved on the
>   Cloud Terrace.
> And for those who have done valiantly rich reward awaits.

First of all, Waley changes several images. In the original, the second couplet literally reads "Green waters stretch over undulating distances,/Vermilion loft-buildings rise up across successive stages." For Waley, "waters" become "canals," and the *lou* type of building becomes a

---

[46]Ibid., 190. A recent introduction to the traditional Chinese views on authorial intent and modern criticism in opposition is Zhang Longxi, *The Tao and the Logos: Literary Hermeneutics, East and West* (Durham: Duke University Press, 1992), 133-87.

[47]*Translations from the Chinese* (1919; rpt. New York: Alfred A. Knopf, 1941), 99.

high tower bereft of its color. Hence, there is no contrasting of the reds of man-made artifice with the green colors of natural waterways. In the next couplet, "lean over" is a weak rendering of a powerful image of the gables on opposite sides of the road "clasping" their rafter-like hands together, embracing the roadway. "Bridle-road" stands for "Express Way," the imperial highway reserved for His Highness or his messengers. "Royal Aqueduct" spruces up the original "Royal Ditch," denoting the imperial moat. In the penultimate couplet, the verbs do not do justice to the activity of a royal procession along the imperial expressway, Waley's "sing" rendering the original "surrounds in protection," and "bang" being an ineffective substitute for "escort."

As for allusions, Waley does note that "Cloud Terrace" was the record office, but neglects to mention that it was located in a Han-period palace and refers less to records than the painting of the portraits of the twenty-eight famous ministers of merit who helped establish the Han dynasty.

Finally, the initial couplet of the poem became a famous reference to the splendor of early Nanking, known as Chin-ling, and was repeatedly recycled in both *shih* and *tz'u* poetry over the ages. As such an evocative image, its importance should be mentioned (and preserved more exactly): Waley's "exalted and kingly province" is less exalted than the original: "province of emperors and kings!" or "imperial and kingly province!"

Overall, we see that Waley was more concerned in this poem, and in many others, with composing an effective, euphonious English counterpart to the Chinese original, even at the expense of an image, an action, or a color. Writing in a style that forswore the use of heavy annotation, Waley has been justifiably faulted at least for not making more of an effort to preserve the original sense and the imagery used to convey it, even at the expense of the bloom of his English prosody. But, in all fairness to his age and sensibility, such aspersions should function more as an orientation to his chosen approach than a just criticism. In Waley's view, the overall effect of the poem was its artistry; he strove, therefore, to preserve its artistry in English form. Where the choice of the translator hinged more on poetic style than semantic substance, Waley was rarely wrong.

Waley combined both the roles of philologist and poet in his many translations. But his philological skills always served to further literary purposes. Because of the exotic nature of Chinese and Japanese literature to English readers of his time, and due to Waley's exquisite command of English, the effects of his translations were strangely exhilarating and refreshingly liberating. In the words of Jonathan Spence, "Arthur Waley selected the jewels of Chinese and Japanese literature and pinned them quietly to his chest. No one ever did anything like it before, and no one will ever do it again."[48] Let Waley send us off, accompanied by a benedictory verse by Yüan Mei in his inimitable translation:

> The first sign of farewell to life
> Is the turning inside out of all one' tastes.
> The great drinker stops caring for wine,
> The traveler wants only to be left where he is.
> My life-long passion was my love of company,
> And the more my visitors talked, the better I liked them.
> But ever since my illness came upon me
> At the first word I at once stop up my ears.
> And worse still, when my wife or children come
> I cannot bring myself even to wave a hand.
> I know that this is a very bad sign;
> My old body has almost done its task.
> But strangely enough I go through my old books
> With as great delight as I did in former days.
> And ill though I am still write poems,
> Chanting them aloud till the night is far spent.
> Shall it be 'push the door' or 'knock at the door'?
> I weigh each word, each line from beginning to end.
> I see to it that every phrase is alive;
> I do not accept a single dead word.
> Perhaps the fact that this habit has not left me
> Shows that I still have a little longer to live.[49]

---

[48]Spence, *China Roundabout*, 329.
[49]*Madly Singing in the Mountains*, 220-21.

10. AMERICAN SINOLOGISTS

"Sufficient weight has not, generally, we think, been given to native authorities. While we would allow them their proper influence, we shall try to avoid the opposite extreme. We have no very strong expectations of finding much that will rival the arts and sciences, and various institutions of the western nations. We do not expect to find among all the almost numberless tomes of the celestial empire, data of such value and authority, as shall enable the wise men of the ages, to 'correct the chronology, or improve the morality of Holy Writ.'"

—*The Chinese Repository*[1]

"Mastering Chinese was regarded in the treaty ports as next to impossible (except perhaps for missionaries with divine guidance) and in any case highly inadvisable; it was felt to require [quoting Milne] *"a head of oak, lungs of brass, nerves of steel, a constitution of iron, the patience of Job, and the lifetime of Methuselah"—which may, for all I know, be quite true. I have not heard of anyone who has 'mastered' Chinese, in China or elsewhere, although it is indubitable that Sinologists become the servants of language, if not its bond servants."*

—John King Fairbank[2]

Path-Breaking Americans

In the United States, a lag similar to that of the British experience existed between the presence of merchants and diplomats in China and the beginnings of language study by the late-arriving missionaries. For instance, of the eleven most prominent American sinologists of the nineteenth and early twentieth centuries noted by Laurence Thompson, all but three came from Protestant missionary background; the exceptions were Rockhill the diplomat, and two scholars, Berthold Laufer and Paul Carus.[3]

---

[1]"Introduction," *The Chinese Repository* 1.1 (May 1832): 3.

[2]*Ch'ing Documents: An Introductory Syllabus*, 2 vols. (1952; 3rd. ed. Cambridge, Mass.: East Asian Research Center, 1965), 1:vii.

[3]See Thompson, "American Sinology, 1830-1920: A Bibliographical Survey," *Tsing Hua Journal of Chinese Studies*, 2 (1961): 244-90; list on 275. On early contacts, see Kenneth Scott Latourette, *The History of Early Relations between the United States and*

As soon as the War of Independence was won, the first foreign market the Americans sought to exploit was that of China. The *Empress of China* left New York on January 15, 1783 and a year later anchored off Canton. One of the original merchants who participated in this joint venture was appointed as the first American consul to China, Major Samuel Shaw.[4] After serving three successive terms, he died in Canton in 1794. The commerce that was initiated by the *Empress of China* led to an increasing volume of trade in tea, silk, spices, bamboo ware, fur, linen, and rice, etc. that expanded throughout the century;[5] but it took until 1830 for the first American missionaries to arrive on the scene.

At this time, the American Board of Commissioners for Foreign Missions sent two missionaries to Canton, Elijah Coleman Bridgman (1801-61) and David Abeel (1804-46); Abeel, however, functioned more as chaplain to American seaman serving on the South China Sea than as proselytizing missionary.[6] But by 1851, eighty-eight missionaries were

---

China, 1784-1844 (New Haven: Yale University Press, 1917); Earl Swisher, *China's Management of the American Barbarians: A Study of Sino-American Relations, 1841-1861, with Documents* (New Haven: Far Eastern Publications, 1951); and Tyler Dennett, *Americans in East Asia: A Critical Study of the Policy of the United States with Reference to China, Japan, and Korea in the 19th Century* (New York: Barnes and Noble, 1941), 63. John King Fairbank, *The United States and China*, 4th ed. (Cambridge, Mass.: Harvard University Press, 1979), with "Suggested Readings" organized thematically, sets the entire course of Sino-American relations within the historical continuum. A recent reappraisal is Ta Jen Liu, *U.S.-China Relations, 1784-1992* (Lanham, Maryland: University Press of America, 1992).

[4]On the mission of the *Empress of China* and the diplomatic career of Shaw, see Josiah Quincy, *Major Samuel Shaw: The First American Consul at Canton* (Boston: Crosby and Nichols, 1947).

[5]Consult Ernest R. May and John K. Fairbank, *America's China Trade in Historical Perspective: The Chinese and American Performance* (Cambridge, Mass.: Harvard University Press, 1986), and the sources cited.

[6]Kenneth S. Latourette, *A History of Christian Missions in China*, 217. Abeel's memoirs were edited by G.R. Williamson, *Memoir of the Rev. David Abeel, D.D., Late Missionary to China* (New York, 1848). Abeel had earlier published his own account of his experiences in China, *Journal of a Residence in China and the Neighboring Countries with a Preliminary Essay on the Commencement and Progress of Missions in the World* (New York, 1834).

busily engaged in China, and after 1870 more than two hundred were present. These all represented Protestant denominations, for American—as opposed to European Catholics—did not arrive on the scene until 1918.[7] By 1930, more than 3,000 American missionaries were present; over $3,000,000 per annum was sent from the U.S. to support the effort there.[8] But, despite the early presence of both American merchants and missionaries, diplomatic relations between the two countries only developed after the first Opium War (1840-42), for the American consuls in Canton, beginning with Major Samuel Shaw, were appointed from among the ranks of the resident merchants and received no direction from Washington. The missionaries soon established their importance as interpreters and go-betweens; three of them, Elijah Bridgman, Samuel W. Williams, and Peter Parker (1804-88), medical missionary in China and later commissioner, assisted Caleb Cushing, earliest U.S. commissioner to China, in negotiating the first Sino-American treaty in 1844.[9]

---

[7]These statistics are cited from the useful survey of Hu Shu Chao, *The Development of the Chinese Collection in the Library of Congress* (Boulder: Westview Press, 1970), 16-17. For this missionary presence, see Latourette, *A History of Christian Missions in China*; Paul A. Cohen, *China and Christianity: The Missionary Movement and the Growth of Chinese Antiforeignism, 1860-1870* (Cambridge, Mass.: Harvard University Press, 1963); Paul A. Varg, *Missionaries, Chinese and Diplomats: The American Protestant Missionary in China, 1890-1952* (Princeton: Princeton University Press, 1952); John K. Fairbank, ed. *The Missionary Enterprise in China and America* (Cambridge, Mass.: Harvard University Press, 1974); and Suzanne W. Barnett and John K. Fairbank, eds., *Christianity in China: Early Protestant Missionary Writings* (Cambridge, Mass.: Harvard University Press, 1985). The special case of the missionary-educators is introduced by Alice H. Gregg, *China and Educational Autonomy: The Changing Role of the Protestant Educational Missionary in China, 1807-1937* (Syracuse: Syracuse University Press, 1946); and Jessie Gregory Lutz, *China and the Christian College, 1850-1950* (Ithaca: Cornell University Press, 1971).

[8]Liu Kwang-ching, *Americans and Chinese: A Historical Essay and a Bibliography* (Cambridge, Mass.: Harvard University Press, 1963), 14.

[9]Tyler Dennett, *American Policy in China, 1840-1870* (Washington, D.C.: The Endowment, 1921), treats the official beginnings of American diplomacy in China. An analysis of early American Chinese policy up to 1898 is John King Fairbank, *China Perceived: Images and Policies in Chinese-American Relations* (New York: Vintage Books, 1976), 85-101.

Of all the missionaries in China during the nineteenth century who contributed to the development of American sinology, two may be considered as most influential, Elijah Bridgman, the founding sinologist, and Samuel Wells Williams, the pioneering lexicographer and historian.[10]

Upon arrival in Canton in February, 1830, Elijah Coleman Bridgman learned Chinese from William C. Hunter, an employee of the Canton factory of Thomas H. Smith of New York,[11] and with "the assistance of Morrison and his great dictionary." Thanks to both Hunter and Morrison, Bridgman was the first American to have the opportunity to study Chinese systematically.[12] A good friend of the founder of English sinology, Robert Morrison, Bridgman set up an English-language periodical in 1832, *The China Repository*, which he edited until 1847. It was underwritten by the American merchant D. W. Olyphant (1789-1851), who had also sponsored the ocean passage of Bridgman and Abeel. In 1841 Bridgman published his encyclopedic *Chinese Chrestomathy in the Canton Dialect*, a massive (728 pp.) reader in three columns: English, Chinese, and romanization with notes and commentary, divided into topical chapters such as Domestic Affairs, Commercial Affairs, the Human Body, Architecture, Agriculture, and the like. It was one of the earliest texts to teach Chinese through romanization. Bridgman became the first president of the newly founded North China Branch of the Royal Asiatic Society, serving from 1857 to 1859. The many articles he contributed to the *Repository*, as well as his chrestomathy, qualify Bridgman as the first

---

[10]These and other early missionaries are introduced by Arthur Hummel, "Some American Pioneers in Chinese Studies," *Notes on Far Eastern Studies in America* 9 (1941):1-6.

[11]Hunter had arrived in Canton in 1825 at the age of thirteen, after attending the Anglo-Chinese school at Malacca. Two of his books are of historical and cultural interest, *The 'Fan Kwae' at Canton Before Treaty Days, 1825-1844* (1882) and *Bits of Old China* (1885); consult See Sung, "Sinological Studies in the United States," *Chinese Culture* 8 (1967): 133.

[12]Hummel, "Some American Pioneers in Chinese Studies," 3; Hu, *The Development of the Chinese Collection in the Library of Congress*, 31.

American sinologist.[13] Lawrence G. Thompson appraises the value of *The China Repository*, the first sinological journal, in glowing terms: "The twenty volumes of this work remain not only invaluable sources of material on the events of those times, but 'repositories' of research on China which may still on occasion be consulted with profit."[14]

In 1833, the year after the founding of *The China Repository*, Samuel Wells Williams (1812-1888) arrived on the scene, and assumed management of the printing office;[15] like Alexander Wylie, he had been recruited to go to China to take charge of a mission press.[16] Almost immediately he commenced to publish in the pages of the journal (in all his total reached some one hundred items), and succeeded Bridgman as editor in 1848, serving until 1851. His most influential publications include *The Middle Kingdom* (1848), still a mine of interesting information today, and *Syllabic Dictionary of the Chinese Language* (1874), not superseded until Giles' *A Chinese-English Dictionary* of 1892. In a letter written to a friend, Professor James D. Dana of Yale University, dated April 22, 1852, Williams remarked at length on the labors attendant on Chinese lexicography:

> Dictionary-making is not one of the most enlivening studies a man can pursue, and I am conscious of having a great deal of boggy ground under my feet which I have not properly sounded, and cannot fully measure, in our present limited knowledge of this

---

[13]Sung, "Sinological Study in the United States," 134; Thompson, "American Sinology, 1830-1920," 245-47. See also Eliza J. Gillet Bridgman, ed. *The Life and Labors of Elijah Coleman Bridgman* (New York, 1864); and Elly Mei-ngor Cheung, "'Bona Fide Auxiliaries': The Literary and Educational Enterprises of Elijah Coleman Bridgman in the Canton Mission (1830-1854)," M. Phil. thesis, Hong Kong Baptist University, 1998. Bridgman is not to be confused with J.G. Bridgman (d. 1850), another American missionary who produced a confusing translation of Prémare's grammar into English; see Christopher Harbsmeier, "John Webb and the Early History of the Study of the Classical Language in the West," in *Europe Studies China*, 338, n. 42.

[14]Thompson, "American Sinology, 1830-1920," 246.

[15]For his life, see Frederick W. Williams, *The Life and Letters of Samuel Wells Williams, L.L.D., Missionary, Diplomat, Sinologue* (New York: G.P. Putnam's Sons, 1889).

[16]He was nominated by his father, William Williams; see *The Life and Letters of Samuel Wells Williams*, 39.

language. It is somewhat like pounding out specimens in mineralogy to puzzle out the meaning of Chinese characters from native dictionaries; the fraction of error which enters into the definition of a vast number of the characters, arising from the difference in habits, ideas, and knowledge between the Chinese and ourselves, renders Chinese lexicography tedious and unsatisfactory. When one has the whole language packed away in a small compass, as Genesis had Hebrew; or when there is no literature at all, as among the Indians and Africans, I sometimes think 't would be easier work than with this ancient speech chipped off the Tower of Babel and its enormous bibliography.[17]

The popularity of his *Syllabic Dictionary*, which consumed eleven years of labor, was immediate among the missionary readers in China, for whom it was intended, and especially praised for its concise definitions of 12,527 characters and a host of phrases, in comparison to the sometimes wordy entries of Morrison.[18] A seventy-page introduction treats such topics as Mandarin or court language, his system of romanization, tones, ancient and obsolete pronunciation, radicals, and dialects.

Fluent in Japanese as well as several Chinese dialects, Williams accompanied Perry's expedition to Japan as interpreter. Later he became the secretary of the U.S. legation in China. Williams eventually returned to the States, and assumed the newly endowed Chinese Chair at Yale University in 1876.[19]

A host of Chinese primers and dictionaries followed throughout the course of the century by various American missionaries, foreign service officers, and educationalists.[20] Probably the only one that retains its usefulness today, aside from the handbooks and manuals on obscure

---

[17]Williams, *The Life and Letters of Samuel Wells Williams*, 179-80.

[18]See the selection of reviews included in Williams, *The Life and Letters of Samuel Wells Williams*, 397-400.

[19]His son, Frederick W. Williams (1857-1928) followed in his father's footsteps at Yale, although lagging behind with regard to his scholarly contributions. His most notable works include *A Sketch of the Relations between the United States and China* (1910) and *Anson Burlingame and the First Chinese Mission to Foreign Powers* (1912).

[20]Noted by Thompson in chronological order.

dialects, is Chauncey Goodrich, *A Pocket Dictionary (Chinese-English) and Pekingese Syllabary* (1891), much reprinted.[21] Goodrich (1836-1925) spent sixty years in China; he first arrived in 1865, and was most active in education and translation, including rendering parts of the New Testament in Mongolian and producing a Chinese version (with Henry Blodget) of the Christian hymnal in 1872. He was the father of the noted sinologist and long-time professor at Columbia University, L. Carrington Goodrich.[22] Each of the 10,587 entries in his *Pocket Dictionary* is arranged according to the alphabetical order of the Wade-Giles romanization. A notable feature of this work is the indication of radical for each entry. Earlier editions included a cross-reference to the corresponding page of Williams' dictionary.

Despite significant contributions to religion, ethnology, history, and of course lexicography and pedagogy, only one scholar of this century contributed theoretically to the development of philology. This was Peter S. Du Ponceau (1760-1844), the first president of the American Oriental Society (founded in 1842). Du Ponceau, in his *A Dissertation on the Nature and Character of the Chinese System of Writing* (Philadelphia, 1838), held that the Chinese script represented words, not ideas, and hence he was the first to attack the heresy of ideology. His theories were not accepted in his day—the reaction of S.W. Williams was typical: his work "is a labored treatise upon a figment."[23] But Du Ponceau's proposition that Chinese characters are "lexigraphs," in the more formalized terminology of "logographs," carries the field today.[24]

William F. Rockhill

The representative sinologist, and indeed most outstanding scholar,

---

[21]Including in Shanghai, 1918; Peking, 1941; and Columbia University, 1943. More recently it was published by the Hong Kong University Press, 1964, with several later reissues.

[22]A short biographical sketch of Chauncey Goodrich prefaces the Hong Kong University edition of the *Pocket Dictionary*, issued in 1965.

[23]*The Chinese Repository* XVIII (1849): 408; cited in Thompson, "American Sinology," 247.

[24]See the discussion on logography in chapter 11 below.

among early American diplomats, was William F. Rockhill (1854-1914).[25] Rockhill was a cosmopolitan man of action: educated in France at St. Cyr, the French equivalent of West Point, he served three years in the French Foreign Legion before starting a cattle ranch in New Mexico. When he embarked on his diplomatic career in China in 1883 he had already learned Tibetan and Sanskrit, and had published several works, including *The Life of the Buddha and the Early History of His Order* (1884), based on a Tibetan source. He became secretary to the U.S. Legation in Peking in 1884. His wife's inheritance enabled him to travel widely. He left for Tibet in 1888, having to resign his post in order to have the freedom to travel. The contributions to the geographic knowledge of Tibet and Mongolia made by both his travels and his published monographs were acknowledged in 1893 with the award of the Gold Medal of the Royal Geographic Society of London.

His travels in Asia, accomplished on foot and under trying circumstances, yielded two travelogues, *The Land of the Lamas* (1891) and *Diary of a Journey through Mongolia and Tibet in 1891 and 1892* (1894). His stature as a scholar is shown by the invitation he received to become professor of Oriental languages at the University of California, an offer he declined. He rejoined the State Department in 1893, serving in a variety of posts, including Assistant Secretary of State, Minister to Greece, and Far Eastern Advisor. He was the chief orchestrator of the Open Door Policy towards China at the turn of the century, and participated as U.S. Commissioner in the negotiations settling the aftermath of the Boxer Rebellion. In 1904 he was appointed by President Roosevelt as United States Minister to China, and was instrumental in applying the Boxer indemnity towards educating Chinese students in America. By this time he had already donated some six thousand volumes of Chinese books to the Library of Congress. In 1909 he became Ambassador to Russia, but was reassigned to Constantinople in 1911; he was ultimately dismissed in 1913 by the new administration of Woodrow Wilson. He served as advisor to

---

[25]Paul A. Varg, *Open Door Diplomat: the Life of W.W. Rockhill* (Urbana: University of Illinois Press, 1952). A full listing of Rockhill's works is found in the bibliography proper on pp. 133-36.

Yuan Shih-k'ai, first president of the Republic of China, until his death in 1914.

Rockhill's interest in international trade and diplomacy led him to produce several relevant articles and compilations, culminating with an important study of William of Rubruck, which he completed in Athens, and which remains the standard scholarly edition used today.[26]   Later publications include *China's Intercourse with Korea from the XVth Century to 1895* (1905) and *Diplomatic Audiences at the Court of China* (1905), both based on earlier publications in periodicals.   His *magnum opus* was published just three years before his death in collaboration with F. Hirth, *Chau Ju-Kua: His Work on the Chinese and Arab Trade in the Twelfth and Thirteenth Centuries, Entitled Chu-fan-chi* (1911).[27]   Apparently the translation was the work of Hirth, while Rockhill supplied the historical introduction and copious notes.   This work laid "a firm foundation" for the later studies in Sung maritime commerce by Paul Wheatley, who concludes that "Their map has provided a framework for all subsequent investigators, and Fig. 1 in this paper is a tribute to their scholarship."[28]

A thread that seems to run throughout the course of English-speaking sinologists, from the beginning until the present, is an interest in technology and the natural world, starting most creatively with Alexander Wylie.   For instance, Wylie's study of asbestos in China, the first of its kind,[29] was taken up by both Herbert Giles and Berthold Laufer. Probably the most accomplished of Wylie's successors in these fields among the next generation of sinologists was Emile Vasilievitch Bretschneider (1833-1901), doctor of the Russian legation in Peking from 1866-1883. Although not American or English, this learned physician published mainly in English. Prized even above his valuable contributions on historical geography, of

---

[26] *The Journey of William of Rubruck to the Eastern Parts of the World, 1253-55, as Narrated by Himself, with Two Accounts of the Earlier Journey of John of Pian de Carpine* (London, 1900).

[27] (Rpt. New York: Paragon, 1966); reviewed at length by Pelliot in *TP* 13 (1912): 446-81.

[28] Paul Wheatley, "Geographical Notes on Some Commodities involved in Sung Maritime Trade," *Journal of the Malayan Branch, Royal Asiatic Society* 32 (1959): 10.

[29] Wylie, *Chinese Researches*, "Part III," 141-54.

which three weighty tomes remain,[30] is *Botanicon Sinicum*, which laid the foundation for historical botany in China.[31] Part I is a general introduction to Chinese historical botany and an annotated catalogue of 1,143 traditional Chinese works on botany, *materia medica*, agriculture, historical geography, etc. Part two analyzes the plants that appear in the Chinese classics. Part three discusses 355 medicinal plants from the *Shen-nung pen-ts'ao ching* and the *Ming-i pieh-lu*. Also of interest is his *History of European Botanical Discoveries in China*, 2 vols. (1898).

Berthold Laufer

Berthold Laufer (1874-1934), another non-native writer in English, worked long before Joseph Needham committed himself to the Chinese sciences; Laufer culminated this tradition founded in essence by Wylie and Bretschneider, and became the most erudite sinologist in the realms of archaeology, technology, anthropology, and the natural sciences.[32]

Berthold Laufer worked most of his life at the Field Museum of Natural History in Chicago, commencing in 1908, but he was completely German trained: at the University of Berlin under Grube, the Berlin seminar with Franke, and the University of Leipzig under Conrady.[33] At his death he was regarded as the foremost American sinologist—even if

---

[30]*Notes on Chinese Medieval Travelers to the West* (1875), *Notices of the Medieval Geography and History of Central and Western Asia* (1876), and *Chinese Intercourse with the Countries of Central and Western Asia during the Fifteenth Century* (1877).

[31]"Botanicon Sinicum: Notes on Chinese Botany from Native and Western Sources," *Journal of the North-China Branch of the Royal Asiatic Society*, n.s. 16 (1881): 18-230; 25 (1890-91): 1-468 (rpt. Nendeln, Liechtenstein: Kraus, 1967); "*Botanicon Sinicum*, Part III: Botanical Investigations into the Materia Medica of the Ancient Chinese," (Shanghai, 1895).

[32]For his life and works, see H. G. Creel, *MS* 1 (1935): 487-96; Walter E. Clark, et al., "Berthold Laufer, 1874-1934," *JAOS* 54 (1934): 349-62; Arthur Hummel, "Berthold Laufer, 1874-1943," *American Anthropologist* n.s. (2nd) 38 (1936): 101-11; and the listing of some thirty-one biographical notices, appreciations and necrologies in *Kleinere Schriften von Berthold Laufer, Teil 1: Publikationen aus der Zeit von 1894 bis 1910*, 2 vols, ed. Hartmut Walraven (Wiesbaden: Steiner, 1976), 1:xxii-xxiv.

[33]His early training in Germany is briefly reviewed in Franke, *Erinnerungen aus zwei Welten*, 148-49.

Herbert Franke did not know how to classify him, German or American?—having been the lone American professional sinologist of any repute during the long gap between Hirth's retirement from Columbia in 1917 and the rise of the generation of Peter A. Boodberg, George A. Kennedy, and L. Carrington Goodrich.

It is entirely appropriate that the foreword to the first collection of his minor works was written by Joseph Needham. Let us extract from it an evaluation of the forces that composed Laufer's scholarly approach:

> Berthold Laufer was professionally an ethnographer and anthropologist. Before the First World War he had spent nearly ten years "in the field," leading four expeditions to China, Tibet and the North Pacific region. It has been said that his strength lay in the application of the principles and methods of ethnology to the historic civilisations of Asia. It was natural enough therefore that he should have interested himself in the material culture, the "realia" with which scientists and engineers occupy themselves, men of humanistic education more rarely....Laufer, then, was an ethnologist, and presumably he thought of himself as such; but in fact he was very largely concerned with the universal history and pre-history of science and technology.[34]

Working in a variety of languages—the most broadly versed of any sinologist since Pelliot and before Boodberg,[35] and the first to exploit Greek sources as effectively as Chinese until Otto Maenchen-Helfen—[36] Laufer made many outstanding contributions: art and archaeology,[37] natural history—especially botany and zoology—,[38] culture,[39] ethnography

---

[34]"Foreword," *Kleinere Schriften*, vii-viii.

[35]Including the Semitic languages, Greek, Latin, Turkish, Persian, Sanskrit, Pali, Malay, Japanese, Manchu, Mongolian, Dravidian, and Tibetan.

[36]Witness Laufer's *The Diamond: A Study in Chinese and Hellenistic Folk-Lore.*

[37]E.g., *Chinese Grave-Sculptures of the Han Period* (London: E.L. Morice, 1911); "Confucius and His Portraits," *Open Court* 26 (1912): 147-68; 202-18; and "Chinese Sarcophagi," *OL* 1 (1912): 318-34.

[38]Including *Notes on Turquoise in the East* (Chicago, 1913); "Arabic and Chinese Trade in Walrus and Narwhal Ivory," *TP* 14 (1913): 315-65, and "Rye in the Far East and

and ethnology,[40] history and technology,[41] literature,[42] linguistics,[43] and bibliography.[44] Among his most valuable works must be included *Chinese Pottery of the Han Dynasty* (1909); *Jade: A Study in Chinese Archaeology and Religion* (1912); *Chinese Clay-Figures, Part 1: Prolegomena on the History of Defensive Armor* (1914); and his peerless *Sino-Iranica: Chinese Contributions to the History of Civilization in Ancient Iran* (1919).[45]

The majority of these works resulted from the effort to catalogue the holdings of the Field Museum, many items of which had been collected in the field personally by Laufer. For instance, most of the 111 pieces of Han pottery discussed in *Chinese Pottery of the Han Dynasty* were obtained by Laufer in Si'an in 1903, supplemented by private collections. His study of jade was expressly intended "to furnish the necessary information on the jade collection in the Field Museum," but "does not pretend to be a contribution to sinology."[46] His extensive field work and many detailed reports made Laufer the successor to Chavannes in epigraphy and

---

the Asiatic Origin of Our Word Series 'Rye'," *TP* 31 (1935): 237-73.

[39]As in "The Bird-Chariot in China and Europe," *BOAS Anniversary Volume* (1906): 410-24.

[40]Witness "Preliminary Notes on Explorations Among the Amoor Tribe," *American Anthropologist* n.s. 2 (1900): 297-338.

[41]Viz. "The Relations of the Chinese to the Philippine Islands," *Kleinere Schriften*, 2:248-84; *The Prehistory of Aviation* (Chicago, 1928), and *Paper and Printing in Ancient China* (Chicago, 1931).

[42]*Milaraspa: Tibetische Texte in Auswahl übert ragen* (Darmstadt, 1922).

[43]Such as "Loan Words in Tibetan," *TP* (1916): 403-552; "The Si-Hia Language: A Study in Indo-Chinese Philology," *TP* 17 (1916): 1-126; and *The Language of the Yüe-chi or Indo-Scythians* (Chicago, 1917).

[44]For example, "Skizze der Mongolischen Literatur," *Kleinere Schriften*, 2:1120-1216; "Skizze Der Manjurischen Literatur; *Kleinere Schriften*, 2:1295-1347; or *Descriptive Account of the Collection of Chinese, Tibetan, Mongol and Japanese Books in the Newberry Library* (Chicago, 1913).

[45]Each of the necrologies mentioned above contains a bibliography of approximately 150 items. A complete bibliography of some 490 titles, including multiple reprints, is included in *Kleinere Schriften*, 1:xxix-lxxx.

[46]*Jade*, i.

archaeology, the scope of which study he considerably expanded.[47]

He once commented on the relationship between textual sources and material artifacts in studying ancient China:

> If it is true that Chinese archaeology must be based on the knowledge of Chinese texts with the same method as classical archaeology, it is no less true that the interpretation of the ancient texts will have a great deal to learn from the facts of archaeological research and its living objects of stone, clay or metal which are harder than any paper-transmitted evidence....If I am obliged to deviate from such authorities as Biot, Legge and Couvreur, I beg my critics not to interpret this necessity as arrogance or a mania for knowing better on my part, but as a suggestion intimated by a consideration of the new material here offered.[48]

Despite the technical nature of many of his works, Laufer was committed to the broader humanistic goal of understanding ancient Chinese culture as both the material manifestation of a particular civilization and the embodiment of its highest spiritual values. He was especially skilled in placing an attitude, an artistic motif, or an artifact in the wider context of Asia. A good case in point is *Chinese Pottery of the Han Dynasty*, which contains a section called "Influence of Siberian Art and Culture on Ancient China."[49] It treats such foreign adaptations into Chinese culture as the mounted infantry formation, falconry, and furniture. Such an attitude is, of course, the spirit behind Laufer's greatest work, *Sino-Iranica*.

In this seminal work, Laufer's purpose is "to trace the history of all objects of material culture, pre-eminently cultivated plants, drugs, products, minerals, metals, precious stones, and textiles, in their migration from Persia to China (Sino-Iranica), and others transmitted from China to

---

[47]Concerning Laufer's contributions to the field of epigraphy, consult Hartmut Walravens, "Berthold Laufer and His Rubbings Collection," *JAOS* 100 (1980): 519-22.

[48]*Jade*, 15-16.

[49]*Chinese Pottery of the Han Dynasty* (1909; 2nd ed. Rutland and Tokyo: Charles E. Tuttle, 1962), 212-36.

Persia (Irano-Sinica)."[50] Apart from Laufer's complete command of the methodologies of anthropology, ethnology, and archaeology mentioned by Needham above, another approach adopted in this work was that of comparative linguistics, applied with great skill and judgement. Working in the era before Bernard Karlgren had codified and presented the results of his researches into Chinese historical phonology, Laufer used his own reconstructions based on the work of Pelliot and Maspero:

> Iranian geographical and tribal names have hitherto been identified on historical grounds, some correctly, some inexactly, but an attempt to restore the Chinese transcriptions to their correct Iranian prototypes has hardly been made....In my opinion, it must be our foremost object first to record the Chinese transcriptions as exactly as possible in their ancient phonetic garb, according to the method so successfully inaugurated and applied by P. Pelliot and H. Maspero, and then to proceed from this secure basis to the reconstruction of the Iranian model. The accurate restoration of the Chinese form in accordance with rigid phonetic principals is the essential point, and means much more than any haphazardly made guesses at identification.[51]

In conclusion, Laufer was not a traditional sinologist concerned with translating a text and presenting it in all of its contextual and interpretive glory. Nevertheless, he exploited the riches of historical documents through his "philological erudition," as Chavannes termed it,[52] and utilized the resources of the material world to throw light upon countless fascinating facets of the culture of ancient China, and fully earned the accolades that accrued to his name upon his untimely death.

---

[50]*Sino-Iranica: Chinese Contributions to the History of Civilization in Ancient Iran, with Special Reference to the History of Cultivated Plants and Products* (1919; rpt. New York: Kraus Reprint Corporation, 1967), 188.

[51]*Sino-Iranica*, 186-87.

[52]*TP* 14 (1913): 486.

L. Carrington Goodrich

L. Carrington Goodrich (1894-1986), son of Chauncey Goodrich, carried on many aspects of the scientific stewardship inherited from Laufer.[53] He was a long-time professor of Chinese at Columbia University, his *alma mater*, emphasizing Ming and Ch'ing history. Although Goodrich is better known for his contributions to bibliography and biography,[54] his *A Short History of the Chinese People* (New York, 1943) managed to discuss the Chinese contributions to science and technology within a narrow compass of political history. It was termed by Hu Shih "the best history of China ever published in any European language."[55] His revision of Thomas Carter's *The Invention of Printing and Its Spread Westward* (New York: Ronald Press, 1955), added so much new material that the work is usually considered to be a collaborative effort. Among the many scientific subjects he treated in article form, I mention plants and foodstuffs,[56] technology,[57] and most prominently, printing.[58]

Arthur W. Hummel (1884-1975)

Among the last representatives of the sinologists nurtured within

---

[53]For a short biography with bibliography, see Thomas D. Goodrich, "Luther Carrington Goodrich (1894-1986): A Bibliography," *JAOS* 113 (1993): 585-92.

[54]*The Literary Inquisition of Ch'ien-lung* (Baltimore, 1935; 2nd ed. with addenda and corrigenda, New York: Paragon, 1966), and *Dictionary of Ming Biography*, 2 vols., editor, with Chao-ying Fang (New York: Columbia University Press, 1976). The latter work won the Julien Prize for 1976.

[55]As cited by Thomas D. Goodrich, "Luther Carrington Goodrich," 585.

[56]"Early Notices of the Peanut in China," *MS* 2 (1936-37): 405-9; "Early Prohibitions of Tobacco in China and Manchuria," *JAOS* 58 (1938): 648-57; and "Cotton in China," *ISIS* 34 (1943): 408-10.

[57]"The Revolving Bookcase in China," *HJAS* 7 (1942): 130-61; "Suspension Bridges in China: A Preliminary Inquiry," *Sino-Indian Studies* 5 (1956): 53-61, and "The Early Development of Firearms in China" (with Feng Chia-sheng), *ISIS* 36 (1945-46): 114-23.

[58]"The Origin of Printing in China," *JAOS* 82 (1962): 556-57; "The Development of Printing in China and Its Effects on the Renaissance under the Sung Dynasty," *Journal of the Hong Kong Branch of the Royal Asiatic Society* 3 (1963): 36-43; and "Movable Type Printing: Two Notes," *JAOS* 94 (1974): 476-77.

the missionary heritage was Arthur Hummel of the Library of Congress.

Arthur W. Hummel was educated at the University of Chicago, graduating in 1909.[59] He received his master's degree in 1911. For ten years, under the auspices of that venerable institution, the American Board of Commissioners for Foreign Missions, he taught at the Boy's Middle School in Fenchow, Shansi. His leisure time was spent amassing a huge fund of antique coins and gathering an equally important collection of old maps, which later formed the basis of the Hummel Collection of Rare Chinese Cartography in the Library of Congress. Based upon his expertise in Chinese artifacts, he was invited to join the Library of Congress and continue his work in building up the Asian collection upon returning to the States in 1927. He was appointed to the newly established Division of Chinese Literature in 1928, later becoming Chief of the Orientalia Division; he retired in 1954.

Hummel received a doctorate from Leiden in 1931, based as much on his distinguished service to scholarship as on his dissertation, *The Autobiography of a Chinese Historian*. Since Hummel knew the leading participants among the rising generation of Chinese historians, J.J.L. Duyvendak encouraged him to work on the autobiographical preface to the first issue of *Ku-shih pien* by Ku Chieh-kang. It was in essence an honorary doctorate confirmed rather than earned through the production of a skilled translation with commentary.

Based upon Hummel's personal experiences, predilections, and expertise, the Library developed particularly strong collections in the areas of local gazetteers, *ts'ung-shu*, and rare books.[60] Indeed, the foundation of the Chinese collection was the collectanea, for the first ten books acquired by the Library, a gift from Prince Kung in 1869, consisted of ten *ts'ung-shu*.[61] A specialized article on the nature and use of collectanea by

[59]See Edwin G. Beal and Janet F. Beal, "Arthur W. Hummel 1884-1975," *JAS* 35 (1976): 265-76, with complete bibliography; and Hu, *The Development of the Chinese Collection of the Library of Congress*, 134-39.

[60]Hu, 137.

[61]Ibid., 43-46. For the foundation on collectanea of the Harvard-Yenching library, see Serge Elliséeff, "The Chinese-Japanese Library of the Harvard-Yenching Institute," *Harvard Library Bulletin* (1956): 73-76.

Hummel, including a five-part classification system, is still of interest.[62] The important guide to the rare-book collection compiled by the noted bibliographer Wang Chung-min was itself initiated by Hummel.[63] But the greatest contribution to the development of sinology rendered by Hummel was his editing of *Eminent Chinese of the Ch'ing Period*.

For this collaborative biographical project, Hummel had to harness much institutional support. But he had already done much on his own to promote the institutionalization of East Asian studies. He was the founding president of the Association for Asian Studies (from 1948 to 1949), and had served as president of the American Oriental Society in 1940. As Chairman of the Committee for the Promotion of Chinese Studies of the American Council of Learned Societies from 1930 to 1934, Hummel took advantage of the fund-raising possibilities of his office to initiate this biographical dictionary of the Ch'ing dynasty. It would serve two purposes. The first was academic, the second, pedagogical, both addressed by Hummel in his "Editor's Note" to the finished volumes:

> The work grew out of the co-operation of the Library of Congress and the American Council of Learned Societies, assisted by the Rockefeller Foundation, in providing the Library a center where advanced students of Chinese culture might have additional experience in research and in the use of historical and literary materials. It was thought that the most valuable experience they could derive from the use of such materials would be the preparation of contributions to a Biographical Dictionary of the Ch'ing Dynasty; for it was not difficult to foresee...that without more detailed guides to the famous names, the great events, and the rich and almost inexhaustible literature of China, we of the West cannot hope to acquire an adequate understanding of the Chinese people.[64]

---

[62]Hummel, "T'sung Shu," *JAOS* 51 (1931): 40-46.

[63]Edwin G. Beal, Jr., "Preface," in Wang Chung-min, comp., *A Descriptive Catalogue of Rare Chinese Books in the Library of Congress*, 2 vols., ed. T.L. Yuan (Washington, D.C.: Library of Congress, 1957).

[64]Hummel, "Editor's Note," *Eminent Chinese of the Ch'ing Period*, 2 vols. (Washington: U.S. Government Printing Office, 1943), viii.

More than eight hundred biographies are included, written by some fifty scholars. According to Hu Shih, who authored the preface, "It is the most detailed and best history of China of the last three hundred years that one can find anywhere. It is written in the form of biographies of eight hundred men and women who made that history. This form, by the way, is in line with the Chinese tradition of historiography."[65]

Homer H. Dubs (1892-1969)

Another American sinologist weaned to the task in China was Homer H. Dubs.[66] Dubs was born in Illinois, but grew up in Hunan where his parents were missionaries. After graduating from Yale in philosophy, Dubs did graduate work at Columbia, M.A. 1916,[67] and the Union Theological Seminary. After a period of missionary service in Nanking and Hunan, Dubs returned to academic life, and received his Ph.D. at Chicago with a dissertation on Hsün-tzu (1925). It resulted in his first major translation, *Hsüntze, the Moulder of Ancient Confucianism*, 2 vols. (London, 1927-28). His many articles, mostly on questions of philosophy,[68] Han history and historiography,[69] early science,[70] or religion,[71] are exemplary in their combination of philosophical acumen and philological skill. Breadth of training, especially in the Greek and Latin classics, served Dubs well in his approach to Chinese history in the Asian

---

[65]Hu Shih, "Preface," *Eminent Chinese of the Ch'ing Period*, 1:v.

[66]See L. Carrington Goodrich, "Homer Dubs (1892-1969)," *JAS* 29 (1970): 889-91, with complete bibliography.

[67]His M.A. thesis was called "Mechanism Versus Vitalism."

[68]Especially notable is "The Political Career of Confucius," *JAOS* 66 (1946): 273-82, and "Did Confucius Study the 'Book of Changes'?" *TP* 25 (1928): 82-90.

[69]E.g., "Wang Mang and his Economic Reforms," *TP* 35 (1940): 219-65; and "The Reliability of Chinese Histories," *FEQ* 6 (1946): 23-43.

[70]Viz. "Solar Eclipses During the Former Han Period," *Osiris* 5 (1938): 499-532; and "The Beginnings of Alchemy," *Isis* 38 (1948): 62-86.

[71]Namely, "An Ancient Chinese Mystery Cult," *Harvard Theological Review* 35 (1942): 221-40; and "The Archaic Royal Jou Religion," *TP* 46 (1958): 217-59.

setting, namely Chinese-Roman cultural contacts.[72]

After teaching philosophy for a time at the University of Minnesota (1925-27) and Marshall College (1927-34), which period produced a general textbook on philosophy,[73] Dubs was commissioned by the American Council of Learned Societies to translate one of the dynastic histories. Along with two Chinese collaborators, Dubs worked at the Library of Congress from 1934 to 1937, later at Duke, and duly produced *The History of the Former Han Dynasty*, 3 vols. (Baltimore: Waverly Press, 1938, 1944, and 1955), rendering into English the basic annals of the *Han-shu* and the treatise on Wang Mang with many learned appendices. Annotated with as much virtuosity as Chavannes' translation of the *Shih-chi*, Dubs' work is a model of accurate translation and thorough commentary. A notable feature of his annotations was his consultation with leading scientists of the natural world to answer questions outside the normal purview of sinologists: Dr. Leonard Stejneger, Head Curator of Biology, U.S. National Museum, addressed the problem of fighting frogs; Dr. T.D. Stewart, Assistant Curator, Division of Physical Anthropology, Smithsonian Institute, tackled the case of hairy soles and palms in the royal Liu lineage; and Dr. George D. Wilde, resident in Shantung, helped discriminate among various species of swans. For going to such lengths to address similar textual questions, scientific queries, and historiographical excesses, providing at the same time a readable rendering of the basic annals of this important historical work, Dubs was awarded the 1947 Julien Prize for volume two.

Derk Bodde reviewed his work very favorably, commenting especially on his translation style:

As for the translation itself, it is accurate and exceeding close to the

---

[72]Notably his short monograph *A Roman City in Ancient China* (London, 1957), and an earlier "A Military Contact Between Chinese and Romans in 36 B.C.," *TP* 36 (1942): 64-80. He even published in classical journals, namely "An Ancient Military Contact Between Romans and Chinese," *American Journal of Philology* 42 (1941): 322-30, and "A Roman Influence on Chinese Painting," *Classical Philology* 38 (1943): 13-19.

[73]*Rational Induction: An Analysis of The Method of Science and Philosophy* (Chicago: University of Chicago Press, 1930).

text. Indeed, the English rendering might at times have gained in smoothness and ease if more freedom from the original had been allowed, but many scholars will probably feel that the accuracy thus gained justifies such literalness. Occasionally, as in almost any translation of a Chinese text, objections may be raised to certain renderings, but these are neither numerous nor important.[74]

Examples of suggested corrections and emendations, for "only a few places," can be found in the review of volume three by Yang Lien-sheng.[75]

In his foreword to volume one, Dubs promised a volume of prolegomena and a final volume containing a glossary of proper names and an index. Apparently, a manuscript of such a glossary was shunted back and forth between various Han specialists, without it ever finding a willing editor to see it through the press. It now is stored in the Bodleian Library in Oxford.[76] Another project Dubs promised was the creation of a classical dictionary in his own peculiar form of romanization. It sought to combine twenty-two Latin letters, five vowel accents, and thirty Chinese radicals. For instance, *tao* "way," would be rendered Ďao㡁, *ti* "thearch," as ĎiÆí, etc.[77] Ten years later, in a review of Watson's *Grand Historian of China*, he dropped the tone marks and added the numerals 1, 2, 3, or 4.[78] In this review (p. 218) he provided a table of characters that he had used, introduced with the following statement: "These alphabetic spellings for Chinese characters are taken from a list of over 16,000 characters with a distinctive spelling for each pronunciation of each one, for which I am now seeking funds for publication." Alas, his card file of dictionary entries languishes at the Bodleian as well. But this same spirit of orthographic adventure, seeking to incorporate as much information in the system of romanization as found in the Chinese graphs, was exhibited by fellow

---

[74]*American Historical Review* 44 (1939): 641-42.

[75]See Yang, *HJAS* 19 (1956): 435-42.

[76]Personal Communication, Anthony D. Hyder, Librarian of the Institute for Chinese Studies, Oxford, England, April 21, 1997.

[77]See "A Practical Alphabetic Script for Chinese," *FEQ* 10 (1951): 284 where he introduces the "Gardner-Dubs" simplification of the Wade-Giles romanization.

[78]*JAS* 20 (1961): 213-18.

American sinologists George Kennedy and Peter Boodberg, as we shall see.

Late in life he assumed the Oxford Chair in Chinese in 1947, which had been vacant since the death of Soothill in 1935 and the inability of Ch'en Yin-k'o to function in office due to eye trouble. He was instrumental in building up the Chinese collection of the Bodleian as well as the library of the Oriental Institute, often corresponding with Gustav Haloun on questions of bibliographical acquisition.[79]

Dubs displayed an aspect to his character that, if not particularly dark, at least conspired to render his public persona something of a laughing-stock. This was a tendency towards buffoonery that manifested itself in various ways, from parking his motorcycle in the hallways of the Oriental Institute to his dabbling in the occult. In the latter activity he joined the select company of his more famous Oxford contemporary, E.R. Dodds, Regius Professor of Greek.[80] Dodd's dabbling in what he variously called the "universal question mark" or "booby-trapped by-ways" of psychical research was well known, and had been shared by his even more famous predecessor in Greek at Oxford, Gilbert F. Murray.[81] I bring up this aspect of Dubs' personality only because it may help explain certain oddities of his scholarship, especially his quirky system of romanization. He also seemed to have had a fixation with numbers, manifested both early and late in his career: on the last page of his master's thesis, he lists the number of words contained in each of five chapters, plus introduction and bibliography (29,360 words in all); and in the edition of the *Han-shu* that he donated to St. Anne's College is this superfluous marginal notation in pencil at the end of the first thematic section of chapter one (1A.1a): "Ca. 35 Chinese characters of text and 1200 characters of annotation."

Although Dubs taught only philosophy in the United States,

---

[79]See, for instance, letter dated 2 May 1949 to Haloun requesting his assistance in purchasing large collectanea; in 1950 Dubs helped the Harvard-Yenching Institute acquire a set of the *Ssu-pu pei-yao* and *Ssu-pu ts'ung-k'an*; see letters filed in "Dubs Papers on Foundation of Oriental Institute Library," Institute of Chinese Studies, Oxford.

[80]Undated letter from J.B. Rhine (author of a book on precognition) to H.H. Dubs, Bodleian Library, MS. English, miscellaneous, d. 706.

[81]See Dodds, *Missing Persons: An Autobiography* (Oxford: Clarendon Press, 1977), 97-111, 194.

except for a year spent visiting the East-West Center at the University of Hawaii in 1962-63, he influenced the growth of American sinology by his many publications; indeed, aside from Laufer, he was the most prolific professional sinologist to publish in English during his era, and the most distinguished historian of philosophy among English or American sinologists.

George A. Kennedy

George A. Kennedy (1901-60), like Dubs, Hummel, and L. C. Goodrich, developed from a missionary background. He was born in Chekiang to missionary parents. He grew up speaking a Wu dialect, and liked to call Chinese his native tongue. After receiving his Ph.D. from the University of Berlin in 1937, probably under Otto Franke, he was appointed an assistant professor of Chinese at Yale. In 1943 he was promoted to associate professor, and reached the rank of professor in 1954. During the war he served as the director of the Military Intelligence School and Army Specialized Training Program at Yale from 1942 to 1944.

In many ways, Kennedy is similar to Peter A. Boodberg. Although lacking Boodberg's incisive genius or range of endeavors, Kennedy shared many of the intellectual qualities and interests of his contemporary at Berkeley.

First of all, he was interested in pedagogy, as the preponderance of his bibliography indicates.[82] This commitment is apparent in every publication. His *An Introduction to Sinology: Being a Guide to the Tz'u Hai (Ci hai)* is the most formal manifestation of this concern. It is a handbook on the craft and conventions of philological work in Chinese texts, introduced through the practical use of the *Tz'u-hai* dictionary. Other tools of the working sinologist are introduced and illustrated in this book, such as biographical compendia, geographical dictionaries, and chronological tables. All in all, it is a convenient syllabus for an introductory course on methodology, methodological rectitude being a theme Kennedy tried to reinforce at every turn:

---

[82]See the complete bibliography in Li Tien-yi, ed., *Selected Works of George A. Kennedy* (New Haven: Far Eastern Publications, 1964), 513-25.

However mysterious and impenetrable the Chinese jungle may have appeared to the early missionaries, its underbrush has been somewhat cleared by generations of devoted scholars, and pathways have been opened here and there. But these ways are nothing else than methods, and those that serve the translator best are the methods of philology.[83]

Second, Kennedy had the same wry tone and ease of expression as Boodberg, even if he eschewed the Boodbergian tendency for coining neologisms. Contra Boodberg, however, his first loyalty was to his readership, not to the texts, as he preferred to make his translations accessible to the average student of Chinese.

Third, he proffered many innovative approaches to linguistics, grammar, and etymology. His interest in the Chinese script, romanization, statistical analysis, and a suggested method for writing Chinese characters in shorthand, all partake of the same spirit as Boodberg's technical experimentations. However, to take a metaphor from music, Kennedy's excursions in this direction rarely exceeded the domain of tonality; even if he sometimes sounded like Alban Berg, he never approached the dodecaphonic atonality of Boodberg's Schönberg. Kennedy even knew Manchu, although he did not exploit it much in his publications.

Finally, an interest in biography gripped them both. Paralleling Boodberg's biographies of eminent Hsiung-nu chieftains of the Sixteen-States period, published mostly in his privately printed series, are Kennedy's seventy-two contributions on Manchu and Chinese rulers and officials included in *Eminent Chinese of the Ch'ing Period*. In these biographical epitomes, Kennedy demonstrates his command of traditional Chinese sources, and of course the secondary literature in Chinese, Japanese, and German; he also exploited Manchurian archival materials.[84] It should also be noted that Kennedy, again like Boodberg, produced his own private series, the *Wennti* papers, which included in his case

---

[83]Kennedy, review of William Charles, *An Album of Chinese Bamboos*, rpt. in *Selected Works*, 488.

[84]Witness his discussion of the textual tradition of the Manchu version of Nurhachi's *Shih-lu*, in *Eminent Chinese of the Ch'ing Period*, 1:599.

contributions of other scholars on sinological subjects.

Most of Kennedy's published offerings deal with questions of either grammar or linguistics. According to E.G. Pulleyblank, his contributions to classical Chinese grammar retain their value today, but his proposed solutions to problems in historical phonology, while accurately pointing out difficulties in Karlgren's reconstruction, do not improve upon Karlgren.[85] Yet his own system of romanization attempts to reflect pan-dialectal features, and even incorporates the distinctions found in Middle Chinese *fan-ch'ieh* spellings.[86]

Several of Kennedy's works deserve re-reading. The first contribution of importance is "Interpretation of the Ch'un-Ch'iu."[87] Kennedy makes heavy use of tabulation and statistics, a feature that characterizes most of his works. On the basis of examining the use of technical terms for the death of rulers in the *Ch'un-ch'iu*, he concludes that, contrary to traditional Chinese views—and that of his mentor Otto Franke in *Studien zur Geschichte des konfuzianischen Dogmas* (1920)—no moralistic lesson, let alone esoteric meaning, can be drawn from the vocabulary in this dreary classic. Kennedy proves that data were included rather on the basis of the availability of facts to the author Confucius in the course of his travels. "Metrical Irregularity in the *Shih Ching*,"[88] continuing in this statistical vein, makes an important conclusion for *Shih-ching* poetics in terms of accentation and meter: when a line deviates from the normal four-character syllables, it was usually metrically equivalent to four beats. In the age when Karlgren was making sweeping conclusions on the basis of statistical studies of one or two vocabulary items or syntactic elements,[89] Kennedy's restrained application of this new tool is an admirable example.

---

[85]E.G. Pulleyblank, review of Li, *Selected Works of George A. Kennedy*, *AM* n.s. 12 (1986): 127-30.

[86]See Hugh Stimson, "About the Transcription System," in Kennedy, *An Introduction to Sinology*, ix-x.

[87]*JAOS* 62 (1942):40-48; rpt. in *Selected Works*, 79-103. It first had appeared in 1935 in *Sinica*, and in 1936 was published in Chinese in the journal *Min-tsu*.

[88]*HJAS* 60 (1939): 284-96; rpt. in *Selected Works*, 10-26.

[89]As in Karlgren, "On the Authenticity and Nature of Tso Chuan," or "The Authenticity of Ancient Chinese Texts."

Perhaps Kennedy's most significant article is "A Study of the Particle *Yen*."[90] While again heavily dependent on statistical tabulation, it reveals another characteristic feature of Kennedy's approach, a presentation that is light in tone and dry of wit.[91] Kennedy regarded particles as more than aids to punctuation, he treated them as words and worked to isolate their precise function: "In tackling a classical text, the first task always is to find the phrasing, that is, to supply the punctuation, and particles that can be depended on to occur at the beginning or at the end of phrases are eagerly seized on as aids in punctuating. But one must be continually on guard against the too easy mistake of concluding that they are there just for that purpose."[92] Analyzing the particle *yen* both through its grammatical use as well as its phonological form, Kennedy determined that it was a fusion of a preposition and a pronoun, *yü* 於 + *chih* 之 .[93] Other words and problems in philological analysis are also broached in this exemplary methodological study.

Kennedy was another sinologue to lay great stress on syntax as the key to reading classical Chinese. His unfinished grammar of *Meng-tzu*, published as "Word Classes in Classical Chinese,"[94] according to Pulleyblank, attempted to analyze the syntactical patterns of the language. It isolated the "relative position" in linguistic context for the two hundred most commonly occurring graphs in *Meng-tzu*: "This context is a quotable segment that can be preceded and followed by a pause, hence it possesses some sort of syntactic unity and independence. There is no better place in which a study of the grammar of Mencius can begin."[95] "In spite of its incompleteness and some points of detail which I would question," concludes Pulleyblank, "this article remains, in my view, the best attempt

---

[90]*JAOS* 60 (1940): 1-22, 193-207.

[91]This Kennedy style perhaps reached its apex with "The Monosyllabic Myth," *JAOS* 71 (1951): 161-66, rpt. *Selected Works*, 104-18; and "The Butterfly Case (Part One)," *Wennti* 8 (March 1955), rpt. in *Selected Works*, 274-322.

[92]"A Study of the Particle *Yen*," *Selected Works*, 30.

[93]Another work that treats fusion words is ""Negatives in Classical Chinese," *Wennti Papers* 1 (1954); rpt. *Selected Works*, 119-34.

[94]*Wennti* 9 (April 1956); rpt. in *Selected Works*, 323-433.

[95]*Selected Works*, 330.

so far to give an account of the grammar of a variety of Classical Chinese."[96] The two famous "Kennedy laws" of syntax, although they had already been noted in the grammars of Julien and von der Gabelentz, came to be firmly associated with the name of Kennedy, and first appeared in "A Study of the Particle *Yen*": 1) if a normally transitive verb lacks an object, it becomes passive; and 2) if a normally intransitive verb takes an object, it becomes causative.[97] All in all, Kennedy did much to professionalize the study of classical Chinese, which he recognized for what it was: a science, not a skill.[98]

John K. Fairbank and the Founding of Area Studies

The efforts of men like Hummel and Serge Elisséeff of the Harvard-Yenching Institute[99] to institutionalize funding for research on East Asia in the 1930s eventually led to the fourth phase of the four-part periodization of the development of American sinology as described by Fairbank.

John King Fairbank (1907-91) was the founder and patron saint of the modern Area Studies movement. As the voice of authority at Harvard in this nascent field, he combined general familiarity with the sources with first-hand knowledge of the contemporary Chinese scene. Through his own seminal works and the careers of the students he mentored, it was his merit to reorient the direction of American historical studies away from what he considered the out-moded treaty-port narrative historiography of

---

[96]Pulleyblank, review of Kennedy's, *Selected Works*, 129.

[97]*Selected Works*, 34-35.

[98]See his "Foreword" to *An Introduction to Sinology*, vii-viii.

[99]Founded in 1928 in Massachusetts, the Harvard-Yenching Institute had as its primary purpose to administer funds received from the estate of Charles M. Hall and Harvard University to strengthen higher education in China, and to establish a center at Harvard for the teaching and study of the Far East. The story of the founding of this institute is recounted in Dwight Edwards, *Yenching University* (New York: United Board for Christian Higher Education in Asia, 1959), 173-77, 274-78; Philip West, *Yenching University and Sino-Western Relations* (Cambridge, Mass.: Harvard University Press, 1976), 187-94; and Egan, *A Latterday Confucian: Reminiscences of William Hung (1893-1980)*, 111-18.

the pre-World War II mode towards the New History of the social sciences. As an historian with a decided anti-philological bias, he makes an interesting foil to contrast with traditional sinologists.

Fairbank was born and raised in South Dakota. In an autobiography that is part introspection, part confession, and part detached reportage, Fairbank recalls the course of his studies at Exeter Academy, Wisconsin, Harvard, and Oxford, his training in Peking, his war-time work for the government, and his career at Harvard.[100] He narrates the story of this life with a tone of breezy self-confidence punctuated on occasion by self-deprecatory asides more indebted to wit than humility. We see Fairbank the Rhodes scholar at Oxford turn into Fairbank the Area Studies father figure by dint of hard work and the avoidance of an accepted academic program: "If I had been properly trained, I could never have put together the combination of approaches I made to China. Language training would have taken all my time.[101] So would thesis research in a well-developed field. I would never have had time for first-hand 'area' experience through casual travel. My combination of approaches was possible only because I was entirely on my own, not under

---

[100]*Chinabound: A Fifty-Year Memoir* (New York: Harper Colophon Books, 1982). Paul M. Evan puts Fairbank's life and accomplishments into the plural contexts of national interest, the Cold War, and the growth of international scholarship in *John Fairbank and the American Understanding of Modern China* (New York: Basil Blackwell Inc., 1988). See also Paul A. Cohen and Merle Goldman, compilers, *Fairbank Remembered* (Cambridge, Mass.: John K. Fairbank Center for East Asian Research, 1992).

[101]His political antipodes the historian C. Martin Wilbur, as staunch in his support for the ROC as Fairbank was for the PRC, expressed the same sentiments: "The years I spent on language study could have been used much better in getting a broader education;" Wilbur, *China in My Life: A Historian's Own History*, ed. Anita M. O'Brien (Armonk, New York: M.E. Sharpe, 1996), 307. This attitude, shared by Fairbank and Wilbur, was not conducive to conducing primary research in Chinese, and led to the sad assessment of Raymond Myers and Thomas Metzger that by the 1980s few American historians working in the field of modern China had a "strong grasp" of the Chinese language, whether for speaking or reading in various genres. Fortunately, their assessment is no longer valid; see their "Sinological Shadows: The State of Modern China Studies in the U.S.," *Australian Journal of Chinese Affairs* (1980), 4:1-34.

anyone's direction."[102]

Despite his scatter-gun approach to China and the language, Fairbank did believe, if not in mastering the literary language for general purposes, at least in obtaining a basic grounding in the material sources of one's own particular corner of the Chinese "area." He chose Ch'ing documents related to foreign diplomacy, specifically the *I-wu-shih mo*.[103] He explained that

> I did not propose to study Chinese classical texts under a scholar like William Hung, or even at the major centers in Paris or Leyden. European sinology was wedded to the idea that a Western scholar of China must be able to handle Chinese texts, using the vast paraphernalia of Chinese reference works, all by himself. It decried the China coast sinology of missionaries and consuls who, when the going got tough, always had their faithful teacher available to refer to in a back room, just as I seemed to be doing.[104]

While much more than a China hand, of course, Fairbank did collaborate with Chinese and Japanese scholars, leaving the details of translation and annotation to their experienced care. For instance, his co-author of *Ch'ing Administration: Three Studies*,[105] S.Y. Teng, helped him produce *China's Response to the West: A Documentary Survey 1839-1923*[106]: "Of the sixty-five key documents, Teng drafted most of the translations and compiled most of the data on authors, which I edited, and I then wrote the final text that links the documents together."[107] The extent of his editing seemed to be limited to polishing up the English, rather than checking on the accuracy

---

[102]*Chinabound*, 94.

[103]On Fairbank's scholarly approach, "documentary history," see Evans, *John Fairbank*, 49-71.

[104]Ibid., 98.

[105]*Ch'ing Administration: Three Studies* (Cambridge, Mass.: Harvard University Press, 1960).

[106](Cambridge, Mass.: Harvard University Press, 1954). A similar compilation is *A Documentary History of Chinese Communism* (Cambridge, Mass.: Harvard University Press, 1952), a collaboration involving Conrad Brandt and Benjamin Schwartz.

[107]*Chinabound*, 329.

of the translations.

His purpose, however, was less the philological treatment of specific texts for their own sake than to develop a data base through background research for more refined interpretive studies at a later date:

> Our main effort, therefore, is to simulate and assist the kind of monographic study necessary to any intellectual progress in this field. It will not be enough for Western social scientists to apply new interpretations to the meager record of modern Chinese history thus far available. Not enough facts are known. We cannot rely on propagandist "scholarship," with its dogmatic disregard for the truth...to give us the real story. It is necessary for trained and competent Asian and Western scholars alone and in collaboration to spend long periods of time in translation and research, else we shall never know what has really happened in China since its opening to the West.[108]

Notwithstanding his endorsement of the work of translation, even in his primer on Ch'ing administrative documents Fairbank was careful to separate the useful tool of language from the onerous, even distracting, task of language study: he warned that "for historians, the problem is to use the language rather than be used by it;"[109] it was "a tool and not an end."[110] His overriding goal was to utilize the facts of Chinese history, culled from whatever source was relevant and accessible, to confirm an interpretive framework designed from the models generated by the social sciences. But this basic gulf between the methodologies of philology and social science were more than mere functional differences of operation and procedure; it marked a more fundamental question of the superiority and utility of

---

[108]Teng and Fairbank, *China's Response to the West*, 5-6.

[109]*Ch'ing Documents: An Introductory Syllabus*, 1:vii. A similar syllabus carries no such strictures against enjoying the literary language; see Philip A. Kuhn and John K. Fairbank, compilers, *Introduction to Ch'ing Documents, Part One. Reading Documents: The Rebellion of Chung Jen-Chieh*, 2 vols. (Cambridge, Mass.: John King Fairbank Center for East Asian Research, 1986).

[110]See Evan, *John Fairbank*, 38-39, for this quote and the intellectual context of Fairbank's attitude towards language learning.

one approach over another. Fairbank regarded traditional sinology as, at base, an individual—and hopeless, if not even vain—effort to master a boundless, pre-modern literary corpus of little relevance for understanding and ameliorating the human condition in modern China; it was an Old World preoccupation, even when imported to American soil. On the contrary, "Regional Studies—China" was a corporate endeavor of an American-led community of scholars, utilizing scientific techniques of universal applicability, regardless of area. In such a view, sinology did not represent a competing methodology, but merely an antiquarian and attenuated one. This is clearly seen in Fairbank's periodization of sinology.[111]

The Periodization of Sinology

Sinology, according to Fairbank's definition, is "the study of Chinese civilization through the Chinese language and writing system. The accumulation of factual bricks to build an edifice of learning (or at least to pile up a heap of knowledge)," continued Fairbank, "created the tradition of micro-sinology, which was nourished by the Chinese tradition of k'ao-cheng hsüeh (establishing textual facts for facts' sake)."[112] Although tacitly recognizing the philological foundation of traditional sinology, Fairbank's periodization focused rather on the application of sinological studies to questions that would satisfy the interests of the social scientist. Hence, the more scientific and institutionalized sinology became at each phase, the more maturity it was granted.

The first phase had been of "distinguished amateurism," characterized by the works of missionary scholars such as Bridgman and Williams. The second phase was introduced with the founding of American learned societies, and we may add, the establishment of chairs in Chinese at American universities: 1876 at Yale, 1879 at Harvard, 1890 at

---

[111]Fairbank, *China Perceived*, 211-15. For another periodization scheme, see John Lam, "The Early History of Chinese Studies in America," *Hong Kong Library Association Journal* 2 (1971): 16-23.

[112]Fairbank, *China Perceived*, 211.

the University of California, and 1901 at Columbia.[113] During the third phase, corresponding to the first third of the twentieth century, "both history and sinology were challenged by social science and suffered comparative slowdown."[114] One manifestation of this stagnation was the infrequency of sinological contributions made by the few active American sinologists, Rockhill, Hirth, and Laufer, to the solitary Orientalist journal in America, *Journal of the American Oriental Society*; for the most part they preferred to publish in Europe instead. To quote L.C. Goodrich, "Until the last decade or so (1920s) there was, it shames an American to say—scarcely any commerce in their wares on the continent of North America."[115] Continues Professor Goodrich, in this period of American sinology the field was ripe for harvest but the laborers were few: "To put it bluntly—we have an extraordinarily fine lot of basic material for our studies: books, rubbings, objects of art and archeology, and sociological materials of many kinds; but we have scarcely a handful trained to their intelligent appreciation."[116] Professional training in Chinese and Japanese until the early twenties, *ad hoc* and sporadic, became more focused with the establishment of the American Institute of Pacific Relations in 1925 and even more so after 1928 with the founding of the Harvard-Yenching Institute and the Committee on the Promotion of Far Eastern Studies of the American Council of Learned Societies. In the 1940s began the massive language school movement to train interpreters and intelligence analysts for World War II. This led to Fairbank's fourth and final phase, that of "self-conscious maturity and coalescence" after WWII.[117]

---

[113]Surveyed in Hu, *The Development of the Chinese Collection at the Library of Congress*, 35-40.

[114]Fairbank, *China Perceived*, 213. This entire period of stagnation and its many causes are reviewed in the first half of Maribeth E. Cameron, "Far Eastern Studies in the United States," *FEQ* 7 (1948): 115-35.

[115]L. Carrington Goodrich, "Chinese Studies in the United States," *Chinese Social and Political Science Review* 15 (1931): 67.

[116]Ibid, 76.

[117]See Cameron, "Far Eastern Studies in the United States," for the growth of this final phase. The development of sinology from this teleological point of view is traced by Richard C. Howard, "The Development of American China Studies: A Chronological

The necessity for dealing with problems in contemporary Asian politics, society, and economy to help rebuild from the devastation of the war led to an intense academic interest in the social sciences at the expense of the humanities, a debate that occurred contemporaneously in Great Britain.[118] The American Oriental Society, first founded in 1842, had always retained a grounding in philology and a focus on pre-modern civilizations.[119] It hence was an unsatisfactory outlet for the new generation of professional scholars interested in the condition of modern Asia. "Asian Studies," instead of the traditional Sinological Orientalism of the nineteenth century or the more focused but still narrowly disciplined sinology, then became the rallying cry after the war. In 1948 the Far Eastern Association was founded to meet this need, changing its name to the Association for Asian Studies in 1957.[120] Its first president was Arthur Hummel[121] The journal *Far Eastern Quarterly* (later *Journal of Asian Studies*), sponsored by the Association, served this new approach through stressing the broad fields of history, culture, geography, economics, sociology, and government. A rejection letter from the managing editor, Cyrus H. Peake of Columbia University, to a would-be contributor from South Pasadena, California, dated March 14, 1940, stresses this commitment to the modern setting: "We feel that we cannot go in for the more literary type of article and translated material as our emphasis is upon

---

Outline," *International Association of Orientalist Libraries, Bulletin* 32-33 (1988): 38-49.

[118]For this debate and the new thrust of the School of Oriental and African Studies away from philology towards the equivalent of the American "area studies," see Michael McWilliam, "Knowledge and Power: Reflections on National Interest and the Study of Asia," *Asian Affairs* 26 (1995): 33-46.

[119]See Nathaniel Schmidt, "Early Oriental Studies in Europe and the Work of the American Oriental Society, 1842-1922." *JAOS* 43 (1923): 1-10; and Elizabeth Strout, ed., *Catalogue of the American Oriental Library* (New Haven: Yale University Library, 1930).

[120]Charles O. Hucker, *The Association for Asian Studies: An Interpretive History* (Ann Arbor: AAS, 1973), 9-19. An earlier intellectual bifurcation in Soviet sinology occurred in the 1920s between the old-school Leningrad sinologists and the Moscow historians focusing on the revolution, according to Gafurov and Gankovsky, eds., *Fifty Years of Soviet Oriental Studies*, 6.

[121]Ibid., "Appendix Three," list all of the presidents until 1970.

historical, economic and political problems in the modern period."[122] The earliest period looked at by this new brand of historian was the Ming, and then only for its foundational role in the rise of the Ch'ing dynasty and the maturation of Neo-Confucianism.

The institutional culmination of this concern with modern China as an "Area Study" was reached with the founding in 1959 of the Joint Committee on Contemporary China.   Organized by the American Council of Learned Studies and the Social Science Research Council, the Joint Committee enjoyed the financial support of the Ford Foundation. According to one researcher, "The grants for faculty research and graduate training given by the Joint Committee, together with larger institutional grants made by the Ford Foundation and the U.S. government, helped stimulate the first wave of American research on the economy, political system, and society of contemporary China."[123]

Area Studies were termed "Regional Studies" in Fairbank's parlance: "Regional was Harvardese, a special name to go with a special place.... Both terms meant interdisciplinary study, more specifically, focusing the skills of the social sciences to study a certain part of the world."[124] To Fairbank, the rise of Area Studies and the marriage of social sciences to history became less an alternate path in the scholarly road than its ultimate termination: "Looked at as modes of thought, history, the social sciences, and area study including sinology seem now to have all met and intermingled. They are no longer in separate intellectual channels, and one

---

[122]Letter attached to the inside cover of the first volume of *FEQ*, Harold B. Library, Brigham Young University.

[123]Harry Harding, "The Evolution of American Scholarship on Contemporary China," in *American Studies of Contemporary China*, ed. David Shambaugh (Washington, D.C.: Woodrow Wilson Center Press, 1993), 14. For a broad historical and institutional introduction, see John M.H. Lindbeck, *Understanding China: An Assessment of American Scholarly Resources* (New York: Praeger Publishers, 1971).

[124]*Chinabound*, 324. Benjamin Schwartz provides a critical assessment of area studies as a type of academic discipline, plus a defense against charges on the one hand that it is the linear descendant of Orientalism and, on the other, that it is too limited in light of the more pertinent "global models" and "world systems" of the school of Immanuel Wallerstein. See Schwartz, "Area Studies as a Critical Discipline," in *China and Other Matters* (Cambridge, Mass.: Harvard University Press, 1996), 98-113.

cannot follow any one stream without getting into the others."[125] Since the few scholarly virtues sinology had enjoyed were now, in the view of Fairbank's followers, incorporated in the new pan-disciplinary and all-embracing "Asian Studies," the term sinology was reserved by many American scholars for retrograde thinking and outmoded approaches to China, even those in the field of modern political history.[126] Yet Fairbank did acknowledge that, at base, area study was not a discipline but an activity, approachable not through an M.A. program, but only through a Ph.D.[127] It took two other Harvard men, one in theory and one in practice, to clarify the conceptual distinction between a field such as history and a discipline such as philology when they recognized that the growth of history and other "modes of thought" did not vitiate the need for philological grounding, that is, accessing the primary data contained in documentary sources—it just expanded what scholarship could do with the texts. The theoretician was Charles Gardner, one of the original editors of the *HJAS*, and second president of the Far Eastern Association.   The practicing philologist was Francis Cleaves.

Charles Gardner

Charles Gardner (1900-66) earned his B.A. and graduate degrees

---

[125]Ibid. The difficulty in applying theories from the social sciences to historical questions based on Chinese sources is touched on by Paul A. Cohen, *Discovering History in China: American Historical Writing on the Recent Chinese Past* (New York: Columbia University Press, 1984), 184.

[126]For instance, Joseph Levenson's brand of historiography in the 1950s and 1960s was thought alien and radical at the time to the traditional "treaty port" historians; now Levenson's superannuated historiography is characterized as the "old Western Sinological tradition;" Maurice Meisner and Rhoads Murphey, eds. *The Mozartian Historian: Essays on The Works of Joseph R. Levenson* (Berkeley and Los Angeles: University of California Press, 1976), 14. Another example: Cohen termed Levenson's perspective as the effort to rise above the "parochialism of American Sinology," i.e., historiography; Cohen, *Discovering History in China*, 62. The stresses and strains in the competing brands of history in general are introduced, with insight and amusement, by Gertrude Himmelfarb, *The New History and the Old: Critical Essays and Reappraisals* (Cambridge, Mass.: Harvard University Press, 1987).

[127]*Chinabound*, 325.

from Harvard (Ph.D. 1955).[128]   His dissertation, "A Chapter of the Basic Annals from the Draft Tsing History," continued his interest in historiography that was first manifested with his most important work, *Chinese Traditional Historiography* (Cambridge, Mass.: Harvard University Press, 1938).[129] He was hired as an instructor at Harvard in 1933, becoming associate professor in 1937.   He lectured at Columbia and Wellesley in 1944-1945. His bibliography lists some ten items, including two privately printed offerings that evince his interest in bibliography and the history of sinology: *Bibliographies of Sinologists* (Cambridge, Mass., 1958), and *Bibliographies of Fourteen American Specialists of the Far East with a Few Biographical Notes* (Cambridge, Mass., 1960).

In his best known publication, a short but densely detailed work, Gardner lays bare the foundation for historical research to be conducted in traditional Chinese sources. *Chinese Traditional Historiography* is basically a crash-course in philology for the historian. Since most historians, it seems, dismissed textual work as, in the words of Mary Wright, "intellectually simple but technically exacting procedures of authentication, dating, etc. of our texts,"[130] Gardner needed at least to underscore the importance of these dull if necessary procedures: "It rather aims at the systematic presentation of a part of those general ideas which are the necessary baggage of any historian who would handle the Chinese sources." Equally necessary is the introduction of principles of historical research for the sinologist: "It is intended primarily to smooth the path of the novice sinologist, to warn him of special perils and difficulties which beset his way, and to remind him of those canons of criticism which may help him avoid some pitfalls."[131]

Chapter II, "Motivation," begins the main part of this study. Here Gardner deals with the origin and motivation for historical writing. The

---

[128]"Charles Sidney Gardner, January 1, 1900 - November 30, 1966," *HJAS* 27 (1967): 329-30, with bibliography.

[129]The second printing of 1961 contained additional notes and corrections by Prof. Yang Lien-shang on pp. 107-110.

[130]Mary C. Wright, "Chinese History and the Historical Vocation," *JAS* 24 (1964): 515.

[131]*Chinese Traditional Historiography*, ix.

first histories can be considered as mnemonic records for use in religious and divinatory rites. These grew into archival court records and chronicles. The only one of these to survive, the *Ch'un-ch'iu* of Lu, already evinced in the manner of its compilation the chief characteristic of all subsequent official and orthodox historical works in China until modern times. For its compiler included in his narrative only those facts which served to illustrate, either positively or negatively, the moral norms and principles he supported. Hence the moral interpretation of history and the responsibility of the historian to support political probity are two of the basic characteristics of Chinese exemplar historiography.[132]

Perhaps the most valuable chapter of the book is the next one, on textual criticism. Chapter Three presents many ways of approaching the problems of textual corruption, filiation of editions, the question of authorship, anachronism, buried scholia and interpolation, bibliography, and the transmission of texts—including the controversy over Old versus New texts. Short chapters on historical criticism, synthesis, and style follow. The final chapter, entitled "Formal Classification," is a detailed discussion of the different categories of historical writings. In this chapter, as in the whole book, Gardner provides explanations for key Chinese terms and how they were used. This discussion is broad enough to clarify which terms were actually synonymous and which reflected functional differences.

Throughout the work Gardner refers extensively to secondary literature which either provides guidance for further reading, or represents the authorities upon whom his claims depend. His analysis of Chinese historiography is based almost entirely upon the scholarly contributions and methodological examples of "the sinological Titans of the Collège de France, Chavannes, Pelliot, and Maspero,"and to a lesser extent Bernhard Karlgren. Indeed, though honoring Karlgren's contributions to the advancement of sinology, there is a definite undercurrent of support for the

---

[132]For exemplar historiography, an approach designed to establish and inculcate a model of ethical and practical behavior drawn from historical examples, see Michael C. Rogers, *The Chronicle of Fu Chien: A Case of Exemplar History* (Berkeley: University of California Press, 1968).

French school of sinology against the rigidity of Karlgren's approach, with his systematizing word studies, and attempts at reducing complex linguistic questions down to a statistical certainty. For example, Karlgren "ignores the fact that history is concerned far more often with probabilities than with facts which are susceptible of scientific demonstration."[133] The canons of historical criticism, concludes Gardner, while never codified or discussed in the abstract, have nevertheless been illustrated by the individual work of brilliant scholars.[134]

Francis Cleaves

Francis Woodman Cleaves (1911-95) was born in Boston on July 14, 1911.[135] After graduating in classics from Dartmouth in 1933, Cleaves studied comparative philology at Harvard (M.A. 1934) and received his Ph.D. in Far Eastern Languages in 1947 with a dissertation on the Sino-Mongolian inscription of 1362.[136] Before World War II, Cleaves attended Pelliot's lectures in Paris (1934-35) and met Antoine Mostaert in Peking during a long sojourn from 1937 to 1941. He began teaching at Harvard after war service as a naval officer, when he resumed his collaboration with Mostaert. They eventually produced facsimile editions or transcriptions of many Mongolian literary texts, produced by the Harvard-Yenching Institute in a scholarly series Cleaves edited, the *Scripta Mongolica Series;* most important were *Altan Tobči* (1952); *Erdeni-yin Tobči* (1956); and *Bolor Erike* (1959). One issue of a *Scripta Mongolica Monograph* was another

---

[133]*Chinese Traditional Historiography*, 22, n. 10. Cf. the next two footnotes, 11 and 12, and the discussion on pp. 18-19.

[134]Ibid., 18-19.

[135]For his life, see the two-page necrology by Elizabeth Endicott-West, "Obituary: Francis Woodman Cleaves (1911-1995)," *Journal of Sung-Yuan Studies* 27 (1997), unpaginated; and John R. Krueger, "In Memoriam Francis Woodman Cleaves (July 13th [*sic*]) 1911-1995 (Dec. 31st)," *Permanent International Altaistic Conference (P.I.A.C.) Newsletter* 25 (May 1997): 2-3. My former colleague at BYU, Dr. David C. Wright, graciously put at my disposal his complete set of Cleaves' *HJAS* publications, and supplied me with Endicott-West's obituary, all of which considerably eased the way for this evaluation.

[136]Later published as "The Sino-Mongolian Inscription of 1362 in Memory of Prince Hindu," *HJAS* 12 (1949): 1-133.

collaboration with Mostaert, *Les Lettres de 1289 et 1305 des ilkhan Aryun ey Öljeitü à Philippe le Bel* (1962). The rationale behind such productions was the same philological impetus that had motivated Fairbank in producing his compendia of documents, and was expressed by editor Cleaves in the opening preface of the first volume in *Scripta Mongolica Series:*

> At the present time, it is either impossible or extremely difficult for a student of Mongolian history or literature to engage in basic research, because the primary source materials, if available in either printed or manuscript form, are practically inaccessible. It is for this reason that the Harvard-Yenching Institute plans to publish reproductions of series of important Mongolian texts, printed or manuscript, but difficult of access.[137]

To reproduce the text of the *Altan Tobči*, Cleaves borrowed the only copy in the United States, one owned by Owen Lattimore.[138]

Cleaves continued to publish rare and inaccessible Mongolian documents, now presented in close translation copiously annotated, often with plates of the inscription or document in question. His approach, whether the concern was historical, biographical, or linguistic, never varied: he took his departure from a specific word, phrase, or text, and annotated it exhaustively, after a lengthy review of the literature usually graced with an open dedication or expression of gratitude in the first few notes.[139] Literally scores of these texts appeared in the pages of *Harvard Journal of Asiatic Studies*, which he edited for over a decade. He frequently collaborated again with Mostaert,[140] sometimes unofficially it is true, but

---

[137]*Altan Tobči*, p. v. The same rueful sentiments and lofty hopes are expressed by James Bosson in the preface to his edition of the biography of Milaraspa, the *Mila-yin namtar* (Taipei, 1967), 23.

[138]*Altan Tobči*, vi.

[139]This format and approach is discerned most conveniently in his first published article, "K'uei-K'uei or Nao-Nao?" *HJAS* 10 (1947): 1-12, with three plates.

[140]"Trois documents mongols des archives secrètes Vaticanes," *HJAS* 15 (1952): 419-506, with 8 plates.

it was to Pelliot that he owed his greatest methodological debt. In fact, both Cleaves' translation-*cum*-annotation approach and the scope of his studies, Sino-Mongolia, were indelibly stamped with Pelliot's personal interests and methodological predilections. Even the density of the notes, and the care taken to set every aspect of the bibliographical, historical, and biographical background, followed Pelliot's lead.

Once Cleaves explained his passion for digging so deeply in the philological soil of the text: "Within the limits imposed by the relative accessibility of the material in question, I have attempted to comply with Pelliot's suggestion: 'reprendre en un travail d'ensemble tout ce qui subsiste de ce monument mongol important.'"[141] It is true, however, that this single-minded attention to philological exegesis was sometimes carried to extremes when he felt compelled to gloss seemingly every term in an edict or poem. For instance, in "The 'Fifteen Palace Poems' by K'o Chiu-ssu," Cleaves provided the *locus classicus* for the common locution "myriad nations" (*wan-kuo* 萬國), surely by his day part of everyday sinological parlance.[142]   And his two-page historical treatment of the "nine ushers"(*chiu-pin* 九賓) is needlessly digressive when the title is used merely for its allusive overtones of grandeur.[143] On the other hand, an even longer note occupying three pages on the practice of viewing a Buddhist ritual perambulation is necessary to understand the setting of the poem.[144] Examples from his glosses on Mongolian texts are found on facing pages of "The Sino-Mongolian Inscription of 1362 in Memory of Prince Hindu," cited above. On page 98, n. 23 we find the superfluous, or at least needlessly detailed note, on a Mongolian term: "The word *jaya γada γsabar* is a *converbum* in -*γsabar* of *jaya γada*-, an old *passivus* in -*da* of the verb *j aya γa*- "to predestine." So far so good; but he continues by introducing irritatingly elementary components of Mongolian grammar that should be part and parcel of every Mongolist's background: "The suffice -*bar* is that of the *instrumentalis* and -*γsa* is a variant of -*γsan*, the suffix of the *nomen*

---

[141]"The Sino-Mongolian Inscription of 1346," *HJAS* 15 (1952):2.

[142]*HJAS* 20 (1957): 391-479; example is from 425, n. 1.

[143]Ibid., 425-26, n. 3.

[144]Ibid., 453-55, n. 124.

perfecti...." The next notes, #24 on p. 98 and #27, p. 99, discuss with profit two *hapax legomena* not found in any dictionary, the words *narbai* "all, entire," and *ümedü*, "north." Cleaves' zeal for annotation is understandable when viewed from the perspective of pedagogy: all his works were eagerly devoured as linguistic cribs by students of Mongolian language and Sino-Mongolian history alike. It is, of course, much easier for readers to ignore a verbose or unnecessary annotation than it is to track down textual or linguistic arcana on one's own. The degree of annotation is left up to the translator, and it is likely that Cleaves indulged his Pelliot-like penchant for exhaustive annotation as much out of concern for his readers as his commitment to philological completeness.

Cleaves was a man of sincere warmth and compassion, enthused with Christian charity and piety, who often expressed his feelings through dedicating individual articles to former teachers and mentors, colleagues, and even students (e.g., Joseph Fletcher and John Bishop). For instance, a dedication to a 1949 publication reads: "IN PIAM MEMORIAM/PAVLI PELLIOT/MAGISTRI ILLUSTRISSIMI."[145] The Latin inscriptions to Mostaert, Władysław Kotwicz, Medhi Bahrami, Boris Yakovlevič Vladirmircov (cleverly Latinized as "BORISII IACOBI FILII"), and Wallace Brett Donham are much longer and expressive.[146] Cleaves' humanity for both his colleagues and the subject of his studies, the Mongols, is movingly expressed in a dedication that foreshadows Peter A. Boodberg's commitment to including nomadic peoples within his global humanism:

> To the Reverend Antoine Mostaert, C.I.C.M., to whom I owe so much and with whom I have been so closely bound in friendship since 1938, I offer this translation of the biography of one of the greatest Mongols of the thirteenth century as an expression of my high esteem and deep affection. In Antoine Mostaert who went to minister unto the Ordos Mongols—descendants of Mongols among whom moved the immortal Friars, Iohannes de Plano Carpini and

---

[145]*HJAS* 12 (1949): 1-133.
[146]*HJAS* 13 (1950): 1; #15 (1952): 1; #16 (1953): 1; #17 (1954): 1; #18 (1955): 1, and #46 (1986): 184.

Willelmus de Rubruc, and whose relations with the Papacy constitute one of the great chapters of the history of the Middle Ages—the Mongolian people has the staunchest of friends and the closest of brothers. "A friend loveth at all times, and a brother is born for adversity." No one has done more than this humble priest to reveal to the Western World the richness of the cultural heritage of the Mongols, the beauty of their way of life, and the magnificence of their history.[147]

Alas, the late appearance of his masterful if archaically rendered translation of the Secret History after a lag of twenty-five years perhaps was due to the depth of his emotions.[148] A gentlemanly reluctance to contravene the opinions of William Hung on the dating of the *Secret History* may have contributed to the delay in publication.[149] Furthermore, he apparently had experienced an abrupt falling out with Fairbank over funding. Cleaves had desired to establish a bilingual translation series for classical Chinese texts along the lines of the Loeb library, while Fairbank wanted to utilize the same endowment to launch his series of historical monographs. Fairbank won out, leaving Cleaves open to further disenchantment with Harvard down the road and in possession of a set of unpublished translations that he had already prepared. Cleaves did not appreciate Fairbank's cavalier attitude towards the Chinese language, nor do I expect that Fairbank enjoyed either the philological orientation of Cleaves' publications or their scope in medieval Asia. Nor could it have helped that many Asian *Han-hsüeh-chia* who visited Harvard preferred to

---

[147]*HJAS* 19 (1956): 185. An equally lengthy and impassioned dedication, to Serge Elisséeff, is found in 20 (1957): 391.

[148]The title was as quaint as the alliterating King James prose of the translation: *The Secret History of the Mongols/For the First Time/Done into English out of the Original Tongue/and/Provided with an Exegetical Commentary, vol. I (Translation)* (Cambridge, Mass.: Harvard University Press, 1982). Inside the title page are appended the explanatory remarks "This work was completed in 1956 and set in type in 1957. For personal reasons it was set aside and not published until the present." The promised volume two of a continued introduction and extended commentary has never appeared; see the review by Walther Heissig, *HJAS* 44 (1984): 587-90.

[149]Krueger, "In Memoriam Francis Woodman Cleaves," 3.

call on Cleaves instead of on Fairbank; it seems that Cleaves' philological acumen in many languages was more serviceable to their work than the theoretical titrations of Fairbank. All of this might have prodded Cleaves' decision no longer to publish in the *HJAS* after 1976, with the solitary exception of 1985.[150] The only articles of his to appear in *HJAS* during the decade of the 1970s were relatively short bagatelles, "The Boy and His Elephant," and "A Chinese Source Bearing on Marco Polo's Departure from China and a Persian Source on His Arrival in Persia."[151] These came after four articles in the 1940s; seventeen in the 1950s, and three in the 1960s. Of course, the hostility of *HJAS* to philological studies *per se* was hard to brook. In fact, an article Cleaves submitted in 1992-93 was rejected on just such grounds. In later years, he turned towards alternative scholarly outlets such as *Asia Major*, *Mongolian Studies*, *Journal of Sung and Yüan Studies*, or *Journal of Turkish Studies*.[152] His splendid personal library, together with many unpublished manuscripts, is now housed not at Harvard but in the basement of a Catholic church in Gilford, New Hampshire. It functions, in the words of Cleaves' former student Dr. Ruby Lam, as "both a treasure house and a shrine."[153]

Contemporary with Gardner and Cleaves was Peter A. Boodberg, a lesser Altaicist than Cleaves if greater sinologist than either. Boodberg and his pupil Edward H. Schafer brilliantly epitomized those aspects of philology first pioneered by Bridgman and Williams: Boodberg in lexicography, and Schafer in culture and the science of the natural world à la Laufer or Goodrich. Together, they initiated the Berkeley school of sinology that took as its point of departure the close reading of texts with

---

[150]"The Eighteenth Chapter of an Early Mongolian Version of the *Hsiao Ching*," *HJAS* 45 (1985): 225-54.

[151]35 (1975): 14-59, and 36 (1976): 181-203.

[152]Among his last works are "The Memorial For Presenting the *Yüan shih*," *Asia Major* 3rd ser. 1 (1988): 59-69; "The Fifth Chapter of an Early Mongolian Verse of the *Hsiao-ching*," *Mongolian Studies* 16 (1993): 19-40; and "The Sixth Chapter of an Early Mongolian Verse of the *Hsiao-ching*," *Mongolian Studies* 17 (1994): 1-20.

[153]Personal communication, May 28, 1997. A report on this library is David C. Wright, "The Papers of Professor Francis Woodman Cleaves, (1911-1995)," *Journal of Sung–Yuan Studies* 28 (1998): 284-91.

ample annotation, grounded as much in culture and the natural world as in philology. They both deserve separate treatment, and will conclude this section on American sinologists.

11. PETER A. BOODBERG (1903-1972):

Philological Humanism and Global Sinology[1]

"I don't remember exactly when Budberg died, it was either two years ago or three.
The same with Chen. Whether last year or the one before.
Soon after our arrival Budberg, gently pensive
Said that in the evening it is hard to get accustomed,
For here there is no spring or summer, no winter or fall.
'I kept dreaming of snow and birch forests.
Where so little changes you hardly notice how time goes by.
This is, you will see, a magic mountain.'"
        —Czeslaw Milosz, "A Magic Mountain," from *Bells in Winter*.

Peter Alexis Boodberg was a brilliant sinologist and altaicist, who profoundly influenced his students and colleagues as much by his personal traits as by his teaching and scholarship. He was one of the few scholars able to match Pelliot's command of languages, strict methodological standards, tenacity of memory, and the brilliance of his imaginative reasoning.[2]

Boodberg was born on April 8, 1903 in Vladivostok, the economic

---

[1]A preliminary version of parts of this chapter appeared as "Philologist as *Philobarbaros*: The Altaic Studies of Peter A. Boodberg," in *L'Eurasie centrale et ses contacts avec le monde ocidental*, ed. M.-D. Even, et al. (Paris: Centre d'études mongoles, 1997), 59-70.

[2]The chief sources for Boodberg's life and career are Edward H. Schafer, "Peter A. Boodberg, 1903-1972," *JAOS* 94.1 (1974): 1-7, and Alvin P. Cohen, "Bibliography of Peter Alexis Boodberg," *JAOS* 94.1 (1974): 8-13; both reprinted in *Selected Works of Peter A. Boodberg*, compiled by Alvin P. Cohen (Berkeley and Los Angeles: University of California Press, 1979), ix-xix, 496-501. A short biographical notice is contained in *University of California: Asiatic and Slavic Studies on the Berkeley Campus, 1896-1947* (Berkeley: University of California Press, 1947), 10; some analysis of his influence on the Department of Oriental Languages is made by Doris Chun, "The Agassiz Professorship and the Development of Chinese Studies at the University of California, Berkeley, 1872-1985," Ed.D. diss., University of San Francisco, 1986.

center of the Russian Far East, and eastern terminus of the Trans-Siberian Railroad. The son of a nobleman, he enjoyed a good education in the classics and in European languages. He attended a military academy in St. Petersburg until the outbreak of World War I, when he was sent to Harbin for safety. Studying at the university at Vladivostok, he made two trips to Japan before being forced to flee during the revolution. In 1920 he ended up in San Francisco, already knowing several Asiatic languages.

In 1924 Boodberg graduated from the University of California with a degree in Oriental languages. He continued his graduate studies at the same institution, but not limited to the same department. His "global" approach to sinology, that is, the study of China within the continental context of the rest of Asia, manifested itself early in his choice of graduate courses, for included along with his East Asiatic classes were advanced Arabic and Assyro-Babylonian (called Akkadian today)—he understood the designation "Oriental" as applying to the Near East as well as the Far East. Hence, by the time he earned his Ph.D. in 1930, he had mastered enough oriental sources to be able to produce significant contributions to "global sinology" almost immediately.[3]

The Continental Context of China and Historiography on the Nomads

The history of Chinese relations with her northern and western neighbors was a very popular field during the first half of this century.[4] Perhaps Boodberg was attracted by this current academic interest, although his own childhood on the Chinese frontier would have steered him naturally enough towards it. He learned Chinese from locals in Harbin, but the legend of Tungusic blood in his veins from a "Manchurian Princess" ancestor derived from the fact that his maternal grandmother was Princess Gautimooroff, a descendant of "the princes that ruled one of the

---

[3]Professors William Popper and Henry Frederick Lutz were both among the members of his final examination committee, in charge of his minor field of Semitic Languages.

[4]See David B. Honey, "The Sinologist and Chinese Sources on Asia," *Phi Theta Papers* 17 (1987): 21-27.

Mongolian tribes in Siberia before the Russian conquest."[5] If anything, then, Boodberg's Altaic heritage consisted of very diffused Mongolian, not Manchurian, blood.

Boodberg understood global sinology to be the heritage of the best French sinologists, Chavannes and Pelliot, and described it as follows:

> The Oriental Department (at Berkeley) and the scholars associated with it have always approached the study of China on the principle that the development of that nation can be rightly understood only as an integral part of that of the Eur-Asiatic continent. This "global" approach reflects itself particularly in the interest paid to linguistic, historical and cultural relations of ancient and medieval China with its steppe neighbors and through them with the Eurasiatic "Far West."[6]

But Boodberg was not content with seeing the Altaics only as they interacted with the Chinese or only through the optical illusion of Chinese eyes: he tried to view them as themselves.

Several factors raised his own work above the level of generalized

---

[5]Letter from Boodberg's sister, Mrs. Valentina Vernon, to Edward H. Schafer, September 30, 1972, in my possession.

[6]Report of work in progress in the Department of Oriental Languages, quoted by Schafer in Boodberg, *Selected Works*, xiii. Cf. Boodberg's rambling response to a questionnaire by Dr. S. H. Leger:

> For the past fifteen years the Department has stressed the necessity of treating China in its proper continental setting that is as a nation which has never, contrary to the popular notion, existed in isolation, but in an ever widening historical and cultural context with its neighbors, immediate or remote while maintaining Chinese studies as the core of its activities, the Department felt that to be true to its name it must...provide competent instruction in relevant languages used within or immediately adjacent to the Chinese cultural sphere. During that period courses of varied length and intensity have therefore been offered in at least ten other Asiatic languages.

The various languages included Japanese, Mongolian, Manchu, Tibetan, Korean, Siamese (Thai), Malay, Turkish, Javanese, Sanskrit, and Annamese (Vietnamese); 8-page typescript from the late 1940s, in my possession, 2.

synthesis and bland translation with superficial notation. First of all, his command of the primary sources was absolute. Besides his mastery of all relevant Oriental languages, his knowledge of the Chinese sources was not limited to such obvious texts as the monograph on the Hsiung-nu in the *Shih-chi* or the biography of Chang Ch'ien in the *Han-shu*. He drew comparative data from everywhere within the dynastic histories, to name just one genre of historical documents. Secondly, Boodberg was a master philologist, treating with equal skill the intricacies of phonetic reconstruction, the identification of loan words, etymologies, and textual criticism and filiation. And this same philological acumen was evident whether the word at hand was Chinese, Mongolian, Turkish, or Tibetan. Of equal importance was the brilliance of his reasoning and sense of judgement—tempered, no doubt, by his personal experience with the cultures—which allowed him to balance the surface or textual-linguistic evidence with secondary considerations of cultural patterns and historical factors.

The theory behind this outlook was enunciated in 1951:

> Pelliot's solution is essentially a reflection of the scholarly spirit of our generation which seeks to solve the manifold of the history of Central Asia in the light of ethnographic and linguistic factors almost exclusively....An older, and often disregarded, approach to the problem of Central Asiatic ethnogenesis...was typical for investigators of the late eighteenth and early nineteenth centuries, notably De Guignes and Father Hyacinth Bichurin, who were inclined to stress political economy as the dominant factor in the formation of the steppe confederacies and were not too much disturbed by linguistic incongruity. Their attitude... evidenced perhaps a surer insight into the political forces that shape human societies and even a certain instinctive prescience of the analytical failures of their successors, who were too prone to give primacy to ethnic and racial factors in the reconstruction of the history of High Asia.[7]

---

[7]"Three Notes on the T'u-chüeh Turks," in *University of California Publications in Semitic Philology*, vol. 9 (Berkeley, 1951): 1-11; 1; rpt. in *Selected Works*, 350-60.

This outlook permitted Boodberg, for instance, to allow for an admixture of linguistic elements within the same nomadic confederacy, and thus to avoid positing the ethnic identity of the whole on the basis of traces of a language that may have characterized only a small element, such as the ruling group or another social entity.

This same flexibility in dealing with other kinds of evidence was apparent in his handling of Chinese linguistic data:

> Our precise reconstructions of ancient Chinese words, particularly in Karlgren's system, are based on the study of rhyming dictionaries, that is, that of the phonetic values of syllables as they occur *in pause*. In the analysis of transcriptions of polysyllabic names, however, these "dictionary" reconstructions are not necessarily valid for every member of the complex and might even be misleading for unstressed syllables.[8]

Among other examples, Boodberg adduced the Chinese transcription *t'siet-nuo* 吐奴 for Mongolian *činoa*, "wolf," with the final -t of *t'siet* quiescent, or the Chinese medial *liuk/luk/lak* 六, 鹿, or 洛 (as in 阿六敦 or something similar) representing nothing more than a medial -l- as in Turkish *altun*, "gold."[9]

Boodberg had an equal skill in dealing with the phonetic reconstruction of Altaic words, for he was a fine altaicist, not just skilled in consulting dictionaries. In fact, Nicholas Poppe called Boodberg a brilliant altaicist in his memoirs. His expertise in Altaic studies being nationally recognized, he was invited, along with his colleague Otto Maenchen-Helfen, to attend the Ural and Altaic Studies Conference held at Columbia University on September 30, 1958 to discuss the expansion of this important but hitherto neglected field. The two, however did not attend, for unknown reasons.

---

[8]"Three Notes on the T'u-chüeh Turks," 2.
[9]See *Selected Works*, 260-61.

Philological Humanism

Boodberg's most important contributions to sino-altaic studies would seem to be analyses of history and historiography. They include "The Language of the T'o-Pa Wei;"[10] "Two Notes on the History of the Chinese Frontier;"[11] and "Marginalia to the Histories of the Northern Dynasties."[12] But Boodberg was much better known for his work in literary, lexicographical, and historical texts. I mention "texts" because even when interpreting T'ang poetry, Boodberg's approach was always grounded in textual explication, that is, the philological approach, a methodology which in fact was a personal creed:

> Now a philologist, as distinct from a specialist in linguistics, is particularly sensitive to tradition operating in language. As a citizen of the present world he knows that revolutionary reform is inevitable. As one who dwells spiritually in the past, and is, one might say, a custodian of the continuity and contiguity that bind together past and present, he feels obliged to do his utmost in insuring the survival of those elements and monuments which, in his opinion, still perform vital functions.[13]

Perhaps it was partly as a vital link with the great scholarly tradition of the past and as living exemplar that Boodberg exerted the most profound influence on his students. In his teaching career, spent entirely at Berkeley, he trained his students to be able to work with Chinese documents as soon as possible. By the end of the first semester of Beginning Classical Chinese, his students were tested on translation but also on the sexagenary cycle, radicals and the classification of characters, the function of *fan-ch'ieh*, and even the method for reconstructing the

---

[10]*HJAS* 1 (1936): 167-85.

[11]*HJAS* 1 (1936): 283-307.

[12]*HJAS* 3 (1938): 223-53; 4 (1939):230-83, all reprinted in *Selected Works*, 221-349.

[13]*UCI: An Interim System of Transcription For Chinese* (Berkeley: University of California, 1947), Introduction. A companion piece to the above immediately followed: *UCJ: An Orthographic System of Notation and Transcription For Sino-Japanese* (Berkeley: University of California, 1947).

archaic and ancient phonological systems.[14]   But in addition to basic research skills, Boodberg tried to instill in his students something of the true spirit of humanistic scholarship, especially as it was exemplified in the work of the best modern sinologists: Chavannes, Pelliot, and Laufer were introduced as soon as Confucius and Ssu-ma Ch'ien in his beginning syllabus, for he wanted to expose his students not only to the problems of sinology but to the solutions as well. In short, he saw himself as training scholars, not merely teaching classical Chinese.[15]

His humanistic approach to the study of nomadic peoples exerted a powerful influence on the research of his students. His presiding genius founded, as it were, a Berkeley school of Chinese historiography on the nomads. Many important texts on nomads found their way into print after initial translation and annotation as dissertations under his direction.[16] He

---

[14]Cf. Boodberg, "Ancient and Archaic Chinese in the Grammatonomic Perspective," in *Studia Serica Bernhard Karlgren Dedicata*, 212: "For some twenty years it has been our ambition at the University of California (Berkeley) to build our course in elementary Classical Chinese on the most solid philological foundation possible by anchoring it on the granite rock of Professor Karlgren's epoch making researches and by devising an effective formula of introduction to *Grammata Serica* that would permit the student to grasp its principles even before he had set his eyes on his first Seric gramma."

[15]Another undergraduate course taught by Boodberg bears this lofty goal in mind: Oriental Languages 188 was entitled "Philological Method: Languages and Literature of East Asia;" *Asiatic and Slavic Studies on the Berkeley Campus 1897-1947*, 30.

[16]Publications by Boodberg's students on nomadic and related studies include the following: Thomas D. Carrol, S. J., *Account of the T'u-yu-hun in the History of the Chin Dynasty* (Berkeley, 1953); Gerhard Schreiber, "The History of the Former Yen Dynasty, Part I," *MS* 14 (1949): 374-480; "Part II," *MS* 15 (1956): 1-141; Richard B. Mather, *The Biography of Lü Kuang* (Berkeley, 1959); Roy Andrew Miller, *Accounts of Western Nations in the History of the Northern Chou Dynasty* (Berkeley, 1959); William G. Boltz, "A Biographical Note on T'an Shih-huai," *Phi Theta Papers* 10 (1967): 44-46; Michael C. Rogers, *The Chronicle of Fu Chien: A Case of Exemplar History*; Albert E. Dien, "Elite Lineages and the T'o-Pa Accommodation: A Study of the Edict of 495," *JESHO* 19 (1976): 61-88; Chauncey S. Goodrich, "Riding Astride and the Saddle in Ancient China," *HJAS* 44 (1984): 279-306; and Dien, "The Stirrup and Its Effect on Chinese Military History," *Ars Orientalis* 16 (1986): 33-56. The wide-ranging work of Edward H. Schafer, including his interest in both the steppes and the tropics, can be credited in part to--or at least was strongly reinforced by--the parallel interests of Boodberg.

also taught Altaic languages, having inaugurated in 1939-40 a course entitled "Introduction to the Study of Manchu and Mongol Texts."[17] This presumably focused on readings in selected Altaic documents for those students who already had begun language study with Ferdinand Lessing, who had joined the department in 1935.[18] Perhaps one manifestation of this course is the partial transcription of a Manchu version of the *Sun-tzu*, printed as *Hu T'ien Han Yüeh Fang Chu* 6 (April 1933).[19]

Michael C. Rogers, a student who later became a colleague, wrote the most eloquent acknowledgment of the intellectual debt owed to Boodberg by his former students, in the preface to his *The Chronicle of Fu Chien*:

> It all began as a Ph.D. dissertation completed under the chief supervision of Professor Peter A. Boodberg, whose contributions to this work and to the author's whole approach to the study of Far Eastern civilization have been too pervasive to be described in a phrase or two. My Boodbergian apprenticeship has served as a cure for complacency and, indeed, a recipe for instant and constant frustration in my handling of Chinese texts; but my apprehension of such things as semantic contour and allusive patterning, dim though it remains, is incomparably keener that it would have been but for his tutelage.[20]

Boodberg influenced his colleagues almost as much as his students. Nor was this influence limited to Boodberg's role as superlative sinologist or even as department chairman (from 1948 to 1950). He was also one of the founders and mainstays of the Colloquium Orientologicum, a monthly meeting of like-minded Bay Area scholars, which included such Berkeley luminaries as Ernst Kantorowicz, Yakov Malkiel, Otto Maenchen-Helfen,

---

[17]Schafer, in Boodberg, *Selected Works*, xiii.

[18]Typescript history of the department entitled "Oriental Languages and Literature," composed by Boodberg on July 15, 1965, 2, in my possession.

[19]The version preserved in the East Asiatic Library at Berkeley contains marginal notes, in the opinion of William G. Boltz, probably added by Albert Dien.

[20]Rogers, *The Chronicle of Fu Chien*, xi.

W. B. Henning, Lynn White, and Leonardo Olschki.[21] He cultivated a close friendship with the founder of Berkeley's sociology department, Frederick J. Teggart, assisting him in his research in Chinese texts for his study *Rome and China*, and expressed his admiration for the Polish poet Czeslaw Milosz before it became the popular thing to do.

Proleptical Philology

Boodberg's scholarly output was not large. He never published a book, although several manuscripts were largely completed before he died,[22] nor was the number of his articles particularly noteworthy. Yet the impact of his publications was felt among sinologists in Asia, Europe, and America. One of Boodberg's most important publications was "Some Proleptical Remarks of the Evolution of Archaic Chinese."[23] This was inspired in part by suggestions found in Karlgren's fertile phonetic studies; but it was written because Boodberg was dismayed by the lack of application and development of Karlgren's work by other scholars, and especially disturbed by the retrograde theorizing of H.G. Creel on the nature of archaic Chinese.[24] Written specifically *contra* Creel's essay, "On

---

[21]Titles of typical presentations delivered at the meetings, foreshadowing eventual publications, included Kantorowicz, "Synthronus, Throne Sharing with the Deity," Maenchen-Helfen, "Hercules and the Swan Maiden in China," Olschki, "Guillaume Boucher: A Parisian Artist at the Court of the Khans in Mongolia," Henning, "The First Indo-Europeans in History," and Malkiel, "The Origin of the Word *Marrano*." Two of Boodberg's presentations were "Chronology of the Danube Bulgars," and "In Search of Analogues," the later being the Memorial Lecture, given on Feb. 24, 1971, at the 236th meeting.

[22]Schafer reports that by 1963 Boodberg had completed in manuscript a biography of Confucius only in need of revision, as well as a study of the *Lao-tzu* (see *Selected Works*, p. xvi); and the table of contents listing four chapters, plus 308 handwritten pages of text from the first two chapters of a projected two-volume work entitled *Studies in Chinese Lexicology*, is listed by Cohen as still preserved (*Selected Works*, p. 500). We may cite Cohen further: "It appears that P.A.B. destroyed several other MSS of books and articles relating to his interest in philology and the history of the Chinese frontier;" *Selected Works*, 500.

[23]*HJAS* 2 (1937): 329-372; rpt. in *Selected Works*, 363-406.

[24]The debate in the journals between Boodberg and H.G. Creel is set into theoretical context by John DeFrancis, *The Chinese Language: Fact and Fantasy* (Honolulu:

the Nature of Chinese Ideography,"[25] this article is an astute attempt to defend and promote the use of phonology as a necessary, certainly equal, companion to graphology in philological investigation.[26] And along the way Boodberg provided some brilliant insights into the operation of both Chinese language and script.

Conceptual Foil: Herrlee G. Creel

Herrlee G. Creel (1905-1994), Boodberg's target in this debate, graduated from the University of Chicago after a short career as a journalist; his travel and study in China gave him access to the most current Chinese archeological research. His first few works rode the wave of excitement that archeological discoveries engender, and introduced American readers to early Chinese history, culture, and thought. Michael Loewe has commented on the function of Creel's work in attracting a readership beyond academic circles:

University of Hawaii Press, 1984), 85-87.

[25] *TP* (1936): 85-161. Boodberg followed up Creel's rejoinder with a surrejoinder called "'Ideography' or Iconolatry?" *TP* 35 (1940): 266-88. Although Boodberg was not normally combative nor abrasive, his review of Derk Bodde's translation of the two volumes of *A History of Chinese Philosophy* by Fung Yu-lan, printed in *FEQ* 12 (1953): 419-22 and 13 (1954): 334-37, provoked another debate when Bodde felt compelled to respond to the philosophical issues concerning translation raised by Boodberg's criticisms. Bodde's response was "On Translating Chinese Philosophical Terms," *FEQ* 14 (1955): 231-44, rpt. in *Essays on Chinese Civilization*, ed. Charles Le Blanc and Dorothy Borei (Princeton: Princeton University Press, 1981), 395-408. Perhaps Bodde was still feeling stung by an earlier review of one of his works by Boodberg that was as even-toned but equally critical; see "*Tolstoy and China*—A Critical Analysis," *PEW* 1.3 (1951): 64-76, rpt. in *Selected Works*, 481-93.

[26] Phonological studies are perhaps even more important than graphologic research in Chinese philology. According to William G. Boltz, "The etymology of a particular Chinese word is best (and perhaps only) determined by its proper placement within a word family;" "Studies in Old Chinese Word Families." Ph.D. diss., University of California at Berkeley, 1974, 30. Usually, however, Boltz combines both phonological and epigraphical approaches in determining word etymologies; see, for instance, his "Word and Word History in the Analects: The Exegesis of Lun Yü IX.I," *TP* 69 (1983): 261-71.

In addition to setting out a theme within which the origins and growth of Chinese civilization could be set, Creel supplied a further invaluable contribution—publication of his findings in a form that would attract the interest of the non-specialist, that would engage the attention of newly aroused students, and that would display to the academic world that Chinese studies merited an active disciplinary approach.[27]

Especially influential in this regard were Creel's *The Birth of China*, and *Confucius: The Man and the Myth*.[28] *The Origins of Statecraft in China*, vol. 1: *The Western Chou Empire*, was the first mature treatment of the institutions, intellectual foundations, and historical background to the rise of the Chou, based on both a thorough knowledge of the documents and command of the evidence from bronze inscriptions.[29] Yet, despite his publication of a widely-utilized primer of classical Chinese,[30] Creel was an historian and philosopher, not a philologist or pedagogue, and his championing of the ideographic nature of Chinese, even in the face of forceful arguments to the contrary, was doomed from the start.[31]

---

[27]Michael Loewe, in *A Service in Memory of Herrlee G. Creel 1905-1994* (Chicago: Division of the Humanities and Department of East Asian Languages and Civilizations, University of Chicago, 1994), 15. Other participants in the service included colleagues Edward Shaughnessy, Anthony Yu, and Tsuin-hsuin Tsien, former student Sydney Rosen, and fellow historian David N. Keightley. This short but informative pamphlet was supplied courtesy of Prof. Edward Shaughnessy. A complete bibliography of the works of Creel through 1977 is included in David T. Roy and Tsuen-hsuin Tsien, eds., *Ancient China: Studies in Early Civilization* (Hong Kong: Chinese University Press, 1978), 343-46.

[28]*The Birth of China* (1937; rpt. New York: F. Unger, 1954), and *Confucius: The Man and the Myth* (1949; rpt. Norwalk, Conn.: Easton Press, 1994).

[29](Chicago: University of Chicago Press, 1970). Many of Creel's articles were reprinted that same year in the collection *What is Taoism? And Other Studies in Chinese Cultural History* (Chicago: University of Chicago Press, 1970).

[30]*Literary Chinese By The Inductive Method*, 3 vols. (Chicago: University of Chicago Press, 1938-1952). See the review by George A. Kennedy, in *JAOS* 73 (1953): 27-30.

[31]For the position of Creel—but not Boodberg—in the development of Western studies in early Chinese paleography, see Noel Barnard, "The Nature of the Ch'in

To counter Creel's theorizing on ideography, Boodberg led off "Some Proleptical Remarks" by encapsulating the essence of Creel's arguments, followed by an overall condemnation on general principles. It was, comments Boodberg,

> A well expressed, but most ineffectual attempt to demonstrate the unique "ideographic" characteristic of Chinese script and to combat the "phonological" investigation of archaic graphs. Professor Pelliot's remarks appended to the article rightly condemn Dr. Creel's habit of divorcing writing from the living language. Apart from the author's impossible thesis, one must deplore the general tendency manifest throughout this article (and, alas, too prominently figuring in Sinological research on this continent) of insisting that the Chinese in the development of their writing...followed some mysterious esoteric principles that set them apart from the rest of the human race.[32]

As the evolution of sound and symbol in archaic Chinese was yet little understood, Boodberg first laid to rest certain fallacies regarding the nature of archaic Chinese; then he posited several phonetic principles, including word contours, the formation of binomes, polyphony, anlaut and dimidiation, and the like. Finally, he illustrated the application of these principles in the solution of morphological and semantic problems—in short, he convincingly demonstrated the use of phonology as a philological tool.

'Reform of the Script' as Reflected in Archaeological Documents Excavated Under Conditions of Control," in *Ancient China: Studies in Early Civilization*, 183-84.

[32]"Some Proleptical Remarks," rpt. in *Selected Works*, 364-65, n. 2. Kennedy, *Selected Works of George A. Kennedy*, 489-93, reviews three textbooks, Creel, *Literary Chinese by the Inductive Method*, vol. 3, John DeFrancis and Elizabeth Jen Young, *Talks on Chinese History*, and John K. Fairbank, *Ch'ing Documents, An Introductory Syllabus*. In the course of the review, he condemns Creel for the same exclusive focus on Chinese graphs rather than the words they represent. The entire debate is put into linguistic perspective, again in favor of Boodberg's position, in Paul Serruys, "Philologie et linguistique dans le études sinologiques."

Ideography as Idolatry

Relatively inaccessible geographic location and historical aloofness, inspired in part by the awareness of her own cultural superiority, combined to make China a veritable utopia for half-informed Westerners. From Marco Polo and the early Jesuits to Diderot and Voltaire, and even to the twentieth-century perigrinator Count Keysling, China has seemed the ideal civilization, teeming with contented masses, protected by wise officials, informed by unique traditions, nourished by profound faiths and philosophies, and enriched by superb art and literature. It seemed a unique cultural phenomenon unparalleled in history. Unfortunately, some modern sinologists, according the Chinese writing system the same unique status vis-à-vis other written languages, have taken to defining Chinese as an "ideographic" script; that is, as representing graphically the ideas of the writer without the intervening mechanism of the sounds of the language.[33]

Boodberg decried the usage of such terminology as being responsible for most of the misunderstanding of the evolution of Chinese writing, and as diverting needed attention from the study of the *word* represented by the graph (phonology) to the study of the physical shape of the graph (graphology). Therefore, he proposed the use of the term "logographic" to characterize Chinese writing.[34] Although he does not use this specific term, George Kennedy describes the nature of logographic writing as follows:

> Every student soon learns that Chinese graphs are constantly and rather indiscriminately "borrowed" for other homophonous graphs,

---

[33]John DeFrancis, an early adherent of the "Ideographic Myth,"—since reformed—discusses it in depth in a chapter by the same name in his *The Chinese Language: Fact and Fantasy*, 133-48.

[34]Chao Yuen-Ren endorsed and supported this new term by calling attention to an earlier proposal for the use of a similar term. See his "A Note on an Early Logographic Theory of Chinese Writing," *HJAS* 5 (1940): 189. Other endorsements followed; see, *inter alia*, Paul Serruys, "Philologie et linguistique dans les études sinologiques," 175 and Franke, *Sinologie*, 59. For the most recent treatment, see now William G. Boltz, *The Origin and Early Development of the Chinese Writing System* (New Haven: American Oriental Society, 1994).

and if he thinks about this at all he must conclude that the only relatively permanent thing about a graph is the sound it symbolizes. Consequently, the information that is pertinent tells what was meant by a particular sound in the language....What particular graph was used is, fundamentally speaking, unimportant.[35]

GSP and Dimidiation

In order to set the stage for a "'new method of attack' on the structure of Chinese characters," Boodberg first formulated general principles that he thought had determined the development of most writing systems, and he introduced and defined a set of technical terms:

1. A graph ideally represents a single *semanteme* (meaning) and a single *phoneme.*

2. Graphs have to be conventionally and habitually associated with certain semantic-phonetic values in order to represent them in a written language.

3. This habitual association of graph (G) with semanteme and phoneme (SP) is only achieved through long usage, but once achieved is stubbornly retained.

4. Logographs often represent more than one sound (polyphony) and thus more than one meaning (polysemy). Single phonemes can also be represented by more than one graph (polygraphy).[36] Such differences often arose due to the graphic ambiguity of representation.

5. The confusing characteristics of logographic writing—polyphony, polysemy, and polygraphy—encouraged its further development into a more refined vehicle for expression by the addition of another graphic element to an ambiguous graph in order to fix either its sound or its meaning.

6. Many phonetic determiners (pd) also function as semantic

---

[35]Kennedy, *Selected Works*, 490.

[36]The principles of polygraphy, polysemy, and a new one—the polyptoton—are developed and illustrated for classroom use in David B. Honey, "The Word Behind the Graph: Three Notes on the Logographic Nature of Classical Chinese," *Journal of the Chinese Language Teachers Association* 24 (October 1989): 15-26.

determiners (sd) and vice versa, which can be designated etymonic determiners (ed).

Having posited these principles and having formulated new terminology, Boodberg proceeded to utilize them in a new study of several old problems in the evolution, and especially the interpretation, of Chinese writing.

One major handicap in the investigation of archaic Chinese has been the ignorance or evasion of the importance of polyphony. This ignorance caused many additional readings (i.e. meanings, for there is no meaning for any graph divorced from its pronunciation) to remain unsuspected. For example, the graph 名 , according to the *Shuo-wen chieh-tzu* of Hsü Shen, was composed of 口 "mouth" plus 夕 "evening, dark;" Hsü's gloss on 夕 [夕者冥也   ] was interpreted by the ideographists as "夕 means 'dark'" when all that was meant by this gloss was that 夕 should be read as 冥 , that is, as *mieng*. By missing the polyphonous nature of 夕 in this instance, the ideographists abandoned the phonetic trail which would have led directly to other homophonous graph– 鳴 "sound" and 命 "command"—and thus failed to perceive that 夕 was the pd of 口 which was also read *mieng*. This additional reading of 口 , of course, gave it an additional meaning, which if not perceived would vitiate the accurate understanding of any context in which it appeared. Thus to ignore polyphony is to ignore a basic philological tool.

Ignorance of the phonetic element of many graphs led to their subsumption into the class of *hui-i* 會意 "ideographs;" but upon closer examination, most of these have to be re-classified as phonetic compounds. The few true ideographs were merely learned creations of idle schoolmen, graphical variations of original pictograms or symbols, or "perverse rationalizations of 'organically' developed phonetic compounds."

Variant pronunciations of graphs also led Boodberg to observe the important development in the phase of Chinese writing where pd graphs were assimilated internally into simplified versions of original graphs. This explains the grotesque appearance of an early pictograph of a capitated horse—its swollen eye (目 *miok*) only served to draw attention to the pronunciation of the graph; no longer a sharp image of a horse, it represented the phoneme *mieg*, homophonous with "eye."

Another phonetic problem, long ignored by sinologists but raised by both Karlgren and Maspero, was the presence of complex consonantal initials in archaic Chinese. Isolating several archaic stems revealed the etymological relationship between many words traceable to such stems. Thus words that at some later time possess different single initial consonants could be shown to be cognate.

The most fruitful result of Boodberg's study of complex "Anlaut" (initials) was his elucidation of the dimidiation process and the nature of alliterative binomes. He showed that these types of binomes were originally the orthographic means to render phonetically the complex structure of a single complex phoneme (an extension of the method of phonetic determination). For instance, in rendering a word with an initial consonantal cluster such as *gleu, "hunchback," two graphs were needed: 句 *gɣu and 婁 *lɣu. The combination of the two graphs merely spelled a word with an initial consonantal complex, and should not be regarded as representing a bisyllabic word, although this was the later result. This method was indigenous to China, and can be seen later in the *fan-ch'ieh* "spelling" system—which was not developed by Buddhist missionary influence, as is generally supposed. Boodberg's binomial studies naturally elucidated the archaic consonantal Anlaut complexes; he postulated two additional series, **DN (dentals/nasals) and **BD (bilabials/dentals).[37]

From the high vantage point of a steady phonetic scaffolding, Boodberg was able to descry the very horizon of graphic etymologies, and thus interpret textual topographies better than most sinologists. In this he was able to further our understanding of early Chinese thought and mythology as it was preserved in the words and language recorded in the early texts. For instance, he demonstrated the etymonic link between 我 *nga "I" and 義 *nga to define precisely the latter as "we-ness", "allegiance to the 'we' group," i.e., loyalty to the immediate clan as opposed to the men 人 *nien of the state as a whole, as represented by the term 仁 *nien,

---

[37]Boodberg's student William G. Boltz fashioned his Ph.D. dissertation around the former phonetic series. The particular example of "hunchback" was adduced in his recent treatment of dimidiation; see Boltz, *The Origin and Early Development of the Chinese Writing System*, 171-72.

"men-ness", "otherliness."[38]

But Boodberg's lasting contribution to sinology in "Some Proleptical Remarks" lay not in the gems of insight and information presented about words, and through them the philosophy and mythology of the early Chinese, but rather in his clearly presented and copiously illustrated principles for the reconstruction and application of archaic Chinese phonology, which helped to raise sinology to the level of a science founded on universally applicable methods. His overall contribution to the study of classical Chinese was praised by Kennedy, who, while expressing reservations about the process of dimidiation—"the theory of (dimidiation) is one to which I have not rushed, but am being dragged"—nevertheless admitted that "no one can pretend to be studying Chinese seriously these days unless he pays a good deal of attention to Boodberg."[39]

Lone Voice Crying in the Wilderness

Perhaps an inevitable result of Boodberg's genius was increasing isolation from the majority of his professional colleagues. His habit of forming neologisms from Latin and Greek roots made for precise translation, as in his treatment of the 214 radicals,[40] but increased the difficulty of access to his work for those who shared neither his talent in classical languages nor his predilection for molding the English language to suit his tastes.[41] Furthermore, with sinological research after World War II tending to emphasize methodologies adopted from sociology, anthropology, and comparative literature, his brand of scholarship

---

[38]Boodberg gave the same thorough treatment to other key philosophical terms in his article, "The Semasiology of Some Primary Confucian Concepts," *PEW* 2.4 (1953): 317-32, rpt. in *Selected Works*, 26-40.

[39]Kennedy, *Selected Works*, 492.

[40]See his privately printed "Cedules From a Berkeley Workshop in Asiatic Philology," nos. 41-51 (Berkeley, 1955).

[41]For instance, Boodberg's translation of "Deer Park Hermitage" by Wang Wei elicited the following dismissal from Eliot Weinberger: "To me this sounds like Gerard Manley Hopkins on LSD;" Weinberger and Octavio Paz, *Nineteen Ways of Looking at Wang Wei* (Mt. Kisco, New York: Moyer Bell, 1987), 51.

—"philological humanism"—was no longer popular.

The reprinting of most of his works, *Selected Works by Peter A. Boodberg*, was greeted by mixed reviews, in part because of the haste in which it was printed, and also due to the preliminary nature of some of its conclusions.[42] Yet in reading some of Boodberg's less accessible offerings, it is evident that not only was his methodology fundamentally sound, even if hard to follow for the less gifted, many of his specific findings are still valuable today. For example, in discussing the first chapter of the *Lao-tzu*, Boodberg surmised that "in probability 妙 *miao* is but a graphically specialized form of 眇."[43] The recently discovered Ma-wang tui *Lao-tzu* manuscripts confirm the emendation he suggested.[44] In a review of D.C. Lau's translation of the *Analects*, Stephen Durrant congratulates a Chinese author on a novel but correct interpretation of the loaded classical term *jen* 仁 .[45] Twenty years earlier Boodberg had arrived at the same conclusion about the word.[46] Finally, attention to Boodberg's "Notes on Isocolometry in Early Chinese Accounts of Barbarians"[47] could have informed Hulsewé's 1979 discussion of textual problems in Chinese accounts of nomads with precise terminology and supplied a methodological approach for dealing with them.[48]

We can see from these few examples the value in reviving

---

[42]Paul W. Kroll, *CLEAR* 4 (1981): 271-73, Albert E. Dien, *JAOS* 102.2 (1982): 422-23, and Sarah Allan, *BSOAS* 45.2 (1982): 390-92 are very favorable; E.G. Pulleyblank, *Pacific Affairs* 52.3 (Fall, 1979): 513-14 is lukewarm; Roy Andrew Miller, *Early China* 5 (1979-80): 57-58 is extremely negative.

[43]"Philological Notes on Chapter One of the *Lao Tzu*," *HJAS* 20 (1957): 598-618, rpt. in *Selected Works*, 460-80; quote on 473.

[44]See Kroll, *CLEAR* 4 (1981): 272 for another example of modern scholarship substantiating one of Boodberg's Taoist interpretations.

[45]Stephen W. Durrant, "On Translating *Lun Yü*," *CLEAR* 3 (1981): 109-19.

[46]"The Semasiology of Some Primary Confucian Concepts," rpt. in *Selected Works*, 36-37.

[47]*Oriens* 10 (1957): 119-27, rpt. in *Selected Works*, 451-59.

[48]Hulsewé, *China in Central Asia: The Early Stage, 125 B.C.—A.D. 23* (Leiden, 1979), 18. In an earlier article, "The Problem of the Authenticity of *Shi-chi* ch.123, The Memoir on Ta-yüan," *TP* 61 (1975): 83-147, Hulsewé did at least admit to the existence of Boodberg's piece, but did not profit from it.

Boodberg's scholarly productions. But of more lasting value would be to revive interest in the principles that guided his research. "Philological humanism" is the term that best captures Boodberg's scholarly aim. No matter the subject, he was careful to highlight the human spiritual or cultural current behind each word or text he worked with. Hence his scholarship always furthered our understanding of the ancients as people, even while discussing technical linguistic problems.[49] He once formulated his principles in a lyrical, almost religious, statement he called "A Philologist's Creed," found among his unpublished manuscripts; it is worth reproducing in its entirety, and is much more concerned with the spirit and intent of scholarship than with its methods:

A Philologist's Creed

Youth speaks, o youth, with the tongues of the angels - as yet unborn. Let me speak with the ancient tongue of the earth.

I believe in Language, chorus of numberless voices, product of myriads of minds, the universal and inclusive art, the massive and enduring monument of ages past; and in the Word, the molder of thought and bearer of truth, the great call of the shrouded dead, my begetters, and in the Light that shines from the beginning of time, through the darkness and silence of tombs unto the heart of Everyman.

I believe in Memory, mother of the Muses and consort of Hope. And this I know: seed fallen on good ground, deep in rich remembrance, will bring forth fruit an hundredfold and unto the number of generations remembered; but seed sown by sowers, self-minded and proud of spirit, and foolish of hope, fall where they have no deepness of earth and wither with the sun of the morrow.

And this I have seen: man brings forth wonders in the travail of his hands, and his goods and his many inventions are increased upon the earth, and behold, there are many new things under the sun. But this generation will pass away and another generation will come, and folly ever abides in the heart of men. And this, I believe, is good: to give heed, and seek out, and set in order the judgment of

---

[49]His "An Early Mongolian Toponym," *HJAS* 19 (1956): 407-8, rpt. in *Selected Works*, 361-62, is a brilliant example of this.

ancients, that the wisdom of man might also endure.

Then I hold fast to the Scriptures of old and the Book of the Ancients, and the parchments and scrolls, and the multiple records of my fathers I revere and I honor, and their voices that speak in the Letters I heed and their signs I interpret, as I heed the voice of the living, as I read the portents of the morrow. On the wonders of my world and your world, o youth, I converse and discourse and take counsel with the ancients and bring fullness of being to them who abide in me and I in them, and on their bones I will lay the sinews of my strength and the flesh of my deeds and I will put in them the breath of my hope and your hope.

And I bless and I ever remember Zion thrice-hallowed and the tower of Nimrod in the vale of Shinar, and the sorrows of Goshen and the prides of the City Eternal, and Hellas, the fair and the wise. I mind me of all tongues, all tribes, and all nations that labored and wrought all manner of works with their hands, and their minds, and their hearts. And I cast mine eyes unto Hind, unto Sinim, and the lands of Gogs and Magogs of the earth, across wilderness, pasture, and field, over mountains, waters, and oceans, to wherever man lived, suffered, and died; to wherever he sinned, and toiled, and sang. I rejoice and I weep over his story and relics, and I praise his glory, and I share his shame.

To-day with you, o youth, I live and hope, yet who, living can stay the sun, for, lo, the night is come, and the noisy flight of today is stilled in the morrow into the silence of yesteryears. So, Janus-faced as mortals be, I gladly learned and gladly teach the truth of earthly time. And for better to serve the living, I, living, but to the past as yet unborn and to my seed a memory forgotten, I serve the living dead with faith, and hope, and charity, in humble expectation of the fulfillment of the Great Design, when time will be no more and we may, united, perceive the plan of our being and our end, our Alpha and your Omega, and may encompass understanding of the Love that moves the sun and all the other stars.

The same brooding humanism in the special case of Asian peoples who competed and interacted in Central Asia is revealed in a lecture presented in 1942 at Berkeley entitled "Turk, Aryan, and Chinese in Ancient Asia," printed as the first entry in *Selected Works* as a thematic and methodological introduction to the entire Boodbergian corpus.[50]   Here Boodberg played the role of cultural middleman to perfection, as he detailed with sympathetic balance and linguistic rigor the historical roles of the steppe nomads, the oasis dwellers along the silk route, and the sedentary Chinese.   Boodberg defined his approach as follows: "In discussing tonight certain aspects of the historical role of these Altaic pastoral nomads I speak as a Philologist, rather than as a historian or anthropologist.   The three epithets I am using—Aryan, Turk, and Chinese—refer first of all to linguistic distinctions."[51]   His historical and cultural explorations traced the evolving pattern of the interaction of these peoples over time, but were based not only on a close reading of the ancient sources as histories but also as repositories of language.   The diffusion of a specialized politico-economic vocabulary, concealed under a number of Asian scripts only discernible to a master philologist, then, provided the interpretive framework for viewing the story of the people of the steppes.   His conclusions on the historical role of the nomads in trying to arbitrate and control the trade in luxury goods in Central Asia between the sedentary Aryans and Chinese, the political formation of nomadic confederacies and the role of great leaders, and the cause of nomadic incursions, have been convincingly confirmed by recent studies, anthropologically by the work of Thomas Barfield, ecologically by John Smith and Joseph Fletcher, and historically by various authors in the *Cambridge History of Early Inner Asia.*

In 1972 Boodberg died, despairing that he had failed to revolutionize sinological studies.   And so he had, for his methods, even if of fundamental importance to philological endeavors, were still of value only as much as philology itself was regarded as the foundation of sinological research in most disciplines.   But to the extent that philology was disparaged, so too were the brilliant but often bewildering works of this virtuoso performer.   He probably underestimated the importance his own intellectual genius played in his success, let alone the influence of his

---

[50]Printed from a hand-written manuscript of seventy-two pages in *Selected Works*, 1-21; manuscript now in my possession.
    [51]*Selected Works*, 3.

deep spiritual concern for humanity; neither his mental processes nor reservoir of humanity were easy to access or imitate.

Three of his most outstanding students exemplify this question. Out of all his students, the most distinguished in terms of quality and amount of publications are most likely Paul Serruys, Edward Schafer, and Richard Mather. The former has had great success as a philologist and linguist, but could not be termed a "humanist." On the other hand, the latter two have produced reams of very humanistic scholarship of equal precision and erudition to that of Serruys. The difference in the innate spirit of the three men, then, not some mechanical flaw in method, accounts for the difference in the type of scholarship they have produced. The same creative spirit that inspired Schafer and Mather was at work much earlier with Peter Boodberg. Because of this, Boodberg was much more than his methods. We can hardly expect to find another like him. But it is his example of rigorous, demanding, bold yet humanistic philology that is important to remember today.

12. EDWARD H. SCHAFER (1913-1991):

Poetic Archaeology and the World of T'ang[1]

"To be a philologist means to believe that language is the greatest achievement of the species, and that literature, even trivial literature, embodies the chief activity of the human mind. A philologist is interested in the names of things, of abstractions and of institutions, and in the life of these words in the stream of literature, their role in the rational, imaginative, and emotional life of man."

—Edward Schafer

Edward Schafer was the grand master of T'ang poetry and the material world of medieval China, who used his world-ranging experience in natural ecology to elucidate the concrete imagery that informed the T'ang poetic visions of the worlds of man, nature, space, and that of the imagination.

Born in Seattle on August 23, 1913, Edward Schafer did his undergraduate work in anthropology at U.C.L.A., finishing at Berkeley where he also earned his Ph.D. in Oriental languages. His M.A. thesis was written at the University of Hawaii, where he was supported by a grant. His studies of Japanese and Arabic, begun at Harvard in 1940, were suddenly interrupted by the onslaught of World War Two. He went on to master Japanese while serving in Naval Intelligence, only one of a final complement of languages that came to include French, German, Italian, Spanish, Old English, classical Greek, classical and medieval Latin, and an acquaintance with ancient Egyptian, Coptic, Arabic, Vietnamese, and other Southeast Asian languages.

His graduate work revealed the themes and methodology that would govern the course of his mature scholarship. "Persian Merchants in China during the T'ang Dynasty," his 1940 Hawaii thesis, and "The Reign of Liu Ch'ang, Last Emperor of Southern Han: A Critical Translation of

---

[1] This chapter is largely based on David B. Honey, "Edward Hetzel Schafer (1913-1991)," *Journal of Asian History* 25 (1991): 181-93.

the Text of *Wu Tai shih*, with Special Inquiries into Relevant Phases of Contemporary Chinese Civilization," his 1947 Berkeley dissertation, already manifest his firm grasp of philology: control of texts and their explication with sophistication and penetrating insight. They set the range—T'ang exotica and foreign influences—and methodology—exacting translations of poetry and prose with annotation and commentary—that were to characterize his scholarly endeavors for the rest of his life.

Later distillations of these works soon found their way into print.[2] Among them, a lengthy article on "Ritual Exposure in Ancient China" is one of the earliest examples of the methodological approach of reconstructing a series of word families to set the linguistic provenance of a given word among homophonous cognates.[3] This concern to utilize various approaches in the philologist's arsenal, to discuss in almost every publication their proper application, and to warn against revisionist or heterodoxic tendencies,[4] exemplified the care he took both to refine and promulgate the gospel of philology.[5]

---

[2]"Iranian Merchants in T'ang Dynasty Tales," *Semitic and Oriental Studies.* University of California Publications in Semitic Philology 11 (1951): 403-22, combines chapters from both thesis and dissertation. "Ritual Exposure in Ancient China," *HJAS* 14 (1951): 130-84, is based on dissertation chapter 4. Other spin-offs include "The History of the Empire of Southern Han according to Chapter 65 of the *Wu-tai-shih* of Ou-yang Hsiu," in *Silver Jubilee Volume of the Zinbun-Kagaku-Kenkyusyo* (Kyoto, 1954), 339-69, and "War Elephants in Ancient and Medieval China," *Oriens* 10 (1957): 289-91.

[3]Among sinologists, the earliest attempts at utilizing this method were in Peter Boodberg's 1937 "Proleptical Remarks on the Evolution of Archaic Chinese" (see *Selected Works*, 398-402), and R.A. Stein, "Jardins en miniature d'Extrême-Orient," *BEFEO* 42 (1942): 54. Unfortunately, only the immediate circle of Schafer's students, chiefly Stephen Bokenkamp and Donald Harper, Paul W. Kroll, an intellectual disciple of Schafer, and Boodberg's pupil William Boltz have followed Schafer's methodological example in consistently employing this linguistic approach with intriguing results.

[4]See for instance, "Non-translation and Functional Translation—Two Sinological Maladies," *FEQ* 13 (1954): 251-60. The book review was a major weapon in Schafer's hands for warning against harmful assumptions and approaches, such as Chinoiserie, Mandarinization—seeing classical Chinese through the veil of the Mandarin dialect or of Sino-Japanese, dependence on author biography and psychology, and the like.

[5]Convenient access to Professor Schafer's methodological maxims, treatment of specialized Chinese terms of flora and fauna, minerals and textiles, etc. plus proposed

The Faith of a Philologist

Educated in the intricacies of sinology by Peter A. Boodberg, Schafer developed a personal style of philology characterized by the exacting control of texts and textual filiation of a Pelliot, the insightful exegesis of a Maspero, the creative recreation of ancient mores of a Granet, the scientific knowledge of the material world of a Laufer, plus the virtuosic command of English of a Waley in realizing, through verbal artistry, the sense and symbolism of the medieval world of T'ang China. Schafer once defined his own scholarly role as follows:

> I am a philologist with a particular interest in medieval Chinese literature relating to material culture, and my standards are set (for example) by students of al-Biruni and Agricola and even of Chaucer. I would prefer to be judged an unsuccessful philologist than to deserve the appellation of impertinent "historian" or presumptuous "linguist." I have been both.[6]

This self-definition was occasioned by the problems increasingly apparent in the field owing to the fuzzy use of the term "sinologist." At the time Schafer wrote this, attacks were exchanged in journals between scholars

---

standardizations for bureaucratic and other technical terms, is provided by David B. Honey and Stephen R. Bokenkamp, "An Annotated Bibliography of the Works of Edward H. Schafer," *Phi Theta Papers* 16 (1984): 8-30. Paul W. Kroll, in the introduction to the *JAOS* issue dedicated to Schafer (106.1 [1986]), effectively encapsulates Schafer's impact and continuing influence on sinology and the brilliant texture of his works. He could scarcely hope in a short encomium to plumb the extent of his oeuvre, however. The bibliography appended on pp. 241-45 does include items up to 1985 and supplies additional entries, mostly book reviews, missing from the annotated bibliography published in *Phi Theta Papers* in 1984. A necrology by Prof. Kroll and Phyllis Brooks Schafer is printed in *JAOS* 111.3 (1991): 441-43 and *T'ang Studies* 8-9 (1990-91): 3-8 which includes (pp. 9-22) a bibliography complete through 1991; see also Stephen R. Bokenkamp, "In Memoriam: Edward H. Schafer (1913-1991)," *Taoist Resources*: 97-99. A more personal portrayal of Schafer and his Taoist studies is Phyllis Brooks Schafer, "Discovering a Religion," *Taoist Resources* 4.2 (1993): 1-8.

[6]"Communication to the Editors," *JAOS* 78 (1958): 120; *JAS* 17 (1958): 509.

who branded other sinologists heretical because they did not practice the particular discipline preached by the attackers themselves—even while both parties called themselves faithful sinologists. Much slipshod methodology was itself excused by evoking the sacred name of sinology, as if the term, like "charity," covered a multitude of methodological sins. Schafer's aim was to remind his colleagues that, after being baptized in the field by learning Chinese, the convert must remain faithful to the commandments of his particular discipline, regardless of its individual tenets. To him, Protestant social scientists, Catholic historians, the ascetic philologists of the stricter orders, agnostic anthropologists, or even atheistic linguists were all alike in the uniqueness of their individual contributions to the worship at the temple of sinology, whether as buyers or sellers. However, he could not countenance born-again literary theorists (as opposed to literary critics), regarding their shallow-rooted faith as merely passing fascination with the gurus of ephemeral cults. At any rate, Schafer's missive was intended not to convert anyone to his individual belief in philology, although he did believe that it was the head of the corner set at naught by the other creeds. Its purpose was rather to call all creeds to repentance and to keep discipline within the ranks: "A scholar who uses one or more Oriental languages for his work is an Art Historian, or a Textual Critic, or a Literary Critic, or a Historian of Science, or whatever. In other words, his work must be judged in comparison with the work of other scholars in the same discipline, not with that of other 'Asian Scholars,' whatever that may mean."[7] Schafer could, of course, be exceedingly caustic in expressing his irritation with dry, unimaginative writing, to say nothing of careless or flawed approaches, or provincial and philistine attitudes.[8] But on principle he granted honorable coexistence for any discipline that was rigorous in its application and that granted the right of philology to practice its fundamental beliefs in peace. In his capacity as chief editor of the *Journal*

---

[7]"Asian Studies," *American Council of Learned Societies Newsletter* 13 (January, 1962): 20.

[8]See, for instance, Schafer's stern review of the anti-philology, anti-humanism clique, as he viewed it, gathered together in *Perspectives on the T'ang*, reviewed in *JAOS* 95 (1975): 466-7.

of the American Oriental Society from 1958 to 1963, inserted between two terms as associate editor for East Asia (1955-58, 1964-67), and as president of that learned society from 1975 to1976, he exercised a firm but fair hand in enforcing, and indeed embodying, the strictest philological grounding for any scholarly approach to China.[9]

For all of Schafer's vocal antipathy to modern literary theorists, he was unavoidably imbued with his own particular conceptual grounding, that of Anglo-American New Criticism, honed and harnessed to pedagogical purposes with a tinge of Russian Formalism. The following extended passage, prelude to his formal definition of what constitutes a poem in "Notes on Translating T'ang Poetry, Part Two: Poetry,"[10] is a revealing program statement of his personal theoretical moorings:

> A poem is a unique thing made of words. We shall leave it to the ephemeral deities of literary theory—the pre-structuralists, the structuralists, the post-structuralists—Frye, Heidegger, Derrida, Bloom, Kermode, Krieger, and all the rest, along with their worshipful acolytes of the moment, to debate the metaphysical (i.e. unknowable) or psychological relationships between poem and author, poem and reader, poem and history, poem and mythology, poem and other poems, and what not. Here we content ourselves with the primary but often neglected task of discovering the poem itself. We shall also avoid such byzantine preoccupations as the possible meaning of the spaces between the stanzas of a poem.

The opening statement, "A poem is a unique thing made of words," locates Schafer squarely in the camp of the Formalists and the New Critics: "The enjoyment and enjoyment *of the best poetry* requires a sensitiveness and discrimination with words, a nicety, imaginativeness and deftness in

---

[9]Schafer's views of his particular discipline of philology and its place as the foundation of the other disciplines in sinology are introduced in *What and How is Sinology?* Inaugural Lecture for the Department of Oriental Languages and Literatures, University of Colorado (Boulder, 1982), rpt. in *T'ang Studies* 8-9 (1990-91): 23-44.

[10]*Schafer Sinological Papers* 31 (Berkeley, Sept. 21, 1985): 1.

taking their sense...."[11]   Both schools regarded poetry as the highest
manifestation of language (witness the epigraph that commences this
chapter); as verbal art, poetry was best analyzed and appreciated through
internal, mechanical literary devices that structure and express its unique
nature.   Extra-literary systems such as politics, ideology, economics,
mythology, history, biography, etc., are ultimately irrelevant for analyzing
poetry, let alone appreciating it.[12]   A favorite phrase of Nabokov, oft
quoted by Schafer—"The word, the expression, the image is the true
function of literature.   *Not* ideas"[13]—easily (and perhaps too airily)
dismissed from consideration all extra-textual literary approaches, whether
psychoanalytic criticism ("poem and author"), phenomenology ("poem and
reader"), Marxist criticism ("poem and history"), myth criticism ("poem
and mythology"), canon criticism and comparative literature ("poem and
other poem") and the like.   But such text-based literary theories as preached
by a Richards or a Jakobson would be naturally conducive to a philologist
of the old school such as Schafer, who delighted in composing learned and
elegantly expressed "annotations of the creative process," to paraphrase
Balanchandra Rajan.[14]   The "practical criticism" preached by Richards
provided a teachable approach in the classroom as well as theoretical
justification for avoiding all manner of fallacies of interpretation.   To those
fallacies isolated in Richards' *Practical Criticism* (which was required
reading in Schafer's class on T'ang poetry), Schafer added his own set of
common sinological fallacies: "the Fallacy of Timelessness, the Genteel or
Imperialist Fallacy, the Etiolative or Sluggish Fallacy, the Fallacy of

---

[11]I.A. Richards, *Practical Criticism: A Study of Literary Judgment* (New York:
Harcourt Brace Jovanovich, 1929), 191.

[12]For convenient entrés into these theories, see Leroy F. Seale, "New Criticism;"
Heather Murray, "Practical Criticism;" and Karen A. McCauley, "Russian Formalism;"
in *The Johns Hopkins Guide to Literary Theory and Criticism*, ed. Michael Groden and
Martin Kereiswirth (Baltimore: Johns Hopkins University Press, 1994), 528-34, 589-92,
634-38.

[13]Cited in "Notes on Translating T'ang Poetry, Part Three: Deponents," *Schafer
Sinological Papers*, 33 (Berkeley, Nov. 6, 1985): 5.

[14]*The Johns Hopkins Guide to Literary Theory and Criticism*, *sub* "T.S. Eliot," 222.

Synonymity, and the Dillettantist or Poetaster's Fallacy."[15]

The close reading of texts, upon which Schafer's practical criticism depended, was itself dependent upon the mechanics of philology, and was introduced in the next paragraph of Schafer's prelude to poetry:

> Classical sinologists are not primarily entertainers, trying to persuade their readers that they can write tasteful English and even, as some actually believe, good poetry; nor are they philosophers or theologians.   They are scholars whose great responsibility is to elucidate THE POEM ITSELF,[16] whose mystery and intricacy is enhanced by the fact that it is written in an ancient, classical, or "dead" language, to which no language now spoken is really comparable.   To translate is to deform: scholarly translation is justifiable only as a mode of explication or commentary; it must be accompanied by other modes, to bring readers as close as possible to understanding the form and the color of that old linguistic artifact.[17]

These "other modes," or all of the technical skills of etymology, epigraphy, paleography, textual criticism, historical phonology, grammar, explication, etc., collectively compose the discipline of philology.   And it is philology that makes close reading possible, an endeavor dear to the hearts of New Critics.[18]   Concludes Richards, "All respectable poetry invites close reading.   It encourages attention to its literal sense up to the point, to be detected by the reader's discretion, at which liberty can serve the aim of the

---

[15]"Notes on Translating T'ang Poetry, Part Two: Poetry," 12-15. Schafer's views on interpretive fallacies were also informed by the work of W.K. Wimsat; see *The Verbal Icon: Studies in the Meaning of Poetry* (Lexington: University of Kentucky Press, 1954), 3-65.

[16]Referring, as Schafer notes, to the title of a book edited by Stanley Burnshaw: *The Poem Itself* (Fayetteville: University of Arkansas Press, 1995).

[17]"Notes on Translating T'ang Poetry, Part Two: Poetry," 1.

[18]For philological work as propadeutic to textual criticism of any sort, see Wilfred L. Guerin, et al., *A Handbook of Critical Approaches to Literature* (Oxford: Oxford University Press, 1992), 18-21, subtitled "Textual Scholarship: A Prerequisite to Criticism."

poem better than fidelity to fact or strict coherence among fictions."[19] That Richards allows extra-textual frameworks of interpretation above the literal level only underscores the fundamental importance of philology in performing an initial "close reading."

A modern philologist of comparable erudition and influence in his own field to Schafer in his, Hugh Lloyd-Jones, admirably distills the essence of this oft-misunderstood discipline:

> For most English people "philology" has come to mean "comparative philology," and "comparative philology" means "comparative study of language." Yet if one uses terms exactly, linguistics is only one section of philology, a word which came into use in Alexandria as early as the third century before Christ and which properly denotes the love of literature, of thought, of all that is expressed in words....It is deplorable that we in England have ceased to use this valuable term correctly.[20]

Ulrich von Wilamowitz-Moellendorff, the Chavannes of classical scholarship, stressed the breadth of the task of philology and its unique power to "recreate the poet's song, the thought of the philosopher...the sanctity of the temple and the feelings of believers and unbelievers, the bustling life of market and port, the physical appearance of land and sea, mankind at work and at play."[21] Wilamowitz was able to do this because, according to his pupil Eduard Fraenkel, he did not compartmentalize disciplines: "For him there was no such thing as a watertight compartment of textual criticism, another of historical grammar, another of metre, another of history of religion, another of ancient law, and so forth. No single subsection of the technique of research was allowed to get the better of the rest: they all had to be subservient and to co-operate to one purpose only, the adequate interpretation of the text in hand."[22] All of these

---

[19]Richards, *Practical Criticism*, 195.

[20]Hugh Lloyd-Jones, in the Introduction to Wilamowitz-Moellendorff, *History of Classical Scholarship*, vii.

[21]Ibid.

[22]Eduard Fraenkel, ed., *Aeschylus: Agamemnon* (Oxford: Clarendon, 1950), 60-61.

subjects in the realm of China and in the wider world of Asia, and indeed most of these research disciplines, received refined treatment and authoritative manipulation by Schafer at some point in his career.

Poetic Archaeology

A series of distinguished books published by the University of California is the center of Schafer's remarkably rich and varied oeuvre.[23] These works created a new genre of scholarly writing, perhaps best defined as "poetic archaeology" because of Schafer's uncanny and inimitable ability to reconstruct the medieval Chinese world through broad field surveys of the literary corpus and site excavations of poetic artifacts. A later fascination with Taoism broadened his scope of research, first foreshadowed in 1963 by the appearance of an analysis of Buddhist poetic visions in "Mineral Imagery in the Paradise Poems of Kuan-hsu."[24] This late immersion in T'ang Taoism, which crested but did not ebb with *Pacing the Void*, did not change Schafer's fundamental philological approach, nor restrain the boldness of his prose, the wit that infused it, nor the penetrating erudition that buttressed all of his conclusions.

The following quotation from one of these elegant but erudite books epitomizes all the best in Schaferian scholarship, with its light tone, wry humor, understated alliteration, breadth of diction, and scrupulous accuracy in translation:

> In T'ang times, the barbarism of female supremacy beyond the expanding southern frontier must have irritated the austerely male sensibilities of the northern aristocrats and made them itch to abolish it. Early in the seventh century the Chams were ruled by a royal princess—did the knowledge of this alien enormity augment the

---

[23] *Tu Wan's Stone Catalogue of Cloudy Forest: A Commentary and Synopsis* (1961), *The Golden Peaches of Samarkand: A Study of T'ang Exotics* (1963), *The Vermilion Bird: T'ang Images of the South* (1967), *Shore of Pearls: Hainan Island in Early Times* (1970), *The Divine Woman: Dragon Ladies and Rain Maidens in T'ang Literature* (1973), *Pacing the Void: T'ang Approaches to the Stars* (1977), and *Mirages on the Sea of Time: The Taoist Poetry of Ts'ao T'ang* (1985).

[24] *AM* 10 (1963): 73-102.

shame of the old guard in Ch'ang-an and Lo-yang, subjected to the Empress Wu later in that century? But if the story of a tribute-bearing embassy from the "country of the Female Man," in the middle of the ninth century is true, glamour might almost compensate for impropriety: "They had steep chignons and golden hats—beaded necklaces covered their bodies. Therefore they were called 'Bodhisattva Man [here Man is the ethnic name]. Accordingly, the gleewomen and players of that time fabricated the 'Song of the Bodhisattva Man.' Literary gentlemen too, now and then, have publicized this air."[25]

The combination of erudition and verbal virtuosity exemplified in this passage from mid-career perhaps reached its apex in Schafer's brilliantly researched and written "Wu Yün's 'Cantos on Pacing the Void'."[26] The "finding list" of Taoist technical terms appended to this article represents his complete mastery of the techniques of textual exegesis, and the poems in mock heroic couplets that he composed as interpretive glosses on Wu Yün's cantos represent his utter command of English diction, style, tone, and the ease with which he exploited the imagery of English—and indeed world—literature in virtually all of his scholarly communications as an aid to exegesis.

One common manner of exploitation was in the use of elegant, apt epigraphs, often as not in the original languages. His preface to *Pacing the Void* contains an enlightening statement on the importance of quoting non-Chinese poets to highlight the imagery of the Chinese:

Sprinkled through these pages—not just in the epigraphs—the reader will encounter tags and fragments quoted from European literature. He will not, I hope, regard these as mere displays of frivolous erudition or feeble wit, but accept them, as I hope he will accept such unusual words as protopsyche and Triaster, as bright foils, partial reflections, and surprising analogies, intended to illustrate, either by accent or by contrast, the unique quality—the oddness, if you

---

[25] *The Vermilion Bird*, 80-81.
[26] *HJAS* 41 (1981): 377-415.

please—of medieval Chinese images, whose special flavor some writer of Spanish, or Greek, or Old English may, by chance, have captured very nicely.[27]

Turning from the verbal to the physical, Schafer's works are invaluable for the historian of China, and not just for providing the basic identifications of birds, beasts, minerals, color terms, and other technical vocabulary.[28] He recreated the richness of the full physical environment in which historical events occurred: the topography of Canton was as faithfully mapped as the Taoist heavens,[29] the development of bathing customs as thoroughly traced as the transmission of a loan-word,[30] the particular qualities of trade products as accurately described as the baubles of the elite.[31] This concentration on the details of the material world of medieval China, for all of its importance to historical studies, was nevertheless bent to a literary aim: students of Chinese literature should, he taught, "strive to become familiar with the particular world of each writer—that is, his specific, real, local world in all of its rich details. Once they have achieved this knowledge they will be able to interpret their writer's unique vision of that world, expressed in his well-chosen images, which in turn reflect his own special views of creation, astrology, sovereignty, duty, magic, food, heroism, and what not."[32] The student of Asian history also benefitted by Schafer's concern for setting the customs

---

[27]*Pacing the Void*, 7.

[28]The following articles are just a sampling: "The Camel in China down to the Mongol Dynasty," *Sinologica* 2 (1950),165-94, 263-90; "Notes on Mica in Medieval China," *TP* 43 (1954): 265-86; "Rosewood, Dragon's Blood, and Lac," *JAOS* 77 (1957): 129-36; "Parrots in Medieval China," *Studia Serica Bernhard Karlgren Dedicata* (Copenhagen, 1959), 271-82; and "The Transcendent Vitamin: Efflorescence of Lang-kan," *Chinese Science* 3 (1978): 27-38.

[29]"A Fourteenth Century Gazetteer of Canton," in *Oriente Poliano* (Rome, 1957), 67-93.

[30]"The Development of Bathing Customs in Ancient and Medieval China and the History of the Floriate Clear Palace," *JAOS* 76 (1956): 57-82.

[31]"Local Tribute Products of the T'ang Dynasty," *Journal of Oriental Studies* 4 (1957-58): 213-48 (with B. Wallacker).

[32]"Notes on Translating T'ang Poetry. Part Two: Poetry," 12-13.

and creature comforts of China within the wider context of Asian culture in order to trace the routes of and rationales for their importation. For this reason, as well as reflecting the heritage of the geographical approach to Asian history inherited from Teggart, Schafer insisted that his students in the classical Chinese program include the history of Inner Asia, Japan and Korea, South and Southeast Asia, and Tibet in their program of written exams for the Ph.D. He was, of course, himself assiduous in setting the historical contexts of his treatment of particular people, places, or things, making thorough use of the historical and anthropological literature; "standing on the shoulders of giants" is the quote he modestly used to sum up his debt to his learned predecessors and contemporaries.

Like Boodberg, Schafer's entire teaching career centered around Berkeley. From 1947, as a new Ph.D., to his tenure in 1953, from full professorship in 1958 to retirement in 1984, he maintained and indeed increased the distinction of the tradition of scholarly teaching associated with the Berkeley school of sinology. He occupied the Agassiz Chair of Oriental Languages and Literature (from 1969 to his retirement) longer than any of his illustrious predecessors. Later in life, Schafer's creative flow was too insistent to be constricted by the slow pace of the publication process. Like Boodberg before him, he produced a series of privately printed *samizdat* termed "Schafer Sinological Papers," distributed to a fortunate inner circle of ten friends and former students. Numbering in all thirty-eight titles, these papers appeared irregularly from January 25, 1984 to August 4, 1989.[33]

The program in classical Chinese that he founded was itself a manifestation of the care he took to conserve the traditional values of the curriculum developed by distinguished scholars at Berkeley from Forke to Boodberg. Alas, his program literally died with him, for after his retirement too few students were willing to brave the rigors of its requirements without the compensating reward of the guidance of his presiding genius. Its *de facto* death was made official by vote of the Oriental Languages faculty just a month before Schafer died.

In the final analysis, it is as practicing philologist, producing highly

---

[33]See "Appendix" to this chapter for a full listing of titles.

idiomatic and learned poetic annotations, that Schafer was best known. His combination of the erudition of a scholar with the taste of a stylist made his writings on literature the most inimitable since Waley. In this endeavor, part scholarly and part poetic, he was the past master of Tang literature.

APPENDIX B: *SCHAFER SINOLOGICAL PAPERS*, JAN 29, 1984 TO AUG. 4, 1989

1. "The Oriole and the Bush Warbler"
2. "Notes on T'ang Geisha. 1. Typology"
3. "Kiwi Fruit"
4. "Notes on T'ang Geisha. 2. The Masks of T'ang Courtesans"
5. "Cosmic Metaphors: The Poetry of Space"
6. "Notes on T'ang Geisha. 3. Yang-chou in T'ang Times"
7. "Notes on T'ang Geisha. 4. Pleasure Boats"
8. "The Anastrophe Catastrophe"
9. "Brightness and Iridescence in the Chinese Color Words"
10. "The Fibrous Stars"
11. "The Other Peach Flower Font"
12. "Table of Contents to Wang Hsüan-ho, *San tung chu nang*"
13. "Annex to 'Combined Supplements to Mathews' part I"
14. "Annex to 'Combined Supplements to Mathews' part II"
15. "Ts'ao T'ang and the Tropics"
16. "Annex to 'Combined Supplements to Mathews' part III"
17. "The Tourmaline Queen and the Forbidden City"
18. "Annex to 'Combined Supplements to Mathews' part IV"
19. "An Early T'ang 'Court Poem' on Snow"
20. "Annex to 'Combined Supplements to Mathews' part V"
21. "The Eight Daunters"
22. "Annex to 'Combined Supplements to Mathews' part VI"
23. "The Moon's Doubled Wheel"
24. "Annex to 'Combined Supplements to Mathews' part VII
25. "Mildewed Apricots"
26. "Annex to 'Combined Supplements to Mathews' part VIII
27. "Notes on Lord Lao in T'ang Times"
28. "The Moon Doubles its Wheel Once More"
29. "Notes on Translating T'ang Poetry. Part One"
30. "Passionate Peonies"
31. "Notes on Translating T'ang Poetry. Part Two: Poems"
32. "The World Between: Ts'ao T'ang's Grotto Poems"

33. "Notes on Translating T'ang Poetry: Part 3: Deponents"
34. "The Moth and the Candle"
35. "A Vision of Shark People"
36. "Moon Cinnamons"
37. "A Chinese Chough"
38. "The T'ang Osmanthus"

ENVOI: TRADITION AND TRUTH IN SINOLOGY

"Tradition is the living faith of the dead, traditionalism is the dead faith of the living....It is traditionalism that gives tradition such a bad name."
—Jaroslav Pelikan[1]

"Philology...is one of the two great opponents of all superstitions."
—Nietzsche[2]

The proto-sinologist Jesuit translators, compilers, and editors, the expatriate consular, commercial, and missionary sinologists of the nineteenth century, and the first French *sinologues du chambre* of the middle to late decades of that era all formed the foundation of modern sinology. This is because they bequeathed to the early twentieth century a methodological outlook, however rough-hewn and chaotic, as well as a research agenda, both adopted from native Chinese scholars and scholiasts. Chavannes inherited this tradition, systematized its working methodologies, and promulgated the new orthodoxy of philology to the next generation. This philological approach and academic program held unquestioned sway, in most circles, until World War Two called into hurried service newly developed disciplines to answer questions of impelling urgency. Sinology today, therefore, encompasses many more disciplines than just philology. The aim all along, however, in past and present sinological enterprises, is the search for truth about China, whether culled from ancient documentary evidence or conceptualized from new scientific paradigms.

In tracing the development of certain fundamental techniques of the philological approach throughout the course of the growth of sinology, I have focused on selected key scholars at each stage of the evolutionary process and the textual studies that serve as exemplars of methodology. They are not my personal choice of the "top ten sinologists," although

---

[1]Jaroslav Pelikan, *The Vindication of Tradition* (New Haven: Yale University Press, 1984), 65.
[2]Quote in Henderson, *Scripture, Canon, and Commentary*, 211. Incidently, the other opponent is medicine.

most of them should be considered so. A "great sinologist," in the "great man" mode of Carlyle, is an abstraction conditioned as much by reader response to what a sinologist had to say about Chinese civilization as by an objective evaluation of the intellectual power that framed a work or the literary value that presented it. The sinologists I have treated are exemplars of the philological tradition, and paradigmatic of its best techniques. This means neither that other sinologists did not make their important contributions, nor that the philological approach is *primus inter pares* among other methodologies that operate above or beyond the level of the text.

Yet, due to this earth-bound grounding in a text—what some call the documentary approach—a question immediately arises: are philologists who habitually ignore the more theoretical considerations of the social sciences inherently narrow in outlook or parochial in approach? In certain respects it seems to be so, especially when occupied with the minutiae of linguistic reconstruction or textual variora. But to the extent that entire works are translated, annotated, and subjected to literary analysis is the philological approach as broad in scope as any other academic field in, say, the discipline of history. All approaches and fields suffer in some respects in comparison with others. For instance, in contrast to certain popular techniques employed by sociologists, historians are viewed as sacrificing the general pattern for the sake of concrete details,[3] a charge first leveled against history by Aristotle in the ninth book of his *Poetics*.[4] And to the extent that the new history of Ranke turned from general, derivative chronicles to the official, primary documents themselves was the new historian of the nineteenth century as text-bound as any traditional philologist.

Peter Burke summarizes the philological basis of the new history as follows: "The historical revolution associated with Ranke was above all a revolution in sources and methods, a shift away from the use of earlier

---

[3]Peter Burke, *History and Social Theory* (Ithaca: Cornell University Press, 1992), 3.

[4]For the context of the debate between the generalizing trends of history versus the universal concerns of poetry, see M.I. Finely, *The Use and Abuse of History* (1971; rpt. New York: Penguin Books, 1987), 11-12.

histories or 'chronicles' to use the official records of governments. Historians began to work regularly in archives and they elaborated a set of increasingly sophisticated techniques for assessing the reliability of these documents."[5] It seems, then, that particular methods of dealing with textual evidence unites, on one level at least, both the historian and the philologist, and protects them both against charges of either narrowness of outlook or parochialism of approach.[6]

The periodization I have incorporated in this work, although roughly presented by national school, has been largely based on the invention, adoption, and maturation of specific research skills associated with the discipline of philology. This periodization is divided into discrete stages in the lengthy process of the development of technique.

First were the Jesuits. Resident in China, they experimented with the first approaches for exploiting the literary tradition of China, aided by their growing command of the spoken language and access to the native scholarly tradition of exegesis, hermeneutics, and applied ethical philosophy. Their philological skills can be characterized as the naive and sporadic application of nascent techniques for translating classical Chinese texts and composing their own scientific essays and missionary tracts. They are appropriately designated as proto-sinologists.

Next came the French *sinologues du chambre*, self-taught and stay-at-home academicians armed with philological acumen but not first-hand experience with either the culture or the living language. Nevertheless, they were the first to develop a sophisticated set of technical approaches designed not only to access the texts in reading them, but more importantly, to assess critically their value and position within the textual

---

[5]Burke, *History and Social Theory*, 6.

[6]Even modes of presentation, according to Hayden White and Dominick LaCapra, should borrow more from literature. For the uniquely literary elements of romance, tragedy, comedy, and satire that "emplot" historical narrative, see Hayden White, *Metahistory: The Historical Imagination in Nineteenth-Century Europe* (Baltimore: Johns Hopkins University Press, 1973); for the debt owed to rhetoric by historians, see Dominick LaCapra, "Rhetoric and History," in *History and Criticism* (Ithaca: Cornell University Press, 1985), 15-44 and Peter Gay, *Style in History* (New York: W.W. Norton, 1988).

tradition and to hazard independent interpretations. Techniques from classical scholarship and comparative philology, and to a lesser extent the Chinese commentarial tradition, aided their sinological efforts, which, after all, were circumscribed by the limited resources of European libraries. Because of the intellectual and methodological milieu of the times, Norman Girardot and Lauren F. Pfister call them Sinological Orientalists. Chief among these was Stanislaus Julien, who not only never went to China, but prided himself on never using a native informant in the "relentless textuality" of his research. It would not be until the post-World War II development of Area Studies that American sinologists, the last holdover among national schools of sinology, abandoned this stay-at-home posture, traveled to China, and began large-scale collaboration with colleagues in China.[7]

British and American consular, missionary, and commercial representatives came to the fore in the next stage which saw the beginnings of the integration of the local expert having resident experience in China with the library-bound *sinologues du chambre*. The first fledgling steps of field-work in the nascent disciplines of archaeology, epigraphy, ethnology, anthropology, and folklore were taken at this time. James Legge was the leading light of the many part-time sinologists resident in China, and at the death of Julien inherited the latter's mantle of the master sinologist. His assumption of the first Chinese chair at Oxford in 1876 confirmed the ascendancy of British-American sinology over the French school which had experienced a short-lived but sharp nadir with the career of Saint-Denys. The Oxford career of Legge, then, inaugurated the period of incipient integration.

Edouard Chavannes founded the first modern school of sinology by harmonizing the different strands of the proto-sinologists, the *sinologues du*

---

[7]Tu Wei-ming, in an interview published in *Shih-chieh Han-hsüeh/World Sinology* 1 (1998): 9, made this point, but did not limit it to American sinologists; he maintained that this insular attitude was characteristic of "famous Western sinologists" in general. The field experience of Chavannes and his star pupils, and such Germans as Grube, Haenisch, and Conrady, refute this assessment which, of course, could not apply to former missionaries or consular men-turned sinologists anyway.

chambre, and the expatriate part-timers. From the Jesuits he derived a deep reverence for the native tradition. The French academicians bequeathed to him a rigorous philological mentality and methodology, and the hoary heritage of French library science. He inherited from the consular-missionary-commercial sinologists the importance of first-hand field experience and expertise in modern Chinese. The resulting brand of scholarship he epitomized helped to transcend the limiting intellectual barriers of Sinological Orientalism and its confining mentalities of religious Hermeticism, cultural parallelomania, and colonial or missionary paternalism. The modern science of sinology and its broad concerns of a multi-disciplinary approach, therefore, is the direct legacy of Chavannes, and is surely due to his harmonizing of disparate old trends and his pioneering of new methods.

After Chavannes, the periodization I have adopted in this book breaks down along national or linguistic lines (e.g., English- or German-speaking and publishing sinologists) in the attempt to trace the development of some of these new techniques. Perhaps, in order to distinguish if not always the methods, at least the aims and outlooks of historians and other social scientists from those of the philologists, a different periodization schema might be introduced. If so, this should be based on the conception of a scholarly task and its intellectual intent, not the progress of the techniques used to carry it out. Just such a schema was suggested by the historian Arthur Wright.

Sinology as a Tradition

In a valuable summation of the ideology of sinologists at different stages of intellectual engagement with China over the last few centuries, Wright hurled down numerous threatening but welcome conceptual gauntlets that continue to challenge philologists. The Jesuits encountered a China that had been interpreted and presented over several millennia by a self-conscious literati that formed, to borrow an intellectual paradigm applied by Benjamin Elman to the Chinese case, a coherent "discourse: a shared system of scholarly articulation and meaning."[8] This discourse is an "'archaeology' of systems of thought or 'episteme.'"[9] Modern sociologists refer to a discourse rather as a "mode of thought," a "belief system," or a "cognitive map." These all are traceable to the Durkheimian approach of isolating a *mentality*, which, according to Peter Burke, is the aggregate of collective attitudes, unspoken assumptions, the common sense in a particular culture, and the structure of belief systems.[10]

Wright characterized such a discourse or mentality (which he calls a "tradition") as the self-image of self-serving literati who perpetuated a tradition of scholarly values and research approaches that upheld their privileged status. Comments Wright,

> As Europeans...began their arduous progress toward some understanding of this remote cultural entity, they were guided in their choice of subject and in their methods and interpretations by the traditions of Chinese scholarship. After all, who could speak with more authority than those Chinese scholars....Thus the Europeans, in their early studies, were in a sense the captives of the tradition they studied and of the self-image of Chinese civilization which the perpetrators of that tradition had developed over the millennia.[11]

In this sense, Sinological Orientalism was adopted, naively and whole-heartedly, from the oriental world of the Chinese, not manufactured out of self-empowering stereotypes of China as part of an attempt at textual colonialism, as Edward Said posits for the mentality of Orientalism in general. Yet, since Europeans stood outside of this insular community of

---

[8]Benjamin Elman, *From Philosophy to Philology: Intellectual and Social Aspects of Change in Late Imperial China* (Cambridge, Mass.: Council on East Asian Studies, Harvard University, 1984), xx.

[9]Cf. Burke, *History and Social Theory*, 92.

[10]Ibid., 91-92.

[11]Arthur Wright, "The Study of Chinese Civilization," *Journal of the History of Ideas* 21 (1960): 233. The same point is stressed in the preface of Girardot, *The Victorian Translation of China*, 2.

literati, they did not participate in the discourse as discussants. Nevertheless, they were influenced by it, in terms defined by Antonio Gramsci as "cultural hegemony."[12] This hegemony exerted its pervasive if hardly apprehended influence as it selected both the means of understanding China as well as the modes of communicating this understanding in writing. Wright therefore judges the progress of sinology, whcthcr Western, Chinese, or Japanese, on the basis of dependence on or emancipation from this entrenched hegemonic tradition. As far as the West is concerned, first came the stage of Romantic Sinophilia, "the legacy of the early Jesuit missionaries and the Enlightenment." Next came the stage of Sinological Orientalism, part of the pan-European preoccupation with things oriental: artistic treasures and philosophical truths enmeshed, like wasps in amber, in an unchanging and static society beyond the capacity—or need—for historical progress.[13]

The methodology adopted by both the romantic sinophiles and the sinological orientalists, not surprisingly, was the same approach advocated by the community of Chinese curators of the tradition: the translation-annotation approach. "The exegetical mode," summarizes Wright, "the subservience to traditional Chinese scholarship, continued to characterize European sinology until the 1890's."[14] It was not until the career of Chavannes in archaeology and history, Granet in sociology, and Franke in historiography, that the "Incubus of Orientalism" was exorcised and sinology freed from the suffocating clench of the tradition.[15]

Chavannes, evaluates Wright, "led the way towards a new critical method in dealing with the past" by seeing beyond the hermetically sealed

---

[12]See Burke, *History and Social Theory*, 86.

[13]Wright, "The Study of Chinese Civilization," 240-42.

[14]Ibid., 243.

[15]One aspect of Western scholarship of China that did seem to partake of "intellectual imperialism" was the effort to compare and contrast things Chinese with European standards. This is most easily seen in early grammars, from Varo to Gabelentz, where the language was analyzed by means of rigid, ill-fitting categories adopted from Latin, not from any study of the laws operating inherently in the Chinese language itself; on this point, see Wolfgang Franke, *China and the West*, trans. R.A. Wilson (Oxford: Basil Blackwell, 1967), 146.

"block" of the tradition to isolate individual epochs and authors. Granet, continues Wright, "read *through* the Classical texts which on the surface mirrored the literati view of the culture and *into* the social reality behind them." And finally, Franke was the first historian to derive his methods from European historiography, not from the literati tradition. As a bonus, Wright adds Maspero, who developed Chavannes' methods to work in fields outside the orthodox limits of the tradition, even studying the "dissident" school of Taoism.[16]

Yet, in spite of Wright's experience in philological work—or perhaps because of a deep psychological conflict between the outer historian and the inner philologist—[17] he neglects the documentary basis of virtually all of the work of Chavannes, Maspero, and Granet. Even more compelling is the championing of the translation-annotation approach by Chavannes, Wright's pioneering historian. Of course, Wright was stressing what one can do with the sources. Philologists may, in the name of fairness, be allowed the same latitude in deciding what to do with the texts, beyond what the commentarial tradition and its exegetical excesses allow. Procedurally, I see little distinction between the annotations of a literary

---

[16]Ibid., 246-47. If the methodology of the earliest sinologists was adopted whole cloth from Ruist classical exegetes, the focus of such methodology, the orthodox and the rational over the religious and the transcendent, was just as eagerly adopted. Students of such non-Confucian traditions as Buddhism blame Matteo Ricci for this initial scholarly prejudice. "In particular," comments Bernard Faure, "his (Ricci's) prejudices against Buddhism and Chinese religion have had enduring consequences; he circumscribed the field of Sinology by excluding entire areas of the Chinese intellectual and religious life. We may therefore wonder to what extent 'every Western Sinologist should recognize his forebearer in him'" (quoting Demiéville); Faure, *Chan Insights and Oversights: An Epistemological Critique of the Chan Tradition* (Princeton: Princeton University Press, 1993), 19-20. In light of this traditional bias, Maspero's pioneering studies on Buddhism also deserve credit for helping to break the Confucianism monopoly on scholarship. For more on this inherent bias of Western sinology, see Norman Girardot, "Chinese Religion and Western Scholarship," in *China and Western Christianity: Historical and Future Encounters*, ed. James D. Whitehead, Yu-ming Shaw, and Norman J. Girardot (Notre Dame: University of Notre Dame Press, 1979), 83-111.

[17]Witness his superbly annotated translations of Buddhist texts contained in *Studies in Chinese Buddhism*, ed. Robert M. Somers (New Haven: Yale University Press, 1990); three of five chapters are philological studies of Buddhist biographies and sources!

scholar on a poem and the "critical comments"on translations of Ch'ing bureaucratic documents by Fairbank or Martin Wilbur's effort to "illustrate and explain" his translations of either Han period historical materials on slavery or Chinese Communist documents.[18] And after all, it was the time-honored application of textual criticism by Ku Chieh-kang and his school of skeptics that inaugurated the "new history" in China, tempered and reined in by Fu Ssu-nien and his colleagues at the Institute of History and Philology.[19] And with the burgeoning of the field of paleography with new discoveries of long-cached texts on silk manuscripts, bamboo strips, and bronze vessels being reported nearly every year in the 1980s and 1990s, philological treatment of such documentary sources is an indispensable propaedeutic to utilizing them as historical sources.[20]

Wright himself acknowledges that, at base, the historical work of even Ku's New Historians was philological:

> In the field of history Ku Chieh-kang exemplifies the reorientation of the study of China in these years. His critical spirit and his use of new methods for the study of China's past reflect an emancipation from the myths on which the culture of imperial China rested and from the methods of inquiry which the old order sanctioned. The Confucian canon was looked at afresh and each text was studied, not

---

[18]C. Martin Wilbur, *Slavery in China During the Former Han Dynasty 206 B.C. - A.D. 25.* (1943; rpt. New York: Krause Reprint Co., 1968); (with Julie Lien-ying How*), Documents on Communism, Nationalism, and Soviet Advisors in China 1918-1927: Papers Seized in the 1927 Peking Raid* (New York: Columbia University Press, 1956), greatly expanded as *Missionaries of Revolution: Soviet Advisers and Nationalist China 1920-1927* (Cambridge, Mass.: Harvard University Press, 1989).

[19]Laurence A. Schneider, *Ku Chieh-kang and China's New History: Nationalism and the Quest for Alternate Traditions* (Berkeley and Los Angeles: University of California Press, 1971), analyzes this revolution in historiography; for Fu and the collaboration between philology and history, see Wang Fan-sheng, *Fu Ssu-nien: An Intellectual Biography,* Ph.D. diss., Princeton University, 1993, chapter two.

[20]Edward Shaughnessy stresses the integration of history and philology in utilizing these new sources in his introduction to *New Sources of Early Chinese History: An Introduction to the Reading of Inscriptions and Manuscripts,* ed. Shaughnessy (Berkeley: Society for the Study of Early China and The Institute of East Asian Studies, University of California, 1997), 1-14.

as a repository of wisdom but as a document with a history, with a greater or lesser degree of authenticity and credibility, with analyzable relation to its time and authorship.[21]

The ironic contradiction between Wright's antipathy towards the translation-annotation approach of philologists on the one hand and his endorsement of it at the hands of historians on the other may be resolved by using his own terminology: Ku's "critical spirit" decides how he approaches the texts. That is, Ku's methodology of textual criticism is directed by a critical spirit to place the text within a new paradigm: as a source, not an icon, as a document to plumb, not a literary work to appreciate. In other words, he uses philology as Nietzsche recommended in the second epigraph to this envoi, as an opponent of superstition—or an entrenched world-view. In the "Orientalism" of modern France, both disciplines of philology and history have equal value as foundational disciplines, because the civilizations of Asia are "written civilizations."[22]

It is true that in the intellectual sphere, the reduction of the classics to historical significance, that is, the turn from philological tending of the classics to historical interpretation, was a painful reorientation, not always negotiated with either conceptual retooling or emotional equanimity. Chang Ping-lin 章炳麟 (1868-1936), for instance, according to Joseph Levenson, "bitterly conceded that the Classics had been reduced from persistent guide to historical source, that they could no longer be taken to dominate men throughout time, but had to submit instead to the scrutiny of men who allowed them only one time in history."[23] This retreat from the classics as repositories of truth, and the ensuing counterattack on them

---

[21]Wright, "The Study of Chinese Civilization," 251. For the paradigmatic shift in studying the classics inaugurated by the New Historians, see Henderson, *Scripture, Canon, and Commentary*, 200-23.

[22]"Ce sont la philologie et l'histoire qui constituent la base obligatoire du champ scientifique, puisque les civilisations de l'Asie sont par excellence celles de l'ecrite;" *Livre de l'orientalisme française* (Paris: Société Asiatique, 1992), 15.

[23]Joseph Levenson, *Confucian China and Its Modern Fate*, 1:93. On Chang, see Shimada Kenji, *Pioneer of the Chinese Revolution: Zhang Binglin and Confucianism*, trans. Joshua Fogel (Stanford: Stanford University Press, 1990).

as mundane documents ready for exploitation, marked a major turning point in modern intellectual history.   As summarized by John B. Henderson, with an interlinear quote from Ricoeur:

> This shift in hermeneutical focus from the classics to the classical era, "from the *chefs-d'oeuvre* of mankind to the historical interconnection which supports them," was one of the most momentous in the history of the human sciences.   Such a transition occurred in eighteenth- and nineteenth-century European historical studies as well as in Ch'ing scholarship....Not all Ch'ing scholars were entranced by the historicist vision.[24]

In the first epigraph above Pelikan makes the same distinction between reverencing a source and utilizing it when he suggests using history not to recover the tradition but to rediscover it: "There have been many, particularly in the nineteenth century and since, for whom the rediscovery and the critical study of a tradition that they had been affirming uncritically has led to the repudiation of that tradition.....Rediscovery can often lead to rejection."[25] If such a rediscovery by Ts'ui Shu 崔述 (1740-1816) did not lead to total rejection of the past as repository of moral values, it certainly did for Ku Chieh-kang.[26]

Philologists can insure their emancipation from the grasp of the past and its tradition by transcending it and working from a critical, not a cultural, paradigm. This can only be done, however, if the purpose of the task is to rediscover the truths of the sources by means of critical methods, not to recover from them, in the misguided spirit of sinophilic identification, the cultural sources of the tradition.

---

[24]Henderson, *Scripture, Canon, and Commentary,* 214-15; cf. Levenson, *Confucian China and Its Modern Fate,* 1:79-94; and Schneider, *Ku Chieh-kang and China's New History,* 188-217.

[25]Pelikan, *The Vindication of Tradition,* 23-24.

[26]See Joshua Fogel, "On the 'Rediscovery' of the Chinese Past: Ts'ui Shu and Related Cases," in *Perspectives on a Changing China: Essays in Honor of Professor C. Martin Wilbur on the Occasion of His Retirement,* ed. Joshua A. Fogel and William T. Rowe (Boulder: Westview Press, 1979), 219-35.

Truth in Sinology

The generation of Pelliot and his classmates and colleagues, especially founders of national schools such as Duyvendak and Alekseev, insisted on fidelity to the texts as final arbiters of truth. This, needless to say, can be a dangerous enterprise, for some texts are inconstant lovers at best, unfaithful to history and impervious to philological coaxing and cajoling. Nevertheless, it was an axiom of the times and is a general rule of thumb for philologists today. For instance, "Alekseev demanded from his pupils a high level of accuracy, and above all precise attention to the text, which he believed to be the main scholarly method of proof—that is to say, he insisted on the primacy of objective data as against all kinds of speculation."[27] The text was, according to this view, the "highest criterion of truth."[28]

This reverence for the sacred nature of the texts, and the need to approach them almost on bended knee, partook of the old positivist historiography of French historians of the late nineteenth century, for whom all truth resided securely—if all too often obscurely—within the texts. It only needed rigorous philological handling, as methodical and deliberate as the chemist in a lab, to free such truths for the benefit of intellectual stimulation, human guidance, and social progress. Witness Numa Denys Fustel de Coulanges, who preached the "positivism of the document." According to Ernest Breisach, in de Coulanges' *Histoire des institutions politiques de l'ancienne France*, 6 vols. (Paris, 1891), he "argued that what was not in the documents did not exist." It was only through the "patient study of the writings and documents that each age has left of itself," claims de Coulange, that one may detach oneself "sufficiently from present preoccupations and to escape sufficiently from every kind of predilection or prejudice in order to be able to imagine with some exactness the life of men of former times."[29]   Pelliot is the most

---

[27]L.N. Men'shikov, "Academician Vasilii Mikhailovich Alekseev (1881-1951) and His School of Russian Sinology," in *Europe Studies China*, 138.

[28]Ibid., 136.

[29]Ernst Breisach, *Historiography: Ancient, Medieval, and Modern* (Chicago: University of Chicago Press, 1983), 276.

representative figure of this tradition.

Maspero, on the other hand, although a gifted philologist, rose above the positivistic preoccupation with the texts to make many synthetic narratives and analyses of ancient Chinese political, social, economic, and religious history, Taoist rituals and beliefs, and the like, which, although based on a rigorous and broad reading of texts, stood outside of them in the end to harmonize and coordinate the available data into general summaries and provisional conclusions. Nor was he constrained with the hesitation of historicism to interpret each period in modern terms, even if he did not go as far as Granet in adopting the models of nascent sociology.

As apart from the philological approach, modern social science finds truth not in texts but in models of understanding. Models have the advantage of being objectively constructed and applied from without the Chinese tradition; this avoids the problem of the early historians who, as Marianne Bastid-Bruguière reminds us, imparted the same uniqueness to Chinese history usually accorded the Chinese language and script by the early sinologists.[30] Such an objective model is immediately serviceable in comparative studies with other cultures and peoples. It also helps to insure that the self-assured Sinocentric view encouraged by the commentarial tradition is transcended.

Because of the culmination of the sinological tradition in Chavannes, the perfection of philological technique in Pelliot, the transitional figure of the historian Maspero, and the importance of the sociologist Granet in introducing the use of conceptual models, we come to the paradoxical conclusion that, while the foundation of modern sinology rests securely and honorably with Chavannes and his three disciples, these three nevertheless mark the bifurcation of the tradition, and the decline in popularity of one branch and the rise of another. Franke in history, Haloun in textual criticism, Legge in classical translation, Karlgren in linguistics, Waley and Schafer in literature, Laufer in the natural world, and Boodberg in Asian etymology—all represented the epitome of uniquely individualized approaches of a tradition that, if not dying, was definitely

---

[30]Marianne Bastid-Bruguière, "Some Themes of 19th and 20th Century European Historiography on China," in *Europe Studies China*, 231.

on the decline after World War II and increasingly marginalized by the growth of other disciplines.

Nevertheless, in an age of burgeoning archaeological evidence, the need for inter-disciplinary approaches today is all the more crucial.[31] Since part of this evidence consists of documentary finds, not only do these new texts need philological scrutiny, but so does the entire textual tradition in light of newly discovered documents and archaeological finds, especially in the face of the increasing sophistication of such fields as historical phonology and textual criticism, and the development of new approaches in literary criticism and comparative literature. "Historians seem to have forgotten—if they ever properly learned—" muses H. Stuart Hughes, "the simple truth that what one may call progress in their endeavors comes not merely through the discovery of new materials but at least as much through a *new reading* of materials already available."[32] Nor do we desire to revert to the blind Cartesian belief in reason alone—artfully disguised as models of philosophy, mathematics, and physics—as the sole avenue to truth. The "myth of methodology" is ever present, as David Hackett Fischer cautions,[33] and is as blinding as it is seductive.

Sometimes the model takes on a life of its own, inspired by the evidence if not necessarily supported by it: extrapolations in "leaps of faith" are as dangerous to the historian as to the textual critic. For example, Theodore Hamerow likens the entire enterprise to the work of the art historian:

> The social-science historian is thus like a curator of ancient art who tries to piece together a Roman mosaic out of a handful of scattered fragments. The result may be plausible; but it can never be more than an imaginative reconstruction. The methodology employed leads to conclusions which are frequently ingenious and persuasive; they may even prove valid. But can we be sure that they represent

---

[31]This fundamental need is stressed by Michael Loewe, "The History of Early Imperial China: The Western Contribution," in *Europe Studies China*, 247.

[32]Quoted in LaCapra, *History and Criticism*, 20.

[33]David Hackett Fischer, *Historians' Fallacies: Toward a Logic of Historical Thought* (New York: Harper Torchbooks, 1970), xx-xxi.

an objective reality, not a subjective perception?[34]

In such a scenario, the means becomes the ends. For philologists, methodology is a means to the ends of physical texts. History and other social sciences, it seems to me, are methodological means to constructing provisional ends that are themselves often mere projections of the means; they are not independent entities, merely elusive and ever changing constructions of abstractions. (I am, of course, begging the ontological question of whether anyone can ever really "read" a text and access authorial intention, an irrelevancy from the point of view of the philologist). On the other hand, Edward Said points out that "it seems a common human failing to prefer the schematic authority of a text to the disorientations of direct encounters with the human."[35] So even if a specific text or body of documents has the advantage of a common point of argument and source of data, the desire to escape to the security and solitude of the written sources must be guarded against, however safe and seemingly secure the haven they provide.

Today, the touchstone for sinologists of whatever disciplinary allegiance should be the continuing search for truth. Truth in this case is not some "objective reality" arrived at by either a rigorous and faithfully applied method or a revelation apprehended in one glorious moment of insight: truth is the method itself, wielded in a truthful manner. This definition of truth is occasioned by the unavoidable gap between the ideal of objectivity and the reality of inherent bias, as forcefully postulated and demonstrated by Peter Novick.[36] In light of this, Paul Ricoeur insists that historians—or any other scholar, for that matter—do not engage in vain

---

[34]Hamerow, *Reflections on History and Historians* (Madison: University of Wisconsin Press, 1987), 187. His entire essay, "The New History and The Old" (162-204), should be read in conjunction with Gertrude Himmelfarb, *The New History and the Old: Critical Essays and Reappraisals* (Cambridge, Mass.: Harvard University Press, 1987), for salutary caution in the face of newly available models and care in their application.

[35]Cited by Clifford, review of Said, *Orientalism*, *History and Theory* 19 (1980): 212.

[36]Novick, *That Noble Dream: The "Objectivity Question" and the American Historical Profession* (Cambridge: Cambridge University Press, 1988).

attempts at embracing abstract, infinite, ultimate truth. Instead, they attempt to grasp concrete, finite, ephemeral answers. Therefore, "truth," to Ricoeur, consists in the ethical "fulfillment of my task as a workman of history."[37] Immanuel Wallerstein clarifies the issues by bringing the discussion of truth back to the definition of objectivity:

> The scholar's role is to discern, within the framework of his commitments, the present reality of the phenomena he studies, to derive from this study general principles, from which ultimately particular applications may be made. "Truth" changes because society changes. At any given time, nothing is successive; everything is contemporaneous, even that which is past. And in the present we are all irremediably the products of our background, our training, our personality and social role, and structured pressures within which we operate.

"Objectivity," he concludes, "is honesty within this framework."[38] Truth for philologists, therefore, is the disciplined and objective application of the best techniques and methods of the philological approach.

The sinologists treated in the present work provide, therefore, much needed examples of the procedural labors of exemplary working philologists. This is why it was important to include a sinologist of such technical brilliance as Berthold Laufer, even if he worked as an independent agent, and founded no school. If I have neglected to outline the development of the institutions of sinology, and do not document explicitly enough schools of sinology or lines of discipleship, let alone attempt a theoretical or intellectual history of sinology, at least the pitfalls and successes of particular approaches have been introduced.

The model I have adopted to orchestrate my treatment of sinologists is a genealogical one. To paraphrase the words of James

---

[37]Ricoeur, *History and Truth*, tr. Charles A. Kelbley (Evanston: Northwestern University Press, 1965), 8.

[38]Wallerstein, *The Modern World System*, vol. 1: *Capitalist Agriculture and the Origins of the European World-Economy in the Sixteenth Century* (New York: Academic Press, 1974), 9.

Clifford, this genealogical approach allows me to avoid intellectual history and instead describe retrospectively and continuously the "structures and methodology" of a philological sinology which achieved its classical form in the nineteenth and early twentieth centuries.[39] If one looks closely, at least at those sinologists to whom I have devoted the most attention, this biographical framework unconsciously yet inevitably breaks down into a personal "great man" tradition, with the unavoidable Chinese twist of a secularized trinity: the triumvirate of British missionary-consular sinologists Morrison, Legge, and Giles; the troika of *sinologues du chambre* Fourmont, Abel Rémusat, and Julien; the trio of master philologists Chavannes, Pelliot, and Maspero; the trey of German sinologists Haloun, Franke, and the expatriate Laufer; and a triple-play of Anglo-American humanists Waley, Boodberg, and Schafer. And this modern sinological series of nine, from Chavannes to Schafer, should perhaps be honored separately, with Spenser's species of angels, as three ranks of three hierarchies, or "trinall triplicities."

Sinology as a diachronic succession of great individual exemplars may be easier to access and to analyze, and perhaps sometimes to imitate, than a seamless and synchronic "hegemony" or "scholarly discourse." But it is institutionalized sinology that will maintain the tradition through a field-wide commitment to excellence by practitioners on many levels, both in method to insure long-term reliability and in readable, informative results to maintain the dialogue with the outside. Yet, without the regular appearance of such heroic figures in the field, it may be increasingly difficult for philology to claim its particular carrel, however modest, in the research library of sinology in the face of growing competition for funds, allocation of resources, and sponsorship. An example of such difficulty is that confronting the modern Dutch school, as Wilt Idema laments:

> Dutch sinology has always prided itself on its fine philological groundwork. This integral approach to the study of Chinese culture finds it hard to survive in view of the ever increasing demands for disciplinary sophistication that accompany the ever increasing

---

[39]Clifford, review of Said, *Orientalism*, 207.

specialization and in view of government measures strictly to limit the periods of undergraduate teaching and graduate work.[40]

In the face of such pressure, a field such as sinology, with the reputation for nostalgic conservatism, out-of-fashion approaches, and the heavy hand of traditionalism, can only resist corporate downsizing and retain its precarious foothold in academia by continually demonstrating its relevance for humanistic endeavors in general, and importance for Chinese studies in particular. "When the past is no longer relevant to the present, occupation with the past becomes antiquarianism," warns LaCapra.[41] We must not let the charge of "antiquarianism" join the other stereotyped epithets made against philological sinologists of this and past centuries. This can be done only through being true to the tradition as pioneered and developed by the authorities treated in this work as we actively engage in reexamining, analyzing, and presenting for our peers the Chinese literary heritage by competently handling and clearly articulating the technical arsenal of the philologist. Just as important, however, is the inspiration they offer, as we pay homage with incense at the altar in reading their works and pondering their methodologies, that redounds upon us in increased technical sophistication and broader contextualization and relevancy of our own efforts. No one can expect more from the past.

---

[40]Idema, "Dutch Sinology: Past, Present and Future," in *Europe Studies China*, 107.

[41]LaCapra, *History and Criticism*, 30.

BIBLIOGRAPHY

This bibliography is limited to modern studies on the history of sinology and its setting, institutions or library holdings, and scholarship. Individual works by the sinologists and relevant biographical sources are too numerous to be included here; they may be found under the individuals cited.

Almond, Philip C. *The British Discovery of Buddhism*. Cambridge: Cambridge University Press, 1988.

Barnett, Suzanne W. and John K. Fairbank, eds. *Christianity in China: Early Protestant Missionary Writings*. Cambridge, Mass.: Harvard University Press, 1985.

Barrett, Timothy. *Singular Listlessness: A Short History of Chinese Books and British Scholars*. London: Wellsweep, 1989.

Barthold, Wilhelm. *La Découverte de l'Asie: Histoire de l'orientalisme en Europe et en Russe*. French translation by Basile Nikitine. Paris: Bovin, 1947.

Bastid-Bruguière, Marianne. "Some Themes of 19th and 20th Century Historiography on China." In *Europe Studies China: Papers from an International Conference on the History of European Sinology*, 228-39. London: Han-Shan Tang Books, 1995.

Bertuccioli, Giuliano. "Sinology in Italy 1600-1950." In *Europe Studies China*, 67-78.

Boxer, C.R., ed. *South China in the Sixteenth Century*. London: Hakluyt Society, 1953.

_____. "Some Aspects of Western Historical Writing on the Far East, 1500-1800." In *Historians of China and Japan*, edited by E.G. Pulleyblank and W.G. Beasley, 306-21. London: Oxford University Press, 1961.

Breisach, Ernst. *Historiography: Ancient, Medieval, and Modern*. Chicago: University of Chicago Press, 1983.

Burke, Peter. *The French Historical Revolution: The Annales School 1929-89*. Cambridge: Cambridge University Press, 1990.

_____. *History and Social Theory*. Ithaca: Cornell University Press, 1992.

Cameron, Meribeth E. "Far Eastern Studies in the United States." *FEQ* 7 (1948): 115-35.

Centre franco-chinois d'études sinologiques. *Deux siècles de sinologie française*. Peking, 1943.

Chalmers, John. "Is Sinology a Science?" *China Review* 2 (1873): 169-73.

Chang, I-tung. "The Earliest Contacts Between China and England." *Chinese Studies in History and Philosophy* 1 (1968): 53-78.

Ch'en, Jerome. *China and the West: Society and Culture 1815-1937*. London: Hutchinson, 1979.

Chou, Fa-kao. *Han-hsüeh lun-chi*. [Hong Kong]: Ke-ta shu-chü, 1964.

Cohen, Paul A. *China and Christianity: The Missionary Movement and the Growth of Chinese Antiforeignism, 1860-1870*. Cambridge, Mass.: Harvard University Press, 1963.

_____. *Discovering History in China: American Historical Writing on the Recent Chinese Past*. New York: Columbia University Press, 1984.

Cooper, Michael. "The Portuguese in the Far East: Missionaries and Traders." *Arts of Asia* 7 (1977): 25-33.

Cordier, Henri. "Les Etudes chinoises sous la révolution et l'empire." *TP* 19 (1920): 59-103.

Crone, C.R. *The Discovery of the East*. New York: St. Martin's Press, 1972.

Dawson, Raymond. *The Chinese Chameleon: An Analysis of European Conceptions of Chinese Civilization*. London: Oxford University Press, 1967.

de Jong, J.W. *A Brief History of Buddhist Studies in Europe and America*. New Delhi: Bharat-Bharati, 1976.

Demiéville, Paul. "Aperçu historique des études sinologiques en France." In *Choix d'études sinologiques (1921-1970)*, 443-87. Leiden: E.J. Brill, 1973.

Drège, Jean-Pierre. "Tun-huang Studies in Europe." In *Europe Studies China*, 513-32.

Dubs, Homer H. *China: The Land of Humanistic Scholarship*. An Inaugural Lecture Delivered before the University of Oxford on 23 February 1948. Oxford: Clarendon Press, 1949.

Dunne, George. *Generation of Giants: The Story of the Jesuits in China in the Last Decades of the Ming Dynasty*. South Bend: Notre Dame University Press, 1962.

Duyvendak, J.J.L. "Early Chinese Studies in Holland." *TP* 32 (1936): 293-344.

_____. *Holland's Contribution to Chinese Studies*. London: The China Society, 1950.

Eames, James Bromley. *The English in China*. London: Curzon Press, 1909.

Edwards, Dwight. *Yenching University*. New York: United Board for Christian Higher Education in Asia, 1959.

Elliséeff, Serge. "The Chinese-Japanese Library of the Harvard-Yenching Institute." *Harvard Library Bulletin* (1956): 73-93.

Elman, Benjamin. "From Value to Fact: The Emergence of Phonology as a Precise Discipline in Late Imperial China." *JAOS* 102 (1982): 493-500.

_____. *From Philosophy to Philology: Intellectual and Social Aspects of Change in Late Imperial China*. Cambridge, Mass.: Council for East Asian Studies, Harvard University, 1984.

Eoyang, Eugene Chen. *The Transparent Eye: Reflections on Translation, Chinese Literature, and Comparative Poetics*. Honolulu: University of Hawaii Press, 1993.

Fan, Tsen-chung. *Dr. Johnson and Chinese Culture*. London: The China Society, 1945.

Franke, Herbert. *Sinologie*. Bern: A. Francke, 1953.

_____. *Sinologie an Deutschen Universitäten*. Wiesbaden: Franz Steiner Verlag, 1968.

_____. *Sinology at German Universities*. Wiesbaden: Franz Steiner Verlag, 1968.

_____. Sinologie im 19. Jahrhundert." In *August Pfizmaier (1808-1887) und seine Dedeutung für die Ostasienwissenschaften*, ed. Otto Ladstatter and Sepp Linhart, 23-40. Vienna, 1990.

_____. "In Search of China: Some General Remarks on the History of European Sinology." In *Europe Studies China*, 11-25.

Franke, Otto. "Die sinologischen Studien in Deutschland." *Ostasiatische Neubildungen* (Hamburg, 1911): 357-77.

Franke, Wolfgang. "The Younger Generation of German Sinologists." *MS* 5 (1940): 437-46.

_____. *China and the West,* trans. R.A. Wilson. Oxford: Basil Blackwell, 1967.

Frèches, José. *La Sinologie.* Paris: Presses Universitaires de France, 1975.

Gafurov, B.G. and Y.V. Gankovsky, eds. *Fifty Years of Soviet Oriental Studies: Brief Reviews (1917-1962).* Moscow: Nauka, 1967.

Gardner, Charles S. *Chinese Traditional Historiography.* 1938; rpt. Cambridge, Mass.: Harvard University Press, 1970.

Guldin, Gregory Eliyu. *The Saga of Anthropology in China: From Malinowski to Moscow to Mao.* Armonk, N.Y: M.E. Sharpe, 1994.

Henderson, John B. *Scripture, Canon, and Commentary: A Comparison of Confucian and Western Exegesis.* Princeton: Princeton University Press, 1991.

Honour, Hugh. *Chinoiserie: The Vision of Cathay.* London: John Murray, 1961.

Hopkirk, Peter. *Foreign Devils on the Silk Road.* London: John Murray, 1982.

Howard, Richard C. "The Development of American China Studies: A Chronological Outline." *International Association of Orientalist Libraries, Bulletin* 32-33 (1988): 38-49.

Hu, Shu Chao. *The Development of the Chinese Collection in the Library of Congress.* Boulder: Westview Press, 1970.

Hucker, Charles O. *The Association for Asian Studies: An Interpretive History.* Ann Arbor: AAS, 1973.

Hummel, Arthur W. "Some American Pioneers in Chinese Studies." *Notes on Far Eastern Studies in America* 9 (1941): 1-6.

_____, ed. *Eminent Chinese of the Ch'ing Period (1644-1912),* 2 vols. Washington: United States Government Printing Office, 1943.

Idema, Wilt L. "Dutch Sinology: Past, Present, and Future." In *Europe Studies China,* 88-110.

Iggers, George C. *The German Conception of History: The National Tradition of Historical Thought from Herder to the Present.* Middletown, Conn.: Wesleyan University Press, 1983.

Ishida, Mikinosuke. *Ō-Bei ni okeru Shina kenkyū.* Tokyo, 1942.

Kennedy, George A. *An Introduction to Sinology: Being a Guide to the Tz'u Hai (Ci hai).* 1953; rpt. New Haven: Far Eastern Publications, 1981.

Kiang, Kang-Hu. *Chinese Civilization: An Introduction to Sinology.* Shanghai: Chun Hwa Book Co., 1935.

Kirby, E. Stuart. *Russian Studies of China: Progress and Problems of Soviet Sinology.* New Jersey: Rowman and Littlefield, 1976.

Kiriloff, C. "Russian Sources." In *Essays on the Sources for Chinese History.* Ed. Donald Leslie, Donald D., Colin Mackerras, and Wang Gungwu, 188-202. Columbia, S.C.: University of South Carolina Press, 1973.

Lam, John. "The Early History of Chinese Studies in America." *Hong Kong Library Association Journal* 2 (1971): 16-23.

Latourette, Kenneth S. *The History of Early Relations between the United States and China, 1784-1844.* New Haven: Yale University Press, 1917.

_____. *A History of Christian Missions in China.* New York: Macmillan, 1929.

Levenson, Joseph R. "The Humanistic Disciplines: Will Sinology Do?" *JAS* 23 (1964): 507-12.

Li, Huang. *Fa-kuo Han-hsüeh lun-chi.* Kowloon: Chu Hai College, 1975.

Lindbeck, John M.H. *Understanding China: An Assessment of American Scholarly Resources.* New York: Praeger, 1971.

Liu, Kwang-ching. *Americans and Chinese: A Historical Essay and a Bibliography.* Cambridge, Mass.: Harvard University Press, 1963.

Loewe, Michael. "The History of Early Imperial China: The Western Contribution." In *Europe Studies China,* 245-63.

Lundbæk, Knud. "The Establishment of European Sinology, 1801-1815." In *Cultural Encounters: China, Japan, and the West. Essays Commemorating 25 Years of East Asian Studies at the University of Aarhus.* Ed. Søren Clausen, Roy Starrs, and Anne Wedell-Wedellsborg, 15-54. Aarhus: Aarhus University Press, 1995.

Lutz, Jessie Gregory. *China and the Christian College, 1850-1950.* Ithaca: Cornell University Press, 1971.

Malmqvist, Göran. "On the History of Swedish Sinology." In *Europe Studies China,* 161-74.

Studies China, 161-74.

Martino, P. *L'Orient dans la littérature française aux XIIIe et au XVIIIe siècles*. Paris: Hachette, 1906.

Maspero, Henri. "La Sinologie." In *Société Asiatique, Le Livre du centenaire, 1822-1922*, 261-83. Paris, 1922.

_____. "La Chaire de Langues et Littératures chinoises et tartares-mandchoues." In *Le Collège de France, Livre jubilaire composé à l'occasion de son quatrième centenaire*, 355-66. Paris, 1932.

May, Ernest R. and John K. Fairbank. *America's China Trade in Historical Perspective: The Chinese and American Performance*. Cambridge, Mass.: Harvard University Press, 1986.

Mote, Frederick W. "The Case for the Integrity of Sinology." *JAS* 23 (1964): 531-34.

Moule, A.C. "British Sinology." *The Asiatic Review* 44 (1948): 187-92.

Mungello, David E. *Curious Land: Jesuit Accommodation and the Origins of Sinology*. Wiesbaden: Franz Steiner, 1985.

_____, ed. *The Chinese Rites Controversy: Its History and Meaning*. Nettetal: Steyler Verlag, 1994.

_____. *The Great Encounter of China and the West, 1500-1800*. New York: Rowman and Littlefield, 1999.

Nienhauser, William H., Jr., et al., eds. *The Indiana Companion to Traditional Chinese Literature*. Bloomington: Indian University Press, 1986.

Novick, Peter. *That Noble Dream: The "Objectivity Question" and the American Historical Profession*. Cambridge: Cambridge University Press, 1988.

Pulleyblank, Edwin G. "How Do We Reconstruct Old Chinese?" *JAOS* 112 (1992): 365-82.

Ronan, Charles and Bonnie Oh, eds., *East Meets West: The Jesuits in China, 1582-1773*. Chicago: Loyola University Press, 1988.

Rowbotham, Arnold H., "A Brief Account of the Early Development of Sinology." *The Chinese Social and Political Science Review* 7 (1923): 113-38.

_____. *Missionary and Mandarin: The Jesuits at the Court of China*. Berkeley: University of California Press, 1942.

edited by Donald Leslie, et al., 176-87. Columbia, S.C.: University of South Carolina Press, 1973.

_____. *K'ung-tzu or Confucius: The Jesuit Interpretations of Confucianism*. Sydney: Allen and Unwin, 1986.

Schafer, Edward H. *What and How is Sinology?* Inaugural Lecture for the Department of Oriental Languages and Literatures, University of Colorado, Boulder, 14 October, 1982. University of Colorado, 1982.

_____. "Rudiments of a Syllabus on Sinological History." Berkeley, n.d. Photocopy.

Schipper, Kristopher. "The History of Taoist Studies in the West." In *Europe Studies China*, 467-91.

Schwab, Raymond. *La Renaissance orientale*. Paris: Editions Payot, 1950. Tr. Gene Patterson-Black and Victor Reinking, under the title *The Oriental Renaissance: Europe's Rediscovery of India and the East, 1680-1880* (New York: Columbia University Press, 1984).

See, Sung. "Sinological Studies in the United States." *Chinese Culture* 8 (1967): 133-70.

Serruys, Paul L-M. "Philologie et linguistique dans les études sinologiques." *MS* 8 (1943): 167-219.

Shambaugh, David, ed. *American Studies of Contemporary China*. Armonk, N.Y.: Woodrow Wilson Center Press, 1993.

Simmonds, Stuart and Simon Digby, eds., *The Royal Asiatic Society: Its History and Treasures*. Leiden: E.J. Brill, 1979.

Skinner, G. William. "What the Study of China Can Do for Social Science." *JAS* 23 (1964): 517-22.

Sorokin, Vladislav F. "Two and a Half Centuries of Russian Sinology." In *Europe Studies China*, 111-28.

Speshnev, Nikolai. "Teaching and Research on Chinese Language at St Petersburg University in the 19th and 20th Centuries." In *Europe Studies China*, 129-35.

Soothill, W.E. *China and the West: A Sketch of Their Intercourse*. London: Oxford University Press, 1925.

Strout, Elizabeth, ed. *Catalogue of the American Oriental Society Library*. New Haven: Yale University Library, 1930.

New Haven: Yale University Library, 1930.

Strianovich, Traian. *French Historical Method: "Annales" Paradigm.* Ithaca: Cornell University Press, 1976.

Swisher, Earl. *China's Management of the American Barbarians: A Study of Sino-American Relations, 1841-1861, with Documents.* New Haven: Far Eastern Publications, 1951.

"Symposium on Chinese Studies and the Disciplines." *JAS* 23 (1964): 505-38; 24 (1964): 109-14.

Tao, C. Y. (T'ao Chen-yü). *Shih-chieh ke-kuo Han-hsüeh yen-chiu lun-wen-chi.* Taipei: Kuo-fang yen-chiu-yüan, 1962.

Ting Tchao-ts'ing. *Les Descriptions de la Chine par les Français, 1650-1750.* Paris, 1928.

Thompson, Laurence G. "American Sinology, 1830-1920: A Bibliographical Survey." *Tsing Hua Journal of Chinese Studies.* New Series 2 (1961): 244-90.

Treadgold, Donald W. *The West in Russia and China: Religious and Secular Thought in Modern Times,* vol. 2: *China 1582-1949.* Cambridge: Cambridge University Press, 1973.

Twitchett, Denis. *Land Tenure and the Social Order in T'ang and Sung China.* London: Oxford University Press, 1962.

_____. "A Lone Cheer for Sinology." *JAS* 24 (1964): 109-12.

_____. *Printing and Publishing in Medieval China.* London: Wynken De Worde Society, 1983.

Varg, Paul. *Missionaries, Chinese and Diplomats: the American Protestant Missionary in China, 1890-1952.* Princeton: Princeton University Press, 1952.

Vissière, Isabelle and Jean-Louise Vissière. *Lettres édifiantes et curieuses de Chine par des missionnaires jésuits 1702-1776.* Paris: Garnier-Flammarion, 1979.

West, Philip. *Yenching University and Sino-Western Relations.* Cambridge, Mass.: Harvard University Press, 1976.

Widmer, Eric. *The Russian Ecclesiastical Mission in Peking during the 18th century.* Cambridge, Mass.: Harvard University Press, 1976.

Wright, Arthur. "The Study of Chinese Civilization." *Journal of the History of Ideas* 21 (1960): 233-55.

(1964): 513-16.

Yuan, Tung-Li. *Russian Works on China, 1918-1960.* New Haven: Far Eastern Publications, 1961.

Zhang, Longxi. *The Tao and the Logos: Literary Hermeneutics, East and West.* Durham, N.C.: Duke University Press, 1992.

Zürcher, E. "From 'Jesuit Studies' to 'Western Learning.'" In *Europe Studies China,* 264-79.

Zurndorfer, Harriet T. *China Bibliography: A Research Guide to Reference Works About China Past and Present.* Leiden: E.J. Brill, 1995.

GENERAL INDEX

PGIL2021USA